Crossovers

Crossovers

Essays on Race, Music, and American Culture

JOHN SZWED

PENN

University of Pennsylvania Press

Philadelphia

10   9   8   7   6   5   4   3   2   1

Published by
University of Pennsylvania Press
Philadelphia, Pennsylvania 19104-4011

Library of Congress Cataloging-in-Publication Data

Szwed, John F., 1936–
    Crossovers : essays on race, music, and American culture / John Szwed.
        p.   cm.
    ISBN 0-8122-3882-6 (cloth : alk. paper)
    Includes bibliographical references (p.) and index.
    1. Music and race. 2. African Americans. 3. Popular culture—
United States—History—20th century.
ML3795 .S98   2005
780′.89′00973—dc22   2005042233

To Erika Bourguignon

Contents

Chapter 1
Introduction

Back when I wrote the earliest essay in this book, there were virtually no college or high school courses on vernacular culture or African Americans. The inclusiveness of the late 1960s was yet to come, as was the all-embracing, culturally leveling idea of text, the time-traveling of post-modernism, and the fearless sweep of culture studies. When we talked in school about art in those days, I longed to be able to use John Lee Hooker as an example, rather than say, Violette Leduc, or Chester Himes instead of Ernest Hemingway. Conventional arguments about creativity and the nature of art badly needed the example of jazz improvisation, but there was no shared body of knowledge among academics that would allow for its entry into discussion. Not that there weren't always some scholars who took popular culture seriously, or who knew and honored the culture of black America, but it cost them: a professor of early English literature such as Marshall Stearns was forced to do his innovative work on jazz, rhythm 'n' blues, and vernacular dance and theater outside of the academy, teaching night classes to those not seeking degrees, and turning his apartment in New York City into an archive he called the Institute of Jazz Studies. An Africanist like anthropologist Alan Merriam could only publish his ideas on the connection between Africa and jazz in fan magazines such as *Down Beat*. And even as things became more inclusive, the eccentric venues pioneered by Stearns, Merriam, and others continued to offer possibilities that academic journals did not. My biographies of Sun Ra and Miles Davis came out of my own crossover experiences—academic work on race and culture, together with reviews and other journalism on jazz and popular culture. The biographies and journalism tapped into my experience as a musician, a scholar, and as a boy growing up in the South, where I discovered the cultural mixtures and separations that have fascinated me ever since.

I was born in Eutaw, Alabama, in Greene County, red clay country, the black belt, one of the birthplaces of the civil rights movement. My mother was born there too, the daughter of a shopkeeper's assistant, and the first person in the county to become a nurse. My father had come south during the Great Depression from western Pennsylvania to work for a pipe foundry in Birmingham, the most segregated metropolis in the United States, a city under the spell of race, one as possessed by color as Johannesburg. I spent most of my early years there. As in South Africa, the culture of Birmingham was perversely and prismatically integrated. Radio was intensely local, and programs aimed at specific groups reached everyone, even if only heard subliminally while dialing from one station to another. To a child listening in bed, the late night aether was a musical utopia, with the disembodied chanka-a-lanka background riffs of gospel quartets, the broken hearts and families of country songs, and the strut and sass of early rhythm 'n' blues. There were still street singers in Birmingham then, and dancers who gathered around them. Hip military drilling could be seen in fields or on empty lots. There was a war on, to be sure, but as Ralph Ellison once said, this kind of drilling went on in the black community even when there were no wars.

In summers I visited my grandmother back in Eutaw, where time seemed to have stopped, and the depression continued on. The antebellum houses still gleamed white, but most folks, like my grandmother, lived in glorified shotgun shacks, often without electricity. My earliest memory is of mules standing motionless in fields, and men in overalls hunkered down outside shops, squinting at the license plates of passing cars—mules and men, as Zora Neale Hurston succinctly put it in one of her book titles.

When I was ten we moved north from Birmingham to Burlington, New Jersey, a historic and gritty ethnic river town. During my family's first summer there, we lived in the only hotel, just across the street from the only movie theater. With no children nearby for me to play with, my mother was always sympathetic when I asked to go to the movies, and I spent many afternoons at matinees where I sat through whatever was showing, most often a cowboy film or a war movie. But I was also there on the days dedicated to black films, many of them shot in glorious sepiatone, a process by which the whole world was made to seem colored. Scattered among the newsreels and cartoons there were also the soundies, short films of musicians with their instruments gleaming in the spotlights, their stage costumes a revelation of glitter and flash. For some reason I fixed on the trombone and pestered my parents into buying one for me, no small purchase for them, and a decision that pitted one against the other. After a few years of lessons, I was into music seriously, taking long bus trips to Philadelphia to study with Donald Reinhardt, a brass teacher with something of a national cult following, and hanging with musicians who whiled away their late-waking afternoons in his studio. Over coffee and pots of baked beans in the Automat downstairs, they filled me with weird stories of life on the bandstand that convinced me this was the only life. I couldn't get enough: I bought and traded records, sent off for self-instruction courses in arranging and composition, and picked up the bass and the vibraphone along the way.

Once I started working as a musician I was happy to play anywhere: high school dances, Christmas parties for Sears and Roebuck employees, Hungarian weddings at American Legion halls, Fourth of July parades, even an occasional symphony gig. But best of all were the jobs on the rhythm 'n' blues circuits with black bands, where I developed a different repertoire, dressed better, and, as B. B. King might say, learned to deal with new clientele. Sometimes I stumbled into magical moments, such as one evening at the Colored VFW Hall of Burlington County, where the piano trio with which I was now bassist played for dancing and the floor show. One incident from the first set stands out: a lady dancing near the bandstand slipped a note to me, the only person of non-color in the room, with a request for "Chopsticks Mambo," an obvious but nonetheless *au courant* little piece loved by dancers. When I allowed that I didn't think we knew it, she smiled indulgently, nodded toward our pianist, and said, "Ask the *man*." During the break I was sternly advised by the pianist never to admit to not knowing *anything*. As the floor show began, we accompanied several acts that had stopped off on their way to New York City, the most memorable of which was a comedy trio of Eddie Anderson (Rochester on the *Jack Benny Show*), Percy Harris (from *Beaulah*, the first black TV show), and Mantan Moreland (of Charlie Chan films and countless other movies). Their act was a short vaudeville skit called the "interruptions," in which a high-speed monologue begun by one of the three was continually interrupted by the others overlapping and talking over his words, so that his meanings were sent spiraling off in unintended and hilarious directions.

When we first moved north I discovered that I was far behind other children in school, a gap I was slow to close, and one that soon was highlighted by my own intransigence. In junior high school I was placed in the lowest of the tracks, as they called them, the holding pens for the disaffected, the troubled, the "late starters" who never got started at all. Various difficulties in high school got me on the principal's list of troublemakers, those who, he assured me, were "unrecommendable" for anything in life. The guidance counselor offered me no guidance. Still, with my parents' urging and a complete lack of alternatives, I managed to get accepted into college on test scores alone and became, as my parents never ceased to remind me, the first person in my family to go to college.

At Marietta College in southeastern Ohio I continued playing music, working road houses, country clubs, college dances, and West Virginia's speakeasies, bars that circumvented the state's peculiar liquor laws by posting a "Members Only" sign (meaning that anyone who came in was a member). The irony was that this public/private solution actually encouraged gambling, b-girls, and drugs. Every night could bring some new excitement to the gig: arrests, fights, a drunk shoved down a flight of stairs, or beer bottles thrown at the ceiling to create a kaleidoscope of shards raining through the colored stage lights. We were finished by three a.m. or so, and I made it back to bed just as the sun was coming up over the Ohio River. It was a thrillingly unhealthy life, and with no time left for anything but studies, my grades soared. Though I was to drift away from the dream of making a living at music in a few years, I never lost sight of the alternative world it offered, the social vision it sustained.

The summer after graduation I followed my girlfriend up to Columbus where she had a job, and I began taking courses at Ohio State University, with no clear purpose. Ohio State in the late 1950s and early 1960s was already as big as a fair-sized town and had a bureaucracy as dense as Communist Hungary, or at least one just dense enough that enterprising students could make it work for them. When fall came I enrolled to work on a master's degree in communication and found a job as a graduate assistant in the Department of Motion Pictures, where I helped with the introductory filmmaking class and ran a campus film series. Then, hearing that the Department of English needed teaching fellows, I somehow convinced them to trust me with a freshman class in composition. Holding two assistantships at once was technically forbidden, but on the other hand I wasn't a graduate student in English either, so nobody seemed to care.

When my academic days were once again nearing an end, I feared leaving the comfortable life I was living, and began thinking about studying for a Ph.D. I sought advice wherever I could. Roy Harvey Pierce, a professor of English, suggested, straight-faced, that I should go to New York City to study with Harry Smith. Never having heard of Smith, and so not having a clue of what life around that underground filmmaker, sometime-anthropologist, collector of hillbilly records, proto-beatnik, and notorious moocher would be like, I must have given a tepid response, for Pearce countered with a safer alternative—the new Annenberg School for Communication at the University of Pennsylvania, where, he fancied (wrongly, it turned out), wild new experiments in media were underway. Then, while on the shoot of a film interview with Marshall McLuhan, I heard the guru of the new media say that graduate schools would soon turn into monasteries in the face of electronic media, and become the last refuges of those who didn't measure up. At some folk affair or other, I met Alan Lomax, and he also warned me off graduate school, suggesting instead that I learn by hanging around cool people such as the maverick psychiatrists, avant-film makers, and alt.social scientists whose names he rattled off for me—people like Ray Birdwistell, Colin Turnbull, Ted Carpenter, and John Marshall. Brewton Berry, an archeologist who had remade himself into a sociologist specializing in race relations, suggested to me that if he were a young person interested in anthropology, he'd become a travel writer instead.

These were all good ideas, I'm sure, but I was too timid to take them up. I was happy right where I was, recently married, making money, taking classes in everything that caught my attention, playing music, running off to jazz concerts in Cleveland, working for a film production company, pumping gas at an all-night service station, racing sports cars, and driving deep into the country on weekends to places like Hillbilly Park in Newark, Ohio, or to folk performances in Ashland, Kentucky. I had just fallen under the spell of bluegrass, a music not yet known outside of its native region. It was country jazz as far as I was concerned, with its instrumental choreography, its distinct schools of improvisation, and its own form of rural hipsterism. Once again I was spending too many nights away from my studies, becoming a regular at Irv-Nell's Bar and Grill in Columbus, where I listened to musicians who had migrated from Pike County, Kentucky chug through "Orange Blossom Special" and cry out "The Long Black Veil."

So I stayed on at Ohio State, now accepted into a joint Ph.D. program in sociology and anthropology, where I also studied linguistics and folklore. I may have drifted off from the program from time to time, but never once did I feel the resentment that is so often the emblem of the graduate student. For me, it was a fresh discovery every day—the beats, Freud, Greek poetry, structuralism, the twin explosions of 1960s free jazz and rock, the folk and blues revival, world cinema, and pop art. I'd spent time as a farm laborer by the age of twelve, cleaned beaches and worked in an ice cream factory during the summers in high school, and worked for a while after graduation in a steel mill. Music and graduate school were my tickets out of all that.

My graduate adviser was Erika Bourguignon, an Austrian anthropologist who had studied with Afroamerianist Melville J. Herskovits, done research in Haiti, and was a pioneer in women's studies. A cosmopolitan with a wicked sense of humor, she cared about art and literature, and had a sophisticated vision of the scholar in the modern world. She encouraged me to bring to my work what I knew and had experienced, and I found that through music alone it was possible to challenge the shabby theorizing that passed for studies of race relations, and to confront the bias against African Americans that was shared by left and right alike. Ellison's phrase about African American culture being surely more than the sum of its brutalization rang in my ears. Whole essays on black manhood were being written nightly on bandstands; histories of empire and human triumph were on display in the makeup of the drum kit alone. How was I ever going to read those sorry accounts of broken men without a culture, after I'd seen the confidence and grace with which black musicians approached the microphone night after night to compose solos on the spot? My epiphany was that if anthropology was really the study of culture, then there were no limits on what that study could include, or how it might be carried out. I had, or imagined I had, the license that would unify my life.

The plan was to do doctoral research in the Caribbean and explore African American life outside the United States, what might now be called diasporic studies. But I found research money for that area hard to come by, and instead I wound up with a Canadian government grant to do an agricultural community study in Newfoundland. It took some reconfiguring, but I thought maybe plan B might not be so bad after all: peasants, fishermen, icebergs, northern lights, whales, a colony older than the United States . . . like Saul Bellow's rain king Henderson, my wife and I could begin life again in our own new found land. So in the fall of 1962 we piled everything we had inside and on top of a used VW bug, and aimed northeast from Boulder, where we had just spent the summer taking courses, riding horseback, and trying to absorb enough heat to last us two years.

Newfoundland did change our lives. We found ourselves in a pre-television, pre-electric outport community, with a mixed Anglo-Scots-Irish-Indian-French heritage of ballads, bagpipes, horse-drawn plows, mumming . . . the very stuff of folklore studies, and a way of life not *that* far away from the rural Alabama of my childhood. Far from experiencing culture shock—what some had led me to believe was the true badge of field research—I felt incredibly comfortable among the people of that tiny village, suffused with an overwhelming sense of generosity and welcome that I had never experienced before. Leaving the community after a year was the true shock. We moved on to St. John's and a research center at the Memorial University of Newfoundland, where I met graduate students from departments around the world, and was exposed to some of the other anthropological perspectives to be had—Claude Lévi-Strauss and Marcel Mauss on the continent, and paradigms from British universities that had been shaped in colonial Africa.

Returning to the United States in 1964, I found a one-year job at the University of Cincinnati, teaching 8:00 A.M. classes five days a week and writing my dissertation late at night; we then moved to Lehigh University, where I worked from 1965 to 1967. Bethlehem, Pennsylvania, was a haven from that alluring storm that seemed to be raging everywhere else: the Vietnam War, riots in the cities, sit-ins on campuses, an explosion of new musics, a sub-cultural efflorescence. . . . Those two bucolic years in New-foundland had cut me off from the scene, as well as some vital changes in American culture, and I was longing for more direct contact with music and the social changes it mirrored. We spent a lot of time driving to jazz and folk clubs in Philadelphia, or to art galleries and off-off Broadway theaters like the Judson or Caffe Cino in the Village. So when I heard that the Department of Anthropology at Temple University was expanding, we jumped at the chance and headed south to Philadelphia.

Still drawn to the Caribbean, we spent some months in Trinidad in the summers, testing what I could find to read about the island against the lavishness of its culture. I also took several trips through coastal Georgia and South Carolina, where connections to the West Indies were apparent everywhere. I was fascinated by the concept of creolization, the first cultural theory developed in the Americas. I understood that the black diaspora formed a great civilization and a powerful cultural en-gine. The roots of those cultures in Africa were still important to me and to the politics of race I espoused, but here was for me the beginnings of a way of understanding the mechanics of these cultures and their changes throughout their history in the New World.

In college I had written a few things for magazines like the short-lived but wonderfully serious *Jazz Review* and "men's" magazines such as *Escapade* (which paid well, and once got me into the same issue as Jack Kerouac). Through a friend, I met Bob Thiele, producer of records by everyone from Buddy Holly to John Coltrane, and I began writing liner notes for his records and articles for his magazine *Jazz*. It was a hard-core fan magazine, an us-jazzers-against-the-world kind of thing, but it soon surrendered to changing tastes, and turned into *Jazz and Pop*. I turned with it, and began writing a column on the blues, about Dylan or the Beatles, and doing interviews with bands like the Animals. It got me into recording studios and concerts, gave me entree to the world of musicians and recording engineers, and forced me to think about the larger world of American music. But it was way too early in the scheme of things aca-demic to claim any of this as research in order to advance my career.

"Musical Style and Racial Conflict" was written for an academic meeting while I was still a student. It was my attempt to bring what I was reading in anthropology to bear on musical issues that were hot at the moment; more to the point, it was a way of connecting my studies with my life outside school. When I sent it to the journal *Ethnomusicology* and it was rejected, I salved my pride by assuming they didn't know what I was talking about. After the essay sat in a drawer for a few years I mailed it off to W. E. B. Du Bois's journal *Phylon*, where to my amazement it was immediately accepted. This was the first of many lessons I learned in matching my interests to those of the branch of social science I had chosen. Incredible as it now seems, African Americans were not of that much concern to social scientists in the early 1960s. It would take almost a decade before even the civil rights movement was to make any real impact on sociology and anthropology. My first attempt to introduce a course on African American culture at one university at which I taught was crushed by a senior professor who dismissed it at a faculty meeting as a "non-course on a non-subject" (and taught, I imagined him thinking, by a non-professor). At another university, I naively wrote a letter to the Dean of the School of Music proposing that I introduce the School's first course on black music . . . for free. But it was the Chair of the Department of Anthropology who replied, telling me that the Dean of Arts and Sciences was annoyed that I had communicated with another Dean without going through him, and no, they didn't want the course. Even years later at another university, my proposed seminar on the life and work of Miles Davis was at first rejected by a faculty course committee who doubted that Davis was worthy of such close consideration, and in any case wondered if it was appropriate for an anthropologist to offer it.

It was classic academic resistance to change, I thought: African Americans, jazz, and popular culture could find no place in the departments in which they obviously belonged. But when anyone from another department attempted to treat these subjects seriously, their credentials were questioned. The development of Black Studies in the late 1960s changed much of this, and also made a new place for me in the academy, but the transition was not without its ironies and pains. On several occasions I was brought in as a consultant to other universities which were under pressure from black students to offer courses on the history and lives of African Americans. It was clear that they had no idea who to ask among black scholars, and that they felt more comfortable dealing with a white person, even if it meant they had to turn to another university.

At times the racial dynamics of academia could become truly bizarre. In the early 1970s I was invited to interview for a job in a new Black Studies program in one of the finest universities in America. Whatever pride I could take from this was quickly erased when no faculty from the social sciences turned up, and my interview was conducted entirely by undergraduate students. Yet after I returned home, there was a letter offering me the job. I tried to think of all this as practical ethnographic experience, more data-gathering for life, but for black faculty members who were also new to these same universities, encounters such as these must surely have seemed even stranger and more unsavory.

Complain as I will, I escaped these problems at several universities. In the Program in Folklore and Folklife at the University of Pennsylvania, I was given the freedom to offer courses on African American folk culture, jazz, blues, and pop music, and still found ways to teach D. H. Lawrence, John Reed, Zora Neale Hurston, Matthew Arnold, and Lafcadio Hearn (all ethnographers in their own ways). The folklore program at Penn had a checkered faculty and a motley body of students, but the mix produced some of the most fascinating and original scholars in America, many of whom went on to fame in other disciplines than folklore. And all the more remarkable that the program managed to pay its own way in the university, something unheard of in graduate studies, and, one imagined, an embarrassment to an administration that largely ignored it.

At Yale I was also able to find this same freedom, now by teaching across departments. Though my primary appointments are in Anthropology and African American Studies, I also have secondary appointments in American Studies, Music, and Film Studies, and have even taught in the Literature Program a few times. My model for all this was Dell Hymes, who escaped his own department at the University of Pennsylvania by joining the Program in Folklore and Folklife and the Department of Linguistics, and later by becoming Dean of the Graduate School of Education. (Erving Goffman, himself a self-proclaimed academic cowboy, once admonished Hymes for his academic restlessness and suggested that he pick, say, six good departments and settle down for good.)

"Musical Adaptation Among Afro-Americans" extended some ideas broached in the *Phylon* article, and emerged from my interest in Alan Lomax's work on the relationship of music and social structure. It was published in the *Journal of American Folklore* and also in a book I coedited in 1970 with Norman Whitten, *Afro-American Anthropology: Contemporary Perspectives*, a set of writings that had their origins in some sessions we had put together for the annual meetings of the American Anthropological Association to spark interest in black studies. The idea of black cultural creativity had become an important political issue in the late 1960s when it served as a counter-balance to social science theorizing on the culture of poverty, or, as it emerged in debates, the "poverty of culture," an idea that some of us found both wrong and pernicious. No surprise, then, that there were those at the time who decried the book as an attempt to separate one group of people out from what they saw as anthropology's global perspective. Apparently the title of the book was especially bothersome: there *was* no Afro-American anthropology, they said: it was all one discipline, one single humanistic (or scientific) vision. But with demonstrations and urban insurrections dominating the nightly television news, the book was bound to become an annoyance to some.

Though I had not written much about the racial controversies dominating American life at the end of the 1960s, and most of what I had done seemed common sense to me, it was nonetheless enough to draw me out

of academia, either as an "expert" or as part of the struggle. I had invi-
tations to talk to activist and student groups, to join in "interventions" in
various academic and governmental meetings, to be interviewed on television, to develop radio programs, and to write a *New York Times* op-ed
piece on anthropology's role in American life. Between the cloistered
walls of the academy and the tumult in the streets it was often difficult to
stay focused. Among other weirdness at the time, there was talk of clan-
destine prison camps being built, of assassination plans underway, and
of police spies in every group with which I was involved. Soon some academics were being asked to become involved with governmental plans to
control racial unrest. Overnight, shadowy research corporations sprang
up to bid for federal contracts aimed at explaining and then quelling
what they were now calling "inner city" unrest. Some in the National In-
stitutes of Health, for example, were looking to academics to provide
theoretical justification for governmental intervention by defining the
pathologies that were behind the strife. The causes were quickly mar-
shaled together: Black English as evidence of failure and incapacity;
the "mother-centered" family as a destructive force; slavery as a culture-
stripping experience. IQ testing was soon back with a vengeance, along
with every other creepy research instrument and pseudo-scientific conception short of phrenology and shock therapy.

But there were others in those same government agencies and research centers who resisted these efforts, argued against them, and some
of them even turned up at the demonstrations and meetings that I
attended. After I spoke at one of those meetings, some of the dissidents
urged me to submit a counter-grant proposal to the ones being called
for: to provide accounts of urban life, and to bring African American
peoples into the mainstream of ethnographic research and out of the
realms of the social problem and the pathological. It all seemed unlikely,
but their urgency convinced me and I wrote a proposal for a major
research center that would make its focus urban ethnography—basic
research on the lives of people in American cities—with African Americans and other ethnic groups at its core. We would encourage graduate
students from across the country to do their doctoral research in
American urban areas by funding them, and provide stipends that would
bring African Americans in to study anthropology, and maybe to redi-
rect its priorities. Surprisingly, the proposal worked, and in 1969 I was
offered a five-year grant.

When some at Temple University opposed the idea (less for ideological reasons than for what they called a "tramp scholar" approach to
research), I resigned. Now out of work, and with no university in which
to house the grant, I began hustling the project to other schools. Erving
Goffman had just arrived in town from Berkeley to assume a chair in

anthropology and sociology at the University of Pennsylvania, and he told me that he was looking for "something to do." We met over corned beef in a South Philadelphia deli and in a few minutes had worked out a plan to form the Center for Urban Ethnography at Penn. Within a week the administration of the University of Pennsylvania bought the idea. The Department of Anthropology chose not to get involved, however, with at least one of its faculty members accusing us of discriminating against white students. It was instead the Program in Folklore and Folklife that welcomed the Center to Penn, and asked me to teach in their unit; and with Goffman, Dell Hymes, and myself as co-directors, we recruited a talented group of young researchers and opened an office in the fall.

One of the first events sponsored by the Center was a conference on what we perceived to be a crisis in the field of anthropology that had been underlined by the chaos of the times. My "An American Anthropological Dilemma: The Politics of Afro-American Culture" was published with the other papers at that gathering as *Reinventing Anthropology*, which Hymes edited. We had great hopes for the book, and for the possibility of transforming the goals of anthropology: we talked of introducing reflexivity into the discourse and practice of the field, and of confronting what we saw as the arrogance with which anthropologists had limited their field to the exotic while at the same time assuming that they knew all that they needed to know about their own societies to do comparative studies. But the book was quickly disposed of in the few reviews it got. "Like a group of Puritan ranters," one distinguished British anthropologist wrote. "If this is the new anthropology, the old anthropology has nothing to fear," said an American scholar. Years later, however, we learned that we had struck a chord, at least among graduate students.

The "reconsiderations" of Melville J. Herskovits and Lafcadio Hearn included here were published in the *New Republic* (the latter written with the literary scholar Carol Parssinen), and were closer looks at the lives and ideas of some progenitors on issues of race and culture in the Americas. Years later, in 1984, art historian Robert Farris Thompson and I wrote "The Forest as Moral Document," a tribute to Lydia Cabrera (1900–1991), doyen of Cuban folklorists and literati alike, but ignored by American social scientists and folklorists. (At the time there had never even been a book review of her work in the United States.) Thompson and I were deeply indebted to Lydia, at whose feet we had sat on many occasions in her Coral Gables home.

These early crossovers into other forms of social narrative led me to pay more attention to the limits and potential of academic writing. The format of the ethnographic narrative had a rather recent, but still unexamined history, one that included the use of experimental writing, fiction, natural history note-taking, lab reports, psychological case studies, travel accounts, the "new" journalisms of both the late nineteenth and late twentieth centuries, autobiography, and the British popular tradition of urban ethnographic reportage (Jack London, Sidney and Beatrice Webb, Friedrich Engels, Charles Dickens, and the like). By the early part of the twentieth century there were already literary critics of anthropology, such as G. K. Chesterton, and even parodies of ethnography. So I began considering the ways in which forms and styles of writing reshaped data; the rhetoric of social science; how methods of description themselves contained theoretical assumptions; and the story of how anthropology had mixed genres to develop the forms of presentation that were now taken to be objective, natural, and timeless.

In the early 1970s the Center sponsored several conferences that explored these issues, generally pursuing the links between literary and scientific writing, and comparing novelists' and travelers' accounts of exotic peoples with those of anthropologists. These forays led me deeper into the history of the morass of race and culture, and when I was asked to be part of what has turned out to be a prescient series of lectures on the body at the Institute of Contemporary Arts in London in 1974, I wrote "Race and the Embodiment of Culture," on British observations of Irish, African, and African American cultures. "After the Myth: Studying Afro-American Cultural Patterns in the Plantation Literature" was the result of folklorist Roger D. Abrahams and myself having read hundreds of travelers'—and planters'—accounts of African American life and culture (as part of bibliographical project published by the American Folklore Society in 1978 as *Afro-American Folk Culture: An Annotated Bibliography of Materials from North, Central, and South America*). This same essay later became part of the Introduction when Yale University Press published our collection of these accounts as *After Africa: Slave Culture in Seventeenth, Eighteenth, and Nineteenth Century British West Indies* in 1983. "Speaking People, in Their Own Words" was written (also with Abrahams) for a catalog of a show of Walker Evans's photos for *Let Us Now Praise Famous Men*, and follows these same interests in a different direction. The reading I was doing in this period later led me to write biographies, or what I think of as ethnobiographies—social science case studies of a sort no longer in vogue.

In what was a daring move for me, I sent Robert Christgau, the fabled music editor of the *Village Voice*, a proposal for some things I'd like to write. He surprised me by calling, but only to tell me that since the *Voice* was a New York paper he didn't hire people from out of town. I persisted, telling him I knew that he used out-of-towners, and tossed out a few names. "They're my friends," he said. I told him that I didn't want to quibble, that I could be his friend, too, but he was not amused. Some months later *New York Times* writer Jon Pareles replaced Christgau while he was on leave from the *Voice*, and he asked me to write a piece on Gil Evans, the arranger most famous for his recordings with Miles Davis. When Christgau returned to work he called and chided me for ignoring what he had told me. When I protested, weakly, he cut me off, saying that since I had gone that far, I might as well keep on writing.

That's how it was with the *Voice* then, contentious, funny, committed, sometimes painfully pompous and arch, but always exciting. Christgau turned out to be a dream editor, open to everything (especially things he had never heard of before), and I wrote for him for years. He insisted on a level of writing higher than I was used to producing, and edits with him were intense and exhausting. (I now understood why he *really* wanted local writers: doing edits while holding the phone and typing at the same time could be truly painful.) Sending an idea straight to print as fast as it was written was something new (up against a deadline, I once finished a piece in a cab riding back from a blues club at five in the morning), rather than waiting years to see it in academic journals, or worse, having it rejected as not being anthropological enough or for being written in the first person. Though I never forgot that whatever I wrote was not likely to be read by my colleagues, and for that matter was thrown out the next day with the coffee grounds by those who did, the discipline of developing a writing style, even a smart-ass style like the *Voice*'s, could be heady stuff.

So heady, in fact, that I found it difficult to return to a fixed, academic style of writing, which I began to see with an outsider's or an ethnographer's eye. The irony was that instead of coming to think of ethnographic writing as needing an infusion of color, or the I've-nothing-to-hide intrusion of personal journalism, I began to see that some the best ethnographic writing had rightly been done in a style of no style—styleless to a fault, stuffed with information, and as bare of metaphor as humanly possible. Some ethnographic accounts are written in such a strange, flat, and colorless rhetoric that the reader is constantly reminded that they were not meant to be read in a conventional mode . . . Charles M. Doughty's *Travels in Arabia Deserta* is a case in point. I still felt that academic writing needed to be demystified, but only to open it up to the variety of forms and rhetorics that suited its many functions.

Most of the articles in the second section of the book first appeared in the *Voice*. Pieces such as "The Lizards Fake the Fake," "As It Is Prophesied, So It Used to Be," "Greenwich's Good Gnosis," and "Free Samples" were opportunities to explore larger ideas about music and cultural memory, as was the tight confines of a festival review such as "Milling

at the Mall." Other articles in this section look at the representation of
music in literature and dance. Sally Banes—now a theater and dance
scholar at the University of Wisconsin, then a weekly columnist on performance for the *Voice*—first encouraged me to write about performance
and dance, and asked me to fill in for her a few times while she was on
leave from the paper. "Childhood's Ends" was my first effort, produced
within the heat of East Village/Soho performance art in the 1980s; and
"Sweet Feet" was a try at live dance, written at the nexus at which postmodern irony meets the exhilaration of the revival of black tap dancing.
Some years later Banes and I wrote "From 'Messin' Around' to 'Funky
Western Civilization': The Rise and Fall of Dance Instruction Songs," on
a subject that is (like much of the African American cultural contribution to the world) at once sublimely arcane and yet hidden in plain view.
"The Afro-American Transformation of European Set Dances and Dance
Suites" (written with the ethnomusicologist Morton Marks) was an attempt
to reconnect dance and music within the broader context of the African
diaspora, and to link together square dancing, the origins of jazz, and
the dances of the West Indies. Again, it was a topic that in retrospect
seems perfectly obvious, and only needed to be pushed a little. "All That
Beef, and Symbolic Action, Too" and "The Real Old School" are the
only pieces I've written on hip hop—both exercises in historicizing pop
music and placing it in a comparativist perspective. The former article
was commissioned by the *Voice* after Bob Christgau was no longer music
editor, but it was killed without explanation. (My best guess is that it wandered too far afield of the *Voice*'s political spectrum.)

The four articles in my third section trace my interests in jazz cross-
culturally, beyond the borders of the United States to Argentina, Russia,
Czechoslovakia, and South Africa. Articles such as these never get written in this country unless some foreign musicians become so big that
they can't be ignored, and even then they are usually treated paternalis-
tically, as aberrations that prove the rule. Here, perhaps, my background
in anthropology and folklore shows through more than anywhere else.

The last group of writings begins with meditations on musicians who
are also intellectuals in their own right, artists for whom performance
is only one dimension of the worlds in which they live and work. Sonny
Rollins, Sun Ra, Ornette Coleman, and Anthony Braxton have long been
recognized as important cultural figures, but their importance has never
been fully acknowledged because of the limits of "entertainment" in which
they are obliged to exist as jazz musicians and African Americans. These
four (and I regret not having written a piece good enough to represent
pianist Cecil Taylor) have all reached far beyond their audiences and
their critics, even beyond the usual boundaries of the arts. Like medieval
monks in an age of ignorance, they have kept alive the achievements of

the past, not by archival repetition, but as citations and allusions transformed within the personal utopias that form their aesthetics. The Braxton piece also hints at my interest in cultural creolization, and the last two pieces explore that idea further, a theme that has been lurking throughout other articles in this collection. Though I've spent much of my waking and dreaming life observing and considering the historical roots of African American culture, I'm also aware that no culture operates in the absence of other influences. (The Brazilian pop singer Gilberto Gil once said that the sign of roots music was the swastika; the sign of *his* music, on the other hand, was the antennae.) The simple binary of black/white that served in the earlier days of the civil rights struggle still has its uses, but also needs to be expanded, complicated, and brought up to date. These articles, I hope, point in that direction.

There are days when I think we are in the Golden Age of my obsessions: the scholarship and popular writing on the contribution of African Americans is now so extensive that you could spend a lifetime reading, looking, and listening, and still never catch up. The discographies for jazz and blues are the most complete we have for any kind of music, and the reference materials developed around these two musical forms are rich far out of proportion to their size. Reissues of earlier recordings are more available than ever, and new DVDs and books appear every week. Respect has even been extended to those who do this work. Still, there is no reason to relax yet. Jazz may now be taught in universities, but seldom in departments of music or black studies. And when it's taught, it's often given cautious treatment, cast in the mold of the "classics," and treated as just one more dead phase in the history of popular musics. Meanwhile, some of the best music now being played is passed over by both the academics and the popular press because it doesn't fit the current paradigm of competing ideologies (the 1940s battle of the moldy figs versus the progressives is being fought all over again), or because it comes from suspicious sources like Europe or the electric socket, or is so innovative that no one seems to recognize it as emerging from jazz tradition.

Jazz and other cultural products of African Americans have never been considered within the same historical framework as the other arts, and are still being ghettoized in isolation from other aesthetic movements. Dissertations and academic articles have now begun to appear by those who would take the subject seriously, but lacking experience or coursework in research appropriate to these materials, they often draw conclusions about the blues from a handful of examples, or use the work of a musician or two to illustrate the latest theories about anything. There is still a general insensitivity to what makes the music great . . . great not just because of who and where it came from, but in the same terms as the other celebrated musics of the world. The musicology of the late nineteenth century still mires us in false dichotomies and sanctimonious fantasies about what constitutes quality. By the 1930s musicians and critics had begun to come to terms with this problem, but their insights and cautions have been lost under other anxieties of our time.

Some of the things I touched on in these pieces—South African jazz, the role of Jews in the creation and spread of the music, the sampler as memory aid and cultural generator, new turns of nostalgia in an age of digital reconstruction and infinite cut-and-paste—were bookmarks to myself and others to pursue and explore. In a few cases I followed up on these ideas, but more often, I did not; now, even some of the documents that incited these articles (such as "The Harlequin History of Jazz and Hot Dance") have disappeared, scarcely leaving a trace—the records were never reviewed or archived in libraries—as if they never existed.

Note to the Reader

The essays gathered together here were written at the intersection of race and art, and chart some of my interests over the last thirty-six years. These pieces return again and again to matters that I think are important, but not always well-served by scholars, critics, and journalists. They also reflect the choices made inside and outside of a certain kind of academic life, the crossovers in my time spent as musician, anthropologist, folklorist, college teacher, journalist, jazz scholar, and biographer. Some of these articles, reviews, obituaries, and panegyrics were aimed at scholarly journals and books, and others were commissioned by newspapers, popular magazines, and journals of politics and the arts; but when they were written I felt them as a single line of thought on related themes, and they have been assembled here with that in mind.

These pieces have generally been reprinted as they were first written, unless the awkwardness of the original prose seemed unbearable. This is just to say that if the originals were old school and anachronistic, they still are. And if they contained tics, repetitions, self-plagiarisms, and shifting names for African Americans and for political alliances, they still do.

Writing Race and Culture

Chapter 2

Musical Style and Racial Conflict

Jazz has always held a peculiar but fond place in the hearts of social scientists. The word, if not the music, conjures up the leitmotiv of the outstanding minority of the United States—its own imported "primitives." In recent years it has also meant the "deviant," or the outsider. When social science has concerned itself with jazz, it has seen it as a case study in acculturation and style, a special personality in a special community, and the medium of protest.[1] All of these conceptions need to be called forth to understand one of the most recent developments within the world of professional jazz musicians: "soul" music—a style consciously revivalistic in form and overtly anti-white in function. In the process of looking at this style through its setting both in the history of jazz and in patterns of cultural change in the United States as a whole, an insight is gained into the linkage between social and artistic change. At the same time, several faulty assumptions about jazz and its purveyors also become clear.

The use of jazz as an example of acculturation has been strengthened recently by findings that suggest that jazz was not a musical phenomenon strictly limited to New Orleans, but one which occurred in a number of areas throughout the United States where Negroes and whites were brought into firsthand musical contact. J. S. Slotkin framed this question with his article, "Jazz and Its Forerunners as an Example of Acculturation." He approached the problem by attempting to illustrate Robert E. Park's thesis "that continued contact between two groups leads to eventual assimilation."[2] Slotkin was not concerned with acculturation occurring between African slaves and native white Americans, but with the "styles" of jazz that later resulted from the contact of the two musical traditions.

Shortly after his paper was published in 1946, a series of jazz styles occurred that clearly showed their debt to assimilation. First, the style known as "bebop" appeared, with its emphasis on the extension of harmonic materials into polytonality and complex subdivision of the rhythm pattern.

In 1949 and 1950 a style known as "cool" jazz arose, thus announcing the rejection of the heated emotion that characterized earlier styles. Many groups dropped the piano from their instrumentation, removing the chordal instrument which previously had determined the melody line, while others totally or partially rejected the rhythm section as a hindrance to "free" improvisation and composition.

More recently there appeared a group of academically trained jazz musicians who expressed their discontent with the progress of jazz by their highly structured compositions which they labeled "Third Stream Music"—a highly conscious attempt to remove final barriers to complete assimilation by writing for chamber and symphonic groups.

From this evidence Slotkin's prediction seems to be an accurate one. A total assimilation of serious music from both Negro and white traditions seems imminent. But all is not so simple. Since approximately 1957, a group of young Negro jazzmen has been involved in what was first called "funky" jazz and more recently has become known as "soul" music, a style which represents a departure from the current trend toward formalization, and thus assimilation. The characteristics of this music are: (1) a conscious effort to bring what these musicians deem to be Negro church music (and to a lesser degree, Negro folk music in general) into the jazz repertoire, as both melody and rhythmic-harmonic framework—i.e., simplified, repetitious, highly rhythmic structures with few stated chords, the harmony being implied through the soloist's melody line; (2) the modification of already existing jazz melodies within these same lines; and (3) its almost exclusive performance by young Negroes.

Some titles from this music indicate its direction: "Better Get It In Your Soul," "Moanin'," "Work Song," "The Preacher," "Spiritsville," "Right Down Front," "Sermonette," "A Little 3/4 for God and Co." Albums have appeared with such titles as "The Soul Society," "Blues and Roots," "The Truth," and "Soul Brothers."

Jazz musicians, both Negro and white, have been notoriously poor historians. Jazz itself has gained its direction from innovators—men who restructured the past in new terms. The major figures in jazz history (Louis Armstrong, Jelly Roll Morton, Lester Young, Duke Ellington, and Charlie Parker) have all been revolutionists, rejecting the work of their predecessors. Few musicians today know the names of Blind Lemon Jefferson, Jelly Roll Morton, or any of the figures commonly recognized by jazz scholars as being significant in the early stages of jazz history. But while Negro musicians have failed to learn their history from primary sources, they have been scrupulously keen in observing their "root" music as reinterpreted by modern performers such as Mahalia Jackson, Ray Charles, the Drinkard Singers, Bo Diddley, and any number of Negro singers whose materials lie somewhere in the midst of blues, gospel, and rock 'n' roll. The music performed by these individuals has been accepted by a large segment of the Negro and white audience and has been quite successful economically. This fact has not gone unnoticed by the young musician struggling to place himself in the tight jazz ranks. Thus, this Negro "neofolk" music has been transposed from its vocal form to the realm of the instrumental. The results apparently have been accepted by the public. The *New York Times* has indicated that "'soul jazz' has created a link between jazz and the pop market that can only be compared to the similar linking that occurred in the days of the vastly popular swing bands," and further, that it "appears to have drawn many of the fugitives from rock 'n' roll into the jazz market."[3]

If soul were merely a musical phenomenon, it would be interesting enough, but it has accompanying aspects that extend deeply into race consciousness and strong anti-white sentiments.

Some recent comments in the press give some idea of the current temperament among a number of Negro musicians:

There is the experience of the young Negro trombonist from Detroit who came close to starvation during several months of trying to establish himself, but nourished himself on the belief that his jazz at least had the authenticity that many white musicians lacked. His playing had "soul," and, as he once explained the term warily to a white jazz critic, "That soul only comes from certain kinds of experiences, and only we—you know who I mean—go through what you need to have the kind of soul that makes real jazz."[4]

"I was on the same bill with Brubeck," a prominent Negro trumpet player-leader has said, "and his combo got nearly all the attention even though they were playing nothing. It's like the people took it for granted that we could swing because we were Negroes, but thought it was something to make a fuss about when whites do it."[5]

In another article Nat Hentoff suggests the social function of the Soul Movement:

The term "I feel a draft" is used by Negro musicians when there's evidence in a restaurant—or elsewhere—of Jim Crow. Ironically, white musicians who have played with Negro groups have sometimes used the same phrase in order to tell each other that they're being frozen out of the conversation or an after hours party. . . . Many white musicians do feel self-conscious, to some extent, because their roots do not include the gospel music, the centuries of field hollers that led to the blues, and the general social and musical environment as a youngster that some Negro jazzmen believe to be necessary for "authentication" as a jazz player.[6]

. . . a Negro bass player joined the trio of a white leader and was severely criticized by friends in the Negro community. "That combo wouldn't swing at all if you weren't there, " he was lectured. "Why do you go with them and make those whites sound good?"[7]

The exclusiveness of soul has even penetrated the language of the Negro musician. John Tynan, writing in *Down Beat* about Les McCann, one of the "earthier" of the young Negro musicians, said:

Indeed the word *soul* itself has become synonymous with the truth, honesty, and yes, even social justice among Negro musicians. In some quarters, if one hears someone referred to as a "soul brother" or even just a plain unadorned "soul," the reference is clear—the individual is Negro.[8]

Soul has a similar usage as the term *heart* among members of adolescent gangs in New York City: as a symbol of the in-group, it represents a complex of characteristics that constitutes the requirements for membership in the elite. Leonard Feather, in *Music 1961*, tells of an incident, not uncommon in jazz circles, that is representative of the attitude among Negro musicians that has been termed "Crow Jim":

An illustrative incident was the hiring by . . . Julian (Cannonball) Adderley, of a sideman whose presence he was afraid might seem unacceptable to other members of his combo. The new man he wanted to hire was Victor Feldman. Not only an ofay, but a British ofay at that.

To convince his men that this was the right pianist for the group, Adderley had to sit them around a phonograph, play some records for them blindfold-test-style, and sell them on what they had heard before he could safely say that this was the man he planned to use.[9]

Feelings of their superiority among Negroes in jazz may not be new, but their overt manifestation of such feeling is. However, it has been obvious for some time that white jazz musicians by and large have been followers of Negro innovators, yet have been given public credit for the innovations. A pointed example would be Benny Goodman, whose very successful band was a carbon copy of Fletcher Henderson's earlier less successful group.

How does the jazz audience respond to soul? As previously indicated, jazz record sales are higher than ever. This boom has encouraged the return to "single" jazz records rather than long playing ones, an indication that this music can reach a larger audience. Certainly overt participation on the part of the audience has increased in the last few years, following the period of emotionless silence that characterized the cool period of jazz. In describing Les McCann's audience, John Tynan says:

The reaction of McCann's audience is sometimes remarkable. Some listeners have come up to touch him and thank him profoundly ("like we've healed them," as he puts it).[10]

Negro audiences, at least, are willing to turn a performance into a quasi-religious experience. I recently had the opportunity to witness singer Ray Charles in a concert before a predominantly Negro audience. Charles (who now affects an organ and a tambourine player) urged on singers and instrumentalists in his group with "play it, son," and "sing the song, girl." Over open chords he chanted, growled, and whined his songs, interlaced as they were with responses of "yeah," "all right," and "it's the truth" from the audience. Eventually the entire audience joined him in his songs, drowning out all but the incessant rhythms.

The significance of this attempted revival of folk elements is increased when we consider that revivals are not the rule in jazz. Only one genuine revival has occurred, that of New Orleans jazz, or dixieland, in the early forties. Curiously, this is a movement that Negroes took little or no part in. In fact, it is difficult to find a Negro band playing dixieland in this country. Further, there is no Negro audience for this music, live or on records.

What are the causes of the Soul Movement? A number of forces enters into this revival—a set of factors as broad as the history of Negro-white contacts in this country. First, it should be obvious that conditions of conflict are severe among jazz musicians. Rewards and positions are scarce and the criteria for the determination of skills change rapidly, making for much instability. Adding to these difficulties is the problem of segregation in jazz. Despite popular belief, racial contacts between musicians have not been particularly successful. A number of incidents make this clear:

(a) As recently as 1955–57, a great number of AFL-CIO musicians unions were segregated. Among such locals were San Francisco, Chicago, Boston, Buffalo, and New Haven.

(b) Of the thousands of jazz recordings made between 1917 and 1932, scarcely a dozen used integrated personnel.

(c) Benny Goodman's hiring of Teddy Wilson, a Negro, in 1935 was considered so radical that Wilson was forced to appear as an "act" with the band.

(d) Popular Negro entertainers, such as Ella Fitzgerald, Lena Horne, Nat Cole, Count Basie, and Duke Ellington, have failed to gain sponsored television shows, despite their efforts in that direction. Negroes are rare in studio bands. In addition, some TV shows still do not allow integrated groups to appear.

(e) There is a general lack of integration in traveling "name" bands today.[11]

There can be no doubt that white musicians have much greater security and success than their Negro counterparts. One is reminded, of course, of such names as Louis Armstrong and Miles Davis, exceptions to the rule, but they are truly exceptions, and are not representative of the mass of Negro musicians struggling to stay employed.

A second reason for the rise of soul might be the musical situation present when the first stirrings began in 1955. On one hand, "West Coast" jazz was in strong favor among the jazz record-buying public. An almost totally white body of musicians in California was capitalizing on an extension of the cool period of jazz. A general slump resulted in jazz activity on the East Coast. As the name implies, this was a "cooling-off" of jazz materials to the point of rhythmic and emotional sterilization. At the same time, rock 'n' roll was just beginning to prove successful with the non-jazz audience. It should be kept in mind that before it received its present title, rock 'n' roll was called rhythm and blues, and was usually issued on "race labels," recording companies entirely devoted to the Negro audience. There is, of course, a fundamental relationship between the blues and Negro church music that at times makes them difficult to separate. Thus many Negro jazz musicians saw monetary advantages in playing a more emotional music, a music built upon simple harmony, strong rhythm, and diatonic melodies. It is not difficult to see the resulting similarities between soul and rock 'n' roll.

It seems that the choice of soul as a means of gaining economic advantage over the white musician was a wise one. Thus far, most white musicians have refrained from playing it, and those that have tried have not appealed to a significant audience. Nat Hentoff commented recently in *Commonweal* that it is not uncommon to hear white musicians in New York wish that they had been born Negro, at least as far as musical possibilities are concerned.[12] White musicians in fact always have been aware of the differences in musical background between themselves and Negro musicians, since they are often called upon to play before Negro audiences. They have thus accepted the right of Negroes to exclusively play soul, even though they may be unhappy at their resulting disadvantage. Upon reading the 1956 *Down Beat* magazine's critic poll (which gave a large number of Negro musicians top awards), white band leader Stan Kenton sent the magazine a telegram expressing his "complete and utter disgust" with the results. He said further there was present now a "new minority group, White jazz musicians."[13]

The fact that soul has been so popular among white audiences is a reminder of Morroe Berger's explanation of the popularity of the spiritual in this country. Noticing the very slow acceptance of jazz, he was led to conclude that "throughout the United States, jazz was not so readily accepted as other forms of Negro music, especially spirituals, since they are associated with religious fervor and, in the eyes of White persons at least, show the Negro in a submissive rather than an exuberant role."[14]

Many Negro musicians express their belief that white musicians are better performers of classical music, but Negroes are "natural" jazz musicians.[15] These Negro jazz musicians thus have utilized to their advantage the stereotype of Negroes as natural singers, dancers, and musicians. This ascription of skills to members of the Negro race has been accepted readily by a large segment of the white musical jazz trade, particularly as it has been applied to a style of music previously untouched by white musicians.

The young Negro jazz musicians today are much more aware of their position in jazz history than were their forebears. Whereas earlier Negro musicians emigrated to France and Sweden to find acceptance for themselves and their music, the younger group, like their contemporaries at lunch counters and on buses, choose to fight it out on home soil. It is significant that, like other strong assertions of civil rights, soul appeared after the Supreme Court decision on segregated schools.

James Baldwin, in his article, "A Negro Assays the Negro Mood," indicates that Negroes of his generation were taught to be ashamed of Africa and its lack of contributions to civilization. In an age of bleaching creams, hair straighteners, and the "carryings on" of Father Divine, Negro Americans were rootless creatures. He continues:

But none of this is for those who are young now. The power of the white world to control their identities was crumbling as these young Negroes were born; and by the time they were able to react to the world, Africa was on the stage of history. . . . They were not merely the descendants of slaves in a white, Protestant, and Puritan country; they were also related to kings and princes in an ancestral homeland far away.[16]

Recent jazz compositions, too, reflect the new sensitivity to African nationalism: "A Message from Kenya," "Africa Speaks, America Answers," "Uhuru Afrika," and "Afro-American Sketches." Greater domestic awareness is notable in "Garvey's Ghost" and "Fables of Faubus."

Despite the special position in society of Negro musicians, they are first of all Negroes and are thus largely a reflection of the Negro community. As might be expected, a number of musicians have taken part in the Black Muslim movement of recent years. As with the advocates of soul music, C. Eric Lincoln estimates that up to 80 percent of a typical Black Muslim congregation is between the ages of seventeen and thirty-five.[17] Older Negro jazzmen, as with the older Negro population in general, have resisted such vigorous and aggressive movements. Most recently, the concern of Negro musicians over the racial situation was demonstrated outside of soul music in the performance and recording (under the auspices of the Congress of Racial Equality) of a Max Roach composition, the "Freedom Now Suite," dedicated to the Negroes of South Africa. Numerous concerts have been presented for the benefit of the National Association for the Advancement of Colored People, the Student Non-violent Coordinating Committee, and other groups.

Even dress and demeanor now show a response to a new image. Many Negro female singers crop their hair short, African style, and Negro jazz musicians are noted for their sartorial splendor; their Ivy League and Italian suits are a sharp contrast to the zoot suit of the forties. On stage many Negro musicians do not acknowledge applause, announce titles, nor, in general, recognize the audience in any way. Nat Hentoff quotes pianist John Lewis on the reaction of young Negroes to the "Uncle Tom" posture of older musicians: "the new attitude of these young Negroes was, 'Either you listen to me as the basis of what I actually do, or forget it!'"[18]

The conjunction of Negro art and race consciousness seen at the present time may have had its counterpart in an earlier period. One is reminded of the racist Garvey Movement of the 1920s and the simultaneous "New Negro" art movement in Harlem. While thousands of Negroes were talking about and saving to return to Africa, Negro poets, artists, and musicians were working intently at what might be called a "modern primitive" fad in New York City. Poet-playwright LeRoi Jones properly assesses the Soul Movement when he indicates that, more than simply an anti-white reaction and revivalistic gesture, it is part of the long-term attempt of Negro Americans to find or make a place in society:

The step from *cool* to *soul* is a form of social aggression. It is an attempt to place upon a meaningless social order an order which would give value to terms of existence that were once considered not only valueless but shameful. *Cool* meant non-participation; *soul* means a new establishment. It is an attempt to reverse the social roles within the society by redefining the canons of value. In the same way the "New Negroes" of the twenties began, though quite defensively, to canonize the attributes of their "Negro-ness," so the "soul brother" means to recast the social order in his own image. White is then not "right," as the old blues had it, but a liability, since the culture of White precludes the possession of the Negro "soul."[19]

From the many stereotypes imposed upon Negro Americans, Negro jazz musicians have selected one of the few positive ones—the "natural" ability for music—and have instrumentalized it for their own purposes of asserting identity. Significantly for an industrialized society, however, this effort was begun only after the essential idea had been tested on the marketplace (through the popularity of Negro rock 'n' roll and gospel-folk music) and had been found economically effective.

Chapter 3

Musical Adaptation Among
Afro-Americans

The earliest Afro-American studies were devoted to the music of African slaves. Nothing about the Negro seemed more fascinating than the mystery of the origins of his music. Was it an African product, reshaped to fit the New World? Or was it Anglo-American music, refashioned by African sensibilities? As basic questions these were appropriate, but instead of leading to deeper understanding the passion to illuminate origins resulted in explanations that frequently were shortsighted and territorially limited. Melville J. Herskovits was interested in origins, but he clearly warned that research suffered from a severe lack of knowledge about both African music and the secular music of the Negro.[1] Part of the problem has been poor observation and selective neglect. If students of Afro-America had been more interested in the Negro in the United States, they would have noted that in some areas of expressive culture—notably music, dance, and oral narrative—"Africanisms" have varied in intensity over time, rising and falling with specific conditions. It is still heard, for example, that African musical influences persist most strongly in sacred contexts, a point belied even by a casual acquaintance with Negro popular music today.

The rest is simply a matter of inadequate conceptualization. Since anthropologists and folklorists have chosen to reject biological-instinctual explanations of musical behavior in favor of cultural explanations, they must offer statements in social-cultural terms that realistically explain long-persisting patterns of musical behavior. Once we move beyond questions of origin to problems of persistence and change, we need answers to questions such as the following. What is the relation between normative musical traditions and those that challenge them? How do individual learning experiences relate to the normative patterns? Is there some direction or drift in the change of musical models? Do the models rise and fall in popularity? What variability from normative models is permitted? In general these are questions that remain unanswered in our understanding of music.

Recently several significant contributions to the study of Afro-American music seem to point the way towards broader understanding. Alan Lomax's cantometric analysis, for example, has richly illuminated the cultural dimensions of music and raised the essential issue of the adaptational nature of song style.[2] Norman Whitten's recent work on Colombian and Ecuadorian Negroes reveals suggestive directions for the study of social change through symbolic musical behavior.[3] What is needed now is a conceptual framework in which changes and retentions of musical style and context can be understood within a synthesis of social and cultural change. Such a framework would not only take into account the social and cultural facts of a musical society, but it would also integrate a people's musical forms and their associated performance roles and styles. It is to this central point that this paper is directed: song forms and performances are themselves models of social behavior reflecting strategies of adaptation to human and natural environments. For Afro-America, then, the problem becomes one of defining the situations within which blacks have found themselves and of relating their musical conceptions to their experience.

I

The distinction between sacred and secular music—the most significant native musical categories of the Negroes of the United States—was possibly set by the middle 1800s, and certainly before 1900. Jeanette Murphy spoke of the opposition between church songs and "fiddle" songs in 1899.[4] Although Calvinist notions contributed to the dichotomy, reformulated African religions were also important in defining the differences between sacred texts and the "devil's music." Alan Lomax has remarked on the widespread belief that skill on the fiddle required a pact with the devil, in a churchyard or at a crossroads.[5] Later, a similar pact was required of the blues singer:

As part of his initiation into the vaudou cult, the Negro novice must learn to play the guitar. He goes to the cross-roads at midnight armed with a black cat bone, and as he sits in the dark playing the blues, the Devil approaches, cuts the player's nails to the quick, and swaps guitars. Thus the vaudouist sells his soul to the Devil and in return receives the gift of invisibility and the mastery of his instrument. These practices may explain why the religious often call an expert Negro folk musician "a child of the Devil" or "the Devil's son-in-law."[6]

The significance of the sacred-secular distinction lies not only in perceived differences between the two categories as music, but also in their mutual exclusiveness in defining the social character of the individual performer. The literature of American Negro music abounds with this musical distinction and its implications as to the nature of the singer and the motivations that underlie the songs.[7] For example, in an interview with the Rev. Robert Wilkins (a former blues singer), Pete Welding summarizes Wilkins's comments on the two musical forms:

Distinguishing between spirituals and blues, Rev. Wilkins remarked that he performs only the former currently because of his conviction that the "body is the temple of the spirit of God" and that only one spirit can dwell in that body at any time. Blues, he feels are songs associated with the devil spirit, that the feeling blues express is not spiritual but sorrowful. It is true that blues help to relieve the "natural soul" of the singer but they fail to provide the sufferer any real spiritual solace; this can come only of praising the Lord and giving Him thanks for all things, good and bad alike. . . . The blues, he said, describe and relieve emotional troubles one might experience during life. The blues singer composes his songs primarily for himself but always is conscious of other potential listeners who might "be happy and enjoy it as I sing it."[8]

It is common even today for religious leaders to exhort their followers "to give up blues singing and join the church." Zora Neale Hurston quotes a sermon in *Jonah's Gourd Vine*, "The blues we play in our homes is a club to beat up Jesus."[9] Even the practicing bluesman may hold this view. Harriet J. Ottenheimer comments on New Orleans blues singer Babe Stovall: "He calls his talent a God-given gift and explains that because talent comes from God, it should be used for the playing of spirituals only, as a way of thanks for the gift. He styles himself as a sinner, however, and so plays other music, especially blues, besides spirituals. He plans to repent someday, and cease playing blues altogether, sinful music, in his opinion."[10] And the mother of infamous Mississippi bluesman Robert Johnson claimed that on his deathbed her son hung up his guitar and renounced his blues life, thus dying in glory.[11]

As these examples reveal, the sacred-secular dichotomy is not as clear as it might first appear to be. Secular function and text are not enough to place a form of music in opposition to church songs. The literature of Afro-American folksong shows that work songs and field hollers, for example, are not objected to by committed church members and religious leaders. Rather, it is the blues and bluesmen that represent the essence of the profane. The basic issue, as American blacks have seen it, is one of a sacred-blues dichotomy.

The importance of this dichotomy has not gone unnoticed. Roger Abrahams in his rhetorical analysis of urban Negro folklore, sees this as another example of the distinction between two types of "men-of-words" or "good-talkers" in the Negro community: the street corner bard and the preacher. Abrahams conceives of this as a contest for verbal power, the street talker addressing himself to the "homosexual, anti-feminine world of the early adolescent," the preacher directing his words "to women as well as men."[12] However, in *Urban Blues*, Charles Keil devotes himself to an intensive discussion of the sociological similarities underlying the two performance roles, commenting on the fact that many blues singers have become preachers (though, as he suggests, the process is not reversible). Common role characteristics, apparently, are the reason why perceived differences in behavior become so necessary, for as Keil notes, "Bluesman and preacher may be considered Negro prototypes of the no-good and good man respectively."[13]

Abrahams and Keil point out a very real opposition in the nature of the roles of bluesman and preacher, but the same opposition exists in the structure, style, and function of their performance. The church songs and spirituals of the Negroes in the southern United States closely resemble West African song style, particularly in their strong call-and-response pattern. An 1867 description of this pattern still remains one of the most succinct:

There is no singing in parts, as we understand it, and yet no two appear to be singing the same thing—the leading singer starts the words of each verse, often improvising, and the others who "base" him, as it is called, strike in with the refrain, or even join in the solo, when the words are familiar.

When the "base" begins, the leader often stops, leaving the rest of his words to be guessed at, or it may be that they are taken up by one of the other singers. And the "basers" themselves seem to follow their own whims, beginning when they please and leaving off when they please, striking an octave above or below (in case they have pitched the tune too low or too high), or hitting some other note that chords, so as to produce the effect of a marvelous complication and variety, and yet with the most perfect time, and rarely with any discord . . . they seem not infrequently to strike sounds that cannot be precisely represented . . . slices from one note to another, and turns and cadences not in articulated notes.[14]

This early description accurately notes the tightly woven interplay between members of the singing group, where a leader sets the pattern for the song but the group shapes its response independently. The nature of the group song-response was such that the song was participatory in nature; it invited the participation of all church members by leaving melodic and harmonic "holes" in the song that could be filled or left empty as the choice was made. At the same time, it was redundant enough to allow easy entrance into the message at any point. The church-song was a group phenomenon, hinged loosely on a leadership pattern, and in this sense the traditional spiritual (or, for that matter, the shout and other religious forms) perfectly paralleled the organizational structure of the American Negro church and the cooperative work team.

The blues, on the other hand, are almost unique among traditional American Negro folksong forms. First, they are sung solo, without the typical vocal call-and-response pattern so well known in other song forms. Of course, other songs than blues are sung solo—for example, the field holler and the lullaby—but these are forms that imply physical or social distance. In the case of the holler, the singers are separated from each other on the work field; the lullaby is addressed to an infant, itself not able to participate in song. Since the blues are solo, the form itself implies authority as much as does the classic Western European ballad; although the audience or the guitar may comment supportively, there is no song space for group participation. But because the blues are completely personalized (an example of what Abrahams calls the "intrusive 'I'"), there is an absence of the "objectivity" so widely commented upon in the ballad form. The blues are the least redundant of all American Negro forms. There is greater concern for textual message and meaning; they are information-oriented.

On the first look, of course, the blues appear wholly distinct from Western European song forms, and commentators have always pointed to the "blues scale" and the improvisatory character of the song as marks of its African character. This is deceptive. The blues performance is in many ways closer to white American folk music than to most other Afro-American song forms. When compared to Lomax's white American and African cantometric song profiles[15]—particularly in the parameters of vocal group organization, wordiness of text, embellishment, melisma, and raspy voice—the blues fall between these two musical orientations. Lomax's analysis is also helpful in suggesting the kinds of "normative messages"[16] carried by the blues. Being solo, rather than in the more familiar style of the interlocked leader-group song, they suggest a tendency towards authoritarian leadership patterns. The lesser use of nonsense words and redundancy present in the blues is another shift towards complexity typical of the music of complex societies. By the same token, solo singing characterizes individualized work patterns, as opposed to the more highly organized work groups of West Africa and American slavery. Since blues were usually sung by men (in the rural setting) as opposed to the mixed female-male singing of the churches, blues suggest that men are being presented as musical models in a shifting social order.

Blues, like religious behavior, are highly ritualized, apparently with the intention of easing or blocking "transformations of state in human beings or nature,"[17] rather than merely "entertaining." That is to say, ritual events attempt to restore social equilibrium, change organizational structures, or ease personal conditions of stress. Thus, singers speak of the blues as "relaxing the nerves," "giving relief," and "kinda helpin' somehow." Gospel singer Mahalia Jackson makes the point: "But he (the Negro) created his songs to lift his burden . . . so those that did not believe in God, they created the blues in the same vein that almost they wrote their spirituals."[18] The blues allow some things to be sung that could not otherwise be expressed. Henry Townsend of St. Louis says,

In other words there's several types of blues—there's blues that connects you with personal life—I mean you can tell it to the public as a song, in a song. But I mean, they don't take it seriously which you are tellin' the truth about. They don't always think seriously that it's exactly you that you talkin' about. At the same time it could be you, more or less it would be you for you to have the feelin'. You express yourself in a song like that. Now this particular thing reach others because they have experienced the same condition in life so naturally they feel what you are sayin' because it happened to them. It's a sort of thing that you kinda like to hold to yourself, yet you want somebody to know it. Now I've had the feelin' which I have disposed it in a song, but there's some things that have happened to me that I wouldn't dare tell, not to tell—but I would sing about them. Because people in general they takes the song as an explanation for themselves—they believe this song is expressing their feelings instead of the one that singin' it.[19]

The blues singer is by no means a shaman, but he performs in many of the shaman's capacities. He presents difficult experiences for the group, and the effectiveness of his performance depends upon a mutual sharing of experience.[20] Another former blues singer, now turned religious singer, L'il Son Jackson, makes the point this way:

You see it's two different things—the blues and church songs is two different things. If a man feel hurt within side and he sing a church song then he's askin' God for help. It's a horse of a different color, but I think if a man sing the blues it's more or less out of himself. . . . He's not askin' no one for help. . . . But he's expressin' how he feel. He's expressin' it to someone and that fact makes it a sin, you know, because it make another man sin . . . you're tryin' to get your feelin's over to the next person through the blues, and that's what makes it sin.[21]

The essential difference between the two means of psychological release focuses on the "direction" of the song: church music is directed collectively to God; blues are directed individually to the collective. Both perform similar cathartic functions but within different frameworks. There is a potential in song for individual and group expiation, as the singers themselves testify. At the same time, there is a means by which the personal conditions of both singers and listeners may be socialized, even under large-scale pressures that threaten individual or group identity.

II

I have briefly described the structure of these opposed musical forms in order to arrive at my central point: that musical forms and their associated performance roles and styles reflect alternative adaptational strategies, and that styles and counter styles can and usually do coexist in a single society.

Blues arose as a popular music form in the early 1900s, the period of the first great Negro migrations north to the cities. The blues were a form of secularized ritual—a breakaway from sacred forms, the spiritual or the gospel song, but performing parallel functions. As such, the formal and stylistic elements of the blues seem to symbolize newly emerging social patterns during the crisis period of urbanization. Unlike the group-conservative orientation of the sacred songs, the blues were authoritarian and aggressive, offering a secular-personalized view of the world; they were a "tough-minded" solution to social problems. Lomax quotes an anonymous informant: "The blues is just *revenge*. Like you'll be mad at the boss and you can't say anything. You out behind the wagon and you pretend that a mule stepped on your foot and you say, 'Get offa my foot, god-dam sonafabitch!' You won't be talkin' to the mule, you'll be referrin' to the white boss. . . . That's the way with the blues: you sing those things in a song when you can't speak out."[22] By replacing the functions served by sacred music, the blues eased a transition from a land-based agrarian society to one based on mobile, wage-labor urbanism. This is made all the more apparent by the characteristics of the blues singer's role. Unlike the stable, other-worldly, community-based image of the preacher (approved by Negro and white communities alike), the bluesman appears as a shadowy, sinful, aggressive, footloose wanderer, free to move between sexual partners and to pull up stakes as conditions call for it.[23] Keil makes this point: "The bluesman is in a sense every man: the country bluesman is an archetype of the migrant laborer; the city bluesman, a stereotype of the stud, the hustler; the urban blues artist, something of an ideal man or prototype for his generation as well."[24] The bluesman, for example, formalizes weak familial ties by making them appear culturally normative rather than just a problem for the individual. To paraphrase a gospel song, although I am inverting its meaning, he "lives the life he sings about in his song." Finally, as a stylistic mode, the blues mediate between the African and North American white musical sensibilities and thus provide an aesthetically satisfying musical statement of social reality, one most adaptive in aiding the transition from African slave to Afro-American.

These stylistic models are more than just descriptive manipulations. In the fullest sense, they have power in symbolizing and reinforcing social behavior. When Martin Luther King and the southern leaders of the Civil Rights Movement sought to collectivize group action, they returned to the older and more stable group orientation of the spiritual to coordinate activity. But when northern leaders of Black Power such as Stokely Carmichael operate, they surround themselves with jazzmen (the instrumental analogue of the blues singer) and singers of updated secular folksongs. In the last few years, however, there has been a conscious rejection of both spirituals and blues by urban Negroes. Spirituals and their traditional performance styles have almost disappeared, replaced by the more complicated, professionally oriented "gospel music," which Arna Bontemps calls a compound of "elements found in the old tabernacle songs, the Negro Spirituals and the blues."[25] A strong rhythmic structure with hand-clapping, shouting, and aggressive interplay characterizes this new type of church song. Gospel music frequently is not performed by the church members themselves but by trained choirs. Since they think of themselves as professionals, they often perform outside the church at quite secular functions. E. Franklin Frazier saw this change in musical style as a change in Negro religious life-style: "The Gospel Singers . . . do not represent a complete break with the religious traditions of the Negro. They represent or symbolize the attempt of the Negro to utilize his religious heritage in order to come to terms with changes in his own institutions as well as the problems of the world of which he is a part."[26]

Blues today—even of the electrified, city variety—are characterized by many urban Negroes as "dirty," "down-home," and "old-time." What has risen to replace both the blues and the spiritual is the broad category of music known as "soul," a popular, secular music, markedly similar to gospel music in everything but its verbal content. Soul music is so very close to gospel music that it often draws criticism from older followers of the sacred-secular distinction. Bluesman Big Bill Broonzy criticized Ray Charles thus: "He's got the blues he's cryin' sanctified. He's mixin' the blues with the spirituals. I know that's wrong."[27] Soul-singing—typified by such as Sam Cooke, Aretha Franklin, and Otis Redding (all of them former church singers)—is a polished, arranged blending of European bel canto and African call-and-response allowing for formalized group interplay with highly developed solo passages. Although it may be premature to see it as such, it appears that soul music draws from the older models of spirituals and the blues and, by unifying the sacred-secular dichotomy, has produced a stylistic mode adaptive to the urban Negro situation—a trend toward stability within self-contained ghetto subcultures based on mutual aid and individualism, best captured in the concept of "Black Power."

Soul music embodies a revival of "Africanisms," really older Afro-American style features, particularly in its rhythmic characteristics and call-and-response features. This borrowing of older musical patterns has been possible because some members of the community have continued to operate with former musical-social models. Although the older patterns have not been popular in the mass media, they have remained operative in some influential and slow-changing social institutions of the Negro community: the store-front church and the neighborhood bar, as well as grandmother's rocking chair and children's schoolyard games. Previous musical forms have been retained by older members of the community, who act as repositories of past traditions and of outdated adaptational features. In short, though, at any given time in a society, there are normative performance styles and roles; there are also counter styles and roles, surviving from the past and available for reworking into new styles.

III

It remains to be seen whether the same model of musical adaptation will hold for other parts of Afro-America. At first glance, it would appear that areas of slavery lacking a strong Protestant reinforcement would not conform to the sacred-secular musical dichotomy found in the United States. Tentatively, however, it appears to have application at least in the West Indies, Colombia, and Ecuador, areas under varying degrees of Catholic and Protestant influence. In Trinidad, calypso—a form often compared with the blues—holds a parallel position in relation to the songs of the cults and organized churches.[28] Like the blues, calypso developed after slavery, during the period of urbanization on the island, and seems to have a similar behavioral and stylistic base. Calypso is sung solo, is minimally redundant, and is highly personalized. Certainly calypso is authoritarian in performance pattern and text, and the combative nature of calypsonians during (and out of) performance is widely noted. It is also clear that the exponents of calypso are drawn from the most independent, "rootless," and aggressive strata of Trinidad society.[29]

Unlike the blues, calypso continues to dominate the urban musical landscape long after its nineteenth-century origins, functioning with immense popular support. The difference seems to lie in the fact that the middle class, regardless of color, has chosen to adopt calypso as a musical-social model for emerging Trinidadian-Tobagonian nationalism, making it the focus of its most important public ritual, the Carnival, and one of its most successful esthetic exports. To be sure, calypso song is a veritable statement of national character for Trinidadian residents and for those of the other islands in the West Indies as well, where Trinidad is identified as the epitome of urbanization and aggressive independence.[30]

In Colombia and Ecuador there is again a dichotomous conception of music, but Norman Whitten's analysis suggests that Euro-American, sacred-secular distinctions are absent or irrelevant.[31] Instead, musical forms and roles are pure statements of alternative behavioral strategies. Here, the marimba dance (*currulao*) and the saloon dance (popular "national" music) are in contrast. In the marimba song male and female singers and musicians are divided both in terms of repertory and performance. A call-and-response style expresses the views about household and sexual realignment of the two sexes, and in so doing provides stability to existing structures. In saloon dances, on the other hand, bands or phonographs provide the musical setting for token exchanges of drinks and dancing partners between males, leading to solidification of cooperative men's groups during times of economic gain and to new sexual partnerships. In both musical events dancers symbolically express contrasting notions of sexual alignment. In urbanized areas these musical oppositions are more intense, and they are staged on the same nights so that a choice of attending one or the other must be made. In fact, individuals attend one and then the other on different occasions. Yet, in doing so, they deny their participation in the other events, and even their existence.

Whitten's observation that individuals do participate in different musical events, even though they see them as mutually exclusive,[32] leads us to believe that our understanding of Afro-American musical categories may be incomplete and even superficial. Further inquiry may reveal that alternative musical forms not only exist simultaneously but may be more available to individual option than we have so far been led to believe. This may indeed be part of what Lerone Bennett, Jr., means when he warns against Euro-American interpretations of the Negro tradition: "The essence of the tradition is the extraordinary tension between the poles of pain and joy, agony and ecstasy, good and bad, Sunday and Saturday. One can, for convenience, separate the tradition into Saturdays (blues) and Sundays (spirituals). But it is necessary to remember that the blues and the spirituals are not two different things. They are two sides of the same coin, two banks, as it were, defining the same stream."[33] But whether or not a dichotomous model of musical social reality is fully applicable to Afro-America, a unified musical form and performance role analysis appears necessary. An awareness of styles and counter styles in all aspects of expressive culture should offer us a richer and more realistic picture of the New World Negro experience.

Chapter 4

An American Anthropological Dilemma: The Politics of Afro-American Culture

"Harlem was never like this!"
—*Mantan Moreland, in the film* King of the Zombies

I

It is more than obvious that anthropology has from its beginnings had some pleasant advantages not available to the other social sciences. Working in distant places, largely with nonliterate peoples, anthropologists have seldom had to face their informants as critics of their published work; and having luxuriated in a sparsely populated discipline, they have often been able to avoid even the critical assessments of colleagues who have worked with the same people. In this comfortable situation anthropology developed smoothly, free to move at its own rate, with subjects of its own choice. Perhaps only in times of national upheaval, such as periods of economic instability or war, have its purposes and findings been seriously questioned. When answers to urgent problems are sought in the society as a whole, anthropology comes under pressure to supply answers, to speak to its time and its people's problems, to be, as they say, relevant. Moreover, it is difficult to avoid these challenges, for the anthropological perspective has already had its effects on American thinking; and reciprocally, the country's particular concerns have had their effects on the kinds of problems that anthropology undertakes and the manner in which it undertakes them.

Unfortunately, it is precisely when societal needs are most pressing that the difficulties of doing research and communicating its results are most pronounced. In recent days, such problems have produced an anxiety and desperation that fill professional meetings and shadow research projects. There is concern with spies among scientists, with malign forces behind research projects. In addition, the exacerbated class, racial, sexual, and political divisions in American society have become confused with the more vulgar facts of professorial competition, so that critical areas of concern are even more difficult to approach. Faced with such strains, some have a tendency to "ghettoize" research and teaching and to demand that anthropologists work only with their "own" people;[1] others, to withdraw in despair from research altogether; and still others, to become mere propagandists.

But in addition to spies, hidden motives, and withdrawal from research, there is loose in anthropology a sense of purposelessness, a lack of direction, and even a growing skepticism about the vision of man that anthropology developed. It is thus a need to restore purpose and personal commitment to anthropology that has lately prompted a variety of impassioned suggestions, perhaps the most appealing of which is a call for anthropology to become involved in the defense of the oppressed peoples of the world and to abandon illusory scientific objectivity: in short, a demand for anthropology to undertake committed, partisan research.[2] This is a serious proposal and it deserves serious consideration. As a beginning, I would like to briefly review in this essay one area of anthropological work of great contemporary relevance—the study of Afro-American peoples in the United States—and to argue that in at least this area just such a proposal has in fact been accepted and acted upon for the last forty years, but with rather dismal results. And I will further suggest that in these respects cultural anthropology's contemporary problems are even more complex and plaguing than we have dared think.

II

We can begin by observing that American anthropologists have done almost no research in the usual sense among Afro-Americans in the United States. Why? Several commentators have addressed themselves to this subject and have agreed that the "impure," "acculturated" nature of American blacks made them poor subjects for a cultural anthropology originally bent on reconstructing the ethnographic past of isolated societies.[3] Less charitable but equally important is the fact that Afro-Americans were geographically too close and of too low status for professional prestige in American society. William S. Willis, Jr. calls attention to other political constraints on the study of Afro-Americans, especially the uncomfortable fit of imported ex-slaves to the usual anthropological image of a proper subject—that is, natives defeated and dominated by imperialistic enterprise on their home soil.[4] Ann Fischer, in addition, suggested that field work among lower-class Afro-Americans lacks the exoticism that so appeals to anthropologists. Further, she argued that love of informant and anthropologist for each other is a prerequisite for sound anthropological research and one that is difficult to achieve among Afro-Americans.

Quoting Margaret Mead, she insisted that it would be impossible for an anthropologist to convince ghetto residents that he has any respect for their way of life.[5] However, there seem to me to be more fundamental factors restricting and circumscribing this research, factors discoverable first in the beginnings of American anthropology, in the ideas of Franz Boas during the early 1900s.

Boas was of course the most influential professional anthropologist of his time, and he also became the chief scientific spokesman on the subject of race and its social implications. Viewing race as a statistical range of a given population, he argued for cultural influences on physique and introduced new evidence on the plasticity of the human organism. In addition, by insisting on the study of particular cultures as functional responses to universal needs, rather than as unique expressions of "racial genius," Boas created an intellectual framework and a body of evidence to support the central premise lying behind all of his work: the necessity for keeping race and culture conceptually distinct.

When Boas encountered arguments for racial determination of culture, he chose to oppose them by using the ethnographic facts of exotic societies such as the Eskimo and, by placing these facts in a relativistic framework. But Afro-Americans—certainly the chief object of racist speculation at the time—seem not to have appeared to him to provide good evidence for this kind of argument, as illustrated by a comment in *The Mind of Primitive Man*:

The traits of the American Negroes are adequately explained on the basis of his history and social status. The tearing away from the African soil and the consequent complete loss of the old standards of life, which were replaced by the dependency of slavery and by all that it entailed, followed by a period of disorganization and by a severe economic struggle against heavy odds, are sufficient to explain the inferiority of the status of the race, without falling back upon the theory of hereditary inferiority.[6]

Similarly, when at W. E. B. Du Bois's request Boas addressed the graduating class at Atlanta University in 1906, he urged black students to become aware of the many cultural accomplishments of Africa and directed the class to confront those who argued for the innate inferiority of Afro-Americans with this reply:

that the burden of proof lies with them, that the past history of your race does not sustain their statement, but rather gives you encouragement. . . . say that you have set out to recover for the colored people the strength that was their own before they set foot on the shores of this continent.[7]

Though this was an astonishingly strong statement of negritude for a white *or* a black man of the period, it is also remarkable in its evasion of the issue of the existence and nature of an Afro-American culture.

Boas's political liberalism is evident in his involvement with Du Bois on many ventures, such as the founding of the National Association for the Advancement of Colored People in 1910, in which he became part of the opposition to the accommodationist strategies of Booker T. Washington. Boas had completed numerous anthropometric studies of both whites and blacks, and having discovered the nonexclusive and overlapping nature of racial statistics, he argued eloquently against the reliability of racial identity as a means of predicting cultural capacity. But when he dealt with Afro-American culture, he was equivocal. It is as if the "hard" data of physical anthropology misled Boas into confusing race and culture in a manner opposite to that of the usual confusion of his era—in other words, the overlapping statistics of the physical features of the two races together with overlapping scores on intelligence tests may have led Boas to infer that blacks, as a group, simply "overlapped" white American culture, if only imperfectly.[8] Much the same argument appears in Boas's student Ruth Benedict's *Race: Science and Politics*:

Their patterns of political, economic, and artistic behavior were forgotten—even the languages they had spoken in Africa. Like the poor whites of the South, they gathered together instead for fervent Christian revivalist camp meetings; they sang the hymns the poor whites sang, and if they sang them better and invented countless variations of great poignancy, nevertheless the old forms which they had achieved in Africa were forgotten. Conditions of slavery in America were so drastic that this loss is not to be wondered at. The slaves on any one plantation had come from tribes speaking mutually unintelligible languages, and with mutually unfamiliar arts of life; they had been herded together like cattle in slave ships and sold at the block in a strange and frightening world. They were worked hard on the plantations. It is no wonder that their owners remarked on their lack of any cultural achievements; the mistake they made was to interpret the degradation of the slave trade as if it were an innate and all-time characteristic of the American Negro. The Negro race has proud cultural achievements, but for very good reasons they were not spread before our eyes in America.[9]

In *Patterns of Culture*, too, she argued that in Northern cities as well Afro-Americans had come to "approximate in detail that [culture] of whites in the same cities."[10]

Meanwhile, other anthropologists, such as Ashley Montagu, attempted to exorcize both the folk and the scientific concepts of race.[11] And as such arguments developed over the years, there was a tendency for scientists to deny the existence of *both* racial differences in capacity *and* any significant cultural differences between members of the two different "races." It is important to reiterate that these anthropologists arrived at their conclusions, not on the basis of ethical neutralism, but through a deep commitment to the need for social change. Indeed, it was in their very zeal to refute genetic racism for general audiences and to demonstrate a universal capacity for culture that they argued that Afro-Americans shared essentially the same culture as white Americans, and where they differed, the differences were to be accounted for exclusively as the result of environmental deprivation or cultural "stripping," but certainly not as the result of any normal cultural processes.

Launched and reinforced by these anthropological conceptions, sociologists took up their own version of the same arguments; they soon went much further, bolstering their position with statistical surveys, while still lacking any ethnographically based insights into black life. The chief work in sociology was done at the University of Chicago, where Robert E. Park and E. Franklin Frazier developed what Charles Valentine has called the "pejorative tradition": the use of social pathologists' data to describe black communities as disorganized and culturally nonadaptive.[12] Frazier, for example, in commenting on the significance of Afro-American culture, said:

To be sure, when one undertakes the study of the Negro he discovers a great poverty of traditions and patterns of behavior that exercise any real influence on the formation of the Negro's personality and conduct. If . . . the most striking thing about the Chinese is their deep culture, the most conspicuous thing about the Negro is his lack of a culture.[13]

But perhaps the key contribution of the sociological approach was the work done by Gunnar Myrdal and his associates, who developed their arguments on the basis of an extensive examination of the degree of damage done to black Americans by racism and slavery. Typical was the section of *An American Dilemma* that deals with the Negro community: Myrdal argued that the Negro is "characteristically American" and is "not proud of those things in which he differs from the white American."[14] Following this, he lists features of Negro life which are a "distorted development, or a pathological condition, of the general American culture." The list includes the "emotionalism" of their churches, the "insufficiency and unwholesomeness" of their recreational activity, "the plethora of Negro sociable organizations," "the cultivation of the arts to the neglect of other fields," and so on.[15]

One might have thought that such views were doomed to easy refutation, since lower-class Afro-Americans continued to manifest patterns of behavior in many domains of activity which were distinctively their own, with a historical and comparative basis in Africa and elsewhere in the Americas. However, these "culturally different" behaviors (i.e., different from white middle-class culture) continued to be treated as evidence of deviance, as social pathology, as failures on the part of individual black people in the face of oppression; and if these behaviors became recognized as patterned and normative, they were nonetheless treated as part of a deficit culture,[16] a kind of negative culture existing in the absence of a real one. Afro-American culture was—in Ralph Ellison's phrase— nothing more than the sum of its brutalization.[17]

By the 1950s and 1960s such views had assumed the status of ortho- doxy, and were nowhere better summarized than in Glazer and Moyni- han's *Beyond the Melting Pot*, where it is said that in America the Negro "has no values and culture to guard and protect." If there was some grumbling over Glazer and Moynihan's straightforwardness, there was, and is, very little objection to, say, Kenneth B. Clark's portrayal of Har- lem as nothing more than a cultural hell;[18] or Christopher Lasch's easy dismissal of "ghetto culture" as "thin" and chiefly characterized by "despair and self-hatred"; or Michael Harrington's or Lee Rainwater's reading of black expressive culture as self-destructive or detrimental to develop- ment; or Grier and Cobb's suggestion that black dialect and speech events are evidence of mental disorder among black males; or Kardiner and Ovesey's diagnosis of black dancing as a product of pure rage.[19]

If prophets of deficit culture were simply unaware of a counter posi- tion on these matters, they might be dismissed as naive and ignorant. But a quick scanning of the literature will show that everyone from Frazier forward has known of the kind of distinctive culture argument mounted by Melville J. Herskovits (see below), and most feel compelled to dismiss Herskovits out of hand. Stanley Elkins, for example, in *Slavery*, after wondering "how it was ever possible that all this [West African] native resourcefulness and vitality could have been brought to such a point of utter stultification in America," dismisses Herskovits' position as concerned with "esoteric vestiges of a suspiciously circumstantial nature."[20] Milton Gordon is more systematic in his dismissal of Herskovits and Afro-American culture, when, in *Assimilation in American Life*, he curi- ously divides ethnic culture into *intrinsic* ("essential and vital") elements such as ethics, religion, music, language, and history, and *extrinsic* (situ- ationally adaptive) elements such as dress, "manner," "emotional expres- sion," and dialect.[21] In this way, he can suggest that Yiddish and Italian as well as Judaism and Catholicism are intrinsic elements for Jews and Italians, while black dialects and the "frenzy" and "semi-coherence" of fundamentalist black churches are extrinsic. ("Were the argot . . . to dis- appear, nothing significant for Negro self-regard as a group or the Negro's sense of ethnic history and identity would be violated."[22] One could, alas, go on at length extending this list, but in all the diagnosis is the same: lower-class Afro-Americans have no distinctive culture or sub- culture of their own and what they do have is a nonsupportive or patho- logical version of "mainstream" American culture. Only on the question of remedy is there disagreement.

Again, the terms of this matter are just those in which anthropologists have some expertise, and it is surprising to see how much has been left to laymen and other social scientists. The fact is that most anthropologists seem themselves to have accepted the conventional wisdom on these matters, especially as it was an unpleasant experience to enter into a field of inquiry in which laymen had preceded them and had given racist interpretations to the same kinds of data the anthropologist is interested in. Anthropologists also avoided the issue of gathering or analyzing data on other ethnic groups that might challenge the assumption of a melting-pot society, except where the "culturally different" groups could be shown to have behaviors clearly positive in white middle-class terms. Consequently, we have dozens of articles in anthropological journals on Japanese Americans, whose enterprise, thrift, and cleanliness are stressed.

Thus, in the main, anthropologists and other social scientists have taken a very special position toward Afro-Americans: they have either ignored them, or, abandoning their most sacred dogmas—value-free methods and the necessity for firsthand empirical evidence—they have proceeded to pronounce on black people in a thoroughly nonrelativistic manner, presumably excusing their departure in the name of social justice. Politicos to the contrary, research in black communities by white or black social scientists has hardly begun, unless, of course, one is willing to grant ethnographic status to studies of "culture at a distance," reminiscent for all the world of those carried out on the enemy in World War II.[23]

If the pathologists' approach were simply a matter of professional infighting, it could perhaps be ignored. But I think that the evidence is that the noncultural and deviance orientations of the social sciences toward Afro-Americans have taken hold broadly across the society, and that it is this view that is hardening as the racial stresses of the society increase. Witness the wide popularity of the notion of "cultural deprivation" among politicians, educators, and social workers by which, in an irony cruel to anthropology, material poverty is grossly confused with ideological poverty, culture now being given a remarkably restricted definition. (One recent study suggested that multipurpose room use in crowded slum housing prevents residents from developing "normal" middle-class kinship relations; or, in other words, house type determines kinship patterns!)

Thus, black Americans, having survived the cruel discrediting of slavers and segregationists and the curiously ambivalent stereotypes of abolitionists, must now confront a new bizarre reading of their lives and traditions. It is startling to realize that in the following quotation Ralph Ellison is objecting not to the crude renderings of traditional racists, but to those of the contemporary left:

Many of those who write of Negro life today seem to assume that as long as their hearts are in the right place they can be as arbitrary as they wish in their formulations. . . . They have made of the no man's land created by segregation a territory for infantile self-expression and intellectual anarchy. They write as though Negro life exists only in light of their belated regard, and they publish interpretations of Negro experience which would not hold true of their own or for any other form of human life.

Here the basic unity of human experience that assures us of some possibility of empathetic and symbolic identification with those of other backgrounds is blasted in the interest of specious political and philosophical conceits. Prefabricated Negroes are sketched on sheets of paper and superimposed upon the Negro community; then when someone thrusts his head through the page and yells, "Watch out there, Jack, there's people living under here," they are shocked and indignant.[24]

But perhaps most disturbing is the fact that many black political activists now find it increasingly impossible to press their case for social justice without evoking this social science fiction monster. Now the jargons of the social worker, the psychiatrist, and the anthropologist have been correctly divined as something, at last, to which the white middle class will respond.[25] (Let no one say that the War on Poverty produced no results!)

III

Yet there is an alternative view of Afro-Americans to that of the pathologists, one which begins by examining the distinctive culture history of black people in the United States. It appeared almost forty years ago in the folkloristics of Boas' student Zora Neale Hurston and later in the research of linguist Lorenzo D. Turner, themselves black Americans.[26] And Paul Radin and Hortense Powdermaker, too, followed the cultural tradition of American ethnography in their studies of Afro-Americans.[27] But it was Melville J. Herskovits who undertook the most serious and systematic study of Afro-American culture in the United States. After years of field work in Haiti, Trinidad, Brazil, and West Africa, Herskovits formulated a comprehensive view of the culture history of Afro-Americans in the United States, which he published in 1941 as *The Myth of the Negro Past*.[28] In this work he chose to oppose the consensus of virtually all of the white and black intellectuals and laymen of his time by presenting an outline of the African cultural background of American blacks and by developing a theory of cultural change that would argue for the persistence and continuity of some aspects of this culture.

Soon after publication of this book, however, interests in anthropology shifted heavily toward the ahistoricism of social structural studies, and as a result the weakest features of the book were dwelled upon critically while its strengths were ignored.[29] And, most unfortunately, Herskovits's *handling* of cultural facts was assailed, while the *facts* themselves were discarded. With hindsight, however, one senses that perhaps the primary objection to *Myth* stemmed from the fear that Herskovits's conclusions might be used by racists and the ethnocentrically inclined to build a case against integration and social equality. Perhaps if a person with lesser antiracism and civil rights credentials than Herskovits had attempted this work, he might have been labeled a racist.[30]

It appears certain that Herskovits was fully aware of the political implications of Afro-American cultural studies. Early in his career he had rejected the possibility of any African-derived or independent Negro cultural reality.[31] Later, once he began to work in what he called the "cultural laboratory" of comparative Afro-American cultures across the New World and reversed his argument,[32] he seems to have been concerned with the impact that his data might have on a white society which already asserted racial-cultural differences from a folk perspective of genetic racism; consequently he chose to present his findings in such an oblique manner as to put the white American reader on the defensive. First, he tried to show that Afro-American cultural behaviors had an honorable and, from the standpoint of cultural relativism, valid basis in African culture; and second, he argued that American whites had already been acculturated to the point that they had unknowingly absorbed a great deal of African culture, even in some of the most sacred of white American domains.[33] But by the time Herskovits wrote *Myth* there was no questioning his political assumptions and goals: (1) "to give the Negro an appreciation of his past" and "endow him with the confidence in his own position in this country and in the world which he must have," and (2) "to influence opinion in general concerning Negro abilities and potentialities, and thus contribute to a lessening of interracial tensions."[34]

After publication of *Myth*, a few scholars such as the black historian Carter Woodson welcomed it as a great breakthrough, but most of them followed E. Franklin Frazier in rejecting it as misguided or exaggerated. Ironically, now, thirty years later, there is something of a drift of black ideology in the direction of Herskovits's thesis, so that those who reject the cultural approach must again at least address themselves to Herskovits. Now, for example, arguing that contemporary Afro-American culture is nothing more than a culture of poverty, Christopher Lasch must complain that "unfortunately the whole question of African survivals has now become involved in the politics of cultural nationalism, and it is hard to argue against Herskovits without being accused of wishing to subvert the cultural identity of black people."[35]

Over the last thirty years no one has dared to attempt a work of the scope of Herskovits's, but scattered through a half-dozen disciplines there is a body of Afro-American cultural data that has been accumulating nonetheless. Though there is less interest in African origins, we now have a sizable literature that provides evidence for the existence of the following distinctive Afro-American cultural domains: aesthetics, including plastic arts, crafts, architecture, music, verbal lore, and dance; speech; oral history; religion; and the vaguely defined but vitally important areas of style and interpersonal behavior.[36] The literature on the slave and the slavery experience has been renewed as improved data on the slave trade appeared.[37] Even though thoroughly muddled by lack of facts, the issue of Afro-American kinship is also being reopened.[38] And the lessons learned among other Afro-Americans in the Caribbean and South America are assuming fresh meaning for the United States, especially as Cubans and Puerto Ricans begin to become major revitalization forces in urban centers.[39] There are even hints that Afro-American data may offer new insights for the understanding of Africa itself.[40]

None of these Afro-American cultural studies is satisfactorily comprehensive, but seen together they offer a substantively alternative view of black people in America. First, they all assert that from the beginnings of slavery Afro-Americans exercised the capacity to perpetuate and create means of comprehending and dealing with the natural and social worlds surrounding them—they were culture bearers and creators as well as receivers and learners. In other words, although slavery, poverty, and racism have severely circumscribed the exercise of this capacity, even sometimes driving it underground, these constraints can in no way be seen as the sufficient cause of Afro-American behavior. All of this is borne out by both the continuities and the discontinuities that exist between black people in North and South America and in Africa. Nor do these studies see Afro-American culture as being exclusively negative, "thin," nonsupportive, or "reactive." Far from seeing black Americans as having "no values and culture to guard and protect," they cumulatively suggest that in some respects Afro-Americans have guarded and protected their culture better than any other ethnic or national group in the United States. In fact, they additionally argue that blacks have elaborated some cultural domains in such a rich and vital manner that they have been the source of a huge portion of unacknowledged American culture. Finally, these studies indicate that one cannot set about describing and measuring black cultural incapacity, pathology, and deprivation by crudely comparing and contrasting black and white behaviors and institutions to see how closely black approximates white (whites forever the "control group"), suspending, all the while, a century of Euro-American criticisms of the pathology of Western behaviors and institutions.

But there are counterarguments raised in anthropology against the notion that Afro-Americans have a distinct cultural heritage and a distinct subculture. Briefly, the first is that the harshness of the slavery experience wiped out all vestiges of African culture and that that experience, followed by segregation and racism, acted to create a deficit or poverty culture. One need only note in objection here that *no one* arguing this point has used any quantity of primary data on slavery or the slave trade; in addition, very few undertaking this argument have been familiar enough with West African cultures to be able to recognize such cultural elements in operation in the New World if they saw them. It is significant that the most serious and competent critic of the African survival thesis, M. G. Smith, set standards for such research that virtually assured that no proof could be established. One such was that "traits regarded as evidence of the persistence of African cultural forms must be formally peculiar and distinct from the customs or institutions characteristic of all other cultural groups within the society of their location."[41] In other words, when in doubt, assume that Africans always turn Euro-American.

Less sophisticated counterarguments simply say that if one suggests that any African cultural elements did survive slavery, or became transmuted, then one is saying that slavery was really not such a bad experience after all; or that if African cultural traditions did persist, they were of a superficial nature (music, folk tales, language, religion, and the like) and not substantive—that is, institutional. Thus, the obsessive concern with the nature of the black family.

The problem with these arguments is clearly evident. At root, they suffer from a lack of ethnographic data on Afro-Americans and an ignorance of existing historical materials on slavery and racial contact in the American South and elsewhere, as well as a refusal to effectively use the second basic tool of cultural and social anthropology: the comparative method. Secondly, they are unabashedly ethnocentric, not only in their bias toward institutions and institutional relationships at the expense of culture, but also in their preoccupation with questions of black-white interaction with no concern whatsoever for black-black interaction.

IV

But, having heard all of this, some will insist that there have nonetheless been gains from politically committed research which stressed the destructive aspects of being black in a society built on racist principles. Doubtless such research has played an important role in "unmasking" the social structure of the United States and in demonstrating the massive human costs of such a society. This should not be gainsaid. But even at this pragmatic level there is reason to doubt the long-run utility of the exclusivity of this approach and the wholesale selection and distortion of Afro-American life which accompanied it.

To take an example, virtually all of the race-relations literature of the last thirty years argued that the way out of the American racial dilemma was clear: integration must be implemented in all areas and changes effected in the life-style of the poor and black—toward white middle-class "enrichment" aspirations.[42] It was on the crest of this research and its policy actualization that a counter movement toward separation and withdrawal from integration began among black people. Many have argued that this was clearly the result of a distrust of white people's willingness to make basic changes in America,[43] and certainly such distrust is massively justified. But might it not also have been that a significant number of black people—especially those poor who were on the receiving end of the change process—also began to tire of the stigmatization and forced change that were attached to these programs? Is it not possible that the rejection of one's whole life-style was simply too dear a price to pay, especially when the reasons for doing so were so spurious and the rewards so remote? Was the rejection of whites from positions of leadership in the civil rights movement merely a matter of a wish to assert black control, or was it in addition a move to resist unreasonable and irrelevant white cultural models of change? The answers to these questions are frankly not certain, for social scientists have not been used to doing this kind of thinking.

But whatever the causes, we are now faced with a situation in which interracial politics are intertwined with social science such that current changes in political strategy and style instantly reverberate through social science. Now research begins to appear that "confirms" that racial separation rather than integration is *the* answer. In this liminal confusion of failure and inadequacy some social scientists call for an end to all research with the black poor, asserting that we "know enough." It would be one thing to recognize that long-distance studies of degradation have begun literally to exhaust their subject, but it is altogether another to arrogantly acclaim a sufficiency of knowledge and at the same time to assume a posture of heroic self-denial! Other social scientists call for a moratorium on Afro-American research by whites in order to establish black hegemony in the field with the expectation that black social scientists' work will be more satisfactory than that of the whites. But thus far most black social scientists have bought the same methods and conceptual approaches which rendered their white nonbrothers incapable of dealing with a major portion of lower-class Afro-American life and culture. (One need only contrast the treatment of black culture by black artists and fiction writers with that of black social scientists to sense the inadequacy.)

Yet another variant of such arguments has it that *any* research on black people—even that of the highest quality done by either black or white with the best of intentions—may be used to further oppress and control with greater efficiency, and thus should not be done. But this is a simplistic and dreamlike argument, one that presupposes the possibility of controlling information about the "black community" and that ignores the everyday interracial contacts through which information passes. It ignores, too, the fact that *where a people lacks sufficient information about another people, the blanks are filled in by fantasy*—as indeed has been happening these many years in social science. Finally, it denies the possibility of research ever being of use to its subjects; even though this appears to have typically been the case of Afro-Americans in the United States, anthropology has been of some importance to Afro-Americans elsewhere in the Americas where it has been pursued in less restricted, politically limited fashion.[44]

V

I have been arguing by example that a politicized and partisan approach to anthropology is not in and of itself an answer to the kinds of dilemmas in which anthropology finds itself today. In short, mere commitment, advocacy, and explicit rejection of injustice are by no means sufficient to make anthropology relevant to the problems of the contemporary world. *In the absence of descriptive honesty and imagination, such a position serves as a smoke screen for simple failure and inadequacy.* Worse, perhaps, in the Afro-American case, the radical position comes to little more than that of the reactionaries.

Political positions are easy to assume in research, especially when the causes are popular among one's peers, but it is another thing to be aware of how one's research relates to one's cause. It was my intention here to show how a veneer of partisanship has allowed shabby research on Afro-Americans in the United States to persist in the face of a continuing racial crisis. Afro-Americans as people, as human, cultural creators, have been sacrificed to serve as causes, as ciphers in an anthropology of pathos.

In my insisting on a cultural approach as a specific corrective to the Afro-American dilemma in anthropology, it should be clear that I am not calling for a period of "benign neglect" of the hard realities of American social structure and racial separation—only a scoundrel or a fool could ignore the country's need to deal swiftly and directly with the poverty and injustices brought on by its racial policies and attitudes. Yet at the same time I would insist that social scientists have also escaped this task by merely preaching, pointing fingers, and using "racism" in a simpleminded explanatory fashion—this, instead of defining and describing racism and the mechanisms and institutions which maintain it, delineating the nature and transmission of racist attitudes, or showing the broad linkages that underlie and support racist thought and policy.[45] For those who would suggest that a concern for Afro-American culture is an evasion of the real issue—racism and the larger American social structure—I can only insist that the ascription of culturelessness and partial humanness to Afro-American peoples is basic to both racism and the social system. In exploring the order and kind of influence of Afro-American culture on the various black and white populations of America, we not only move a step closer to the working of "the system," but we also lay a basis for attaching a humanistic conception of man to efforts at social and economic change.

I am asking, then, that we "desegregate" anthropology, giving Afro-Americans the best we can as observers of human cultural capacity and achievement. If we treat Afro-Americans without political posturing, hidden assumptions, and smuggled motives, I am convinced that their cultural accomplishments will not need the spurious defenses and the eleventh-hour apologies that we have been in the habit of offering in the name of research. Lastly, I am of course not arguing that commitment and political partisanship have no place in social science, merely that the links between advocacy and research be clearly articulated, related, and executed. If this is done, it will not be necessary to belabor the obvious—that partisanship and bias are by no means the same thing.

Beyond all of this, anthropologists should be concerned with the need for what Alan Lomax calls *cultural equity*, the rights of a people to maintain, choose, and create cultural alternatives. To do this, it is necessary to develop and make known the kind of descriptive and historical materials which anthropologists can provide, especially to those colonized peoples who have for so long been cut off from their own histories and traditions, and from each other. It should be remembered that cultural stripping was by no means limited to slavery days, but still continues in the classroom and on television, as well as in anthropological journals—in fact, wherever a narrow vision of man and his creative, expressive power is held.

It might be inserted that a cultural approach to Afro-Americans will not be without its own rewards to anthropology as a discipline. By coming to terms with the spurious characterizations of diverse cultural behavior—those which explain cultures as being "reactive," or as nothing more than those of poverty, or of the oppressed—the role of the individual in society can emerge with greater clarity here in our midst than it ever did abroad. Basic anthropological concepts such as acculturation can also take on new meaning when applied here at home. It was, after all, Malinowski, nowadays increasingly dismissed as an imperialist, who, in a discussion of the acculturation of Afro-Americans, warned that the concept was ethnocentric and fraught with moral connotations :

The immigrant has to *acculturate* himself; so do the natives, pagan or heathen, barbarian or savage, who enjoy the benefits of our great Western culture. . . . The "uncultured" is to receive the benefits of "our culture"; it is he who must change and become converted into "one of us."

It requires no effort to understand that by the use of the term *acculturation* we implicitly introduce a series of moral, normative, and evaluative concepts which radically vitiate the understanding of the phenomenon. . . . Every change of culture . . . is a process in which something is always given in return for what one received . . . a process in which both parts of the equation are modified, a process from which a new reality emerges, transformed and complex, a reality that is not a mechanical agglomeration of traits, not even a mosaic, but a new phenomenon, original and independent.[46]

With the exception of some brief comments by Herskovits and a few literary critics, the influence of Afro-Americans on American "mainstream" culture remains mysteriously unwritten, a part of our own "preliterate" period. It may be difficult to bring middle-class academics, those who find so little meaning in their own ethnicity and traditions, to the point where they can see that others may have seen their own lives in a different manner. But the task is necessary, and it grows more necessary every day, particularly as we must now begin to think of the influence of Afro-American culture and history on the entire world, as mediated by the influence of the United States.[47]

The dilemma comes to this: despite their clearly recognized non-European source and their unique history of enforced isolation from the rest of society, some 25,000,000 American people are not subject to understanding by anthropologists in any terms except as dependents or appendages of a vaguely defined white social structure. And the justification for this is the power and dominance of the economic and social systems of the United States. But since most of the non-Western world is in the process of coming within a similar relationship with the United States and the other developed nations, just such logic means that the anthropology of the immediate future will be nothing more than a particularly narrow and sterile sociology and the study of antiquities.

One could feel comfortably *au courant* if the inability of anthropologists to come to terms with Afro-American life could be dismissed as simple ethnocentrism or worse. But there remains an uneasy feeling that the Afro-American dilemma is merely a special case of a much larger problem. It is no accident that the closer the anthropologist comes to his own society the more culture escapes him as a viable concept. In knowing, or rather believing he knows, the sources and processes of his culture, he loses interest in it and readily abandons its study to the hegemony of the sociologist. The apparent demystification of our own culture—a demystification evidenced in the explanations implicit in concepts such as "mass culture"—easily leads to dismissing it as unimportant, unreal, or even externally provided. It thus becomes paradoxically remystified. It is then not only Afro-American culture that is escaping our grasp, but American culture.

Chapter 5

Reconsideration:
The Myth of the Negro Past

If life among the footnotes can tell us anything about a book, it's that *The Myth of the Negro Past*[1] is one of those anomalies, the negatively influential book, one whose message is so disagreeable or so significantly wrong that all who would pass it by must first confront it. So it has seemed these last thirty years, a bothersome obstruction for integrationists such as Harold Issacs, for racialists like Carlton Putnam, for historians Christopher Lasch and Stanley Elkins, for the Panthers, for the Black Muslims. Thirty years ago, as now, there was paradoxical comfort to be found in treating the history of Afro-Americans as an exercise in morality, by discovering and cataloging the costs of American racial injustice and assigning the blame where one would: Western imperialism, capitalism, American aristocratic leanings, the nightmare sexual cravings and guilts of Anglo-Saxon blood, whatever. The black man all the while was treated as a cipher, a casualty of the sociology of pathos. No one was more aware than Herskovits of how whites were expected to write about blacks, for in his close involvement with W. E. B. Du Bois, the NAACP, and the National Urban League, he had achieved impeccable civil rights credentials by doing just such writing. Still, when he began the first chapter of *Myth* he made virtually everyone in the country his intellectual enemy by taking another course.

To say what Herskovits's book is about is easy, but it is not so easy to show how he was about it. He starts with what he saw as the problem with both popular and scholarly conceptions of Afro-American history and society: the ambivalence towards Africa. At one moment, he says, there is a willingness to dismiss the parts of American black behavior and culture which are "different" (from that of Anglo-Americans) as residues of African savagery and backwardness, and at the next instance to treat them as simple American-grown deviance. It was the latter view that formed the core of Gunnar Myrdal's *An American Dilemma* (1944), when he said that "American Negro culture is a distorted development, or a pathological condition of the general American culture." But how, Herskovits asked, can both things be true at the same time, and more important, how can either be said to be true when American knowledge of African history and culture is so limited, and white conceptions of black life-styles almost as bad?

The upshot of this American historical ignorance and arrogance is a fully developed mythology of the Afro-American past which Herskovits summarized this way: (1) Negroes are childlike in character, and, unlike the American Indians, adjusted to and accepting unpleasant circumstances; (2) only the poorest elements of African peoples were caught by the slavers and shipped to the New World; (3) the diversity of slaves, their lack of a common language and native culture left them with no basis for a common culture under slavery; (4) even if the slaves had had such a common culture and had been able to sustain it under the conditions of slavery, the relative inferiority of African culture in the face of Euro-American culture would have led them to abandon their own; consequently (5) Afro-Americans are people without a past. It was this mythological sequence that *The Myth of the Negro Past* was intended to refute. Using a mass of historical and anthropological material on Africa and many of the countries of the Americas, Herskovits set out to document the nature of the slave trade and the culture of American slaves more fully than anyone had done. He offered a radically different picture of the origin of slaves and how they coped, one that provided a basis for seeing that there were many means—both nonviolent and violent—by which slaves resisted the complete cultural brutalization of slavery. He offered examples of African cultural continuities and derivatives in Afro-American religion, politics, social structure, child care, art, music, food, speech, dance, work habits, folk literature, interpersonal style, and even body posture and gestures, and while doing so he also built a stronger case for rejecting racial arguments for the sources of these behavior patterns. If this were not enough, he called attention to something that European observers and the slaveholders themselves had fretted over and that white America secretly feared: that blacks had begun to influence and radically alter the lives of white Americans. In the South, especially, white cuisine, speech, manners, music, religion, sports, all had been tarred by the brush.

Throughout, Herskovits took many black cultural practices and put them in a new frame of reference. More, he transvalued the slave experience and Africa itself. Substantiation of his claims came in his unprecedented anthropological approach to the United States as well as to primitives. By using slave history from Africa, the Caribbean, and elsewhere he was able to show parallel processes at work everywhere that Europeans had attempted enslavement of African peoples. He demonstrated, for example, that there were similarities in the vocabularies and grammars of black peoples throughout the Americas, and that they systematically differed in part from whites'; and the demonstration made it difficult to continue saying that black dialects were nothing more than broken, bastardized, ignorant versions of European languages. Similarly, he showed that the high ceremony and pomp of Afro-American burial societies and social fraternities had their parallels in the cooperative work groups and secret societies of West Africa, Haiti, and Brazil; hence they could no longer be dismissed as the foolish extravagance of inferiors wistfully mimicking their betters.

While the book did have a few influential black and white supporters, it encountered virulent opposition from so authoritative a sociologist as E. Franklin Frazier of Howard University, and from the very Carnegie Corporation-Gunnar Myrdal project for which Herskovits had first written the book as a memorandum. It was clear from the disquieted reactions that followed the publication of *Myth* that anthropology was a subversive science.

What made this book so unsettling? First, its method. It was Herskovits's insight that to understand what had happened to blacks one had to start over again and find new ways to discover and use Afro-American history and culture. To accomplish this, he cut on the bias and drew information from civil libertarians and racists, from defenders of slavery and social reformers, from anyone who had made direct observations of black life and reported it. But in doing so, he turned around and scored redneck and radical alike for misunderstanding or maligning what they had seen and not understood. Just as disturbing was Herskovits's insistence that in a variety of ways, by a variety of means, Africa was still alive in the Americas. The specter of Africa was a little too much for a middle-class black readership who, like other upwardly mobile American ethnics, were in the process of disidentifying with their parents, with the South, with slavery and white stereotypes of what black social behavior meant.

But there was perhaps a more pointed objection to Herskovits's thesis, and one which assumes greater importance today. It was then becoming unpopular to refer publicly to blacks as having defects or failures as a *race*, and it was becoming customary to tally and specify failures, real or imagined, in infinite and sordid detail as long as the blame for those defects was laid at the doorstep of whites. Indeed, the study of race relations in America has seldom been more than this. While some blacks—notably Albert Murray of late—have complained that this apparently enlightened form of diagnosis in the name of social justice looks suspiciously like a continuation of the old American custom of the denigration of everything black, many other Afro-Americans have accepted the practice as a necessary prelude to social redress. But Herskovits did something altogether different. He stressed black accomplishments and black influences and attributed these achievements to blacks themselves and the African resources their ancestors brought with them. No one had done this before, and likewise no one knew how to deal with such an argument. Who knew what to do with the contention that what blacks did with one another was equally important as what whites did with blacks?

But all of that was three decades ago. Now we know, or should know, that the economics of social segregation, not physique and genetics, give us the insights we need into America's "dilemma." But what has become of the "myth" Herskovits sketched out? Doubtless there are many whites who still accept the old mythic explanations as the truth. But for most people a new myth now holds—that the slavery experience was so harsh and systematic as to have eliminated every aspect of each slave's previous life in Africa. Black culture by this argument can be nothing but slave culture or the negative culture of poverty and racism. Though the new myth puts the blame on the oppressors instead of the oppressed, the cultural outcome is much the same as that of the old myth. Except for ambivalent exceptions such as music and dance, virtually all other elements of black cultural tradition and development are treated as deviances and pathologies, not the resourcefulness of human beings. With assumptions such as these, black culture for most people appears (to use Ralph Ellison's terms) to be nothing more than the sum of its brutalization.

For blacks, it was the fate of *The Myth of the Negro Past* to come too late for the romantic primitivism of the Harlem Renaissance and too early for the cultural revitalization of the Black is Beautiful 1960s. Many years have passed without the common-sense scholarship which Herskovits called for, and it is thus no wonder that talk of Black English, a black spiritual community, and a New World tradition of African art, manners and politics looks madly out of touch with the American realities of the War on Poverty, OEO, and Early Childhood Intervention.

Meanwhile American blacks continue to have to reinvent their past every generation, at the moment seeking what they can find of African cultures. Like Richard Wright leaving his father standing on the red clay of Mississippi for the greener pastures of the North, they remain ambivalent towards their Southern roots. And while whites shake their heads like bemused Reconstructionists, Arthur Jensen tells us in the *New York Times* that only the poorer elements of Africa were brought to this country by the slavers . . .

Chapter 6

Reconsideration:
Lafcadio Hearn in Cincinnati

WITH CAROL PARSSINEN

At the age of nineteen, Lafcadio Hearn arrived in newly urban Cincinnati, an Irish immigrant, without money, a job, or connections, and happened onto newspaper reporting as the best compromise between his talents and necessity. During the six years that Hearn wrote for the Cincinnati *Enquirer* and the Cincinnati *Commercial,* he assumed the peculiarly public pose expected of journalists in the 1870s. He traveled with night shift policemen, climbed with steeplejacks, attended a "ladies only" lecture disguised as a lady, and trailed after rag pickers in the city dumps; with the care of a Henry Mayhew reporting on the London poor he interviewed sweatshop seamstresses and ex-slaves, giving them a public forum to speak of their plights; he assaulted pawnbrokers and spiritualists, meat cutters and missionaries, pimps who moonlighted as abortionists, even the YMCA. He reported riots, visited opium dens, exposed body snatchers, wandered in insane asylums. Again and again Hearn returned to his special obsessions, the lack of sanitation among food producers, the ghoulishness of undertaking practices, the filth of the housing of the poor. He could pity the police for the public abuse and violence they endured (they were called "pigs" in the mid-1800s) and at the same time expose their corruption and brutality. Similarly, he could be revolted by murders, as well as by the murder of murderers at the gallows.

Ghettos, stockyards, madhouses, brothels, cemeteries—these were Hearn's controlling images. And for this he paid a high price to critics and literary historians, who have cast him as a youthful sensationalist, another Yellow Kid, a teller of dirty city jokes lacking a muckraker's moral in the punchlines. But sensationalism is too easy a charge, and a suspiciously obvious way to explain away attractive prose that finds its way into newsprint. Do they mean to suggest that Hearn's metropolitan metaphors were inappropriate, that he had a poor sample, that our cities were not, after all, "that bad"? Whatever the case, time has been on Hearn's side, and we know that despite the dreams of Henry James and Walt Whitman, the city that Hearn, Theodore Dreiser, Frank Norris, and Upton Sinclair imagined has not gone away. We speak in newer images now, but the ecologists' tropes of the rat cage and the behavioral sink add little to what bedlam and the slaughterhouse suggested.

There is yet another way in which the sensationalist label misses the point in Hearn's early writings. Where some might seek out the under-life of society only to better know the distance between the earthly real and the transcendent, Hearn descended into the depths of urban life to revel in its unseen glories and to unmask humanity in its apparent ugli-ness. So, Hearn in "Levee Life," recounting the excesses of a black long-shoremen's sporting house (the "fiery drinks and drunken dreams," the interracial prostitution), suddenly shifts to describing the grace of the black dancers and the ritual qualities of the scene; and then to further drive home the transvaluation he is attempting, he turns to the white females and says that they "seemed heavy, cumbersome, ungainly by con-trast with their dark companions; the spirit of the music was not upon them; they were abnormal to the life about them. . . . Amid such scenes does the roustabout find his heaven and this heaven is not to be despised."

In the same manner in one of Hearn's most radical essays, "Pariah People," he defended the uncommon beauty and strength of those "great violators of nature's laws," those who practice miscegenation or are the products of it. Characteristically, always the participant observer, Hearn himself married a Cincinnati black woman, an act as startling for a pub-lic figure as it was illegal by Ohio's laws. If Nabokov could observe in the afterword to the 1958 edition of *Lolita* that successful mixed marriages were one of the three most tabooed topics in American literature, it must have been heavy stuff indeed for those who read their newspapers over breakfast in 1875. Hearn gained access to every level and segment of the city, but he found a sense of community only in the niches of industrial-ization, among the Jews and the Negroes. And though he wrote lauda-tory essays on "Cincinnati's Hebrews," their leaders, their scholarship and morality, and though he retranslated portions of the Talmud, and even condemned anti-Semitism at home and in Russia, he remained a distant commentator on their activities, more their historian than their anthropologist. It was among the blacks that he felt most at ease.

Starting in Cincinnati and continuing after 1877 in New Orleans and in the French West Indies, he transcribed the folksongs of Afro-Americans, described their dances and their theater, collected their be-liefs and proverbs (published as *Gombo Zhèbes* in 1885), studied black dialects and Creole languages, and learned their cuisine so well he wrote a cookbook (*La Cuisine Créole*, 1885) and even briefly ran a restaurant. Instead of recounting these customs with intellectual detachment or putting them in the mouth of some Negro-manqué like Uncle Remus, he recreated in narrative form the atmosphere in which one might wish to believe in these things.

Publicly, then, Hearn was a popularizer and an interpreter of black life for whites and perhaps the most sensitive and least affected that America has known. Privately, however, he saw himself as a scholar. His letters show him to have been studying the West African roots of black culture and, with musicologist H. E. Krehbiel, tracing the effects of the African diaspora on both whites and blacks in the Americas. All this, incredibly, he began less than a decade after the end of slavery. Now, ninety years later, black studies or no, it is doubtful that anyone has this kind of knowledge.

In 1890 Hearn left the United States, retreating in successive moves from industrialization to Martinique and Japan, where he turned his attention to belles lettres and produced the collections of descriptive sketches, occasional essays, and folk tales for which he is principally known and reputed as a minor man of letters.

Although Hearn is generally listed as an "American" writer, critics have followed his lead, giving least attention to his writing about America. Henry Goodman's edition of Hearn's *Selected Writings* places the typical emphasis on Hearn's interpretations of Japan for the West and includes only a handful of his pieces revealing the American city to Americans.[1] Hearn has been at the same time too literary and too scientific for American critics, producing too little hard data for social scientists and too little standard literature for literati. Perhaps more to the point, Hearn in Cincinnati was a journalist, an occupation still understood as tarnished by its immediate connection with business and a popular audience and severed from literature by its subservience to fact.

But now that the "new journalism" is upon us we have new criteria to assess Hearn's special skill as a writer, as well as renewed reason to grasp the significance of what he said. By experimenting with different kinds of language, narrative style, and points of view—with standard literary devices—he combined objective reporting with the subjective life of the characters. And as if the nature of his subject matter freed him from art as distortion—from inflated rhetoric or programmed pathos—Hearn learned to make his material live as only fiction is supposed to do.

In retrospect, then, we can dispense with some false parallels which have been thrown up to show us who Hearn was. He is often seen as having artistic kinship with Zola, Poe, or Baudelaire, to all of whom he appears a weak second. If comparisons are inevitable, it is not his contemporaries but ours who best reflect his significance. Indeed, it is Norman Mailer who continues the line of Hearn's tradition—the Mailer who saw psychopathy as an emerging lifestyle, the Mailer who made Chicago interesting *because* of its stockyards and the tumult in its streets and convention hall, who can tell us that it is the blacks, after all, who are the protean urbanites, the omni-Americans. Mailer's cities, like Hearn's, are populated by the mad, the occult, the diseased, the addicted, and the pariah, and the tedium of filth and poverty is lightened only by the excitement of racial and class turmoil and the arts of survival they breed. Hearn, Mailer, and a few others constitute something of an American literary tradition, a corps of writers with ethnographers' sensibilities who have been obliged to tell us that some of the most despised elements of American city life are not divergencies and evolutionary dead ends, but are the very parts which are converging to make America what it is and what it will be for some unknown time to come.

Chapter 7

The Forest as Moral Document:
The Achievement of Lydia Cabrera

WITH ROBERT FARRIS THOMPSON

It is said that the jazz style of Charlie Parker, blowing cool, blowing hot, blowing all the points between, was so complex that several musicians, indeed schools, were needed fully to explore his implications. This point applies to Lydia Cabrera, in the richness of her Afro-Cuban scholarship. Only a task force, working day after day for years, could effect the just estimation that her work demands, as surely one of the twentieth century's most important bodies of urban anthropological research. We say urban because the two main Cuban cultures from Africa, Yoruba and Kongo, were urban, and anciently so. The creolizing of these cultures, and their fusion with elements of Spanish, French, and even Chinese in the history of Afro-Cuban art and music, largely took place in the port cities of Cuba, notably Havana and Matanzas. The famed stylishness of Cuban blacks is a function, we would suggest, of their tropism toward the city. Afro-Cubans, like Yoruba and Bakongo, appreciate the parlance of the city, the verbal lore and gossip, the continual elaboration of tradition in a situation where an artist or musician might move, in a given week, from Yoruba to Dahomean to Cross River Efik/Ejagham to Kongo to commercial *musica cabaretera* to playing trumpet solo at a wedding to Yoruba *bembé*. In fact, polyvisuality—a world of Catholic chromolithography and Yoruba sacred stones—and polymusicality—where Kongo society members are called upon to play Abakuá (Cross River drums)—may well be a black pan-Caribbean phenomenon, as suggested by Kenneth Bilby in his account of a Jamaican musician:

Starting one morning by playing guitar in a coastal *mento* band for tourists, he returned later that day to his rural village to join in a fife and drum performance, playing the leading drum, and then in the evening added his voice to a Revival church chorus. . . . The easy movement between styles was not unusual for this man.[1]

Nor was it unusual for Lydia Cabrera. Modest, completely free of any self-conscious sense of her exalted status in Afro-Caribbean studies, she has given us a unique body of vividly written works.

In 1954, Cabrera published *El Monte*, a monumental compendium of the lore of herbal healing and associated African-influenced worship among the blacks of western Cuba. Ever since, the book has remained continuously in print. For *El Monte* ("The Sacred Forest") has become a holy book for thousands of servitors of the Afro-American religions derived from the Yoruba, Kongo, Dahomean, and Ejagham cultures. Among other things, the book provides a key to Afro-Atlantic herbalism, not only in its western Cuban manifestation, but in today's broader universe of Afro-Cuban influence, involving thousands of worshippers of Yoruba-Cuban deities and practitioners of Kongo-Cuban medicine and Yoruba-Cuban herbalism in Florida (Miami, Hiahleah, Tampa), New Jersey (Elizabeth, Union City), New York City (especially the South Bronx, Spanish Harlem, the lower East Side), and the Cuban and Puerto Rican barrios of other major northeastern industrial cities. The range of these religions is enormous. This book helps us comprehend them.

El Monte defines a history of brilliantly effected change whereby the worship of more than twelve major goddesses and gods (*orishas*) of the Yoruba (a people who live in what is now southwestern Nigeria and eastern Benin Republic) was transmuted into La Regla de Ocha, the worship of the same deities in Afro-Cuban terms, a worship also known as Santería, after the "masking" of *orisha* with Catholic saints (*santos*) where both shared highly similar or identical visual attributes. For example, Ogun, the Yoruba deity of iron (the charismatic metal), lord of the cutting edge and today patron of metallic wonders like oil rigs, speeding locomotives, or taxicabs, blended with the image of St. Peter because the latter was depicted frequently in Roman Catholic chromolithographs holding an iron key to the gates of heaven. Similarly, the playful propensities on one side of the complex Yoruba trickster-deity, Eshu-Elegba, found a ready avatar in "the child of Atocha," shown with a round object which Yoruba almost inevitably would associate with *àdo*, calabashes of transforming power that are one of the deep signs of the presence of Eshu and his power-to-make-things-happen (*às/.e*, called *aché* in the creolized Yoruba of Cuba). In addition, the dreaded deity of pestilence and social conscience, Obaluaiye, blurred into the picture of St. Lazarus supported by crutches, dogs licking his numerous wounds. Meanwhile, the equally tumultuous and beautifully conceived deities of Dahomey, the *vodun*—the same deities that elsewhere in the Caribbean helped spark one of the world's most conceptually complex and misunderstood religions, Haitian Vodun—were transmuted into Arará worship, in which god and goddess again served with and without carefully selected Catholic masks and counterparts. To this day both Yoruba and Dahomean deities are worshipped with a wealth of vernacular drums, costumes, beadwork, and dance, all combined. In the process, Cuba became a marvel of the Black Atlantic world, with an elaborate and continuous tradition of decorated *batá* drums, beaded necklaces, and ritual beaded garlands (*mazos*) in symbolic colors. Yoruba is still spoken and sung in Cuba, albeit in a creolized fusion form. The Yoruba-born linguist, Dejo Afolayan, maintains that this fusion brings together Kétu and Ijésha dialect forms separated by hundreds of miles in Yorubaland itself, in strength of reblended cultural flavor.

The rise of Yoruba-Cuban and Dahomean-Cuban circles of artistic culture in Cuba would be accomplishment enough, but there were two more surges out of anonymity, misery, and economic deprivation. First, there is the rise of apparently the only male "secret society" of African type in the New World, a transformation of the important Ejagham male society called Ngbe, from the hinterlands of the notorious slave port of Calabar. Many slaves from this part of Africa arrived in Cuba in the first half of the nineteenth century, where they were called Carabalí (linguistic metathesis transformed the word, but not to such an extent that most persons could not sense a relationship binding such people to Calabar and its hinterlands). In Calabar proper, the Ejagham are known as Abakpa or Qua, and it is from the first term, almost beyond doubt, that the creole term for the Ejagham-Cuban male society, Abakuá, derives. The Ejagham are famed for skin-covered masks and a supple ideographic writing system called *nsibidi* ("the dark letters," "the serious signs"), plus powerful women's arts including, again, ideography and remarkable ceremonial plumed calabashes (*echi okpere*). High-ranking initiates of the Ngbe society also used plumed drums of silence, drums to be "heard" visually at funerals and other most important events but not actually sounded. And many of these subtleties of act and envisionment passed intact to Cuba, where Lydia Cabrera for years was alone in rendering full justice to the presence of Ejagham-derived Abakuá practices, not only in two chapters in *El Monte* but also in two later works, *La Sociedad secreta Abakuá* (1959) and *Anaforuana* (1975), the latter a landmark publication in the history of the study of Black Atlantic graphic scripts and ideography. Cabrera, with the exception of Argeliers León and Sosa Hernández, remains the sole and brilliant scholar of Ejagham impact on the New World, as mediated through the culture of Ejagham-influenced slaves and freed slaves, who were concentrated in the sugar ports of western Cuba (Havana, Matanzas, Cárdenas), their environs, and the sugar plantations themselves, linked to these termini by rail and road. Finally, we are confronted by the mighty Kongo and Angola presence, less evident linguistically, perhaps, but massive and profound in the making of charms (*minkisi*), incantations (*mambu*, creolized to *mambo*, a word further borrowed to name one of the most multi-metric Afro-Cuban musics of the twentieth century), and dance and musical instrumentation. That presence is especially felt in the hundreds of plants that bear creole Ki-Kongo names in Cuba and are linked with interlocking circles of Kongo-derived or Kongo-inspired folklore, without which the world would have never heard of rumba, never danced to the conga drum.

El Monte also forces the recognition of a parallel medical system in the Western Hemisphere. Most of the 400,000 Cubans now settled in Dade County, Florida, as Mercedes C. Sandoval points out, rely on standard health care systems for the treatment of infections and organic diseases. But many consult Cuban-Yoruba traditional herbal medicine in dealing with problems emerging from spiritual or emotional stress.[2] For pneumonia one goes to the hospital, but for psychiatric disorders, caused by the destruction of a love affair or bitter jealousy, one goes to the herbalist-diviner. There are serious skills involved in the latter realm of medicine, for the Yoruba of Nigeria, for example, are believed to have known, classified, and used the tranquilizing properties of *rauwolfia* years before it was adopted in the Western pharmacopeia. Moreover, a team of Western doctors reliably report from Yorubaland that "one can say further that the criteria employed to distinguish particular kinds of mental and emotional disturbance are very similar to the criteria employed by Western psychiatrists."[3] In other words, the folkloric substance of this book, largely rooted in herbalism, is not a quaint collection of archaic, vanished happenings, but a vibrant reality, a design for right living, which exists parallel to Western diagnostic medicine in Nigeria and in the Nigerian-influenced New World. Patients involved in this popular medicine sometimes remark on their close and cordial relationships with the healer-diviners, recalling a fictionalized account of the encounter of a North-American black woman with a prophet-healer in which her consultation contrasted vividly with the relative perceived coldness of official medicine:

The satisfaction she felt was from the quiet way he had listened to her, giving her all of his attention. No one had ever done that before. The doctors she saw from time to time at the clinic were brusque, hurried, impatient.[4]

Among the folklorists of the twentieth century, Lydia Cabrera is distinguished by her special attention to Black Atlantic herbalism. We say Atlantic, instead of Afro-Cuban, because some of the herbs she documents are linked to cognate herbs and healing practices among Afro-Jamaican, Afro-Brazilian, and Afro–United States systems. Conventional wisdom cites music, dance, oral literature, religion, and revolutionary politics as the key black contributions to world culture. But here is the beginning of understanding perhaps the finest contribution of them all, Black Atlantic medicine. *El Monte* lists more than five hundred herbs, the ailments that they are alleged to cure, the spirits that preside over their healing powers, and the creolized Yoruba, Ki-Kongo, and Ejagham (Abakuá) words that name the leaves in Afro-Cuban terms.

In addition, we find whole legends associated with certain leaves, miniature narrations. "Truths that can be rendered in a dissociated moment," Susan Sontag points out, "however significant or decisive, have a very narrow relation to the needs of understanding. Only that which narrates can make us understand."[5] And, in fact, *El Monte* is a miracle of narration, brought into being by a woman who uniquely combined the powers of a painter, an interior designer, a sculptor (her painted stones were exhibited in New York in the spring of 1984 at the Intar Gallery), a writer, a linguist, and a passionate student of the folkways of black people. The result is a major work of twentieth-century Cuban literature in the depth of its vision and the quality of the writing, with interviews embedded like "found conversations" (Black Spanish phrasing and all) in the flow of her discourse and summation. It is also a major document in the history of popular Afro-American art, for no place else does one find photographs of major Kongo-influenced charms in Cuba, or photographs (in color, in the original edition) of Yoruba initiatory body painting in Cuba or the characteristic hands-crossing gestures of the Ejagham—and Efik-derived *íreme* (cf. Efik: *idem* "spirit") masker in action, or the only full-color portrait of an *íreme* showing Calabar-influenced details of appliqué and decoration. It becomes immediately comprehensible why this uniquely talented and spiritually knowledgeable woman would attract the friendship and admiration of some of the finest minds of twentieth-century literature.

Lydia Cabrera was born in Havana on Independence Day, May 20, 1900, the last of eight children of Raimundo Cabrera y Bosch and Elisa Marcaida y Casanova. Her father was a distinguished lawyer, journalist, playwright, poet, and novelist, as well as a leader in the movement for Cuba's independence, and the Cabrera home was a gathering place for intellectuals, painters, lawyers, and politicians. It was a climate that helped shape the range of interests characteristic of her later work.

Educated first in public school and then as a painter in the San Alejandro Art Academy, Cabrera completed her education in Cuba outside of schools. Her expanding interest in art led her to become a successful interior decorator (she designed the interior of the Capitolio in Havana), to organize art exhibits, and to establish a furniture workshop and antique store on her family's estate. Already having gone far beyond what young, well-bred Cuban women were supposed to do in life, she sold her successful business interests and left for Paris in 1927 to live in

Montmartre and study at the École des Beaux Arts, where she painted, traveled, and moved in a widening circle that included the poets Federico García Lorca and Gabriela Mistral, and the Venezuelan novelist Teresa de la Parra.

Her studies expanded to encompass Chinese folklore, Buddhism, and Eastern cultures at the École du Louvre. This was of course in the Paris of surrealism, of the cults of the primitive and the exotic, of Picasso and Dérain. But it was not until a trip back to Cuba in 1928 that Cabrera began to tie Afro-Cuban culture into the same framework of cultural universals she was encountering in the comparative study of religions in Paris. Why, she wondered, study distant cultures in the abstract, when there was an undocumented culture quite literally at her doorstep in Havana? For despite her upper-class family—or perhaps because of it—Cabrera had experienced something of a black childhood. Like a Jean Rhys in Dominica in the West Indies or a Truman Capote in South Alabama, she initially learned Afro-American culture through servants and their children. And if it was Afro-American culture of the patio and the kitchen rather than the living room, it was nonetheless an exposure that included daily talk, songs, games, proverbs, beliefs, threats, and bedtime stories—in short, some of the fundamental conduits of cultural transmission.

In addition to childhood daily learning, Cabrera's older sister Estelle was married to Fernando Ortiz, who had published (when Lydia was six) the first major work on Afro-Cuban culture, *Los Negros brujos,* a study of magic workers. Ortiz's Afro-Cuban studies had begun with the assumption (like much conservative and liberal scholarship of the 1960s in the United States) that people of African descent lacked a true culture and, if anything, practiced a culture of poverty (or a culture of pathology). But the sheer corrective power of Afro-Cuban culture fused with Ortiz's basic integrity as a scholar, so that he ultimately came to spend much of his life documenting the splendor and normativeness of this culture, and what's more, to use his documentation as a means to justice for Cuban blacks. Cabrera of course knew Ortiz's dozens of articles and books: still, her contribution was ultimately to prove of greater bite and substance, for in submitting to the responsibility, the incredible repetitiveness of her informant's valuable, pithy arguments, she made an even greater contribution to the cause of Afro-Cuban studies. For she collected whole texts, as it were, whereas Ortiz pigeonholed his facts and worked up essentially an etymology of the main traits of Afro-Cuban lore.

Nevertheless, Ortiz's work was something of a foundation on which the Afro-Cubanist movement of the 1920s and 1930s was built, a movement that spliced together European primitivism, Cuban nationalism, and the growing thrust towards Afro-Cuban rights and freedom. It was a period that saw the writing of from-the-bottom-up novels such as Alejo

Carpentier's *Ecué-Yamba-O*, the culturally black poetry of Nicolás Guillén, and the composition of classical music (Amadeo Roldán and Alejandro García Caturla) and popular music (Ernesto Lecuona) based on Afro-Cuban folk song and dance.

In the spirit of the times, Cabrera's first works were literary retellings of Afro-Cuban folktales, works of local color. But she also knew the creolization of European surrealism and Afro-American political consciousness that had produced *négritude* (she had herself translated the classic of this movement, Aimé Cesaire's *Cahier d'un retour au pays natal,* and was friendly with the Martiniquan poet Leon Damas). Cabrera refers to her four books of Afro-Cuban tales—*Cuentos negros de Cuba* (Havana: La Verónica, 1940); *Por que?: cuentos negros de Cuba* (Havana: Ediciones C.R., 1948); *Ayapá: cuentos de Jicotea* (Miami: Ediciones Universal, 1971); and the more recent *Cuentos para adultos ninos y retrasadas mentales* (Miami: Ediciones C.R., 1983)—as "fiction," with no claim to folkloric validity. At best, she says, they are loosely based on Afro-Cuban originals (as are some of the stories of Alejo Carpentier), while some are totally invented, perhaps inspired—like some Afro-Haitian paintings—by black folk song. Nonetheless, these tales and the anecdotes and dialogues within them are rooted in ethnographic realism. Indeed the glossaries of Afro-Cuban terms that Cabrera includes with some of these books absolutely suggest a more than casual concern with accuracy. Her ear for dialogue—at the margin between fiction and ethnography—is also displayed in *Francisco y Francisca* (Miami: Peninsula Printing, 1976), a collection of humorous anecdotes and short tales in Kongo-Cuban idiom. In fact, it is at the borders of conventional literary genres that Cabrera works most comfortably, as illustrated by *Refranes de negros viejos* (Havana: Ediciones C.R., 1955), a collection of proverbs, and *Itinerario del insomnio: Trinidad de Cuba* (Miami: Peninsula Printing, 1977), a blend of folklore, politics, and mystical nostalgia, a literary raising of the dead in the city of Trinidad at the turn of the century.

In 1938, fleeing the rise of the Nazis, Cabrera returned to Cuba to live and work, though her travels often took her back to Europe. Here at home again, she began persistent research in the black barrios of Havana and Matanzas in the tradition of field ethnography. And while she has always distanced herself from anthropology (she claims merely to "repeat" culture, not interpret it), she approached research on her own country in a highly sophisticated, relativistic fashion, and managed to bridge the "native," the amateur, and the professional anthropological points of view. In addition, she counted among her friends anthropologists such as Melville and Frances S. Herskovits, William and Berta Bascom, Pierre Verger, and Alfred Métraux. In fact, it was Métraux, the distinguished French ethnographer of Haitian *vodun,* at first skeptical of her findings of African languages in Cuba ("Quelle imagination, Lydia!" he said), who aided her in confirming the Yoruba sources of the Lucumí material she had encountered, and who encouraged her to expand her research to include Kongo, that is, *palero* material. And for a time, the French Afro-Brazilianist scholar Pierre Verger joined her in field research, especially aiding her with photography. Most of the research was done by Cabrera herself, however, though sometimes in the company of her companion, paleographic scholar Maria Teresa de Rojas.

In disagreement with the direction taken by the Revolution, Cabrera left Cuba for Miami in 1960. Though her exile was intended to be temporary, her Coral Gables residence became permanent. Isolation from Cuban tradition sharpened her consciousness, and like an anthropologist writing far from the field, she produced eleven more books, each breaking new ground.

Cabrera's ethnographies of Afro-Cuban religious life are the heart of her later work. These include research on the Yoruba in Cuba published as *Yemayá y Ochún* (New York: Ediciones C.R., 1974), an account of the verbal arts surrounding the goddesses of the seas, sweetwater, and love; *Koeko iyawo: aprende novicia: pequeño pratado de regla Lucumí* (Miami: Ultra Graphics, 1980), concerning the structure of the Afro-Yoruba religion, its rituals, sacrifices, and cures; *Anagó: vocabulario lucumí* (Havana: Ediciones C.R., 1957), a lexicon of creolized speech in Cuba; *Otán Iyebiyé: las piedras preciosas* (Miami: Ediciones C.R., 1970), on the beliefs of the priests of the *orishas* about precious stones; *La laguna sagrada de San Joaquín* (Madrid: Ediciones R., 1973), about the rituals of the followers of Iyalosha, the water goddess; and *La medicina popular de Cuba: médicos de Antano, curanderas, santeros y paleros de Hogaño* (Miami: Ediciones Universal, 1984), a study of folk medicine among Afro-Cubans. The seminal work on the Efik and Ejagham male "leopard society" (Ngbe) in Cuba is represented by *La sociedad secreta Abakuá: narrada por viejos adeptos* (Havana: Ediciones C.R., 1959), an account of the myths, rituals, ideography, and organization of the Abakuá religion and their influence on Cuban religious life; *Anaforuna* (Madrid: Ediciones R., 1975), offers an ideography of initiation, funeral leave-taking, and membership in the Abakuá society. Cabrera's research on a creole-Kongo society in Cuba appears in *La regla kimbisa del Santo Cristo del Buen Viaje* (Miami: Ediciones Universal, 1977), a close look at a nineteenth-century creolized Kongo-Catholic religious group and its leaders; and *Reglas de Congo—Palo Monte Mayombe* (Miami: Peninsula Printing, 1979), on the creolized Kongo-Angolan ritual, religion, ideography, and folklore of Cuba.

But *El Monte* is the centerpiece of Cabrera's enterprise. When it was first published in Havana in 1954, it was issued as part of what Cabrera called the *Colección del chichereku* (a *chichereku* is a wooden "doll" made by a *santero* to create "nocturnal mischief"); when she reprinted *El Monte* in

Miami in 1968 she made it a part of the *Colección del chicherekú en el exilio.* In 1954 most Cuban intellectuals treated it as something of a national embarrassment—a tarnishing of Cuba's image as a modern nation state. European and North American folklorists and anthropologists then, as now, took little interest in the scholarship of Cuba, so its publication went unnoticed abroad.

Yet *El Monte* was not lost by any means. Afro-Americanists such as Melville J. Herskovits, William Bascom, and Roger Bastide recognized its importance and kept it alive in their footnotes as part of the growing corpus of comparativist black studies. And Cabrera's skill with local languages and characterization did not escape the notice of Cuba's novelists, for whom she became both a model and a source. Even the folkloric content of *El Monte* influenced Cuban fiction: Alejo Carpentier's *Explosion in a Cathedral* (1962), for instance, is indebted to Cabrera's detailed herbal descriptions and classifications.[6] Most importantly, *El Monte* was immediately recognized to be the first printed guide, the Bible, of Santería worshippers, and began to sell widely. It has been in print now for 50 years, in two countries, an underground best seller if ever there was one, and some kind of assessment in terms of the ethnographic tradition is long overdue.

Just what constitutes a successful ethnography is far from obvious, even after a century of professional anthropology. Exactly what the relationship should be between a culture and its analysis and representation in a book is at best understood only in general terms by anthropologists. But if there is no clear, formalized standard, there are nonetheless stated and unstated paradigms of what ethnography should accomplish and how it should proceed. First, ethnography should be based on fieldwork by trained scholars—a form of disciplined, relativistic, direct observation of life in a given society. Though this work is often called participant observation, the amount of participation that an ethnographer can actually achieve is usually quite limited or at least circumscribed by the nature of the societies typically chosen for study. The second general rule of ethnography is that research should only be carried out far from the observer's own society, ostensibly to take advantage of the objectivity which such cultural alienation ("culture shock") bestows on the researcher, and to further our knowledge of the world's least-known societies. Anthropology continues to be uneasy about "native ethnographies"—accounts of one's own people written for outsiders—but the unease seems to be located more in questions about the motivation for such studies and the rhetoric in which they are rendered, than it is in issues of validity. A third general rule is that field research should be based on an extensive stay in a society—a year or more—and on the ability to communicate in the society's language.

Field research should also report or at least take into account and totalize as many aspects of a people's life as possible, represented by a number of conventional analytical categories such as economy, kinship, law, and the like. And where research focuses on just one of these categories, it must at least respect the holism of social life and not treat other dimensions of life as totally separate phenomena. Lastly, ethnographic research should be conducted within a comparative perspective. An ethnographic study of a particular religion, for example, should ideally understand its subject within the framework of all known systems of religious belief.

Beyond these general strictures, disagreements persist over what ethnography should be. In part this debate is the result of the discipline's history. By and large, ethnography developed as an ad hoc discipline constructed by amateur scientists. Anthropologists such as Franz Boas, Alfred Kroeber, and Paul Radin had no social science training, and came to the discipline from backgrounds in other fields, such as geography, literature, and history. Lacking an agreed upon firm sense of what ethnography should be and how it should be done, early anthropologists experimented with a variety of approaches and even a variety of genres for rendering the results: laboratory-inspired reports, diaries, travel accounts, native autobiographies, and even fictional forms were all tried. And much of the strength of anthropology developed within this sense of experimentation and reflexivity.

Yet as anthropology developed institutionally, the lack of clearly defined goals has led many to put their emphases on the rigors and minutiae of the field experience, while the form of the ethnographic account—now conventionally the monograph—has come to be written in a flattened, "no-style" style of presentation closer to the lab report than to pictorial forms, with no apparent sense of conflict between the extreme subjectivity of the field research experience and the contrived objectivity of the written product. And the question of what makes for successful (or convincing) ethnography continues to remain in contention. For some anthropologists, an adequate ethnography would allow one the knowledge to act acceptably as a native in the society represented (needless to say, no such ethnography has yet been written for any society). For other anthropologists, a good ethnography would offer a "reading" of native texts along with natives' reading of those texts. For still others, ethnography would set a given people, a given culture, into the comparative community of peoples within the conceptual world of anthropologists. Much of the training of anthropologists is taken up with discussions over the various merits of these and other approaches.

What, then, are we to make of *El Monte*, which is now, more often than not, very closely read by the "natives," the followers of Santería in a number

of countries in the Americas. What are we to make of a book so powerful that it continues to be pirated and plagiarized year after year? A book
that has left the disciplinary realms of literature, science, and folklore
and has joined in the very processes of cultural influence and change
itself? A book written, after all, by a native Cuban untrained either as
anthropologist or as *santero*, and yet someone who is often sought after
in both roles by two worlds of people? A book which, though written outside the usual academic and disciplinary frameworks, is based nonetheless on over ten years of field research and is supremely sensitive to
cultural variety? Finally, what are we to make of a book whose complex literary originality is matched only by its subject, a culture so complex that
it resists complete understanding by means of any known theories of cultural change?

What *El Monte* shows us is no fusion-culture in which African cultural
particularity is shredded and kaleidoscoped, thus remaining incomprehensible. The assault on such cultural fatalism begins on the title page.
There we find a kind of cabalistic anagram of the secret cultural pro-
fundities, distinct and independent, that make up the culture of the
blacks of Cuba. The title of the book, *El Monte*, is standard Spanish for
hill or mountain. But in the vernacular the term refers to the country,
to bush or forest, to wild vegetation, plants growing in their natural,
undomesticated state. Cabrera deepens and confirms the sylvan associations by causing the letters that compose the phrase *El Monte* to be illuminated, on the cover of both the Cuban and Miami editions, in green.
And she immediately follows the symbolically illuminated letters with reinforcing glosses from the two major African languages in Cuba, IGBO
(Yoruba: "bush," "grove for worship") NFINDA (Ki-Kongo: "woods," "forest," "wooded country"; "place of the spirits of the dead [from time
immemorial]"). The semantic range of both these important African
words makes plain that the forest in two African civilizations important
to Cuba is charged with spirituality, a cathedral buttressed by the trees
and lit by herbal stained glass, as it were, a cathedral such as William
Faulkner glimpsed in "the big woods, bigger and older than any recorded document." And like Faulkner before her, Cabrera was guided to
the forest in black terms, and this is the way she opens her book:

An astonishingly tenacious belief in *el monte* persists among Afro-Cubans. In the
woods and scrubland of Cuba, as in African forests, dwell ancestral deities and
powerful spirits that today, as in the days of the slave trade, are most feared and
venerated by Afro-Cubans, whose successes or failures depend upon their hos-
tility or benevolence.[7]

The book's concentration upon the healing essence of the forest, the
herbs and roots, is rendered explicit by other Yoruba and Ki-Kongo

phrases that illuminate the cover and the title page: EWE ORISHA (creolized Yoruba: "leaves of the divinities") and VITITI NFINDA (creolized
Ki-Kongo: "herbs of the forest"). The literal, trunkal (root, branch, twig)
and herbal (the leaves) elements of the forest are involved in these
phrasings, but elements of sitting, high and low, are also understood
from the Ki-Kongo spatial references. Thus in classical Ki-Kongo pharmacopeia, according to Fu-Kiau Bunseki, the Kongo scholar, *makaya* (a
word that turns up in Kongo-influenced Louisiana and Haiti as well as
Cuba) refers to "vertical leaves," fluttering high within the branches,
whereas *bititi* refers to "horizontal leaves" attached to vines and creepers.
But in Cuba *bititi*, creolized to *vititi*, refers simply to leaves. Cabrera has
said that *monte* refers to "the bush, to many plants" and that its literal
meaning of mountain is not to be taken *al pié de la letra* (literally) except
in a metaphoric sense of *altura*, height, ascendant source of power, a
mountain-mortar in which the leaves of the gods are ground and worked
for the good of all mankind.

A sense of spiritualized rightness and organic sequence permeates
the book's chapters, which flow from forest to herbs to doctors to fees to
medicines and magical constructions, to chapters literally built around
specific trees, like the turning of Afro-Haitian *vodun* dance about the
trunkal middle-post sited in the center of the peristyle. Thus the first
chapter introduces the forest and its spirituality, source of all wild herbs
and roots, and the second talks of *bilongo* (Ki-Kongo: "the medicines")
or the actual force of the forest in action. The third chapter introduces
the spiritual lords and masters of the leaves (*oluwa ewe*), Osanyin, the
Yoruba deity of herbalism, and Eshu-Elegba, who is the spirit of the crossroads and of spiritual communication with the goddesses and gods—
great trickster and holder of the powers to make things come to pass.
The divine tribute that one owes to such spirits, for the privilege of
plucking and working leaves, unfolds in the following chapter. Then, in
the fifth, we actually learn how to make an Angolan charm (*como se
prepara una nganga*) and various Kongo-influenced charms, a tour de
force of magical reportage, with one informant sometimes contradicting
or correcting another, until the whole point of miniaturizing the forest
essences to make the healing medicines of God (*minkisi*) is memorably
made plain. Soul-embedding earths and spirit-commanding objects or
fluids, mercury for spiritual flash and fleetness, stones for immortal
presence, are classified and revealed in long and absorbing passages
about the building of Kongo charms, major charms like *mpungu*, with
details which further research will probably identify as witty but culturally and historically appropriate local invention and improvisation.

There follows a brief but remarkable chapter on the magical, medicinal treasury of the lord of medicine, Osanyin, and a corresponding creole Kongo figure called "father of the forest" (*tata nfinda*), and in these pages, among many illuminations, one learns to what extent black Cubans believe that the forces of the forest are morally neutral, shaped by the particular character of their users, even as "breeze is cool and hurricanes kill and both are air." Then the book modulates into a tree-centered stanza of four chapters, two on the cottonwood tree in Yoruba and Kongo rites, and two chapters built around the royal palm, rendered in the lore of the Abakuá and a sign par excellence of the Yoruba thundergod. Grounds-people working in the parks of Miami today, so it is said, sometimes come across sacrificial remains at the base of the noblest and tallest royal palms.

In the climatic final section, the leaves themselves are listed by their vernacular Yoruba-Cuban and Kongo-Cuban and Abakuá names, with legends and stories that detail the strong mystic links between the leaves and the deities of Yorubaland, for as Cabrera herself has said, "each orisha has its series of leaves which transmit its power-to-make-things-happen (*aché*)." Whence came this incredible ethnographic abundance of testimony and folkloric evidence? The answer: from an exemplary scholar-informant relationship rendered in terms of long-time mutuality of service and favor, without the self-serving fanfare that marks some scholars' attempts to set themselves up as paragons of cultural camaraderie and inside observation. After Cabrera returned to Havana from Paris, already primed to investigate more fully the black roots of Cuban culture, she began to interview Omitomi, the black seamstress of her grandmother. Omitomi (Yoruba: "I am satisfied with god of water") is a "water name" in Yoruba, indicating in all probability that she was a devotee of the riverine-healer spirit, Eyinle or Erinle, called Inle in Cuba. At first Omitomi feigned total ignorance of the Afro-Cuban world of worship: "I don't know nothing. I was brought up with white folk." Gradually, it developed—and her name was a strong hint of this—that Omitomi was one of the most respected Afro-Cuban religious authorities in all of Cuba, and she introduced Cabrera to her friend, Odedeyi (Yoruba: "Hunter-has-made-us-this"). The two of them, Omitomi and Odedeyi, saw to it that Cabrera traveled to Matanzas. This city, "the Ile-Ife of Cuba," was reputed to be home to the true spiritual overlords of the Afro-Cuban religion. The priests and priestess there, many in their eighties and nineties, were deeply erudite and spoke the three major creolized African languages of Cuba. Odedeyi made Cabrera swear that "no one was to touch her head" (i.e., no one was to initiate her into the Lucumí or Kongo religion, "so that you can write freely about our traditions, for once an *yawo*—a bride of the gods, an initiate—you will never be allowed to speak"). And so a pact was sealed and word spread that Cabrera was a white person of distinction who truly respected black culture and who was quite generous with her informants, in gifts, services, and favors. As her network of informants grew in the 1940s and 1950s, she found her house, the Quinta San José, was admirably sited, built as it was in Pogolotti, a barrio of Marianao, a western suburb of Havana. For Pogolotti is famed to this day for its African-influenced religious activities. It is the site of one of the most prestigious and culturally important Abakuá lodges. Cabrera comments: "In fact Pogolotti was a barrio entirely enlivened with blacks and black culture. There were Abakuá, there were *paleros*, there were Yoruba diviners (*babalaos*), excellent people, no? I had but to cross the street to be in Africa."

These and other informants taught her that *el monte* was a Bible, that the great Kongo kettle-charms, *prendas*, spoke through the bodies of their priestly mediums. Through black friends of friends she was put in touch with perhaps the most holy—and feared—of all the Kongo *banganga* of Cuba, Baró, who worked with two or three ritual assistants in Pogolotti, and, Cabrera thinks, was descended from blacks who worked on the Baró plantation in the province of Matanzas. Gradually her photographs and her documentation grew, each illustration, each legend not a coldly analyzed object but a gift, gestures of good will by black women and men. Cabrera gave room and board to three black elders, led by the incredible Saibeke, who was at once *mayombero*, a *lucumí*, and an Abakuá. Without question, part of the special power of Afro-Cuban culture, the engine behind its world conquest of the dancehalls of the planet, is the fluent, constant creolizing exchange between the three great African traditions that surged forth upon the island, as exemplified by Saibeke's multi-religiosity. Saibeke fell ill and Cabrera brought in a doctor who cured him. And then one day he crossed the compound to Cabrera's door and said: "Niña, ¿tu quiere saber Abakuá? Coge libro" ("Girl, you want to learn Abakuá? Pick up your notebook"). And so began the lengthy seminars that resulted not only in *El Monte*'s magnificent chapters on the Abakuá and their lore of the palm tree and the cottonwood, but also Cabrera's full-scale books on the Abakuá and their ideography.

Her fluency in art and language (speaking excellent English and French in addition to her native Spanish) prepared her for the daunting challenge of making sense of a sea of creolized black speech in the provinces of Havana and Matanzas, where she did the bulk of the work in preparation for *El Monte*. She took down remarks and observations not only in Black Spanish, but also in creolized African languages: Yoruba (*lucumí*), Fongbe from Dahomey (*arará*), Ki-Kongo mixed with words in Black Spanish (*lengua palera*), Efik (*efí*), and Ejagham (*ekoi*). With the vision of a novelist she saw this incredible linguistic landscape whole. And not unlike a filmmaker, she used "establishing shots" or introductory paragraphs along with moments where a single black woman or man dominates a page with a string of texts. Her informants, working-class blacks, came to her with their noble memories and legends. She quickly recognized the strength and validity of their traditions. She saw creative vision, *grands initiateurs*, where others saw only stevedores, household domestics, common fieldhands, or ex-slaves.

We cannot repeat too many times that the great source of the strength of this book is linguistic, involving the patient documentation of texts and phrases from five major African languages spoken or chanted in black Cuba. The author made constant contact with black women and men, particularly in Matanzas, who spoke creolized Ki-Kongo and Yoruba fluently. In fact so creatively challenged was Cabrera by the vibrant linguistic tumult that she found about her, that she matter-of-factly compiled, as parallel projects to the making of *El Monte*, lexicons of the different African languages that came to Cuba in the nineteenth-century slave trade. With *Anagó* she rendered the lexicon of the Yoruba language spoken in creole form in Cuba. But she also published the texts that will establish lexicons for Ki-Kongo and Ejagham Efik creole languages in Cuba. And behind *El Monte* itself we sense the authority of carefully and painstakingly rendered documentation: myriad texts in creolized Yoruba, Ki-Kongo, and Abakuá. Cabrera's mastery of the feel and distinctiveness of each idiom, her pride in mastering them as a genuine intellectual accomplishment, like learning Greek or Hebrew, is an important source of the authority of this book. There is such linguistic abundance, so much linguistic variety, that it is almost as if Lydia Cabrera had been confronted with Ki-Lele, as was Mary Douglas, Samoan, as was Margaret Mead, and Japanese, as Ruth Benedict might have been had she actually gone to Japan, and somehow brought together ethnographic reportage from all these languages within the compass of a single book. Hers is an exquisite art of sharing of hours and afternoons with her informants, some of them, to judge from the quality of their remarks and the fluency of their citations of folk authority in songs in Yoruba or Fongbe or Ejagham or Ki-Kongo, among the most fertile sources of modern Afro-Cuban culture. Untied to a single social scientific vogue or theory, laced with insights internal to Afro-Cuban artistic culture and its amazing languages, her work is a fabric of timeless presences.

This book establishes, once and for all, that the descendants of Yoruba, Kongo, Ejagham, and Dahomean slaves in Cuba never were in their private minds mere pawns or tokens, objects shorn of creative spirit or will. *El Monte* is a mirror of collective resistance and ingenuity, by which the black women and men of Cuba elaborated a secret island within an island, wherein they were free to think and act differently from the whites around them and, more to the point of their own recaptured creativity, differently from one another as well.

Chapter 8

Race and the Embodiment of Culture

One of the ironies of this not-so-happy century is that although it was the first time in human history in which a concerted effort was made to discredit racist ideology, it was also the occasion on which an enormous number of lives were sacrificed in the name of race. Surely now we realize that science and humanism have scarcely scratched the primordial notion that people with bodies different from our own must also be different in culture and character; nor has the converse belief been touched, that people culturally different from ourselves must also have bodies of a different order from our own. So banal is the restatement of this belief in the equation between physique and behavior, and so obvious its refutation in the world around us that it embarrasses me to mention it, even in passing.

Nevertheless, I'd like to try to say something different about race, or try to say the same things in a different way, just once, before we again find ourselves moving to an acceptance of the inexorable intertwining of race and destiny.

1

Let me begin by calling up a few of the terms that we associate with race: physique, culture, and stereotype.

First, far too much emphasis has been given by students of race relations to the idea of race as a cluster of physical features—skin, color, hair form, nose shape, and the like. This they do because these seem to be the core of what people talk about when they speak of races. But physical features are also things that scientists can see, and feel that they can accurately describe and classify through systematic observations and measurements. For example, in order to better show who was or who was not a member of a particular race, or, on the other hand to demonstrate that race was so unscientific a concept as to warrant abandoning it, scientists of the early 1900s relentlessly pursued tests and measurements with a single-minded goal of showing the laymen to be wrong:[1] nothing delighted an anthropometrist more than finding a light-skinned Negro or a dark-skinned Caucasian, unless it was the discovery that the odor of a vial of Caucasian perspiration was offensive to an Oriental. At its thinnest, then, the method was one of discovering racial anomalies or prejudices of non-Westerners toward Euro-Americans. Alas, as is too often the case with scientists, they were not in touch with the laymen. The average person is not so much bothered by the repulsiveness of physical differences, but rather with their seeming cooccurrence with behavioral differences. Exotic appearance accompanies exotic behavior, or so it may seem. And where this is not true on the surface of things, where one may exist without the other, the equation is completed by fantasy.

Perhaps an example would be useful. A perusal of early English writings on the Irish shows that although the Irish were initially seen to be physically much the same as the English (as early illustrations show), Irish culture was seen as alien and threatening. In 1617 Fynes Moryson, for example, found the Irish more than a little offensive. Their language was crude, if indeed it was a language at all, their clothing almost animal-like, if they wore any at all: Moryson noted with shock an Irish lord, seated at the fire with his women, all of them naked, or, again, corn being ground by nude maidens, "striking off into the tub of meal such reliques thereof as stuck on their belly, thighs, and more unseemly parts."[2] From the same period one also thinks of Edmund Spenser's bestial Irishmen or of William Camden, who, in 1610 recounted the profanity, cannibalism, musicality, witchcraft, violence, incest, and gluttony of the "wilde and very uncivill" Irish.[3] In fact, in many ways the Irish sound remarkably like Africans as described by the nineteenth-century English—sensual, slothful, affectionate, garrulous, excitable, humorous, etc.—except that the English appear to have initially often found Africans preferable to the Irish.[4]

The unasked question for the Elizabethans was simply, were the Irish, with their different culture, truly human? And the question was not to be settled quickly, as the following several hundred years show. But by the late 1800s the English physiologist James Redfield could distinguish the Irish as a lower form of life by reinterpreting even their most appealing human qualities in animal terms. Irish "verbosity" for example:

Compare the Irish man and the dog in respect to barking, snarling, howling, begging, fawning, flattering, backbiting, quarrelling, blustering, scenting, seizing, hanging on, teasing, rollicking, and whatever other traits you may discover in either, and you will be convinced that there is a wonderful resemblance.[5]

In the same manner, it was common for the nineteenth-century English to see the Celts as apes, as cartoons in *Punch* (and in America, in *Harper's* and the *Atlantic*) showed the Irish as boasting, drunken, lower-level hominoids, bent on the destruction of civilization.[6]

It remained only for John Beddoe, president of the Anthropological Institute, to develop an "index of Nigresence" which showed the people of Wales, Scotland, Cornwall, and Ireland to be racially separate from the British. And to be more specific, he argued that those from Western Ireland and Wales were "Africanoid" in their "jutting jaws" and "long slitty nostrils," and thus originally immigrants from Africa.[7] The equation was complete: what was at first seen as behavioral (that is to say, cultural) difference between two peoples was now rooted physiologically, these differences having their origins on a distant continent, if not at a lower level of animal development.

The fantasied equation works in reverse, too, as in South Africa, where special schools and curricula are required of those with "black" identity, regardless of whether or not the student has a European or, for that matter, a European *and* African cultural repertoire; or in Nazi Germany, where cultural identity was assumed of those of Jewish descent, even though the Jewish "race" was so poorly defined that special names and dress were required by law in order to complete the equation. This process of stigmatization is one which we meet again and again through history and across nations, and if we object to the process, one name we commonly give it is stereotyping.

It is generally agreed that a stereotype is a distortion or exaggeration of the facts.[8] It would seem then that if only positive stereotypes had emerged in the world we might well have never felt the need for the term. However, some decidedly negative characteristics have been subsumed under stereotypes, as the pejorative connotation of the word suggests. Thus it is worth considering that the process of stereotyping is not itself clearly distinct from the kind of everyday social typifications we make of individuals as members of classes such as "Englishmen," "educated," "farmers," and so forth. All are forms of classification by which we quickly summarize the social information of human encounters as to render social life predictable, or at least less chaotic. And all social types are theoretically subject to correction and individualization as we get to know individuals through direct contact. But here we meet some differences between stereotyping and other forms of social typing. "Everyday" typing characteristically grows out of interaction with individuals, where stereotypes, particularly those of races and foreigners, may often historically precede these individuals and are often a function of the physical or social distance between them and ourselves. Consequently we may simply never get close enough to the people we stereotype to correct or modify the original typification. And since there is some form of distance between ourselves and the others implied in this latter process, there is also typically some form of social hierarchy implied in the stereotype.

But this much about stereotyping is obvious. What is perhaps less obvious is that there are two distinct forms of typing operating within the stereotype. The first is the reading of a person or a group of persons as being known by a set of physical characteristics or behaviors which are quite concrete and subject to some kind of verification. Thus, a people may be said to have red skin, or blue eyes, or to be musically inclined, or to avoid facing each other when they talk. All of these can be measured or checked if we care to do so. But there is also a second level of stereotyping, one which offers observations about a people's laziness, ugliness, childishness, stupidity, dishonesty, lack of self-control, and the like. In these latter forms, we see virtual moral ascriptions or accounts of deviancy, assessments of how far another people's behavior is seen to vary from the observers', and even a sense of how much conflict seems implicit in these characteristics. Obviously in practice this second level of stereotypification is dominant, but related to the first, and forms with it a complex, myth-like whole. Any part of the whole, whether empirically "correct" or not, tends to call up the whole ideological cluster.

Stereotypes also concentrate on the very domains of human behavior and values that are basic to a society's performances and order. Thus they focus on work practices, health and eating habits, means and style of communication, sexual and kinship conceptions, notions of etiquette and law, notions of the supernatural and the eternal. And since relatively few people have ever been exposed to a wide variety of human behaviors, there is a tendency to view another society's behaviors as the polar opposites of one's own, even if they are in reality only small variations on a common human theme. Viewed as opposites, they are typically understood as a *lack* of those behavioral values.[9] Thus, a people may be seen as promiscuous (that is, lacking a sense of sexual propriety or a kinship system), or seen to "babble" and "jibber" (to lack a true communication system, to speak a "broken" form), to be superstitious or fetishistic (to lack a real religion), and the like. And even where the people may be recognized as having certain domains of behavior in which they excel—ritual, openness to friendships, musical or dance skills, whatever—these, too, are seen to have been achieved at the cost of "proper," more important domains of human endeavor, such as rationality, order, discipline, work, etc. Thus it was that early writers on Africa and the slaves of the West Indies, while observing in great detail some of the exotic strengths of black people, seem to have concluded that these people lacked a proper human culture as well as a soul, much as St. Augustine had once wrestled with the question of whether apes were worthy of salvation.

It might appear that I am saying, like most other commentators, that stereotypes are merely the results of lack of information or faulty perception of an alien and exotic people, or simply the natural reaction of an isolated and insular people to outsiders with different physiques and means of organizing their lives; in other words, xenophobia. From such a point of view, however, the function of the stereotype would be simply to *exclude* a people from one's perception. But the function is really *inclusory*; it seeks to explain the presence of other peoples in our midst or in the natural order of the world. In this sense stereotypes are one of the results of normal classificatory thinking, the practice of measuring alien characteristics against existing taxonomies of humanness. It is sobering to recall that such processes are not limited to Western explorers and imperialists. While Europeans were debating the humanity of their "discoveries" in Africa, their discovered peoples were pondering the same questions in reverse. They were repelled by white skin, associated as it was with "peeled" skin and leprosy, its ugly blue-veined surface shamefully covered by many clothes; these offensive-smelling Europeans with the wild-animal hair on their long heads, bodies, and red faces, these savage-looking men who could live so long without their women, were seen to be cannibals.[10]

It should be obvious that stereotypical folk-notions of races arose out of early historical contacts in which it was found that an alien people not only looked different from oneself, but also performed differently, behaving in exotically stylized, recurring presentations of self. Never mind that another people's institutions—law, polity, family, and the like— might be profoundly different, it was their use of their bodies that had the most impact.

To most people, then as now, motor habits—the way one moves, blinks eyes, stands, and walks—the way one pitches one's voice, laughs, cries, and collectivizes with others socially—are seen to be rooted in some mysterious racial, or at least "instinctive" fact.[11] For who ever "learns" such things? Who "teaches" them? As easy as these things are to sense, they are even difficult to describe accurately. Surely, if anything was peculiar to the "genius" of a race (as nineteenth-century writers put it) these things were. But as Professor Ray Birdwhistell[12] stresses, one of the great discoveries of the last twenty years is that even these micro-behaviors are systematically learned and patterned, even though, like language, at a very early age and largely out-of-awareness. Further, they can be unlearned or changed. But as we know them, they are the underlying communicative baselines of what we in the West at least consider to be the *real* communication—words. Thus, the finding of students of kinesics, paralinguistics, proxemics, and microcultural behavior is that the communicative and fundamental level of humanness is as plastic and variable as other forms of human behavior—it is, in the fullest sense in which E. B. Tylor used the word, *culture*.

What makes this matter all the more complicated and interesting is that it is just this level of human cultural variability that also makes up the basis of what we call artful human behavior. In *Folksong Style and Culture*[13] Alan Lomax has elaborated the argument that song, dance, ritual, and other artistic performances are high-level statements of these very microcultural patterns. The arts rest not so much on words and ideas as on these largely out-of-awareness communicative codes. And since the arts are the supreme collective statements of what a people seem to think life is about and what they feel is their place in that life, artistic behavior reaches down into the bases of communication which appear most mysteriously human. Further, since history demonstrates that the stylistic components of the arts are slow to change and difficult to destroy, it is often easy to feel that particular performances are "natural" to particular races. Let me give an example from Lomax's work. His studies of the styles of song and dance suggest that, far from it being the case that the world has as many different systems of these arts as there are peoples, there are in fact a limited number of ways in which these modes of artful communication may be expressed. Indeed, the world is characterized by a limited number of style areas and means of organizing and presenting performances. To use only one case, there are people whose song and dance performances are characterized by a high level of interpersonal synchrony, by great cohesiveness and complementarity of performers.[14] These are people whose performances typically include both men and women at the same time, whose songs are well-blended and rhythmically coordinated, who can organize relatively large groups into complex, multi-parted choruses and dance groups usually without leaders, whose members submerge their individuality into a precise collectivity. Perhaps the three most pronounced areas of the world in this respect are sub-Saharan Africa, Polynesia, and portions of Eastern European village areas. The same peoples use similar schemes and stylistic means for organizing work activities. When these people are compared in their performances with those of Western Europe, Euro-America, and the civilizations of the Middle East—all of whom put emphasis on the non-complementarity of sexes, and either on individuality of performers or on highly stratified, collective performances under the rigid control of a leader, both in art and in work—the degree of the stylistic contrast becomes apparent. Indeed, as Lomax has suggested, Westerners are people who find conscious synchrony—talking at the same time, walking in stride, and the like—embarrassing, "monkey-like," or childish, on the one hand, and on the other they reserve it for rather frightening and coercive mass events such as training soldiers for war.

Other kinds of stylistic variables offer similar societal contrasts: some cultures use heavily worded song texts, some use only sounds; some cultures articulate all parts of the body in dance, others use only the trunk and feet; some sing in unison, some in harmony, some in fugue, etc. And similar kinds of contrasts turn up in between different societies' characteristics of work, ritual, and speech events. All of this simply says that art symbolizes (and thus reinforces) "non-artistic," everyday behavior. And art styles, like behavioral styles, can be mapped across time and geography. What we may have thought of as behavior caused by physical form is rather learned behavior organized at many communicative levels, each cross-referencing the other. It is possible to see from this way of looking at the world that throughout history we have been confusing cultural styles with race.

2

One advantage of looking at race conceptions and relations from a cultural point of view is that it opens up new ways of looking at old phenomena. Consider this: when two "races" find themselves in close and relatively stable social contact, typically where one has power and high status and the other does not, two kinds of problems emerge for the high-status group. How, on one hand, to maintain its genetic status quo, in order to prevent a dilution of the dominant racial group; on the other hand, how to prevent a dilution of the dominant group's culture? The first of these problems has been given considerable attention, and as a consequence we know that although racial "dilution" and "intermixing" occurs in biracial societies, there are elaborate and varied established means for maintaining the fiction of racial purity: to name just one technique, traditionally in the South of the United States the offspring of parents of different and unequal racial status are assigned to the descent group of the lower-ranking parent.[15] But surprisingly little attention has been to the second of these problems, the question of how to prevent the "bastardizing" and "mongrelizing" of the high-status group's culture.

If we can be sure of anything throughout history, it is that two peoples—regardless of the lines drawn and the barriers between them, whether socially unequal or not—will in the process of everyday close interaction learn and adopt some aspects of the other group's behavior. And some of each group will become proficient to the point of being capable of assuming at least the cultural if not the racial identity of the other group. We are less conscious of the high-status member skilled at low-status behavior and culture, perhaps, but it is just such skill and proficiency of low-status members in high-status culture that has drawn attention to inequities in the United States, Great Britain, and elsewhere.

If the low-status member or group borrows from or learns from the high group (even where the high group may deny that true learning goes on, and may see it as merely imitative or "aping"), the high culture is said to become degraded, cheapened, and misunderstood, and attempts are made to carefully guard it and institutionally lock it out of reach. But since more characteristically the high group considers the low as lacking such capacity, such efforts are often not made until it is too late.

On the reverse side, the high group views borrowing and learning from the low to be so personally polluting, and to be such a naked recognition of merit in the low, that few—even the scholars of race contacts—even discuss the possibility. Nevertheless, it goes on. Again, hear the complaint of William Camden discussing the effects of Irish customs on the English: "But the Irish are so wedded to those, that they not only retain 'em themselves, but corrupt the English among them; and it is scarce credible how soon these will degenerate: Such a proneness there is in human nature, to grow worse."[16] Even earlier, in 1366, the preamble to the Statutes of Kilkenny bemoaned the fact that

now many English of the said land, forsaking English language, manners, mode of riding, laws and usages, live and govern themselves according to the manners, fashion and language of the Irish enemies and also have made divers marriages between themselves and the Irish enemies.[17]

Similarly, travelers to the colonies of the New World were fast to condemn the "degeneration" of European and English culture there. A visitor to the United States in 1746 noted:

One thing [the American planters] are very faulty in, with regard to their Children, which is, that when young, they suffer them too much to prowl amongst the young Negroes, which insensibly causes them to imbibe their Manners and broken Speech.[18]

Even an American planter's child, however, could be aware of these cultural influences. Commenting on the influence of slaves' culture on whites, one Mississippi slaveholder's son wrote: "It was as though another Civilization had been wiped out, and a set of Goths and Vandals with shaggy hides and wooden bludgeons were stalking around amid the ruins, in lieu of the inhabitants whom they had slaughtered."[19] Occasionally, there even appeared a detailed chronicle by which one can trace at least the partial personal acculturation of a white European to slaves' culture. In the case of Matt Lewis, the English playwright and novelist who inherited a plantation in Jamaica, the process he recorded took only a year.[20]

But such public admissions are rare. So profound is the potential, so awesome its consideration, that the idea of high turning low is usually left to fiction that borders on myth. The corrosive effect of the stigmatized is richly documented in Joseph Conrad's *Heart of Darkness* or in

William Faulkner's novels. And the madness of the first Mrs. Montgomery in *Jane Eyre* was well understood by Brontë's contemporaries, who knew the corruption and degeneration likely in a Creole, a white person born in the Caribbean.[21]

But the high do learn and borrow from the low, and they have developed elaborate techniques and justifications to skirt the pollution and degradation involved in the transformation. Perhaps the best-known such technique is what might be called *minstrelization*, the process by which the low are characterized or emulated within a carefully regulated and socially approved context. Thus, on the nineteenth-century stage, English and American white minstrels could publicly display the extent to which they had mastered what they assumed to be Negro cultural forms and behaviors, and could for a short time at least participate in what they conceived of as Negro life. (Complicating this process was the fact that before the Negro was mimicked on the stage the Irishman had served the same purpose; in fact, in the transition period in America, Negro speech was simply grafted on to Irish tunes.)[22] That these minstrels and their later followers—Al Jolson, Amos and Andy, Eddie Cantor et al.—became the most popular entertainers in the United States within their time underscores the mass participation in the minstrelization process. And the fact that, say, a Mick Jagger can today perform in the same tradition without blackface simply marks the detachment of culture from race and the almost full absorption of a black tradition into white culture. This form of "passing" is distinctly different from that available to the stigmatized racial group. Where the low-status member must first possess a physique at least marginally similar to the dominant group's and must additionally master the high-status group's cultural devices, always risking discrediting, the high-status minstrelizer has only to learn a minimal number of cultural techniques and *temporarily* mask himself as a subordinate—literally a Negro *manqué* in this case.

A recent example illustrates how rapidly the same process can take place artifactually. A South African wine, "Rock 'n' Roll Sherry," carries on its label an exact reproduction of a 1923 photograph of King Oliver's New Orleans jazz band with Louis Armstrong — except that the faces are shown to be white![23]

Although such examples are dramatic and grand in scope, the cultural plagiarism process is essentially one of everyday occurrence and in many cases a part of the normal educational process of an elite. Willie Morris, in speaking of his childhood in Yazoo, Mississippi, said:

There was a stage, when we were about thirteen, in which we "went Negro." We tried to broaden our accents to sound like Negroes, as if there were not enough similarity already. We consciously walked like young Negroes, mocking their swinging gait, moving our arms the way they did, cracking our knuckles and whistling between our teeth. We tried to use some of the same expressions, as closely as possible to the way they said them, like: "Hey, m-a-a-n, what you *doin'* theah!," the sounds rolled out and clipped sharply at the end for the hell of it.[24]

Morris further documents the way in which other stages of growing up are identified with Negroes, perhaps the most profound of which is the pre-adolescent understanding of sexual intercourse as something one does with Negro women only.[25]

Both individually and collectively then, the high group becomes intimately involved with the low.

In our very lives, we have come to repeat this pattern, individual biography recapitulating cultural history. Born theoretically white, we are permitted to pass our childhood as imaginary Indians, our adolescence as imaginary Negroes, and only then are expected to settle down to being what we really are: white once more.[26]

What makes this kind of cultural borrowing different from that across national lines is the paradoxical denial of the existence of low culture by the high. Often in history this has been accomplished by the simple argument that the low are not quite human. During the earlier years of New World slavery such a paradox was in full flower: slaveholders and travelers wrote extensive journals documenting the beliefs, attitudes, habits, and behaviors of slaves all to demonstrate by their "differences" their nonhuman, or at best "savage" status. Indeed the more carefully the observers noted what we would today easily recognize as a coherent, viable human culture, the more likely they were to use it as negative evidence.

Although such crude readings of human behavior are less likely today, the tendency to treat minority or low-status peoples as lacking culture turns up in different guises, especially in history and the social sciences. The Pygmies of the Congo, for example, were initially understood to lack indigenous song, language, and ritual—simply because the dominant Negro peoples in contact with them used the same forms and the direction of influence was assumed to be one-way—but recent research has shown the process of influence to be just the reverse.[27] Again, Frank M. Snowden's research on blacks in ancient Greek and Roman art turned up abundant proof that Africans regularly performed the roles of jugglers, wrestlers, servants, jesters, and the like, all of which he took as evidence that Africans were acculturated and integrated into these societies.[28] But his assumption that the Africans had lost their cultures is unproved, and it could equally be argued that certain roles, and thus the Greek and Roman societies themselves, had become "Africanized" to some degree through the cultural styles and skills of their alien occupants.

What is more remarkable is that the strategies of the anti-racists among social scientists in the West show a peculiar similarity to the ideologies of the racists. As I suggested in the beginning, early scientific anti-racists in the United States addressed the folk equation of race and culture by specifying and delimiting the concept of race so as to discredit or at least transvalue what they conceived to be the everyday stereotypes of races. All the more strange, then, was their response to the other side of the folk equation. Though anthropologists such as Franz Boas understood that cultures needed to be described and reinterpreted so that their alien qualities could be understood as human responses to universal human problems, and though Boas did such a translation of the culture of the Eskimos, he and other anthropologists took a different approach to American Negroes. So, instead of historical studies and descriptive accounts of cultural practices, anthropologists chose to either completely deny the cultural practices of American Negroes or to treat them as stereotyped fantasies of white people.[29] That is, they attempted to dispel the negative Euro-American *readings* and *valuings* of culturally different behavior of Afro-Americans by denying the existence of the behavior itself. This meant that they were forced to treat black dialects, music, dance, interpersonal style, and the like as non-existent just at the point where these phenomena were beginning to flood the country through the mass media, when they were in fact becoming the basis of an American vernacular culture.

Strange as it appears on the surface, this anti-racist strategy was perfectly in tune with the liberal politics of the times. Since liberals assumed that America was a successful cultural melting pot, they saw variations in culture to be the results of poverty and racism. All that remained was for barriers against racial intermarriage to be removed for racial distinctions to disappear. So, like the racists they hoped to rebut, anthropologists very early fell into the habit of confusing equality with sameness and inequality with difference. Faith in the equality of all people was not inconsistent with a disrespect for unassimilated peoples in our midst, a disrespect that assumed that they would not be different from us had we not prevented them from being like us.[30] How unlike the anthropological brief for Negroes was G. K. Chesterton's forthright plea for the Irish:

The tendency of [Yeats's Celtic] argument is to represent the Irish or the Celts as a strange and separate race, as a tribe of eccentrics in the modern world immersed in dim legends and fruitless dreams. Its tendency is to see the Irish as odd, because they see the fairies. Its trend is to make the Irish seem weird and wild because they sing old songs and join in strange dances. But this is quite an error; indeed it is the opposite of the truth. It is the English who are odd because they do not see the fairies. It is the inhabitants of Kensington who are weird and

wild because they do not sing old songs and join in strange dances. . . . In all this
the Irish are simply an ordinary sensible nation, living the life of any other ordinary and sensible nation which has not been either sodden with smoke or oppressed by money-lenders, or otherwise corrupted with wealth and science. . . .
It is not Ireland which is mad and mystic; it is Manchester which is mad and mystic, which is incredible, which is a wild exception among human things. Ireland
has no need to pretend to be a tribe of visionaries apart. In the matter of visions,
Ireland is more than a nation, it is a model nation.[31]

To sum up, then, in arguing against the equation of race and culture,
social scientists have properly refuted several notions: that race determines culture; that there is a natural affinity between the two categories
or between any particular race and any particular culture; and that there
is thus a cultural means of determining what an "inferior" race might be.
But at the same time, having denied any capacity for developing viable
culture to peoples amongst us whose physiques happen to be different,
they leave them with only stigmatized bodies, since it appears difficult to
transvalue race without transvaluing culture. Now, American social science finds itself facing a people identifiable by body, but having no "real"
culture. Is it any wonder, then, that we have recently begun to see race
re-enter social science research as a variable with explanatory power?
Now, again, race, not culture, is being argued to be the source of low
I.Q. scores.

But social scientists are not alone in having become confused by racist
interpretations of body and culture. Marxists, too, have encountered
difficulties with the notions of ethnicity and culture, since they conceive
of them as false consciousness and as smoke screens of class (though this
theoretical distinction did not keep Engels or the Webbs from detest-
ing the Irish and seeing them as "degrading" influences on the English workingman!).[32] What strikes me as so curious about the Marxists is
that although ostensibly concerned with the exploitation of workers,
they have failed to notice that the cultural products of the lower classes
have also been pooled and in turn exploited. At once limited in the variety and forms of occupation open to them and at the same time isolated from the central resources of the society, often ghettoized or kept
on the margins, the low-status groups live largely on their own cultural
resources. The irony of the situation is obvious: the low-status group,
though cut off from the sources of power and production in the larger
society, is at the same time less alienated from its own cultural productions. The twist is that the elite of the society is free to draw on the lower
group's cultural pool. Were there ever more massive examples of the
conversion of community life and culture into commodity than those in
which black folk-life has been turned into national culture in the United
States, Brazil, or Cuba? Or where an entire people has been made the

entertainers and bearers of another people's folk-art, as with the tinkers of Scotland or the gypsies of Europe?

Finally, the circle comes round: in their efforts to demystify race social scientists and revolutionaries have abandoned culture and grouped the stigmatized and excluded peoples of many races and cultures together in a concept larger than race, one variably called the "lumpenproletariat," the "wretched of the earth," members of the "cultures of poverty," or simply "the masses." One more cynical than I might recognize these as moral characterizations based on lacks, and thus as classical stereotypes.

3

To many, I fear, the anecdotal history I have sketchily drawn here will appear to be a gratuitous exercise in irony. In a world hell-bent on the destruction of cultural variety and integrity through industrialization, "wars of pacification," Common Market, revolution, and the like, the niceties of racial and cultural definition look academic and madly out of touch. But there is also an odd sense in which these questions are taking on critical significance. It is customary to regard the development and spread of racist ideology in the nineteenth and twentieth centuries as simply an elitist ploy in the effort to maintain and establish control over workers and slaves. Certainly the rationales of racist thought tell us as much. But was it not also this very period which witnessed the rise of assertive racial and ethnic consciousness and cultural revitalization on the part of the peoples who were massively dislocated and dispossessed? And was this also not the period in which these outcast groups had their greatest influence? As the native and the peasant began to tentatively abandon aspects of traditional identity for whatever cultural forms industry, city, and the "West" might provide, those who ran the industries and metropolises began to search out alternatives, not from their own severed and truncated pasts, but among those workers, peasants, and slaves in their midsts. As Roger Bastide has said of the spread of African and Afro-American cuisine, dance, music, art forms, religion, and speech in the Americas:

That spiritual void which the city creates at the heart of each human individual is resented, naturally, just as much by the European as by the Negro. As a result the European turns increasingly to Africa or Black America for the satisfaction of those vital needs which industrial society can no longer answer.[33]

There is something pathetic and perhaps ill-fated about the spectacle of Euro-America "Africanizing" and England "Celticizing" under industrialization, but what was the choice? As we have increasingly come to discover that our own past was as dislocated and discontinuous as those very "traditional" societies which we have observed in the throes of "modernization," we have thrashed about in the search for some kind of meaning and identity that will at least last us for even one generation.

If we are to survive in an age in which technology has freed man from the necessity of enslaving other men in order to progress, then, as Claude Lévi-Strauss has suggested,[34] we must unlearn much of what we have accepted since the dawn of the Neolithic and look elsewhere for our models of salvation. Perhaps we are the butt of our own historical joke: we now find ourselves desperately studying the discredited and displaced, and stumbling nakedly into a pastoral of ludicrous dimensions.

After the Myth: Studying Afro-American Cultural Patterns in the Plantation Literature

WITH ROGER D. ABRAHAMS

The difficulty of describing the cultural relationships between Afro-American peoples and their African progenitors is not due to any lack of data. Any argument about culture-flow is difficult to present, and needs as much ethnographic bolstering as possible, but the problems of describing the forced dispersal of African peoples in the New World is made all the more difficult because of the inadequacy of the models of culture contact and resultant change which have been used to explain such diaspora situations. Although many other massive movements of peoples have occurred analogous to the confrontation of Europeans and Africans in the New World, no clear statement exists of the variables that operate in such situations. Instead, a casual, anecdotal approach has been taken in which the encounter is seen from the viewpoint of the politically or economically superordinate people as against the subordinate, with the assumption that such subordination leads to cultural as well as political and economic dominance.

No case undercuts this model of acculturation so clearly as that of Afro-American peoples, because many of the most basic features of plantation and modern New World life have been obviously influenced by Afro-American cultural practices. Subordination was asserted and rationalized through an entirely false stereotypical concept of the slaves' cultural resources. For instance, the Africans often possessed a more highly developed agricultural technology than the Europeans, especially in tropical gardening, so that the Europeans often found themselves in an environment more alien than did their slaves. The planters not only had to exploit the physical energy source of the Africans, but also cultural practices from Africa as well as those brought from Europe, or developed subsequent to their arrival in the New World.

The planters found it convenient not only to allow African practices but actually to encourage them, especially in such noninstitutional dimensions of culture as work practices, ways of playing, and systems of magic and curing. These could be encouraged because they assisted directly or indirectly in the maintenance of the plantation and could be accommodated within the stereotypical concept of Blacks as perpetual children or as animals. In this context, active and self-conscious deculturation was used only to break down residual African modes of asserting community because of their potential power. Thus, the various Old World types of extended families were indeed discouraged, as were the larger economic, political, and social units of African society. From our perspective, desocietalization rather than deculturation resulted, and even here total brainwashing could not have occurred.

Wherever Afro-Americans could interact with each other (whether or not in the presence of Euro-Americans), shared expectations, attitudes, and feelings emerged drawing upon the commonalities of past experience in Africa and in the New World. Wholesale carryovers of community-based culture need not be posited to argue that African cultural continuities are obvious and long-lasting. Many Euro-American observers recognized this cultural persistence from the earliest plantation days, and provided a large, if selective, record of African and Afro-American cultural practices as filtered through their stereotypical rationalizations. We will look, then, at Afro-American life through the documents of the planters and European travelers. In *African Civilizations in the New World*, Roger Bastide states that "the current vogue for the study of African civilizations in America is a comparatively recent phenomenon. Before the abolition of slavery such a thing was inconceivable, since up until then the Negro had simply been regarded as a source of labour, not as the bearer of a culture."[1] Afro-American communities could not be studied in a methodical and holistic manner, because the techniques for analysis of cultural continuities and discontinuities are comparatively recent developments. But whether or not Afro-Americans have such a thing as culture, an ongoing debate on this issue dates back at least two centuries.

To anthropologists, the idea that a group could be forcibly divested of their culture, yet maintain themselves and even proliferate, seems a strange argument indeed. Yet this deculturation argument is still an article of faith for most scholars studying Afro-Americans. Perhaps Euro-Americans are still unwilling to consider the ways of Black peoples as authentic manifestations of culture unless these ways are close enough to European practice to appear as misunderstandings or corruptions. The deculturation argument, an unexamined set of assumptions, was applied equally to other immigrant groups under the control of capitalist economies. Their loss of culture, it is implied, happens to all traditional peoples when they are forced off the land in search of wages. This divestment provided the raison d'être of sociological study and appears as a constant rationalizing thread of argument from Tönnies and Durkheim through Parsons and Merton even to Frederick Barth. This is not to say that anthropologists have been blameless in their treatment of "the dispossessed." Redfield's folk-urban continuum is an obvious extension of Tönnies's Gesellschaft-Gemeinschaft distinction, and Oscar Lewis's conception of a "culture of poverty" is directly related to such "negative pastoral" arguments as are found in Durkheim and Marx, for the pastoral is the literary castigation of city-life while extolling simple country existence.[2]

The "Africanisms" Controversy

The most frustrating line of argument against the distinct features of Afro-American cultures arose in response to the work of Melville J. Herskovits. In 1941 in *The Myth of the Negro Past*, Herskovits listed many possible projects investigating the cultural relationships between Africans and Afro-Americans, and in the process gave a barrage of illustrations of "Africanisms."[3] At that time the idea that American Blacks might be culturally distinct was widely rejected, and two types of counter arguments arose. On the one hand, specific Africanisms were postulated, debated, and largely rejected, a classic baby and bathwater problem. On the other, some scholars demanded that the putative African elements be demonstrated as retained from a specific African ethnic group. The Africanness of traits was not so much rejected as ignored as being incapable of adequate testing.

The frustrations of defending the cultural continuities argument have not diminished since the famous Melville Herskovits-E. Franklin Frazier confrontation after the publication of *Myth of the Negro Past*. The basic lines of argument have not altered very much since the early 1940s, as Afro-Americanists have found to their sorrow. The following recorded conversation between Frazier and Herskovits catches the direction of the arguments and the sense of frustration:

Mr. Frazier : *I* have not found anyone who could show any evidence of survival of African social organization in this country. I may cite a concrete case. You will recall that in reviewing my book, *The Negro Family in the United States*, in the *Nation*, you said that the description I gave of the reunion of a Negro family group could, with the change of a few words, be regarded as a description of a West African institution. But it also happens to be equally adequate as a description of a Pennsylvania Dutch family reunion. What are we to do in a case like that? Are we to say that it is African?

Mr. Herskovits: Methodologically, it seems to me that if in studying a family whose ancestry in part, at least, came from Africa I found that something they do resembles a very deep-seated African custom, I should not look to Pennsylvania Dutch folk, with whom this family has not been in contact, for an explanation of such a custom. I may be wrong but that seems elementary.

Mr. Frazier: But where did the Pennsylvania Dutch get their custom that resembles the one I described? Did they get it from Africa too?

Mr. Herskovits: May I ask if the methodological point at issue is this: is it maintained that if we find anything done by Negroes in this country that resembles anything done in Europe, we must therefore conclude that the Negroes' behavior is derived from the European customs, the inference then being that the traditions of their African ancestors were not strong enough to stand against the impact of European ways?

Mr. Frazier: No I wouldn't say that, but I believe it should be the aim of the scholar to establish an unmistakable historical connection between the African background and present behavior of Negroes, rather than to rely on *a priori* arguments.

Mr. Herskovits: We will be in agreement, if you will add to your statement that neither should the scholar deny any such connection on *a priori* grounds.[4]

Even when such arguments emerge today among social scientists, M. G. Smith's 1960 call for the tracing of specific cultural practices to a specific ethnic group in Africa is still heard; never mind that highly cognate forms of behavior exist between West Africa and the New World. There is considerable evidence of direct and specific retentions. Sea Island basketry, for instance, can be shown to be made with the same techniques and similar materials to those from Senegambia.[5] Similarly, Bascom has surveyed the wide range of retentions of Yoruba and Dahomean deity-names in such New World cult religions as Vodû, Candomblé, and Shango, even while he demonstrates why such continuities have been maintained in so many culturally distinct parts of the New World.[6] Many other practices still to be observed in Afro-America, such as dancing, drumming, and funeral rituals, are obviously close to African antecedents. However, Richard Price has noted that there is greater potential in seeking such "development within historically related and overlapping sets of . . . ideas" than in restricting our search to "direct retentions or survivals."[7] Or as two students of Herskovits, George E. Simpson and Peter Hammond, commented:

Both past records and an examination of the contemporary situation in the New World indicate that beneath the relatively superficial level of form there is a significant, non-conscious level of psychological function. On this level there is an important basic similarity [for instance] between varieties of religious practices both throughout West Africa and in the various New World Negro communities.[8]

In their subsequent discussion of spirit possession, they account for its cultural tenacity through its basic commonality with West African religious behavior. Finally, rejecting M. G. Smith's assertion that continuities can only be established through commonality of form from one specific place in the Old World to one in the New, Simpson and Hammond state that:

Form is the most superficial level of cultural reality. Since it is consciously realized, it is often much quicker to change than the profounder philosophic principles and psychological attitudes which are frequently more persistent and tenacious because they exist beneath the level of consciousness.[9]

But such opinions are all too rarely encountered in Afro-American scholarship. Though less strident than E. Franklin Frazier or M. G. Smith, a number of recent commentators maintain the deculturation argument while carrying out some impressive ethnographic reporting. Diverting attention from African continuities in the New World and the professed intent of the slavers to strip the slaves culturally, these scholars argue rather that if there are New World Negro cultures, they must arise for the most part from the common experiences by Blacks of enslavement and social exclusion. For example, Sidney Mintz argues that

enslaved Africans were quite systematically prevented—with few exceptions . . . from bringing with them the personnel who maintained their homeland institutions; the complex social structures of the ancestral societies, with their kings and courts, guilds and cult-groups, markets and armies were not, and could not be transferred. Cultures are linked as continuing patterns of and for behavior to such social groupings; since the groupings themselves could not be maintained or readily reconstituted, the capacities of random representatives of these societies to perpetuate or to recreate the cultural contents of the past were seriously impaired. Again, the slaves were not usually able to regroup themselves in the New World settings in terms of their origins; the cultural heterogeneity of any slave group normally meant that what was shared culturally was likely to be minimal. . . . [However,] the slaves could and did create viable patterns of life, for which their pasts were pools of available symbolic and material resources.[10]

Certainly African institutions were vulnerable to elimination in the New World, at least where they were incompatible with slavery. Still, too much contrary evidence exists for one to accept Mintz's argument without some real qualifications. One thinks, for instance, of the widespread West African practice of *susu* ("sharing group"), which not only has been encountered under the very name in several places in Afro-America, but provides insight into the importance of such Afro-American voluntary associations as Friendly Societies, lodges, burial societies, rent parties, and the like.[11] The religious domain, too, continued in modified form in a variety of cults in Brazil, Cuba, and elsewhere.[12] Numerous expressions of apparent African nationalities occur in such festivals as the Nation

Dances of Carriacou, the "dance in Place Congo" in New Orleans, the "jubilee" in Washington Square in eighteenth-century Philadelphia, and many other places.[13] Admittedly the intricate African kingship organizations could not be widely maintained in the Americas, but the relatively independent and complementary position of men and women widely observed in the slaving areas of Africa must be considered a formative force in the development of the "matrifocal" household system.[14] This is what we mean by the deeper forms of culture that seem to bind Afro-Americans together.

Expressive Continuities

Just such expressive continuities are crucial to an understanding of the institutions developed by Blacks in their various New World situations. The great diversity of New World settings in which Africans found themselves—plantations, cities, mining areas, escaped slave outposts, etc.— makes it impossible to demonstrate parallel developments in such areas as religious practice, community governance, economics, and even the family, simply in terms of the shared experiences of plantation slavery. These similarities reflect a common conceptual and affective system of which the slave could not be stripped—shared practices, beliefs, and behavioral patterns that not only survived but were developed further in the New World setting. The importance of performance in the stylization of individual and group relationships cannot be overemphasized. These patterns of performance of simplified models of social organization in the Old World provided the basic groundwork on which African-like community interactions would be generated in spite of the loss of the details of their institutional renderings.

If one uses only the literature of white journalist and traveler, the area of Black life most fully documented for continuities from the African past would be folk beliefs and practices and ghost lore. In the United States under the name of "hants," "hags," "rootwork," "conjuring," or "hoodoo," and in the West Indies as "duppies," "jumbies" (among many others) and "obeah men" or "wanga," accounts of plantation life include large sections devoted to the depth and persistence of such "superstitious" beliefs and practices.

The reasons for this interest are various. Most obvious, such practices were evidence for maintaining the stereotype of Blacks either as simpleminded heathen nature-worshipers or—even worse—as pawns of the devil. But each observer had different reasons why this subject was of interest. For the planters, these practices were seen as a threat to their operation, and they tried to militate sporadically against them, though one suspects that the folk medical practices and ceremonies were encouraged

or overlooked as a way of keeping the slaves alive and happy. For abolitionists or their foes, the strange practices were proof of the presence or
absence of human feeling and culture; for missionaries, they provided
evidences of what had to be fought.

For whatsoever reason the observations were made, they form a large
body of data that has not yet been utilized effectively in the study of cultural continuities.

Two other aspects of plantation literature of even greater interest—
the materials on work and on play—will be surveyed to show the complexity of the sociocultural situation wherever African ways were transformed into Afro-American ways.

Work

As noted, the Africans brought to the New World were often master
tropical gardeners. The journal-keepers noted again and again the remarkable abilities of the slaves not only in working the cane fields and
melting-houses, but also in providing their own foodstuffs even to the
point of marketing the excess on their one day off, Sunday. John Luffman's account of Antigua life of 1788 is typical of such often begrudg-
ing descriptions:

every slave on a plantation, whether male or female, when they attained their
14th or 15th year, has a piece of ground, from twenty five, to thirty feet square,
allotted to them, which by some is industriously and advantageously cultivated,
and by others totally neglected. These patches are found to be of material
benefit to the country, their produce principally supplying the "sunday market"
. . . with vegetables. They are also allowed to raise pigs, goats, and fowls, and
it is by their attention to these articles, that whites are prevented from starv-
ing, during such times of the year as vessels cannot come to these coasts with
safety.[15]

Although the contribution of the slaves to the development and operation of the plantation is yet to be studied extensively, suggestive work
has been done by Peter H. Wood on South Carolina, where he shows
Africans to be the source of rice agriculture, new forms of cattle breeding and herding, boat building, inland water navigation, hunting and
trapping, medicine, and other skills.[16] Indeed, the agricultural success of
South Carolina seems more a function of the slaves' knowledge and technology than it was of their masters'.

The slaves often found themselves in a position to teach their masters
and to carry out their agricultural tasks in agricultural time or tempo.
Numerous European observers recount with amazement the coordination
of activities in Afro-American work gangs, and recorded the songs sung

while carrying out the work tasks. "Their different instruments of husbandry, particularly their gleaming hoes, when uplifted to the sun, and which, particularly, when they are digging cane-holes, they frequently raise all together, and in as exact time as can be observed, in a well-conducted orchestra, in the bowing of the fiddles, occasion the light to break in momentary flashes around them."[17] Observers noted that this work was carried out through the use of songs in classic African call-and-response pattern, by which the work gangs both coordinated movements and created and maintained a sense of common purpose. Such descriptions as this, from J. B. Moreton's *West Indian Customs and Manners*, are a commonplace of the genre:

When working, though at the hardest labour, they are commonly singing; and though their songs have neither rime nor measure, yet many are witty and pathetic. I have often laughed heartily, and have been as often struck with deep melancholy at their songs:—for instance, when singing of the overseer's barbarity to them:
   Tink dere is a God in a top,
   No use we ill, Obisha!
   Me no horse, me no mare, me no mule,
   No use me ill, Obisha.[18]

Such activities, of course, were given as indications that the slaves were a happy, childlike people who loved their work. As one especially lighthearted observer describes it, the harvest provided "a scene of animation and cheerfulness" in which the ear and the eye are suffused with evidences of "the light-hearted hilarity of the negroes" in which "the confused clamor of voices in dialogue and song, present a singular contrast to the calm response which nature seems to claim for herself in these clear and ardent climes."[19]

However, it was not just the working styles that made Africans the ideal slaves in the plantation system. As a gardening people, they already measured time and apportioned energy by the cycles of the crops. They understood the necessity of working long and hard hours during planting and harvesting seasons, but they were also used to working considerably less hard during the other seasons. This disparity was often noticed, but without much comprehension of the system of time and energy allocation that lay behind it.[20]

From the perspective of racial stereotyping, this cycle was particularly convenient. When the Blacks were working very hard in the sun or in the heat of the building where the sugar was boiled, they could be portrayed as brute work animals. But during other seasons, when they resisted what they regarded as senseless work, they could be accused of being lazy. One way or another, the stereotype could be applied.

Play

Continuities of African work practices are, then, relatively easily accounted for since they fit the needs of the planters while in no way challenging the European image of Blacks. The aspect of play is more problematic because of a longer history of Black-White relations and imaginings involving a range of behaviors viewed by some as anathema to enterprise. For centuries before colonization, Europeans had associated Africans with festival entertainments; and music, dance, and public performances were ideal opportunities to judge whether or not Blacks might acquire culture. The existence of a great many detailed descriptions of Black play activities enables us to explore the deeper levels of cultural continuity, and may thus help in understanding the creation of Afro-American culture. Play materials tell us about patterns of behavior going far beyond the realm of play, for playing involves a selective stylization of motives also found in other domains of activity. For instance, Alan Lomax and associates' studies in choreometrics have demonstrated high correlation between work and dance movements within specific groups and culture areas.[21] Equally important, however, in discovering deeper cultural patterns is how and to what play activities are contrasted.

Even before there was direct contact between Europeans and Africans, Black peoples from the south held a special symbolic importance for Europeans. As Henri Baudet pointed out, this interest was occasioned by a pre-Rousseauvian primitivism that included all non-Europeans, who were envisaged as simpler people living closer to nature, and therefore closer to a state of primal innocence and harmony. As travel increased, Black Africans were contrasted positively with the Muslim who had become a feared enemy during the Crusades.

However, with the beginning of the Renaissance, Europeans became more knowledgeable about Muslims and came to admire them and their Culture. Baudet describes the consequences of this change:

Unlucky Negro: our culture has always presented him in unequivocal opposition to the Muslim. But now, quite suddenly, Islam is found to merit admiration. Rapidly and unexpectedly, its star moves into a new orbit and the traditional contrast between Negro and Muslim is reversed. For a century or more Islam, and not the Negro, has been the subject of scientific interest. . . . A new reputation for the unfortunate Negro has its origins here, and he approaches the next two centuries as typifying the lowest stage of human development . . . an altogether inferior creature, a slave by nature, lacking all historical background.[22]

Of course, during these "next two centuries" Africans and Europeans were brought together in huge numbers, at a time when the negative image of the primitive was convenient for rationalizing enslavement.

However, during the earlier period, the fascination with Africans had caused Europeans to associate "Moors," "Blacks," and "Negroes" with parades and other kinds of festival behaviors. Eldred D. Jones's *The Elizabethan Image of Africa* brings together a number of illustrations of this fascination: blackface characters identified with Africa appeared in medieval mummers plays or in the courtly "disguises" of the sixteenth century; Henry VIII and the Earl of Essex marched with such "Moors" in 1510; blackface figures led the pageants and cleared away crowds during the same period; Edward VI took part in a Shrovetide masque in 1548 in which the marchers' legs, arms, and faces were all blackened; and Queen Anne appeared as a Negro in Ben Jonson's *The Masque of Blackness.*[23] Numerous other Elizabethan dramas—most notably *Othello*—also contained important Black roles.

Later, after the beginning of the slave trade and the increasing presence of "real" Africans in Europe, the cultural impact became even greater. For example, Black drummers were popular in European military and court bands in the late eighteenth and early nineteenth centuries.[24] Their music, style of performance, and costumes had important and lasting consequences for Europeans and Euro-Americans. And though it has been recognized that African and Turkish drum corps were the inspirations for compositions by Gluck, Mozart, and Haydn, it is not so well known that the source of the "Turkish music" (seventh) variation of the "Ode to Joy" theme of Beethoven's Ninth Symphony was not Turkish drummers, but more likely the African drum corps active in Germany at that time who played what was called "Turkish music."[25] Surely part of the shock value of Beethoven's last movement for Europeans lay in its images of African drums and drummers gathering with the heavenly hosts around the throne of Heaven!

This association of Blacks with public entertainments is characteristic of marginal groups who are stigmatized because of being culturally strange. One of the few roles available to outsiders in European culture is that of the performer because it does not undermine the stereotypes. Performance abilities are utilized as one of the few ways they can survive economically. For instance, among Gypsies in Europe, this performer role has been developed into an entire way of life, as it is with the Bauls in Bengal and the Arioi society in Melanesia.

In any case, Black parades and festivals were encouraged by the plantocracy and used by them on most important entertainment occasions. Such Euro-American interest and occasional participation simply gave an unofficial stamp of approval to practices that came to fill a central role in Afro-American communities throughout the New World. In Bahia, Rio de Janeiro, Havana, Port of Spain, New Orleans, and, in past times, Mexico City, Philadelphia, Wilmington, North Carolina, Hartford, and other cities, Afro-American carnivals, processions, and street parades have been performed annually for many years. Though such events were often dismissed by puritanical members of Euro-American societies as licentious bacchanals, they are in fact highly structured performances based on religious cults and social clubs, many of which have continuity of more than three hundred years. The characteristics of these events are well known: clubs of maskers organize around a variety of exotic themes, elect kings and queens, make banners, and focus on such special performances as stick fighting, baton twirling, and group dancing and singing on the streets and roads. In some areas, sacred and secret symbols are displayed on this day, while in others group spirit possession occurs before the clubs make their appearances. On these days groups and their symbols are moved from the privacy of *favelas* or ghetto neighborhoods where they have been part of their street life throughout the year into the public areas where Euro- and Afro-Americans come together. The significance of these events is well recognized and feared by the guardians of public order, the police, because they know these "backstreet" social organizations rule their streets after dark.

Some have dismissed these arcane and "Africa-like" institutions as the results of partial and incomplete acculturation, as way stations on the road to national homogeneousness; in other words, Blacks attempting to join or parallel Euro-American festivities with whatever cultural resources they can muster. We might better take our lead from the sociolinguists who speak of multiple codes in language systems. In the case of festivals, the codes are not linguistic ones, but instead are performance rules governing musical, motor, and religious behaviors which are the legacy of a wide variety of African peoples brought to Spanish-, Portuguese-, French-, and English-America. These Afro-American processions and carnivals might best be described as rites of passage, not between positions in single societies, but between the performance rules and social hierarchies of two different segments of single societies. These festivities exist because of the cultural dualities present in New World societies, and they have survived through the distinctions between public and private areas of urban life. During those festivities these boundaries are broken down, and the performances become more creole, more "country," more "down home," more African as the effects of license take hold.[26]

Certainly the organizations that give life to these Afro-American festivals in no way approximate the complex institutional arrangements that characterize West African societies, but their existence illustrates the ways in which identification with the African homeland was maintained and how this contributed to a sense of ethnicity and cultural identity in these various Afro-American societies.

Playing carnival, JonKanoo, and other such festivities is regarded as the most public, unrestrained, and hence backward and most African of all of the Afro-American performance occasions with the possible exception of *Shango* and other religious practices. While it is easy for Euro-Americans to be carried into the spirit of such occasions, to be able to understand how very different these performances are for Afro-Americans, it is necessary to understand the world order of Black communities, especially their contrasts between *work* and *play*, and between *private* and *public*. To relegate such expressive behavior as JonKanoo to the periphery of culture is to ignore the centrality of interpersonal performance in Black communities, and its use as a countervailing force against enslavement. In this context, an institution-centered definition of culture must give way to a study of micro-behaviors and the larger interactional system, which provide the formal and informal rules by which these groups live on a day-to-day, minute-to-minute basis.

Basic cultural differences exist between Euro- and Afro-American attitudes and behaviors in play and work or seriousness. Since playing is a departure from everyday behaviors especially with regard to the intensity and self-consciousness of its stylization, it is crucial to note to what play is contrasted.

Play generally has been used by Euro-Americans to describe activity free from the need to be productive within the so-called real or serious world. Although this freedom to be unproductive is often confused with freedom from rule-governed constraints, the most casual observer of play knows that the opposite is true—that playing is acting in accord with a self-consciously articulated and tightly circumscribed set of rules. Although less apparent in contest-games where winning takes precedence, the rule-governed and stylistic dimension of games nonetheless remain paramount. This concept of play is apparently characteristic of all groups, not just Euro-Americans, but Euro- and Afro-Americans differ in their use of the term and in their practices.

Euro-Americans employ the term *play* primarily in contrast to *work*, and Afro-Americans use the same terms, but what is meant by them differs sharply between the two groups. In Euro-America and elsewhere in the Western world, work is what one does to distinguish oneself as an individual. One learns to work successfully by most fully employing one's individual intelligence on a presented task. One proves one's worth by one's works, as it has been voiced until recently. Play, on the other hand, is the activity by which one progressively learns how to coordinate with others. Our values emphasize that the older we get, the more we must learn the importance of "team play." In an admittedly simple rendering then, working comes to mean, as one grows up, developing one's individual abilities, while playing during the same period comes to represent the subordination of individuality in favor of coordination and cooperation with others. Work is one's most *public* set of behaviors, and play is as private as one can maintain, unless one chooses one of the two most deviant of all our acceptable roles, the entertainer or the athlete, he who plays in public. Even here, we attempt to redefine their behavior as work. Thus, the most individual of all our behaviors, work, is also the most public.

Almost exactly the reverse characterizes Afro-Americans. Work tends to be identified with family and, by extension, with home with its relative privacy. Work is learned within the home as the most important feature of extended family living, and is identified with the maintenance of the familial order of the household. Commonly under the direction of *Mama*, children learn to work from older children in the household. Work is thus defined as a cooperative activity. Conversely, play, which is used to refer primarily to performance in this context, is learned from one's peers, commonly outside the home, and comes to be *the* activity by which Afro-American individuality is asserted and maintained. Thus, *playing* or performing is associated with public places, while work begins in the home and remains a kind of private or at least guarded range of behaviors. This accounts in part for the relative lack of discussion of work by Blacks, especially in those public circumstances in which verbal playing is regarded by them as more appropriate.

The distinction parallels that between the female-dominated household world and the male street-corner way of life, in terms of the difference of orientation, activity, and value systems between female respectability and male reputation maintenance.[27] In the Afro-American sense of the term, *play* is not commonly practiced in the house, being more appropriate in public where masculine, crossroads, reputation-centered values may be celebrated. In this sense play means highly unruly behavior, noisy verbal dueling, and using a dramatic speaking style known in the West Indies as *talking bad* or *broken*. When the noise, unruliness, and speaking style are brought together, the result is called *nonsense* or *foolishness*, evaluative terms derived from the household values but usually accepted by the male speakers themselves. Being public and individual, playing is regarded as inappropriate in areas dominated by respectability values, especially the house.[28]

Undoubtedly, the term *play* is used by Afro-Americans with many of the same meanings as other speakers of English. But in Black communities in the United States and the West Indies it has developed another range of meanings that point to an important social feature of Afro-American public behavioral style. Specifically, *play* describes situations of style- and code-switching, changes that have consequences reaching far beyond mere stylistic or esthetic dimensions of culture to the assertion of value- and culture-difference in performance terms. Although these generalizations derive from contemporary ethnographic research, old travel literature indicates that these differences have long existed, both in the use of the word "play" and in the concept of what playing is and how it should be properly carried out. As early as 1729, A. Holt mentions that the slaves in Barbados had gatherings on Sunday, "which they call their plays . . . in which their various instruments of horrid music howling and dancing about the graves of the dead, they [give] victuals and strong liquor to the souls of the deceased."[29] Peter Marsden similarly noted in 1788, "Every Saturday night many divert themselves with dancing and singing, *which they style plays*; and notwithstanding their week's labour, continue this violent exercise all night."[30] Such festivities were more commonly associated with the major holidays, especially Christmas. Another commentator, William Beckford, noticed:

Some negroes will sing and dance, and some will be in a constant state of intoxication, during the whole period that their festival at Christmas shall continue; and what is more extraordinary, several of them will go ten or twelve miles to *what is called a play*), will sit up and drink all night, and yet return in time to the plantation for their work the ensuing morning.[31]

This different approach to time, this all-night and unrestrained performance of play, seems to have most troubled these spectators, for, almost formulaically when they mention the term, they discuss its nocturnal aspects: "The dance, or play as it is sometimes called, commences about eight o'clock . . . and . . . continues to daybreak with scarcely an intermission."[32]

Nothing troubled the planters more than the nighttime activities of their slaves, relating to a whole group of stereotyped traits such as nighttime, diablerie, and supersexuality. Every effort was made to cut down on excessive nocturnal ceremonials, night-burials and wakes, the practice of *obeah*, and, of course, these *plays*. Yet, as anyone knows who has worked in the West Indies, the high value placed on playing any celebration all night remains to the present. Whether it is a wake, Christmas, Carnival, *tea meeting*, or *thanksgiving*, a celebration that can't be sustained all night is a disgrace to the performers and the community.

The designation of these all-night performances as *plays* was only one of the Black uses for the term, possibly fastened on by whites because it departed so fully from their own usage. In *A View of Jamaica*, James Stewart gives us some glimmer of the Afro-American domain of the term when he mentions that "plays, or dances, very frequently take place on Saturday night" and also suggests that "play" is their term for any licensed nonsense occasion.[33] Any holiday was called a *play-day*, as was a wake![34]

This set of practices, although persistently defined as bad and often illegal, has been maintained and even recently intensified throughout the anglophonic West Indies. Significantly, the most licentious of these celebrations are still referred to in play terms. One "plays" wake, Carnival *mas'*, *Christmas sport*, or any of that range of performances generally termed *nonsense* or *foolishness*.

Playing, then, means the acting out of behaviors regarded as *bad*, yet which provide a means of channeling the energies of all those in the performance environment. This acceptance of a negative self-image by at least one segment of Black communities during these "licentious" occasions has been widely noted by ethnographers. Karl Reisman has pointed out the "duality of cultural patterning" between positive (usually European) forms and negative (usually old-fashioned, country, or African) forms.[35] It is an integral part of this performance system to seek power by playing out in public these negative roles. These *bad* performances, regarded as appropriately masculine, embody male reputation values. This kind of nonsense behavior is acted upon constantly by the *sporty fellows*, *bad-johns*, and *rude boys*, but only when *playing* is sanctioned are the *sporty* ones permitted to perform before the community as a whole, and then only by dressing up or dressing down, taking unaccustomed roles into which they channel their antinormative (i.e., antihousehold) *nonsense*.

Thus *playing* in anglophonic Afro-America means not only the switching of styles and codes characteristic of all types of play, but also the switching downward to roles and behaviors regarded from household (and Euro-American) perspectives as "bad" or improper. Furthermore, as Morton Marks has noted of this switching in other parts of Afro-America, it is "always from a 'white' to a 'Black' style" and in music and dance at least, "from a European to an African one."[36] The juxtaposition of the implicitly "good" household-based norms of the Black community with the "bad" activities produces the kind of mass release of energies noted by all observers of Afro-American celebrations. *Playing* then means playing bad, playing Black, playing lower class. It is no coincidence that playing Christmas often led to insurrection, as was noted by the planter-journalists and travelers. The play world with its nonsense, masculine, defensive, and regressive Black motives simply began to break down the boundaries and rules of play, spilling out over the fences into the yards of the great houses.

Play is used in an analogous but somewhat more restricted sense in Black talk in the United States. Here *playing*, *playing the dozens*, and other similar locutions refer to code-switching into *baaad* varieties of speaking and acting which call for the same kind of performative acceptance of the negative role to obtain the power inherent in such behaviors. Thus, throughout Afro-America, playing is equated with a powerful but negative image of the performer. The power in the liminal world is a means of *getting into it*, setting up *the action*, but such playing provides a constant threat to the household world.

This speaking frame of reference acts both positively, in establishing the street environment as an appropriate place of witty and inverted performances, and negatively, in restricting speaking behavior within the household and other places dominated by respectability values.[37] In the Afro-American order of behaviors, "play" is not distinguished from "real" or "work" but from "respectable" behavior. Play is thus conceived in a very different way in Afro-American communities than it is in Euro-American. It is an important element of public performance of Black communities, by which Black men-of-words are able to establish and maintain their "reputations." The descriptions of West Indian *plays* give an indication of the depth of interest in such entertainments. Through these accounts we can gain insight not only into the alternative attitude of playing, but also into the ambivalence of Euro-Americans to such energetic practices, and the ways in which the slaves gradually incorporated European play occasions and in the process developed an Afro-American Creole culture.

With *plays*, as with the performance events introduced into Afro-American life from Europe, the focus and uses of the performances were changed in accord with the ethical and esthetic conceptual system shared by Africans and Afro-Americans. This process can be better understood by reference to the "Creole language hypothesis," which seeks to demonstrate that English, French, and other New World Creole languages are all developments from a West African Creole tongue used by traders and combining Portuguese and West African features.[38] Those who pursue this line of argument point to the large number of underlying similarities between the various New World Creole systems accounting for the major differences in vocabulary by reflexification, the simple substitution of a different (European) word into the phonological and morphological structure of the West African-based language. This word (or phrase) substitution does not necessarily mean that the vocabulary substituted is used with the same system of reference. Indeed, there is good evidence that the process of relexification cannot be understood without taking into account the *calque* (or "loan translation"), words that are translated into their nearest Western equivalent, but that continue to be used in the same system of reference as in Africa. This process of vocabulary substitution has ramifications in the entire semantic realm, in joking and oratory as well as in song and dance.[39]

Whether or not the Creole language hypothesis proves valid, something like reflexification seems to have operated on this larger communication level. One can observe in speech-making events throughout English-speaking Afro-America the utilization of the oratorical variety of Standard English, but in contexts that demand a different performer-audience relationship than can be found in British usage, and for purposes that are in many ways diametrically opposite to the British practices. A similar pattern holds true with song and dance, in the adaptation of the "sentimental song" and European formal dances such as quadrilles for marking formal, more respectable public occasions.

Conclusion

In the process of exploring Afro-American cultures through material such as these journal accounts and histories, the object should not be simply to search out "Africanisms" as survivals of African traditions, but rather to use Africa as a base line, as a starting point, as in fact it was historically. The numerous Afro-American cultures of contemporary North and South America provide important points of comparison. Instead of searching out the *sources* of this or that pattern of behavior, parallel *processes* and *functions* must be searched out in Africa and Afro-America after European colonialism and slavery. As Hortense Powdermaker pointed out long ago in *After Freedom*, her study of a Mississippi community, in taking on new cultural values from the whites, the Blacks did not simply replace older "African" values, but rather added newer patterns onto older ones. This is what Paul Radin meant when he suggested that the "Negro was not converted to [the white Christian] God. He converted God to himself."[40] Both implied that African sensibilities were the starting place and that European values were selectively adapted to the specialized need of Afro-Americans. While all of this is rather elementary anthropology, in taking up the politically charged subject of the roots and nature of Afro-American culture, we must remind ourselves of the universal principles operating in the most diverse groups of the earth's peoples.

The demands of Afro-American students for a cultural history that is relevant to Black people—that is, one that considers both the past and the present of Blacks—have often been dismissed as lacking substance. Such dismissals depend entirely on the view that no unique Afro-American cultural past exists beyond that of Africa and the plantation's institutional requirements. This connection between the two is at best considered more discontinuous than continuous, and at worst nothing more than (to use Ralph Ellison's phrase) the sum of a people's brutalization.

Herskovits recognized this view for what it was, the myth of the Negro past. We would add that it also constitutes the myth of the Negro present, and it is to this myth and its debunking that we have addressed our argument here.

Chapter 10

Speaking People, in Their Own Terms

With Roger D. Abrahams

Let Us Now Praise Famous Men is a book so many have found for them-selves and to whom the work remains a special personal experience.[1] So it has been for us, but for somewhat different reasons than for most. We are by inclination ethnographers, ourselves observers of the mak-ings and doings of people in groups. But as omnivorous readers of fiction, travel accounts, letters, and journals, we are concerned not just with lives but how life can be written about. *Let Us Now Praise Famous Men* for us is ethnography raised to high art, a virtuoso demonstration of how the discerning eye and ear can bring significance out of detail, and force us to register the aesthetical orders of everyday living.

But strangely enough, there is little behavior in this book, and a great deal of paraphernalia. Like the church of the community, all the things populating the book lose "nothing in stasis"; but common sense and personal experience make us miss the laughter and the tears, the working in the fields and noises of the trip to town. Now, here, with this show at the Michener Galleries of Evans photographs from the *Let Us Now Praise Famous Men* Project, we see some of what we have missed; what a relief to find that Fred Ricketts smiles. We can little doubt that Walker Evans was his own man artistically, and that the book records two men's reactions to an experience. But how much broader seem Evans' interests and how much more full of vitality the world he depicts in the full range of pictures than just the one he has in the book.

In a way, these new pictures change the meaning of the title for us. *Let Us Now Praise Famous Men* announces a praise-poem, but it is difficult for us to discern whether it will be an epic, an encomium, a benediction, or an elegy. (Can there be elegiac ethnography?) Both Agee and Evans draw upon such a question, inviting us to witness their witness, continuing to wonder whether the personal pronouns we receive refer to the authors or to the more universalizing "I" and "thou"; for the diction is suffic-iently elevated and deliberate, and the tone often enough modulates between the reverential and the hieratic, that we feel called on to give testimonial to the dignity of life if not exactly these particular lives.

Even if we are to read the words and pictures as a prayer, we still must find the prayer's occasion. And the worship often seems more like a mourning than the blessing before a celebration. Are these men making witness really observers, or do they see Death as their companion in this journey to the heartlands?

It is the quality of the witness which most fascinates us as ethnographers. These men posed for themselves the questions of propriety that morally concerned outsiders who come to look must ask. Behind the external profession of observation there always lies the fear of the double victimization: of forcing the poor to serve as universal ciphers; and of violating whatever sanctity the tenants still have. First, there is the human intrusion itself, the acts of espial, bad faith (at least in potential), and plain nuisance, performed by every social scientist, journalist, and artist, in the name of some higher (or at least different) truth—an intrusion made all the worse by photography. Agee suggests that, from the beginning, the camera was part of an inescapable con, part of what he said Negroes could grasp more quickly than whites, "a weapon, a stealer of images, and souls, a gun, an evil eye." Then there is the violation potential in the telling and the showing. To say that the question of accuracy, adequacy, and righteousness in description is a central theme in the book comes short of the mark: it is an obsession closer to possession. "A lust," Agee called it.

First the writing. How to convince and evoke without plot and invention, that is, without fiction? How, in short, to treat impoverished people and things with integrity and without turning them into works of art, and yet to recognize (and have recognized) the artful where it exists? One of the answers is their focus on the most cosmological of the fixities (those which, almost by convention, lose nothing in stasis): the house and the face. One becomes the metaphor for the other, or at least the analogue, the face registering as the house of the spirit, the house as the facing of their world's tenancy.

Evans and Agee recorded, photographed, excavated, investigated, yes, and spied on and pried into these houses (there is no morally neutral language for such close "caring for" someone else's lives). Venerative spies, devotional peepers. Search literature for a parallel, and only the most reverential of voyeurs living up next to greatness, fattening on it, come to mind—only these draw with such careful awe or awesome care. The Peeping Tom in Henri Barbusse's *Hell* says it this way:

How is it that you can't say what you have seen? How is it that truth flees from you as if it were not the truth, and as if, however sincere you are, you could not be sincere? You haven't conjured up a thing when you have called its name. It's no use having known words since your childhood. You still don't know what they mean.

Let Us Now Praise Famous Men is the masterpiece of the age and the genre because it discusses such themes openly, providing some personal and wholly satisfying (if evanescent and untranslatable) solutions. Most important, it admits to a fascination with the lives of these tenant-farmer families for their ability to endure and to give order harshly, bravely. In their endurance (not the product of any necessary *goodness*, Agee insists) these people bespeak not only man's adaptive facility but his ability to illustrate positive possibility in his most marginal states. But to pull this off, you have to buy the blurring of the distinction between intransigency and the intransitory, between dumbness and persistence or between inadvertent backwardness and some eternal verities. The conjunction is risky, but here it works without becoming sentimental in the least.

Sentimental! The very word is almost unthinkable in relation to this book, and mainly because of the answer the authors provide to their (and our) fears of complicity in victimization. The answer: if there is a risk of importuning and profaning your subject, then first demystify your methods, thus enshriving yourself; bare your techniques (openly in the text, but just as obviously in the pictures), thus making every image a witness of your self-purge. The risk involved is great, and every page of *Let Us Now Praise Famous Men* is a dizzying walk on the edge of sanctimony, the fall into hypocrisy prevented only by the enormity and serious rendering of the personal task. By universalizing the subject, and injecting self into it, the purgation becomes more complete. Present pictures unfiltered, then, and description in its own terms. Tie everything to the larger life processes: to night; to the sky; to the land; and to the objects that surround the people, fashioned somehow naturally. Make the actors people and more than people, never merely role-players (as other documentaries are wont to do). Thus the observer-victimizer and the victim meet and interpenetrate in the very act of documentary.

Voices from Music and Dance

Chapter 11

The Lizards Fake the Fake

The Lounge Lizards first announced themselves as a "fake jazz" band, a conceptual new wave group. Performing in loose-cut, thin-lined suits and knit ties, they might pass as quintessentially cool white West Coasters from the late 1950s. But the giveaway is their music: they play '50s jazz tunes and vaguely reminiscent originals, all distorted by an excess of postbop clichés, forced climaxes, cartoon motions, and punk guitar enrichment. In a word, I suppose, fake.

The critics, who like a good joke as much as anyone, have been laughing along. And why not? Ever since the beboppers, with their strident individualism and hipper-than-thou stance, the drive for constant innovation in jazz has made for a lot of ponderousness and not a little shuck. It's no accident that the first public jazz humor came with the cult of bebop and the cool regression which followed it: there was Sid Caesar's impression of Cool Cees and Henry Jacobs's Shorty Pederstein, which won him an Academy Award for the animation *The Interview*, as well as the bop fables and bop one-liners. What began as a critical mode of living, a surreal alternative, became imitable, a subject for features in *Life* and *Ebony* ("How To Roll a Pork-Pie Hat," by Lester Young) and comedians' shtick.

But a "fake" jazz band? There is of course a tradition of fakery in rock 'n' roll, a line of stagecraft which extends back to vaudeville, and which includes lip-synching, white minstrelsy, Presley's fake guitar playing, imitation psychopaths, and sexual come-ons (demystified, as it were, by Jim Morrison's actual onstage exposure of himself). But this is not what the Lizards are about. And if "fake" implies the lack of jazz chops, that's not quite it either. True, their rhythm at times seems ill-defined and strained, but at others it's adequate to the job, and if saxophonist John Lurie uses the trills, whole tones, and half-time with which inexperienced players tread water in difficult tunes, he nonetheless brings enough tone control and facility to suggest an array of saxophonists, especially the Stan Kenton altoist Boots Mussulli (and for that matter Boots Randolph). And the group does navigate the troublesome changes of Monk's "Well, You Needn't." Even the new wave component of this group—the barbed wire the guitarist strings between melodic phrases—has jazz models in Derek Baily and Sonny Sharrock.

I prefer to think of the Lizards as faking "fake," as foregrounding a weakness in themselves while mocking others. This is an old and honorable technique of parody: When it's successful, it exposes weaknesses in the parodied subject as well. But it's a tricky device, for if the parody becomes too close, too loving, the parodists devour their subject, while if it gets too far away it becomes kitsch. All of this should be clear from their record, *The Lounge Lizards* (Editions E.G.), where they move from letter-perfect copies (Earl Bostic's 1956 "Harlem Nocturne"), to suggestions of Mancini-like TV themes ("Incident on South Street"), to open laughter over Monk's "Epistrophy." Yet there are also creative energies at work as well as deconstructive ones. On "Demented," Lurie's soprano briefly develops Steve Lacy–like intensity against the dense tone-clusters of DNA guitarist Arto Lindsay; "You Haunt Me" evokes Ornette Coleman's melodies without ever quoting them; and "Do the Wrong Thing" alludes to the eccentric grooves of Blood Ulmer and James Chance.

Like Lords of Misrule who got the dates of Lent wrong, the Lounge Lizards played the Bottom Line the day after the massive Kool celebration of jazz. Perhaps it was that, perhaps it was having to follow Dewey Redman's quartet (with saxophonist Redman's masterful control of the Coleman songbook and Ed Blackwell's polymetric recasting of bebop drumming, Baby Dodds, and the Grambling-Morgan State halftime show bands); perhaps it was because the presence of a new and almost inaudible guitarist, Dana Vlcek, signaled Lurie's determination to completely control the band. Whatever the reason, the Lizards played their humor very broad, with some Brubeck 5/8, some stripper music, and some campish Ellington and swing, like "Stompin' at the Corona." Live, they sometimes seemed to be parodying the role white musicians have always assumed in jazz—their stiffness, their distance from the black patrimony. At other times they seemed to be playing what white college students *think* jazz sounds like (and the Bottom Line audience responded with suspicious warmth, it seemed to me).

Whatever they are, the Lounge Lizards are not jazz—their solos are too short and over-prepared, their rhythms too manic, their parody too close yet disembodied, their ambitions too ambivalent. Still, at their best they make jazz seem strange and yet evoke it in an eerie way. And in some quarters that's called art.

Chapter 12

As It Is Prophesied, So It Used To Be

Whatever the daylight ruts of *la vie quotidienne*, at night America dreams pluralistically. In Dade County, Florida, Cubans wash off the grit of the land of *Creem* and Honey-Fried Chicken and sleep in the memories of Matanzas and Habana. In Chester County, Pennsylvania, DuPont executives escape the stench of Delaware's plants to dream of seventeenth-century America, a dream which spills over into their weekend whimsies of raising strange breeds of cattle, riding in ancient oxcarts, and patronizing their local visuals man, Andrew Wyeth. In all the counties of America the dreaming goes on, taking its material shape in airport folk-art gift shops, oldies shows, Victorian doll houses, theme parks, Ethan Allen furniture, folk-look fashion, Greco-Tudor diners—all exercises in the aesthetics of crypto-memory, the raising of the dead from the back of the collective mind. In a word, nostalgia, a social disease.

In 1688, a French physician turned the emotion of homesickness into an illness by renaming it and formalizing its symptoms, much as lovesickness had previously been turned into melancholia. What had begun as a problem of Swiss travelers and soldiers missing local milk, the Alps, and folk songs became a disorder of the imagination. Within a hundred years, Rousseau's *Directory of Music* was suggesting that "disquieting sorrows," "passions du souvenir," could be caused by cowherding songs. And within another hundred, Baudelaire, Balzac, and other sensitive souls could fear death by longing. Romantic aesthetics had demanded romantic illnesses, or at least interesting illnesses that expressed character; nostalgia, along with TB with which it shared every symptom except coughing up blood, arrived with the era. Sontag's *Illness as Metaphor* describes TB as the West's first great individualized disease, a break with the medieval collective diseases of plague, cholera, and the like. Nostalgia, too, was a very personal disorder, and like TB involved deep passions, with the suggestion that the victim caused the disease. And both first became obsessions in the eighteenth century, when Europe's social order went through a terrific wrenching, leaving social status a question mark. Nostalgia, like other illnesses, became a trope for the self—and, not incidentally at all, wonderfully adaptive for life in the colonies of expanding empires.

The disease has come to be demedicalized and demystified: the Freudians spotted Mom hiding behind the milk, mountains, and music. And after soldiers started seeking nostalgia discharges in World War I, the French removed it from their medical books. Nowadays, only kids at summer camp, college students away from home, and other malingerers can be seriously diagnosed as nostalgic. Meanwhile, the term has gained popular currency and lost much of its force.

Today, what we call nostalgia is, like boredom, a form of anxiety over the fragmentation of the social order. And the stuff we feel nostalgic for is usually loot taken from the victims of progress. This reverent trash-picking is part of the search of the displaced for some perspective on what's happened, a kind of crazed, inverted cargo cult where we are the primitives whose culture has been destroyed by our own institutions, and where we long for the return of the old within the framework of the new. There is something of a radical potential in this quest for a totalizing point of view—nostalgia after all represents an incomplete commitment to our own society. But overwhelming these critical sentiments is a tradition of false tradition, a recycling of an imagined past to fill up cultural space. America is not unique in this. And if England's longing for its more substantial history has made it more a museum than a country, the United States has become a flea market, albeit one whose merchandise is largely imported from Taiwan or Nowhere.

This brings us to the matter at hand, a "swing revival" which appears to have been foretold in the dreams of Sid Zion and the editors of *Billboard*. And though one more cynical than I might say that what these performers are nostalgic for is the class gigs in Vegas and Atlantic City that they've never known, they nonetheless announce themselves as serious about the past and must be judged by it.

Producer Richard Perry, guided by Sid Zion's prophecies, has gone forth into the California desert and returned with even less then he went in with: a monstrously slim project called *Swing* on his own Planet label. Imagine, if you can, this made-for-TV scenario: assemble a first-rate band of studio musicians capable of recreating swing, and then make Tom Scott the soloist; pick some of the best swing compositions, and then hire an arranger to monkey with them, discofy the rhythm, and double the horns with a synthesizer so that their acoustic quality is lost; for the singing, get the son of a crooner (Steve March, out of Mel Torme), the daughter of a jazz critic (Lorraine Feather), and a person of color (Charlotte Crossley, whose unnamed parents might well be more important people); finally, abandon the original idea and throw in some flat originals by the producer and the singers, and add local-color lyrics to some classic instrumentals (Fletcher Henderson's "Big John's Special" becomes "Big Bucks," a parody so thin that it winds up celebrating the hot-tub life it started out to skewer). Metonymically put, Richard Perry is to swing what California is to culture.

Carly Simon's *Torch*, on the other hand, tries harder to be honest. She's told interviewers about meeting the great ballad writers as a child, claiming the songs as part of her personal tradition. And here she's taken on five of the most difficult: "I Got It Bad and That Ain't Good," "Body and Soul," "I'll Be Around," and "Spring Is Here" require extraordinary range and a good ear, and "I Get Along Without You Very Well," requires considerable interpretation, tending as it does toward harmonic tedium. All are given earnest, respectful readings but they seem listless and studied, and despite the competent fills behind her from the Brecker-Sanborn-Woods studio saxophone crowd, the obbligatos sound, well, obligatory. Though I don't doubt Simon's sincerity, it's the sincerity of the coffeehouse.

Echoes of an Era is a project of enormous promise. Producer-drummer Lenny White brought together pianist Chick Corea, bassist Stanley Clarke, saxophonist Joe Henderson, and trumpeter Freddie Hubbard with Chaka Khan to do an album of tunes from the 1930s forward, and to do them in the style of the Blue Note recordings of the 1960s—with no rehearsals, no overdubbing, and minimal editing. Each musician is formidable. Joe Henderson's heated, twisted lines have remained unique and exciting through a period of change in tenor saxophone playing. Hubbard is a formalist of a different sort, a careful builder of structures with grand technique and a warm, intimate tone. The rhythm players are expert at shifting between pop and jazz. And Chaka Khan, whose early work with Rufus I admire, has a voice of considerable range and flexibility. Yet this is one of the most discomfiting recordings I've ever heard. Khan's voice—like the big voices of Minnie Riperton or Melba Moore—is too often pushed to its limits, and, impressive though those limits may be, without interpretation and shading the effect is desperation. Only on "Take the A Train," where she takes the Betty Roche–Betty Carter approach, does she seem in full touch with these songs. Putting words to Monk's all-but-unsingable "I Mean You" was an effort doomed from the start. There is also serious trouble in the rhythm section, much movement but no propulsion, and over this slippery deck even those master horns have trouble finding purchase.

What all three records share is this: though they start out to recreate the past, they wind up disdaining and distrusting it. Each patches on incompatible current musical cliches; each defaces an older instrumental work by adding absurd lyrics, poorly sung; and each slips in among the treasured ballads ersatz new product, usually written by the singers. If these records are a clue to the future, what a past we have to look forward to!

Chapter 13

Greenwich's Good Gnosis

Rock scripture tells us that 1961 to 1964 (*anno* Presley, before Beatles) was a time of aesthetic famine and plagues. But then, for r'n'r hagiographers of a certain persuasion, adolescent Afro-American females do not offer a lot to conjure with. So it has come to be that the Chantels, the Shirelles, the Crystals, et al. are footnotes in the Book of Rock to Phil Spector, boy prophet and macher. Yet with 20 years behind us Gnosticism has arrived in the form of Alan Betrock, whose *Girl Groups* (the book, the record, *and* the video) has restored this peculiar period of cooperation between black performer and white composer-producer to its rightful place.

Pop songs freeze a moment in life and develop a universe of meaning. Like novelists—who often mine their late teens and early twenties for the rest of their lives—pop songwriters lock into brief moments within an individual's and an age's development and generate epiphanal portraits of those moments. But the pop song of the 1940s and 1950s at least operated somewhere near the adult mode of authority. When it wasn't black, the post-Elvis pop song was modally adolescent, operating in the domains of pain and becoming, representing an epistemic break as radical in its own way as the one between Hegel and Marx. It made it possible to syncretize black blues with white love songs in a nonminstrelized fashion, and also to fuse traditional black singing and instrumental ensembles with those of whites. So the female trio within the black church choir surfaced with the Chantels and the Shirelles, replacing white sisters' groups (sisters like McGuire, Andrews, and Boswell, that is) in American music. And when soloists like Ronnie Spector and Darlene Love stepped forward within these groups they made it possible for younger women singers to challenge the hegemony of white male pop stars.

The success of early 1960s pop songs is usually attributed to their simplicity and directness. But their simplicity is deceptive. Though they're easier to hum than a Monk tune, we remember them not just as tunes but as compete arrangements. Try to recall "He's So Fine" without hearing the background riffs, or "River Deep, Mountain High" without strings, tambourines, and rim shots. This organic quality makes them seem like hymns, although oddly more Catholic than Protestant. Phil Spector's cavernous production style accounts for some of this, but not all: there are drones beneath open chordal movement ("Da Doo Ron Ron," "Then He Kissed Me"), large choirs ("River Deep"), and church bells (et passim). After progressing from the Chantels' "The Plea" (based on a Gregorian chant) to the Toys' "Lover's Concerto" (based on a theme by Bach), we were ready for the Moodys and Sankeys of the great soul awakening of the late 1960s. It was truly, in Greil Marcus's words, a music for the gods and the girls' bathroom. This organicism seems strange when we recall how this music came to be. Inspired by street corner rhapsodizing, white lower-middle-class composers wrote songs for black teenage girls and taught them the parts by singing them, thus helping to shape a black generation's musical sensibilities. To me the most interesting of these was Ellie Greenwich, a composer so canny that she could turn the Shirelles' "I Met Him on a Monday" into "Da Doo Ron Ron" and improve it; an arranger who made Aretha Franklin's "Chain of Fools" the most Baptist of that lady's work; and a backup singer the equal of the young women she produced. Greenwich knew how to tap the sentimental side of black culture and still produce a tough product. Yet she too failed to survive the British Invasion and the rise of the singer-songwriter, and has been submerged these many years in the world of TV commercial jingles.

Leader of the Pack, the Bottom Line's recent revival of Greenwich's songs, made good musical sense, even though the problems posed by pop revivals have never satisfactorily been solved. A night of songs in an oldies setting serves no one well, and a new dramatic setting for already familiar songs creates unintentional irony. The chosen solution—to set the songs into a thinly dramatized treatment of Greenwich's life—was not an especially happy compromise, especially as it involved two male singers who were irrelevant to the music. But after some awkward and campish scenes the book withered away and the songs started coming edge to edge, offering a chance to hear how rich the harmonies were, how much excitement those nonsense riffs could generate. Unfortunately, a medley which led from "Today I Met the Boy I'm Going to Marry" to "Then He Kissed Me" to "Chapel of Love" also offered a chance to hear the ideals which fueled a generation's sexual and domestic illusions. But reviews of false consciousness are out of my league.

The songs were the stars of course, but the singers weren't bad either. Darlene Love recreated her own hits (in their original keys and tempos) with charm and energy, and Ula Hedwig gave deadpan but accurate readings of "I Have a Boyfriend" and "You Should Have Seen the Way He Looked at Me." The big surprise was Karla DeVito, who sang "Be My

Baby" and "Leader of the Pack" unaffectedly and powerfully and then did a "River Deep" that was a credit to her race. In the second half Ellie Greenwich debuted as a performer. Far from the usual composer-who-can-sing-her-songs, she sang with the authority of someone who's spent years in the studios. She introduced her work shrewdly and matter-of-factly and managed to undercut some of the foolish business that had opened the show.

I was left with the cheery feeling that these songs—some of which have lyrics so silly as to bear no exegesis at all—have transcended their limitations, and like the blues or lieder might be with us forever, lifting us up in times of trouble. They may be thin on eschatology, but you got to believe in something.

Chapter 14

Free Samples: Roy Nathanson and Anthony Coleman

With the literal bushes of the world being beaten for fresh samples and new forced alliances, you'd think that everything was ripe for pillage. But some musics remain out of reach: free jazz and academic chamber experimentalism, for example. Both are tough to pry loose from context because each is shaped by goals that can only be stated metaphorically and evocatively. And in an age in which freedom to cut-and-paste seems limited only by the demand for virtuoso technique, monster bass lines, and concrete forms, musics with subjective aims—energy, spirituality, space—are doomed to languish.

But then along comes Roy Nathanson and Anthony Coleman's *The Great Coming Millennium* (Knitting Factory Works), a kind of free chamber experiment shrewdly disguised with klezmer inflections (at least I choose to hear it as disguise, for klezmer—like bluegrass—is a bit too culturally specific for my taste). Whatever the intention, the klezmer references here serve as reminders that it, too, is an improvising music, and that parallel musics—those of African Americans and Eastern European Jews—ultimately converge in performance. From such assumptions, Nathanson and Coleman launch a set of subtle homages to Monk, La Monte Young, Ellington, Mingus, and pop song itself.

In the process they face questions raised by sampling and nostalgia: how do you play jazz in an age in which its social underpinnings are almost dead, but its aesthetic still intimidatingly alive? How to perform beautiful melodies that evoke their eras invidiously? One of their answers is to make these musics seem hard-bought, earned, by virtual recomposition. For Nathanson and Coleman this means opening up older songs by reducing their harmonic structures to a few pedal tones; making each use of a note seem different from every other; and repositioning conventional phrases and cadences until form itself comes into question. Such were the lessons of Ornette, Monk, and Morton Feldman. So, Ellington's "U.M.M.G." and Charles Mingus's "Orange Was the Color of Her Dress, Then Blue Silk" are mined for characteristic phrases or intervals, and, by means of Coleman's sampling and keyboard manipulation, looped, displaced, and conceptually enriched. Monk's "Reflections" and "You Took Advantage of Me" get the kind of halting lyrical awkwardness that Steve Lacy might bring to them (although Nathanson's soprano more often suggests Sidney Bechet). And some original pieces ("By the Book") have a Feldman-like sparseness in which disparate notes seem to be uncalculatingly seeking each other.

But what to do with swing, a pulse hooked to a dead dance form? Their solution (on "Like Anthony") is to express its tension and forward propulsion by minimalist staggering and repetition, an idea not so bizarre when you recall that the minimalists all grew up in the swing era (in fact, Steve Reich, La Monte Young, Terry Riley, and John Adams all did time in jazz groups before the avant-garde abandoned the beat).

The sampler is the star here, but not as it is in fill-in-the-blanks pop music. On "Orange," for example, Coleman samples whole phrases from Nathanson's saxophone, reassigns them to different keyboard octaves, and plays them back in part or whole, suggesting the sighs and moans of the Mingus band. Elsewhere, in "The Faker," the instability of a low-tech Mirage sampler produces randomly de-tuned intervals that in turn become the organizing principle of the piece. And on "Sadegur Khossidl," a 1917 recording by band leader Abe Schwartz is intermixed with bits of Fanny Brice and some swing band chords to create a kind of klezmer "Rite of Spring."

Cross-generic borrowing, sound for its own sake, repetition—as if I need to tell you—can make for some truly boring music. But in the service of a witty aesthetic of reassembly such as these worldly Downtowners muster, it can be made to charm, indeed, to waken the American inner ear, where the truly multicultural is stored.

Chapter 15

Milling at the Mall

Until recently, the Knitting Factory's annual summer festival was called "What Is Jazz?" The question was whimsically rhetorical and implied that Downtowners know what they like. But things have changed, and the Bell Atlantic-sponsored festival now aims for the Downtowners of the suburbs and the world. Judging by this year's festival, the "what is" question should be revived, maybe as a cry for help. More and more music is slipping under the big tent of jazz, and in the tradition of the Newport/JVC Festival (which always found a way to include ringers like the Kingston Trio or Led Zeppelin), the Knit festival is now voracious— almost 200 acts this year. Fact is, jazz alone has never been able to support a large festival in this country. So whether in the spirit of proselytization or greed, jazz festivals now embrace the rock values and spectacles they once fought against.

Audiences have joined in this ecumenical spirit, enjoying the conceit that we no longer label music, and that nothing could be strange enough to surprise us. Yet this hypercosmopolitanism puts a strain on audiences, turning crowds into gatherings scattered to the point of nonrecognition and plagued by nostalgia for a time when an audience formed a community, shared a history, and had knowable standards. Audiences in an alleged age of simulation are themselves becoming simulations, remakes, tributes to what were once real audiences.

The Knit has valiantly tried to keep alive the communal sense of the club. But as things expand, the struggle for affordable performance space in the city guarantees that every year's festival will have a different character, with new ways of testing an audience's resolve. Take the Atrium at the South Street Seaport, basically a shopping mall with bad acoustics and a poor excuse for a food court: on "Jazzelectronight," Friday, June 4, 1999, the promising idea was to survey trends in technological music. Synthesizer wizard Don Buchla and saxophonist Peter Apfelbaum opened on an assortment of intriguing homemade instruments. But as in a 1950s hi-fi demonstration, the music came in second to the intrigue. After a 45-minute setup, trumpeter Nils Petter Molvaer brought the chill of ECM Records to music explored by Jon Hassell long before anyone knew it was acid jazz. Turntablist-tabla-ist Talvin Singh was a no-show because of immigration problems, and after another long setup, an ethnically equivalent replacement (Karsh Kales' Futureproof Meets Jojo Mayer's Nerve, whew!) was destroyed by the sound system. What's a techno audience to do in a darkened mall during long dead stretches, or even during the music? Dance? Eat? Engage in some frottage? Most milled, or hung around aimlessly, like the shoppers in *Dawn of the Dead*. Meanwhile, as if to drive home the awkwardness of the occasion, a convention of the hearing-impaired was visible through the Atrium's floor, oblivious to the music but busily signing like hip-hoppers, seemingly having a good time.

On June 10, "Tropical Night" at the Atrium, just getting there was a trial; you had to weave through an actual energized street audience, dancing and singing along to Domingo Quiñones's band and Brenda K. Starr out front on Pier 17. But if you made it through, and waited another hour, Conrad Herwig's Latin jazz group segued in nicely—John Coltrane's "Un Supremo Amor" worked just fine in Cuban dress. And when Eddie Palmieri—the Cecil Taylor of Latin music—joined them, he took Coltrane's "Africa" and "Impressions" out. Marc Ribot's Arsenio Rodriguez tribute band followed, and got that cheesy sound that 1950s Havana shared with early rock. For a few minutes, they turned the mall into a high school gym.

But is it the mall or the audience that makes the difference? Last Tuesday night, the Deadheads who packed the Seaport to see Gary Lucas and the Bob Weir–Rob Wasserman Trio managed to warm up the space. Lucas's solo guitar set ranged from his anthemic "Rise Up and Be" (the seed of Jeff Buckley's "Grace") to country-blues slide, and when he later joined Weir and Wasserman the crowd kept whooping. If Deadheads are an anachronism, it's because they're still a real audience.

At the Knit's Main Space, more surprisingly, Steve Coleman also filled the house. He hears music differently from almost everyone else, rhythm determining (some would say overdetermining) melody and harmony—working in a narrow range, sometimes moving sideways, up a slow trajectory, rigorously following his exhaustingly relentless yet infectious logic. When Greg Osby, Gary Thomas, and Ravi Coltrane joined him at evening's end, you knew not to expect a garden-variety quartet nostalgia for the lost family of saxophones. Some of the material was simple—vamps spinning off soloists—but on some pieces one horn's phrase was picked up, swirled, and harmonized to a conclusion by the others.

Some big names would have been better served had they played in a more intimate room than the Main Space: Charlie Haden and John Scofield, for example, who performed a charming but not sparkling acoustic set. But in the much smaller, sometimes freezing, sometimes sweltering

Alterknit Theatre, Trio X held forth brilliantly, their rich textures embracing Joe McPhee, one of the last saxophonists working in the great tradition of vocalized tonality and instrumental storytelling. Likewise at the Alterknit, the Far East Side Band made a music that, in spite of its potential exoticism, could be from nowhere else than New York City. Their performance buzzed, sang, and cried, Jason Kao Hwang's violin driving against bowed kayagum, frame drums, and tubaist Joe Daily, who turns every group he plays with into something special.

But it was in the Old Office, the basement acoustic room with its own bar, where the club feel could be found. The room was just right for the tight arrangements, full sound, and witty asides of Chico Hamilton's Euphoria. And it worked well for the much underrated saxophonist Sonny Fortune, who with bassist Santi Debriano and drummer Steve Johns turned in some of the finest musicianship of the festival, each piece a gem of energy and unity. The downside of the room was that the groups playing there were abandoned by management, and forced to introduce themselves and to see to their own sound. But there's something to be said for the adult authority with which these musicians took control and shaped their own performances, removing the music from the junior high school talent show aesthetic which has for too long dominated and depressed audiences all across the Village.

Chapter 16
Childhood's Ends

The Kitchen offered two evenings of super-8 mm film and related performances a couple of weeks ago under the title of "Super 8 Motel," the idea being, I take it, that everything to be seen owed something to the traditions of *noir* and the B film. On the Friday I went it was not always easy to see how things came to be there.

After the first hour and a half of films, the performances began with Lydia Lunch. She has been doing a set of monologic variations on the theme of abuse with herself as both victim and victimizer, and the Kitchen appearance continued the theme, first in a performance which pitted a woman (of uncertain ethnicity) against the verbal and then physical assaults of black males, and second in a film she recently completed with Richard Kern, *The Right Side of My Brain.* The monologue began with Lunch discoursing on New York attitude in a style reminiscent of early Patti Smith, but without Smith's evocative bite and wit. She sidled towards talking about how things are in "her" neighborhood with what seemed at first to be a black woman's response to an increasingly violent street rap. There is no denying the force and anger of her words, but if this was meant to be a vignette in the manner of Shange's *For Colored Girls . . .* , it was not "colored" enough to override the racial gap; if, on the other hand, this was intended to be a white woman's response to black males (as her speech and rhythms sometimes suggested), then it at least appeared crypto-racist. Still, if it made me this edgy, there was something successful in her daring to finger the jagged line that allegedly separates eros from agon, courtliness from sexual assault in male-to-female public repartee.

If the Lunch performance was ambiguous, her film was not much clearer. Announced as a "survey of a woman's somewhat unsatisfying sexual fantasies," it was more raw melodrama than *noir*; and from what I could make out of the voice-over narrative, there seemed to be considerable talk about vile and unsavory acts, though the nastiest things in sight were three bare-chested boys from New Wave bands. But even if considered as a romance, there was nothing in this film to match the sexual violence that, say, a best-selling Rosemary Rogers could spin out in her novels with both hands tied behind her.

Tony Conrad and Joe Gibbons followed, and ignoring the evening's theme, disassembled the two-dimensional surface of the conventional performer by means of halting starts, puffed-on pipes, exposed seams, and reflexive patter. They told us what fun we were going to have, practiced some lighthearted mass hypnotism, described what a particular song would sound like *if* they could sing it, showed an unprojectable (5000 mm) and unviewable (with flash bulbs as light source) film on "sex-education," discussed a list of what they *might* perform, gave away a sizable amount of money to an audience all too suddenly come alive, threatened us with discipline, and, throughout it all, talked continuously about what was going to happen and what had happened.

Conrad and Gibbons were so at ease in their roles, so sweetly placatory and saturated with good will and graciousness towards their audience, that they undercut the apparent reflexivity and irony of their stance and restored a sense of dialogic wholeness to the evening. None of which was very good for the hour and a half of films yet to come.

The range of films which sandwiched in the performances was enormous but most of them were characterized by obliquely or directly threatening imagery: Saturday-morning-TV cartoon ducks danced to ominous sounds in the rain; cars drove endlessly through the night with mysterious rear-seat passengers appearing and disappearing; a couple of toddlers cast as Sid Vicious and Nancy Spungen played out a playpen version of the murder; an eleven-year-old boy lectured on new Air Force weaponry in an Arbus-like scene and was swallowed up, along with two younger girls, by great swatches of found war and horror film footage.

But what made the evening all of a piece for me was the continual appropriation and decontextualization of the past, especially the past that is childhood.

Appropriation and decontextualization are by no means unique to the avant-garde—the Museum of Modern Art's primitivism show last fall was a confection built on the premise of snap-on, snap-off aesthetics. Nor are they limited to the arts: decontextualization is the operating principle of nightly TV news, the *National Enquirer*, and the fashion industry. What is special about the current avant-garde's version of this practice is the borrowing, shredding (sometimes literally), and transvaluation of thirty- to forty-year-old commercial and pop iconography and a refusal or failure to put things back together in a new configuration. This lack of resynthesis forces us to cast these cultural shards into whatever generic mold we're predisposed to—now retro, now allusion, parody, tribute, whatever.

Maybe what is most salient here is that these truncated, homeless images are drawn from the real and fantasied experiences of youth. And for America of the last several generations much of the sense of being young has been derived from popular culture and the media. Childhood is a respectable source of art, but what makes this version of American youth so unusual and perhaps disturbing is that its incomplete, unsynthesized representation (coupled with shadows of apocalypse) suggests that the door on this particular childhood is closing fast. But like the loops so beloved of many super-8 filmmakers, this door keeps closing again and again and again.

Chapter 17

Sweet Feet

With the sound it generates as its defining feature, tap dance may seem to be an art with a very narrow scope. But its variety is enormous: in addition to the iron-on-the-floor stompers, there are dancers who work with light, barely audible ballroom effects, while others, such as soft shoe dancers, are conceptual tappers, their art coming from the sound we know *might* have been there. Even taps that strike the floor vary in pitch as well as rhythm: you can hear rim shots; horses' hooves on stone; stuttering; dentist-drill whines; and dropped silver chains of sound.

Sound is only one dimension of tap. The personae adopted by its dancers are complex and varied. Among others, there are brisk, efficient hustlers; drummers surprised by their own rhythm figures; challengers overflowing with sass; fastidious specialists studying their own feet for flaws; as well as the flirts, mimes, ingenues, klutzes, and suicidal acrobats. And—typical of Afro-American artistic practice—tap provides the potential for switching persona in a single dance.

What I particularly liked about Changing Times Tap Dance Company's "Sole Sisters" revue last month was the way it played with these variations and saw the possibilities of their permutations. Producer Jane Goldberg and Sarah Safford's "topical taps," for instance, set the key for the evening. These taps with near-raps (concerning, in this performance, their relationships with men) were especially affecting in the way they toyed with political incorrectness and self-pity, seeming always about to stop the dancing and begin a melodrama. Goldberg has developed a very personal style from a mix of ballroom, tap, and comedy, and she was in wonderful form in a piece on the dilemmas of career versus family, accompanying herself on colander and spoon. Yet she can dance straight ahead, too, and her reading of Chick Corea's "Spain" was exceptionally witty and graceful. Safford's humor is broader and more physical, as when in her own "Post-Partum Blues" she schlumped her way in front of a chorus line with her own recently born child on her hip and head.

Following Changing Times's custom of celebrating and learning from older dancers, "Sole Sisters" featured Marion Coles (once a member of

Restina Banks's Number One Chorus Line), who recreated a couple of numbers from the old Apollo Theater. Coles herself, little and low, built up from the ground, did a creditable "Shiny Stockings," full of sweet eccentricities and sudden angles. Harriet Brown sand-danced, and Mabel Lee, a brassy lady who filled in the few slow spots of the evening with her salty spoken obbligatos, did some high-heel tapping and sang a very warm and assured "How Am I To Know" with the chorus tapping while seated in chairs behind her.

Brenda Bufalino's appearance on stage was abrupt and stunning, not merely because she interrupted a weird suite of hora-tap, Irish step-dancing, and Appalachian clogging, but also because she works with attitude received from black male dancers of the past. In contrast to the whimsy and lyric nostalgia which preceded, she cracked out crisp aggressive accents, modulated the tone of her taps, hurled out challenges, and generally let it be known that she prefers an atmosphere of risk and high energy.

On the evening of the benefit, guest dancers ended the performance, the last of whom was Gregory Hines. Energized by all that had come before, he enacted, deadpan, a parade of social types and stereotyped characters which evoked old movies, after-hours clubs, and city promenades, all against a tapped history of drumming, from high school drill team to late bebop.

Chapter 18

From "Messin' Around" to "Funky Western Civilization": The Rise and Fall of Dance Instruction Songs

WITH SALLY BANES

Listen while I talk to you
I tell you what we're gonna do
There's a new thing that's goin' around
And I'll tell you what they're puttin' down
Just move your body all around
And just shake . . .

"Shake," by Sam Cooke, was recorded at the height of the dance instruction song craze of the 1960s. In this genre—which originated in African American dance and music traditions—choreographic instructions are given or "called" while the dance is in progress. This article will focus on the dance instruction song wave of the 1960s, tracing its roots and its decline. Along the way we will analyze the rhetoric of the song, in terms of both its lyrics and its music.

In her book *Dance Notation*, Ann Hutchinson Guest calls notation "the process of recording movement on paper."[1] The development of written notation for dance since the Renaissance in Europe and America has been a fluctuating process of analysis in which the dance is described in terms of a body of shared dance values. For instance, Baroque dancing masters in Europe wrote down floor patterns and the ornamentation of footwork and turns with the assumption that arm movements, carriage, and other aspects of dance style were common knowledge, while Laban sought ways to describe scientifically information that was not only quantitative (body parts in use, divisions of time and space), but also qualitative (for example, energy use).

The use of notation for theatrical dancing requires a system that is fully descriptive, since the choreographer's patterns are not necessarily shared by others. Social dancing, however, may be encoded in much more abbreviated ways, partly because of its close relationship with its music and partly because its sequences are redundant in several ways. However, the dance instruction song is a form of dance "notation" that is part of an oral, rather than written tradition, and is popular, rather than elite.[2] This popular genre of American song, which clearly has African roots, has appeared in mainstream culture in successive waves, beginning just before World War One with songs such as "Messin' Around" and "Ballin' the Jack." It has spread from the United States to become an internationally known phenomenon. Thus in the twentieth century, the broad dissemination of African American social dance instruction to audiences of all ethnicities and classes through the mass media—by means of sheet music, records, radio, television, and cinema—has taken its place alongside the dance manual and the private lesson of the Euro-American elite that dated at least from the Renaissance.

The dance instruction song, spread via these modern mass technologies, has a privileged place for the historian of culture and performance, because it is *about* the mass distribution of dance and bodily knowledge, and thus has served crucial aesthetic, social, and political functions. It has played an important part in the democratization of social dancing; it has spread African American dance forms and styles throughout Euro-American culture and other, subaltern cultures; and it has helped create a mass market for the work of black artists. In short, the dance instruction song has contributed to the formation of a syncretic dance culture—and bodily culture—in multicultural America.

The dance instruction song in mass culture may be traced at least to the beginning of the twentieth century, although it has longer vernacular roots in the African American community. Even though songs have occasionally been used to teach European dances—the Beer Barrel Polka, or the Lambeth Walk—it is important to note that the dance instruction song primarily comprises African American dances, from Ballin' the Jack and the Black Bottom, to the Twist, the Loco-Motion, the Mashed Potato, and the Funky Broadway, to the Hustle, the Smurf, and the Vogue. The song/dance titles range from the internationally recognizable, like the Charleston, the Shimmy, the Madison, the Boogaloo, the Frug, the Limbo, the Jerk, the Watusi, and the Bump, to the more obscure, like the Georgia Crawl, Stewin' the Rice, the Clam, the 81, the Lurch, the Bounce, and the Boomerang. As well, in the African American dance and song tradition, many of these dance instruction songs make reference to "animal" dances: the Bird, the Duck, the Funky Chicken, the Horse, the Pony, the Raccoon, the Dog, the Funky Penguin, the Monkey, and so on.

This genre is so powerful that it has not only spawned various series of dances, like the entire Twist, Jerk, or Dog successions,[3] it has also given rise to a metagenre—a group of songs commenting on or parodying the dance instruction song. These songs create instructions for dances that are physically impossible, either because of the limitations of human physiognomy—for instance, Dr. Hook's "Levitate" (1975), which commands the listener, "I want you to raise your right foot . . . Awright, now raise your left foot . . . No no no no no, don't put your right foot back down!"—or because they are far too general and large-scale—for example, Tonio K's "Funky Western Civilization," which, after cataloguing the evils of western history, instructs its dancers to do all sorts of nasty things to one another: "You just grab your partner by the hair / Throw her down and leave her there" or "You just drag your partner through the dirt / Put him in a world of hurt." And Loudon Wainwright III's "The Suicide Song" (1975) gives new meaning to the dance of death by mixing instructions for shaking one's hips with those for cutting one's wrists. It seems that the parodic dance instruction song has been around nearly as long as the genre itself. But we also want to suggest that one symptom of the dance instruction song's decline during the disco era—the late 1970s and early 1980s—was a disproportionate increase of parodies compared to the number of "actual" or "serious" dance instruction songs.[4]

Roots of the Dance Instruction Song

Dance instruction songs, in the form of dance rhymes and rhythmic verbal-movement games, were already long-established practices when they were first recorded in African American communities as early as the mid-nineteenth century. One of the fullest and earliest accounts of slave dancing records a portion of a dance song from Virginia: "She *bin* to the north / she *bin* to the south / she *bin* to the east / she *bin* to the west / she *bin* so far *beyond* the sun / and she is the *gal* for me."[5] Thomas W. Talley collected a number of what he called "dance song rhymes" in *Negro Folk Rhymes*, and typical is "Jonah's Band Party," which he saw developed at various occasions as a child:

Setch a kickin' up san'! Jonah's Ban'!
Setch a kickin' up san'! Jonah's Ban'!
"Raise yo' right foot, kick it up high,
Knock dat Mobile Buck in de eye."

Setch a kickin' up san'! Jonah's Ban'!
Setch a kickin' up san'! Jonah's Ban'!
"Stan' up, flat foot, Jump dem Bars!
Karo back'ards lak a train o' kyars."

(Talley notes that "Jonah's Ban'," "Mobile Buck," "Jump dem Bars," and "Karo" were dance steps.)[6]

The roots of this genre reach back to the instructions and commentary by slave musicians at both slave gatherings and white plantation balls; to the African American folk song, game, and dance tradition; and earlier to the close relationship between West African dancing and the musicians' cues.[7] There is a link here with Euro-American forms such as square dancing, quadrilles, and play party games, but there is also strong evidence that there is a hidden history of these Euro-American forms—that in the United States, they were partly shaped by African American interventions, including black musicians, callers, and prompters at square dances and contra dances, as well as African American games or styles of game-playing.[8]

That the dance instruction songs are related to rhythmic games synthesizing Euro-American and African American traditions is nicely illustrated in a song from the 1960s—Rufus Thomas' "Little Sally Walker," which is a virtual catalogue of free-floating, recombinative formulaic game and song phrases, mixing an Anglo-American traditional children's chanting game with standard African American vernacular dance calling phrases such as "Put your hand on your hip / Let your backbone slip," all set to a rhythm-and-blues beat.

Little Sally Walker
Sitting in her saucer
Rise, Sally, rise
Wipe your weepin' eyes
Put your hand on your hip
Let your backbone slip
(I want you to) Shake it to the east
Shake it to the west
Shake it to the very one that you love best . . .
Little Sally Walker
I see you sitting in your saucer
Rise and do the jerk
I love to see you work . . . [9]

Roger D. Abrahams recorded girls' jump rope rhymes from Philadelphia in the early 1960s that were parallel to or derivative of dances of the period, such as the Madison and the Baltimore.[10] Since these girls taught their younger brothers and sisters how to play these games, the interaction between dance and games is difficult to unravel.

There is also a connection between these songs and military marching chants—or cadence counting, or "Jody calls," introduced to the U.S. Army by African Americans—which help coordinate the drill movements of large numbers of troops: "Jody was here when I *left* / You're *right*."

Sheet music renditions of dance instruction songs were printed before the turn of this century. Nearly twenty years before "Ballin' the Jack" (1913), which Alec Wilder calls the first dance instruction song, black audiences were dancing to "La Pas Ma La," introduced by the African American dancer-comedian Ernest Hogan in his Georgia Graduates minstrel show and published in 1895.[11] Less explicit in its choreographic instructions than later songs marketed to whites, "La Pas Ma La" often simply names or calls other dances to be performed, like the Bombashay and the Turkey Trot. According to Marshall and Jean Stearns, this served as a shorthand for those who knew black dance conventions. But the choreography for the Pas Ma La itself *was* given, if somewhat elliptically, in the chorus:

Hand upon yo' head, let your mind roll far,
Back, back, back and look at the stars,
Stand up rightly, dance it brightly,
That's the Pas Ma La.[12]

But if "La Pas Ma La" was marketed primarily to black audiences, during the first American mass dance craze "season" of 1912–1914, many other dances and their notation—in the form of music and lyrics published in sheet music, as well as live demonstrations in Broadway revues and musicals—began to find commercial viability among mass white audiences (that is, both consumers at theatrical spectacles and participants at parties and dance halls). In fact, live performances and sheet music (or instructions, with pictures, published in newspapers and magazines) all formed part of a package that provided a network of verbal, aural, and visual demonstrations of the dance.

There were occasional early efforts to reach Euro-American audiences with conventional oral instruction—as in "One Step Instruction" (c. 1915), a Columbia record of dance music with an instructor interrupting the music to describe the steps. But these were short-lived failures.[13]

The song "Ballin' the Jack," written for the Ziegfeld Follies of 1913 by two African American musicians, Chris Smith and Jim Burris, describes traditional African American vernacular dance steps, and it is a paradigm of the early dance instruction song. It contains a great deal of information about various aspects of the choreography.

First you put your two knees close up tight
Then you sway 'em to the left, then you sway 'em to the right
Step around the floor kind of nice and light
Then you twis' around and twis' around with all your might
Stretch your lovin' arms straight out in space
Then you do the Eagle Rock with style and grace
Swing your foot way 'round then bring it back
Now that's what I call "Ballin' the Jack."[14]

Here we have choreographic instructions that describe the structure of the step, call a figure (in the form of an already known dance, the Eagle Rock), and also give advice on style and energy use ("nice and light," "with all your might," "with style and grace").

Similarly, Perry Bradford's songs "Bullfrog Hop" (1909) and "Messin' Around" (1912) provide explicit choreographic instructions, including some similarities to the later, more widely disseminated "Ballin' the Jack." In "Messin' Around," for instance, Bradford explains:

Now anyone can learn the knack
Put your hands on your hips and bend your back,
Stand in one spot, nice and light
Twist around with all your might
Messin' round, they call that messin' round.[15]

Bradford's "Original Black Bottom Dance" (1919) encodes instructions in a catalogue of other figures, including previous dances by the song-writer:

Hop down front and then you Doodle back,
Mooch to your left and then you Mooch to the right
Hands on your hips and do the Mess Around,
Break a Leg until you're near the ground
Now that's the Old Black Bottom Dance.

Now listen folks, open your ears,
This rhythm you will hear—
Charleston was on the afterbeat—
Old Black Bottom'll make you shake your feet,
Believe me it's a wow.
Now learn this dance somehow
Started in Georgia and it went to France
It's got everybody in a trance
It's a wing, that Old Black Bottom Dance.[16]

In addition to the description of the steps and the calling of other figures or dances, the dance explains the timing (like the Charleston, it is on the "afterbeat"), promises positive psychological affect, and makes reference to altered states of consciousness.

Even though these dance instruction songs were published in the form of sheet music, prior to the introduction of recording and broad-cast technologies, they were part of an oral tradition of instruction through popular performance, at first in minstrel shows and black vaudeville, and then in both black and white revues and musicals. The African American musician Clyde Bernhardt describes a 1917 performance by Ma Rainey and her black minstrel company. In the finale, Bernhardt remembers:

The whole chorus line come stepping out behind her and she dance along, kicking up her heels. The song had dance instructions in the lyrics, and as she call a step, everybody would do it. Soon the whole cast was out on stage, jugglers, riders, singers, comedians, all dancing wild with Ma Rainey shouting and stomping. She call "WALK!" and everybody walked together before breaking out fast. She call "STOP!" and everybody froze. After many calls she finally holler "SQUAT!" and the whole group squatted down with a roar. Including Ma Rainey.[17]

Audiences, that is, learned the dance visually and aurally in public performances, rather than by learning to read cryptographic notation or taking private lessons. Accessible to all, this was a democratic form of dance pedagogy. Eventually, as the mass medium of television edged out live popular entertainments like vaudeville and traveling shows, broadcast programs such as American Bandstand and MTV replaced the live visual demonstrations.

The Rise of the Dance Instruction Song

By the 1920s, Broadway musicals with all-black casts regularly introduced new dance crazes to whites by demonstrating the steps and singing songs exhorting spectators to do the dance, such as the Charleston, danced to the song by James P. Johnson, in *Runnin' Wild* (1923).[18]

The Stearns give an account of the process by which the African American dance rhyme, a folk form, was transformed into the commercial dance instruction song. At first, the structure was "a *group* dance performed in a circle with a few 'experts' in the center." As these experts improvised, inserted, and invented steps, the chorus on the outside repeatedly executed the steps named in the title of the dance. Often, the dance was simply named, rather than described, and if there was description, it was cursory. Later, however, as the dances reached the commercial market, "editorializing . . . as to its purported origin, nature, or popularity" began to appear as part of the song's format. And the group dance with improvised steps metamorphosed into a couple dance with a fixed choreographic structure and order. "Although the verse names new steps, and the chorus describes the main step, the aim is simply to sell the dance," they lament.[19]

According to the Stearns, it was the Tin Pan Alley appropriation of these vernacular African American dances, in the form of the dance instruction song, that fostered their surfacing to the mainstream from black folk culture, and indeed, their survival. But oddly enough, although they were writing at the height of a new dance instruction song craze in the 1960s, the Stearns claim that by the end of the 1920s, "the days of the dance-song with folk material were passing" and "the demand for dance-songs faded. The practice of including instructions in the

lyrics of a song dwindled and gradually hardened into a meaningless formula." And, they claim, with the advent of the blues, "dance-songs were
forgotten," although the dances themselves persisted.[20]

But it is our contention that, far from being forgotten or hardening
into "a meaningless formula," dance instruction continued in the blues
(and beyond). William Moore's "Old Country Rock" (1928) has shouted
instructions sprinkled through the record:

Young folks rock.
   Boys rock.
Girls rock.
   Drop back, man, and let me rock.
. . .
Now let's go back to the country again
   on that old rock.
Rappahannac, Rappahannac,
   Cross that river, boys, cross that river.

And boogie-woogie pianists continued to simulate the ambience of live
dances on recordings up until the 1950s.[21] During the course of the twentieth century, the dance instruction song consistently re-emerged in times
of heightened racial consciousness or change—times like the 1920s, the
1940s, and the 1960s—as a subtle component of an ongoing cultural
struggle between black and white America that includes provisional and
partial reconciliations. Even as white America violently resists political
and social progress by African Americans, a steady, subterranean Africanization of American culture continues, and emerging generations of
white youth eagerly learn the bodily and cultural codes of black America
by practicing its dances. And even where whites sang songs that presented
black dances derisively or stereotypically—as in the case of rockabilly
Carl Mann's "Ubangi Stomp" or Johnny Sharpe and the Yellow Jackets'
"Bombie," both of which apply the "n-word" to Africans—the description
and instructional elements were there nonetheless.[22]

While European Americans had danced to music performed by African Americans for generations, they did not as a group perform black
moves or dance to exactly the same music enjoyed in the black community. When whites did so, it was either in an exaggerated, stereotyped
way, in the context of the blackface minstrel show, or it was an individual matter, done either in the black community or in private. The dance
instruction song "crazes" seem repeatedly to have served the function of
both teaching and licensing whites to do black dance movements wholesale, in public spaces in mainstream Euro-American culture, to African American music.[23] That an African American movement style, done
to a 4/4 beat, was utterly alien to whites accounts for the necessity of
these songs' explicating not only steps, but also aspects of dance style,

even bodily style. (It must be noted, however, that the dances are doubly coded, for embedded in the instructions are often allusions to aspects of black culture—particularly to religious experience—that would not necessarily be understood by the average white listener.) The repeated infusions of black style into white mass culture, which dance instruction songs enable, have allowed for temporary resolutions of racial conflict to take place on a deeply embodied cultural level, paralleling shifts in political and legal strata. The (as yet uncompleted) democratization of American culture has depended, in part, on the Africanization of American culture. And the dance instruction song has been both a reflection and an agent of that process, although this has not been unproblematic, as we will discuss below.

Taxonomy: Structure and Function of the Dance Instruction Song

In order to analyze the dance instruction song in more depth, it is useful to establish a taxonomy of the structure and function of the songs and their component parts. For example, some songs do little more than urge the listener to perform the dance by naming it, like Rufus Thomas' "The Dog" and Van McCoy's "The Hustle." However, the majority of the songs begin with the premise that the listener has to be instructed in at least one or more categories—not only in the steps, spacing, timing, or other particulars of the dance, but in the style as well (that is, in a specifically African American dance style). Although in this section we concentrate on the directions given in the lyrics, a great deal of instruction in these songs takes place through aspects of the musical as well as verbal text.

In the beginning stages of the waves of the 1920s and 1960s at least, the detailed instructions of the songs seem to indicate that the white mass audience/participants needed tutoring in all the moves, postures, and rhythms of black dance. However, in each wave, as it progressed, the songs begin to assume some mastery of the black dance style, naming only figures or other coded instructions; sometimes they even assume mastery of previous dances, naming them specifically as comparative references, as we will illustrate below.

Most of the song structures, despite their apparent simplicity and their repetitions, are quite complex. They contain information about the quantitative and qualitative content of the dance—its steps, gestures, and style—but also, they make reference to its novelty, popularity, and/or venerable history; to the dance's psychological affect; to other practitioners of the dance; to the dancer's agency; and to aspects of teaching or learning the dance. They may also make reference to religious practices, sexual pleasure, or altered states of consciousness. Sometimes the songs use the dance as a mask or metaphor for those other experiences; sometimes they overtly frame the dance as a social activity connected with courtship; but at other times they simply offer the listener the chance to learn the dance, with no strings attached.

(Strangely, the wording of the instructions given in Irene and Vernon Castle's 1914 book, *Modern Dancing*, seems very similar to that of dance instruction songs, perhaps suggesting that in the process of learning these dances from African Americans, they also absorbed the pedagogical rhetoric.)[24]

The dance instruction songs usually begin, almost obligatorily, with a formulaic *exhortation* to learn or perform the dance. These range from the paternalistic ("Listen while I talk to you / I tell you what we're gonna do" ["Shake"]) to the pedagogical ("C'mon baby want to teach it to you" ["Mashed Potato Time"]) to the factual ("Come on let's stroll, stroll across the floor" ["Stroll"]); from the encouraging ("Come on baby, do the Bird with me" ["Do the Bird"]) to the wheedling ("Come on mama, do that dance for me" ["Come on Mama"]) to the aggressive ("Hey you! Come out here on the floor / Let's rock some more" ["Baby Workout"]) to the tender ("Come on baby, let's do the Twist . . . Take me by my little hand / And go like this" ["The Twist"]).

It's striking that when inviting the listener to do the dance, narrators of the dance instruction song often sweeten the offer with the promise that the dance will be easy to do. Sometimes this assurance comes in the form of pointing out that other people have already mastered the dance: "I wish I could shimmy like my sister Kate"; "My little baby sister can do it with ease"; "Goin' to see little Susie / Who lives next door / She's doin' the Pony / She's takin' the floor"; "You should see my little sis / She knows how to rock / She knows how to twist"; "Mama Hully Gully, Papa Hully Gully, Baby Hully Gully too"; "Pappy knows how . . ." These are aspects of the formulaic part of the song that reflexively calls attention to its *pedagogical function*. In fact, in "The Loco-Motion," Little Eva makes literal the connection with learning, simultaneously guaranteeing user-friendliness, when she remarks that the dance is "easy as a line in your abcs." And the many allusions to little sisters also seem to literalize the idiom that these dances will be child's play. At least as early as "Doin' the Scraunch" (1930), Robert Hicks (aka Barbecue Bob) promised that "Ain't much to it an' it's easy to do."

But these references to teaching and learning also come simply, without any warranties of easy mastery: "Bobby's going to show you how to do the Swim"; "C'mon now, take a lesson now"; "Now if you don't know what it's all about / Come to me, I'll show you how / We'll do it fast, we'll do it slow / Then you'll know the Walk everywhere you go." As the song progresses, words of encouragement and positive feedback are frequent: "Oh, you're lookin' good, now"; "That's the way to do it"; "Well, I think you've got the knack."

Related to the promise that the dance will be user-friendly and the coaching offered by way of positive feedback is the part of the song—not obligatory but still quite frequent—that speaks to *psychological affect*, either that of the listener or that of the narrator. In "Finger Poppin' Time," Hank Ballard sings "I feel so good / And that's a real good sign," and in "Bristol Stomp," the Dovells predict, "Gonna feel fine" and conclude the song by noting "I feel fine." Sam Cooke, in "Shake," exclaims "Oh I like to do it . . . Make me feel good now," and Little Eva, in "The Loco-Motion," guarantees, "It even makes you happy when you're feeling blue." The lyric "Twist and fly / To the sky" is one of many invocations of euphoria in "Do the Bird." There is a connection here, to be sure, between the kinetic pleasure of the dance and other forms of ecstasy—sexual, romantic, drug-induced, and religious.

On the other hand, a few songs tell of failures to learn the dances, but always within special circumstances: some blame their partners, as in "My Baby Couldn't Do the Cha Cha," or in Buddy Sharpe and The Shakers' "Fat Mama Twist," where the singer's girlfriend is too fat to do it. In other songs, the singer is culturally unprepared for the dance: in Frankie Davidson and the Sapphires' "I Can't Do the Twist," the singer (in a fake Spanish accent) confesses he can't do it, though he can do all of the Latin dances; Benny Bell & His Pretzel Twisters' "Kosher Twist" follows much the same pattern, but in Borscht Belt dialect.

Sometimes, at or near the beginning of the song, the narrator makes references to the *popularity, novelty,* and/or *venerability* of the dance. Although the Stearns consider this aspect of the song a symptom of commercialization and decline, we see it quite otherwise. This is an African-derived practice, clearly in the tradition of the African American praise song. (Indeed, some of the dance instruction songs—like the "Ali Shuffle"—also function as praise songs for other objects than the dance itself. Similarly, in "It's Madison Time," both Wilt Chamberlain and Jackie Gleason are celebrated with a step.) "Down in Dixie, there's a dance that's new," Barbecue Bob announces in "Doin' the Scraunch." Blind Willie McTell's "Georgia Rag" sets the scene "Down in Atlanta on Harris Street," and insists that "Every little kid, that you meet, / Doin' that rag, that Georgia Rag . . . Come all the way from Paris, France / Come to Atlanta to get a chance . . . Peoples come from miles around / Get into Darktown t' break 'em down." In "The Loco-Motion," Little Eva notes that "Everybody's doing a brand new dance now," while in the background the chorus exhorts "Come on baby, do the Loco-Motion." In "Popeye," Huey Smith and the Clowns tell us that "Everywhere we go, people jump and shout / They all want to know what the Popeye's all about." In "Peppermint Twist," Joey Dee and the Starliters announce, "They got a new dance and it goes like this / The name of the dance is the Peppermint Twist." In "The Bounce," the Olympics assert, "You know there's a dance / That's spreading around / In every city / In every little town." And in "Hully Gully Baby," the Dovells characterize the dance's popularity somewhat ominously: "There's a dance spreadin' round like an awful disease . . . " Perhaps in "Mashed Potato Time," Dee Dee Sharp puts the praise of the dance most succinctly: "It's the latest / It's the greatest / Mashed Potato / Yeah yeah yeah yeah." She then goes on to trace the roots of the dance and to bring the listener up to date on its vicissitudes. Similarly, "The Original Black Bottom Dance," "The Bristol Stomp," and "Popeye" provide mythic accounts of origins.

Once the dance has been invoked and/or praised, the lyrics indicate the *steps, gestures,* and *postures.* Usually this information is stated in the imperative mode, as a command—"Just move your body all around / And just shake" ("Shake"); "You gotta swing your hips now . . . / Jump up, jump back" ("The Loco-Motion"); "All right, now, shake your shoulders now / All right, wiggle your knees now" ("Hully Gully"); "You just shake your hips and close your eyes / And then you walk" ("The Walk"); "Shake it up baby" ("Twist and Shout"); "Now you sway at the knees like a tree in the breeze / Then buzz around just like the bumblebees" ("Scratchin' the Gravel"); "Oh, shout you cats, do it, stomp it, step you rats, / Shake your shimmy, break a leg, / Grab your gal and knock 'em dead" ("Shout You Cats"). Sometimes, however, the instructions are more in the manner of a description: "Round and around / Up and down" ("Peppermint Twist"); "We're moving in we're moving out" ("Baby Workout"). And occasionally, this is stated as an invitation: "Now turn around baby, let's stroll once more" ("Strolling"). At times, the narrator actually counts out the sequence: "One, two, three, kick / One, two, three, jump" ("Peppermint Twist"); "Oh my mama move up (first step) / Honey move back (second step) / Shuffle to the left (third step) / Wobble to the right (fourth step)" ("Baby Workout"). In Charles LaVerne's "Shoot 'Em Up Twist" a freeze is ordered every time a gunshot is heard on the record.

One subcategory of this part of the dance is what might be termed *calling the figure.* As in contra dancing or square dancing, the narrator instructs the dancers to perform a phrase or move that itself has already been named, either during the current dance or by common knowledge because it exists in other cultural arenas (like dog paddle or back stroke, or hula hoop, or "a chugga-chugga motion like a railroad train"). "It's Pony Time" is a very good example of first teaching, then calling the figure. The narrator explains: "Now you turn to the left when I say 'gee' / You turn to the right when I say 'haw.'" Then he sings, "Now gee /

Yeah, yeah little baby / Now haw."[25] Or, in "It's Madison Time," the narrator commands, "When I say 'Hit it!' I want you to go two up and two back, with a big strong turn, and back to the Madison."

As suggested earlier, one way of calling the figure is actually to invoke another dance already popular and, presumably, known and available as a standard measurement. The dance may then simply be repeated: "Let's Twist again / Like we did last summer." Or, in a *mise-en-abŷme* structure, the song may direct the listener to do other dances as part of the dance being taught (as noted above in "Jonah's Band Party" and "Original Black Bottom Dance"): "Do that Slow Drag 'round the hall / Do that step the Texas Tommy" ("Walkin' the Dog," 1917); "When I say 'Hold it!' this time, I want everybody to Gully . . . / When I say hold it this time I want everybody to Sally Long" ("Fat Fanny Stomp"); "Do the Shimmy Shimmy" ("Do the Bird"); "Do a little Cha-cha, then you do the Buzz-saw" ("Hully-Gully"); "Do a little wiggle and you do the Mess Around" ("Popeye"); "Hitchhike baby, across the floor" ("The Harlem Shuffle"); "We Ponyed and Twisted" ("Bristol Stomp"); "Think we'll step back now /And end this dance with a Shout" ("Baby Workout").[26] Indeed, Bradford's "Bullfrog Hop" is a veritable catalogue of other dance titles:

First you commence to wiggle from side to side
Get 'way back and do the Jazzbo Glide
Then you do the Shimmy with plenty of pep
Stoop low, yeah Bo', and watch your step
Do the Seven Years' Itch and the Possum Trot
Scratch the Gravel in the vacant lot
Then you drop like Johnny on the Spot
That's the Bullfrog Hop.[27]

Sometimes, the called dance may serve as a model from which to deviate. For instance, in "The Swim," Bobby Freeman explains how to do it: "Just like the Dog, but not so low / Like the Hully Gully but not so slow." "The Walk" mentions the Texas Hop, the Fox Trot, the Mambo, and the Congo, but all as dances that are now out of fashion. In a very complex example, Junior and the Classics' "The Dog," the dancer is asked to "do" various breeds of dog—the poodle, the scotty, et al.

Oddly enough for songs that were usually distributed over nonvisual channels such as radio or records, sometimes the lyrics indicate that the narrator is also demonstrating the dance along the visual channel, as in "The Swim"—"Kind of like the Monkey, kind of like the Twist / Pretend you're in the water and you go like this"—or as in "The Twist"—"Come on and twist /Yeah, baby twist / Oooh yeah, just like this."[28] The radio or record listener has to fill in the visuals, based on a general knowledge of the appropriate vocabulary and style.

This indication of visual demonstration seems to make reference to earlier times, when dance instruction was routinely done as part of live entertainment in black vaudeville and tent shows, as described above. Long before he became a recording artist, Rufus Thomas was a member of the Rabbit's Foot Minstrels, a black vaudeville group that showed its audiences the latest steps. "I sing, I do a step or two, and I'm a comedian," Thomas later described his act.[29]

On the recordings, the residue of a live show with visual demonstration is evident during the musical break, when the time seems right either for the listener to watch the narrator demonstrate the dance (saving the breath he or she would otherwise need to sing) and/or for the listener to practice the movements just learned. Then, when the lyrics are repeated after the musical break, the listener does not find the repetition boring or redundant, because he or she is ready to test the progress made during the (nonverbal) practice time against the instructions once again.

This is nicely illustrated in the Pearl Bailey/Hot Lips Page version of "The Hucklebuck," in which, partly because of the duet form and the dialogic patter, we have the distinct sense that Bailey is teaching Page how to do the dance. In fact, even before she begins singing, Bailey formulaically initiates the dance event by confiding in Page that she has learned a great new dance. According to their conversation, they're in a club, and not only do they comment on the abilities and looks of the musicians, but also Bailey at one point complains that Page is dancing right on her feet. This song seems to record a performance within a performance, for certain lines cue the listener also to set up a scene visually that puts Bailey and Page onstage in the club, teaching the audience how to do the dance. That is, in the fictional drama of the song they are a couple getting together on the dance floor in a club, but in the frame they are the featured club performers singing the fictional romance narrative. In any case, they repeatedly sing the chorus together, exhorting the listener to do the dance and describing the steps and other movements:

Do the Hucklebuck
Do the Hucklebuck
If you don't know how to do it, boy you're out of luck
Push your partner out
Then you hunch your back
Start a little movement in your sacroiliac
Wiggle like a snake
Waddle like a duck
That's the way you do it when you do the Hucklebuck.

As the band plays in between the stanzas, and Bailey and Page trade patter, it is clear that they are *doing* the dance, especially when Bailey scolds Page: "No, not now! I'll tell you when. Right here!"

As noted earlier, dance instruction songs teach not only the quantitative aspects of the dance (the steps, postures, and gestures), but also the qualitative aspects. One of these aspects is *timing*. For instance, "The Walk" is very specific in teaching the proper timing for the moves. Walking may be an ordinary act, but turning it into a dance requires the proper rhythmic sequence. So Jimmy McCracklin notes that "We'll do it fast, we'll do it slow," and later regulates the speed even further as he marks the exact moment in the music when the dancer should take his or her step: "You'll then walk / And you'll walk / *Now* you walk . . ." In "The Harlem Shuffle," Bob and Earl often qualify a step by indicating its proper speed (which, of course, the slow and steady music underscores): "You move it to the right (yeah) / If it takes all night" and they frequently admonish the dancer: "Don't move it too fast / Make it last . . ." In "Slow Twistin'," reminiscent of the "Slow Drag," Chubby Checker and Dee Dee Sharp recommend: "Baby baby baby take it easy / Let's do it right / Aw, baby take it easy / Don't you know we got all night . . . Let's twist all night! / You're gonna last longer, longer / Just take your time . . ."[30] The music, especially its percussive beat, plays an important role in all the songs in indicating timing.

Another qualitative aspect of the dance is its *spacing*; this too serves as an aspect of instruction. Again in "Slow Twistin'," Chubby Checker and Dee Dee Sharp advise the listener that all one needs is "Just a little bit of room, now baby." Spacing refers not only to ambient space, but also to levels of space, as in "The Swim": "Just like the Dog, but not so low . . ." It also refers to relations with one's partner, which can be difficult to negotiate. In "The Walk," the narrator warns, "But when you walk, you stand in close / And don't step on your partner's toes." Several songs recommend, once one has learned a step, doing it in "a big boss line" or "a big strong line." In "The Loco-Motion," Little Eva instructs the listeners, once they have mastered the step, to make a chain. This clearly invokes earlier African American vernacular and communal roots, when the dances were done as group folk forms, rather than as couple forms in the dance hall.

Yet another aspect of style is the category of *energy use*—what Laban movement analysts refer to as effort qualities, such as strength and lightness, boundedness and unboundedness, directness and indirectness. This too is a stylistic characteristic that the dance instruction song sometimes teaches. For instance, "The Loco-Motion" tells us to "Take it nice and easy, now / Don't lose control," while in "The Shake," Sam Cooke gives us quite a few clues: "Shake shake with all your might / Oh if you do it do it right/Just make your body loose and light / You just shake." In "The Duck," Jackie Lee gives some sense of the energy invested in the dance when he describes performing it as "like working on a chain gang" or "busting rocks." Less easy to characterize are other references to *overall style*: the many songs that recommend, for instance, that the dance be performed "with soul."

One of the oldest forms of African American dance instruction is that given by the instruments themselves. The role of drums, for instance, in "talking" to dancers, or in signaling states of possession is a well-known phenomenon, both in Africa and the Americas.[31] The role of instrument as caller or instructor is not so well understood in American dance music, but its presence is undeniable. Barry Michael Cooper describes both horns and singers calling instructions to dancers at Washington, D.C. go-go dances in the 1980s.[32] And dance music critic Michael Freedberg suggests that instruments enact gender roles, both in the blues and in dance music performances.[33]

Dance instruction songs vary in the amount of choreographic information they impart, and they obviously serve a range of functions. Some actually teach the dance from scratch; some serve as prompts or mnemonics, recalling for the listener previously demonstrated and learned dances; some serve to co-ordinate ensemble dancing; some merely praise a dance or exhort the listener to perform it. But it is possible for a dance instruction song to "notate" all ten elements in the taxonomy: exhortation; pedagogical function; psychological affect; popularity, novelty, and/or venerability; steps, gestures, and postures; calling the figure; timing; spacing; energy use; and style. Thus the amount of information can be quite complete.

Doin' the Hermeneutics

Certain aspects of the dance instruction song have nothing to do with learning or remembering to perform the dance. In fact, sometimes even what serves as explicit instruction seems also to have subtextual, metaphoric, or "secret" meanings. So, while the dance instruction songs have partly served to teach the rest of the world African American dances and dance styles, they also allude to other aspects of knowledge and experience. Some of these allusions are highly coded in terms of African American custom, emerging for white consumers and participants only through familiarity with African American history and culture. That these references are also formulaic and appear repeatedly in the songs, in succeeding generations, shows the extent and tenacity of their roots. They are often unrecognized, sturdy traces of long-standing cultural traditions.

Some of the metaphors of African American dance instruction songs are merely pedagogical in function, since traditional dance language lacks names for the steps. So "mashed potatoes," "ride your pony," "walk like a duck," "walk pigeon-toed," and the like are means of directing the dancers away from the received, conventional steps of western dance.

Not all the extrachoreographic references have to do with experiences that are uniquely African American. Often, social dancing serves as a metaphor in these narratives for other kinds of partnering—either romantic or sexual. And, since dancing—especially to slow music—often involves sustained body-to-body contact between partners, the metaphoric leap can be but a tiny one. When white teenagers danced the Twist, they were accused of moving in overly erotic ways and raised the ire of their parents. The lyrics of "Slow Twistin'" are full of double entendres, underscored by the male-female vocal duet: "Don't you know we got all night . . . Let's twist all night! / You're gonna last longer, longer / Just take your time . . . " Perhaps the extreme case is Ronnie Fuller's "Do the Dive," where cunnilingus appears to be the move taught. In some songs, however, the dance serves not as a metaphor for sex, but as a love potion. Performing the dance itself is guaranteed to bond the partners romantically, as in "The Bristol Stomp": "We'll fall in love you see / The Bristol Stomp will make you mine, all mine."

The ecstatic body consciousness of sex, however, is easily conflated with that of another high—from drugs or alcohol. The word "trance" does not only show up in these songs because it rhymes with "dance." Thus, in "Do the Bird," as we have seen, it is not clear whether romance or drugs, or both at once, are in effect when the singer urges:

Come on take me to the sky above (fly-y-y-y-y)
Come on baby we can fall in love (fly-y-y-y-y)
. . .
(Do the bird do the bird) You're a-crazy flying
(Do the bird do the bird) You're going to fly higher.

Similarly, the lines "Let's go strolling in Wonderland," or "Baby, let's go strolling by the candy store," in "The Stroll," also ambiguously suggest some kind of euphoria, whether sexual, drug-induced, or religious.

And yet "Doin' the New Low-Down," while acknowledging rapture—even invoking dreams and trances—specifically rejects other, non-dance forms of euphoria, either chemical or sexual, insisting on a surface reading: for "It isn't alcohol / No yaller girl at all! Thrills me, fills me with the pep I've got / I've got a pair of feet / That found a low-down beat . . . Heigh! Ho! doin' the New Low-Down."

Another line in "Doin' the New Low-Down" invokes a crucial category of cultural invocations: specifically African American signs of *religious* references. "I got a soul that's not for savin' now," this song's narrator admits, since his feet are "misbehavin' now." But more often, dance and religion are seen in the dance instruction song not as exclusionary opposites but as integrally linked. In fact, the frequent references in the songs to black religious practices, in particular the shaking or trembling associated with religious possession, suggest that many secular African American folk dances or social dances are derived directly from religious dances; they may even be the same dances performed in a different context. These are movements that originated in sacred rituals in West Africa, were associated with Yoruba, Ashanti, Congo, and other West African spirits, and shaped the syncretic worship formations of the African American church. In fact, instruction in appropriate physical response among Afro-Protestants is seen when ministers direct the congregation verbally ("Everybody raise your right hand and say 'Praise Jesus!'"); and in eighteenth-century Cuba, among Afro-Cuban religious orders, when leaders directed initiates to "open their ears, stand straight, and put their left hand on their hip."[34]

Thus the Eagle Rock, mentioned in many of the songs beginning with "Ballin' the Jack," and described by the Stearns as "thrusting the arms high over the head with a variety of shuffle steps," actually took its name from the Eagle Rock Baptist Church in Kansas City. According to musician Wilbur Sweatman, worshippers at the church "were famous for dancing it during religious services in the years following the Civil War," and the Stearns note that although the Eagle Rock eventually adapted itself to rent parties and other secular venues, "it has the high arm gestures associated with evangelical dances and religious trance."[35]

Similarly, the Shout often crops up in the steps invoked by dance instruction songs, from "Twist and Shout" to "Do the Bird" to "Baby Workout." Also known as the ring shout when done in a group form, this was not a strictly vocal performance, but a religious dance with chants. It involved a rhythmic walk or shuffle in a circle, tapping the heels, swaying, and clapping as one advanced. In several accounts, observers noted that the shouters moved increasingly faster, working themselves into a trance.[36]

Indeed, Jones and Hawes explicitly make the connection among children's ring plays, adult secular dances, and religious ring shouts in the African American tradition. They include in their chapter on dances the religious ring shout "Daniel," which includes lyrics, sung by the leader, strikingly reminiscent of several dance instruction songs:

Walk, believer, walk,
Walk, believer, walk,
Walk, I tell you, walk,
Shout, believer, shout,
Shout, believer, shout,
On the eagle wing,
On the eagle wing,
Fly, I tell you, fly
Rock, I tell you, rock
Fly the other way,
Shout, I tell you, shout,

Give me the kneebone bend,
On the eagle wing,
Fly, I tell you, fly
Fly back home.[37]

Finally, the all-over body trembling called for and described in various songs—and known as the Shake, the Shimmy, and the Quiver, among other dances—bears a striking resemblance to the movements seen, especially among women, during religious possession in gospel churches.[38] Terms like "workout," "work it on out," "rock my soul," "turn the joint out," and "tear the house down," as well as the instruction to "go down to the river" ("The Duck"), all make explicit reference to ecstatic forms of African American religious worship.

In addition to these markedly African-derived dance practices, yet another set of associations reveals the presence of African cultural practices in dance instruction songs. Although the songs do give choreographic directions to the dancer, space is often made for *improvisation.* Thus, in "Shake," we are told "Dance what you wanna"; in "The Swim," we are assured "Do what you wanna, it's all right"; in "The Loco-Motion," we are told "Dance what you wanna"; in "The Swim," we are assured "Do what you wanna, it's all right"; in "The Loco-Motion," we are instructed "Do it holding hands if you get the notion"; and in "It's Pony Time," we learn that "Any way you do it / You're gonna look real fine." These lyrics not only reveal improvisation as a standard component of African American dance, suggesting that during the musical break it will be perfectly appropriate to "go crazy folks for a minute."[39] They also suggest, in a deeper vein, the metaphoric meaning of that improvisation. That is, the songs promise more than simply feeling good; they imply freedom and agency.

It should be acknowledged that the cross-cultural pedagogy of dance has been neither static nor one-way. Hip-hop, go-go, and ska are only the latest African American dance forms assimilated by white America. On the other hand, European dances like the quadrille have been absorbed, albeit in modified form, into the African American repertory.[40] For instance, the Stroll involves forming two facing longways rows of dance partners, as in a European contra dance configuration. But there is a difference. When each couple goes down the column of space between the rows, they improvise virtuosic inventions in a characteristically African American vein.

One way to understand dance instruction songs is as a kind of summing-up of a musical period. There is considerable self-consciousness about them, and by the time the songs are commercially available it is likely that the original people involved with the dance have moved on to other dances, or will soon do as popularization sets in.

What is striking about most of these songs is that they offer a thin read-ing of the dance that lay behind them. Especially among Euro-Americans there is a tendency to reduce a complex physical-verbal-musical phe-nomenon to the merely verbal. Thus the shout is often discussed as a kind of folk song. And the same reduction has been worked on rap, where the dance components of the form are almost always ignored in favour of the verbal.[41]

The Decline of the Dance Instruction Song

At the end of the 1960s popular music was developing at a remarkable rate. Yet, dance per se was not the focus of forms such as psychedelic music, heavy metal, and art rock. Increasingly, songs about dances became not merely wanna-be dances, but conceptual dance instruction songs—songs about dances that didn't exist. The genre became some-thing of a joke. *Mad Magazine*'s "Let's Do the Fink," by Alfred E. New-man, which came with illustrated dance steps, was typical.[42] At the same time, however, black and Latin music continued a commitment to "the beat," so that when the white gay community encountered strongly grounded dance music in clubs and ballrooms in the 1970s, it seemed a totally new phenomenon. It was as if rock had never happened.

When dance music made its comeback as disco, it did so with a vengeance. New dances were developed apace, but instructional songs were minimal at best, with exhortation and novelty/praise functions carrying the weight of the lyrics. The names of dances were repeated riff-like in songs: "Do the Hustle," "Do the Jaws." Professional dance teachers returned, and a ballroom formality replaced the home-made, self-help atmosphere of many earlier dance eras.

The 1990s are certainly a time of acute racial tension and heightened race awareness in the United States. And yet, dances are being invented and reinvented at a slower rate, and no dance instruction song craze has emerged thus far in this generation. The Electric Slide, one of the few to have appeared in recent years (accompanied by a song of the same name by Marcia Griffith in 1989), was immediately challenged by an older gen-eration of dancers as a thinly disguised remake of the Madison, espe-cially as it, too, emerged from the Baltimore-D.C. area.[43] Similarly, the Lambada was attacked as a commercially fabricated generic Latin dance, and its accompanying song debunked as plagiarism. The current gener-ation of African American kids still knows some dance instruction songs, like the currently popular "Tootsie Roll" by The 69 Boys. But these have not crossed over into the mainstream. In hip hop, one of the few dis-tinctive music forms of the current era, MCs (especially in the early days of the form) may direct dancing and crowd behavior, but usually in an improvised rap, with routinized calls, and seldom in the form of a fully structured song for a distinctive dance. Madonna's appropriation of Voguing from the black gay community in the early 1990s was a sudden, singular—and spectacularly popular—resuscitation of the genre, but it did not spark a new wave.[44]

Dance instruction songs are still with us, though, in truncated, restricted forms. Country and western line dances—a remarkable case of cultural lag—still retain something of the calling of steps used in black popular dancing of the late 1950s and early 1960s (at least in the instructional videos), and aerobics and jazzercise do struggle mightily to get the feel of the discotheque into their routines. But there is a sense here of the end of an era. Two items of nostalgia—"Time Warp" (a camp parody of "Ballin' the Jack") from *The Rocky Horror Picture Show* (1975) and the commemorative scenes from John Waters' 1988 film *Hairspray*—indicate that for the mainstream, the dance instruction song is truly a relic from the past.

Conclusions

There is a school of mass culture criticism, most notoriously represented by Adorno, that condemns popular music as an opiate.[45] The dance instruction song, however, clearly contradicts that position. Far from assuming a docile listener, it galvanizes audiences into action with both its swinging beat and its lyrics. It is a dialogic form, requiring interaction between artist and auditor. Thus, even though the form of dissemination—especially after the invention of the phonograph—has been mass production or broadcast, the dance instruction song does not promote passivity. Rather, it provides a means for individual agency and creativity, especially with its improvisational component. Moreover, it insists that listener response can be bodily, not just intellectual, participation. And, unlike the Castles' gendered ballroom choreography instructions, the dance instruction songs make no gender distinctions in the movements. In fact, unlike the Euro-American style of couple dancing, where the man leads and the woman follows, in the pedagogy proposed by dance instruction songs, women and even girls are often cited as authorities.

The question arises as to whether people actually *listen* to the lyrics and, further, whether listening to the lyrics enables people to learn to do the dance. Several theorists of popular culture claim that people screen out the words in popular music and hear only the rhythm or the emotional contours.[46] And many cultural critics condemn the lyrics of popular songs, claiming that since the words are banal and predictable to begin with, auditors don't need to pay attention to them.[47] The dance instruction song seems unlike other genres of popular music, in that here it *is* important to listen to the words, and not just to sense the beat, melody, or emotional content of the song. This is not to say that the words alone supply the entire set of choreographic instructions, for as we have pointed out, the music also directs the dancer. But the words *are* important, even if not all of them need to be heard or understood, because the dance is "overdetermined." That is, listeners may not hear or comprehend every single word (and indeed, not every song makes every word clear enough to understand). But, given the various ways people learn to dance, the redundancies, both in terms of the repetition of the lyrics and the parallel teaching across various channels—verbal, rhythmic, melodic, and visual—allow for successful instruction.

The dance instruction song is laced with esoteric references to African American culture—especially to ecstatic religious experiences—that have been inaccessible to most Euro-Americans. Nevertheless, during the course of the twentieth century the dance instruction song, while keeping black vernacular dances alive, has had a mass appeal to white audiences. Through the dance instruction song, white bodies have learned—and loved—black moves, from the practice of performing separate rhythms with diverse body parts, to stances like akimbo arms and bent knees, to specific movements like all-over body quivers or hip rotations. Despite the recondite allusions, there is enough accessible material in the songs, both in the music and in the lyrics, for Euro-Americans to learn the dances and the dance style. The genre has become part of mainstream American culture.

We want to close by raising the issue of cultural appropriation. On the one hand, the dance instruction song, besides its own formal pleasures, is an attractive genre for all the reasons we have already mentioned—not only its preservation of vernacular black dance, but also its dialogic character, its role in the democratization and Africanization of American culture, and the economic opportunities it has created for African American musicians. By introducing an African American bodily habitus into mass white culture, thereby stirring up racial, generational, and sexual threats, it has even been subversive. But on the other hand, the dance instruction song *crazes* have been problematic, for they commodified and naturalized the dances, appropriating them for white culture without fully acknowledging their cultural source—their African roots—and sometimes totally detaching them from black bodies and black communities. The dance instruction song crazes created the impression that these dances have no roots—that they always have been and always will be. We hope that this article will in part redress that misperception.[48]

Chapter 19

The Afro-American Transformation of European Set Dances and Dance Suites

WITH MORTON MARKS

It is well acknowledged that the court dances which developed in Europe from the seventeenth century onward spread to the rural areas of Europe and to the New World.[1] What has not been properly recognized is that these dances—the quadrille, the cotillion, the contradance, and the like—were taken up by Afro-Americans in North and South America and the West Indies and were modified and adapted to local cultural circumstances. In many cases—especially in the West Indies—they continue to be found today. Yet as similar as these dances may look or sound, their functions are not always necessarily the same as those of their European sources. At one extreme, they were "Africanized" for sacred purposes; at the other, they were re-formed and became the basis of a New World popular culture. An example of the former occurs on the island of Montserrat.[2]

There *country dance* orchestras made up of various combinations of fife, fiddle, concertina or accordion, triangle, and two drums known as the *woowoo* and the *babala* (or *babla*) play for social dancing, but the same music is also used for inducing possession on other occasions, called "jombee dances."[3] On these latter occasions quadrille dance rhythms are intensified and gradually "Africanized"[4] in order that individuals may become possessed and convey the messages of the spirits. Secular customs such as suppers for guests are transformed into ritual sacrifices for spirits, and the mundane lyrics of quadrille songs become part of the mechanism for possession. But the ritual occasion has become "masked," reinterpreted so extensively that the traditional European elements of the dance seem predominant to the casual observer.

On other West Indian islands, dance suites and set dances are also associated with the spirits of ancestors, as on Trinidad, where the *reel* is danced prior to a wedding to ask for the ancestral spirits' consent, and the quadrille danced at a healing rite is associated with African ancestors; or on Carriacou, where libations may be poured for ancestors during a quadrille dance (*reel engagé*); and on Tobago, where the spirits are invoked during the *reel dance*.[5] (The Tobago *reel* is performed mainly by people of Kongo descent and is said to be similar to the *danse Kongo* of Haiti.)

The best example of the transformation of set dances and dance suites into popular culture is their use in the creation of jazz in the United States, through the slow mutation of the quadrille/cotillion from music for social dancing to a purely abstract musical form. Sometimes, even where these dances seem in other respects similar to their European antecedents, they at least differ in setting, as on St. Croix in the Virgin Islands, where quadrille is danced in the streets instead of indoors.[6]

The chief problem in working with Afro-American folk dances is their lack of visual or written documentation. As in any folk dance tradition, these forms are passed down in an "oral"—i.e., body-to-body—tradition. But there are additional problems, beyond those of transformation, in the documentation of Afro-American dances. While dance is frequently mentioned in historical, travel, and ethnographic literature, it is treated briefly, quite often in negative comparison to European dancing.

And even where descriptions exist, they are often minimal and confusing; a European dance name may refer to an entirely different dance; or a native New World term may disguise a well-known European form; and the European name for a step may label a complex dance in its own right. On the other hand, descriptions of the music for these dances are fuller, and the audio documentation is quite rich, especially as the recordings of folk music in the West Indies began well before that of the United States, in the first decade of the 1900s.

This uneven documentation has had the unfortunate result of reinforcing Western scholars' tendency to think of dance and music as separate. But in the Afro-American tradition, they are thought of together, the steps and the music inextricably intertwined—in theory, the same. It may be possible for dance scholars to recover some of the dance from the music and musical descriptions alone, since in this tradition, the dance is embedded within the music. For this reason, we offer here a capsule view of Afro-American set dance and dance suites (that is, what in Euro-American terms might be called "the music for set dances and dance suites"), in order to encourage their recognition and systematic study.

The Dance Suite in the Circum-Caribbean

The island of St. Lucia is one of the best-documented New World areas for the continuing presence of set dances such as the quadrille, *belé*, and mazurka.[7] The quadrille was probably first introduced there in the early

1800s by the French, or at least by the English after they took control in 1814. Quadrilles—more than other adapted European dances—require considerable learning and rehearsal, both to dance and to play. The performance of the dances thus requires a kind of planning and order different from other dances done on St. Lucia, and a system of values are attached to quadrilles which contrasts with those associated with other local dances. The St. Lucian *kwadril* is understood as essentially European, as associated with economic and social power, as something inherited from the plantocracy which can now be participated in and controlled. In this respect, *kwadrils* are to local dances what standard languages are to creole languages.

Contemporary St. Lucian *kwadrils* are made up of five dances, four of them strictly prescribed, the fifth a round dance of choice. The orchestra, at least during the early 1900s was composed of a violin, tambourine, and *chakchak* (maracas), but is currently made up of violin, banjo, *cuatro* (a small ten-string guitar), guitar, mandolin, and *chakchak*. No callers are used. Despite the dance's identification with Europe, St. Lucians have made considerable adaptations. *Kwadrils* are more complex in structure than the European quadrille, often have improvised melodies, are accompanied by percussion instruments, use off-beat phrasing, and often involve singing.[8]

In Martinique and Guadeloupe formal European dances such as the mazurka, the waltz, and the polka exist in both rural and urban areas, all of them having undergone considerable creolization in the last 100 years or so. The quadrille remains especially important in Guadeloupe, where beneficial societies hold *balakadri* (quadrille balls) for fund raising and social activity.[9] *Festival de Quadrille* (Debs HDD 512) is a commercial recording of such a folk quadrille from Guadeloupe.[10] It documents two sets of four figures, the dance directions provided by a rhythmic, monotone chant from a *commandeur* over a band of accordion, hand drum, triangle and maracas, a group which sounds remarkably similar to a *zydeco* band from rural black Louisiana.[11] Yet, it oddly does not include the "fifth" figure of each set (which may actually be a sixth, seventh, or eighth figure), the concluding dance of which is always of local origin and is in this case usually a *biguine*. It appears that throughout the Caribbean the last dance of a set is typically a local form. Whether this indicates the chronological order of the appearance of each dance in the culture (as Marie-Céline Lafontaine suggests),[12] or is another illustration of the Afro-American performance style of turning "European" performances into "Afro-American" ones as they progress, remains to be seen.

In neighboring Martinique a bewildering variety of European-derived dance suites exist, including the quadrille, *belair*, or *belé* (with eight

figures), *haut taille*, cotillion, and *rejane*.[13] One of the urban developments of this kind of music in Martinique are orchestras such as Malavoi
(*Malavoi*, Musique des Antilles 4710), with its six-piece string ensemble
and two rhythm players. This is certainly *au courant* quadrille, with
phrasing drawn from the Cuban *charanga* (music played by string, flute,
and *timbales* orchestras) and bebopish chords. But their quick changes
of tempo and melodies within single songs suggest miniaturized dance
suites, and in fact on "Quadrille C," they switch back and forth from a
lively dance tempo to slow, baroque-like ensemble playing, while a jazz
violin solo surfaces in between. Again, though it is too soon to say for
sure, single songs with changing melodies and rhythms often seem to be
reduced versions of older dance suites.

For Haiti, the music of the older *contredanse* tradition can be heard
on Maya Deren's recording of "Bal Li Chaise Pou Moin" (*Meringues and
Folk Ballads of Haiti*, Lyrichord LLST 7340), a piece played for the dance
called the *Martinique*. It can also be sampled within a more recent big
band setting on Nemours Jean Baptiste's *Musical Tour of Haiti* (Ansonia
ALP 1280), complete with accordion.

In Jamaica, the quadrille (pronounced "katreel" or "kachriil"—a linguistic creolization also suggesting "scotch reel") is danced and played
in virtually all of the parishes, but with different emphases. Five or six
figures are used in the set, and may include European-derived dances,
steps, and figures such as the waltz, polka, schottische, vaspian, mazurka,
jig, chassé, balancé, and promenade, as well as local dances such as *mento*
or *shay-shay*, especially as the last dance in the set.[14] Two basic forms of
quadrille are distinguished in Jamaica: the ballroom (or European type)
and the "camp" style, with two facing lines of dancers; but various combinations of the two appear in different parts of the island.[15] Samples of
Jamaican quadrille music are included on *John Crow Say* . . . (Folkways
4228), where the instrumentation is harmonica, wooden trumpet, and
cassava grater; *Black Music of Two Worlds* (Folkways 4602), a fife and drum
band; and *Bongo, Backra & Coollie: Jamaican Roots*, Vol. 2 (Folkways 4232),
where a fife, guitar, and banjo play most of the figures of a set. (In earlier
years Jamaican bands might also be made up of combinations of one
to three fifes, two tambourines, big drum, grater, triangle, horse jaw-
bone, and possibly violins, accordion, or concertina. At the end of the
nineteenth century the most popular part of the quadrille was the fifth
dance, an apparently local form, possibly similar to *mento*).[16] The *mento*
was a local development, a looser, hotter form, with certain parallels to
Trinidadian calypso, but also having elements of European and local folk
tunes within it. Recorded examples include *Mento: Jamaican Calypsos 1950*
(Ethnic Cassettes KA 5), a collection of commercial recordings; "Mango
Time" on *Caribbean Island Music* (Nonesuch H-72047); "Wheel and Turn"

on *Black Music of Two Worlds* (Folkways 4602); "You Tell a Lie" on *From the Grass Roots of Jamaica*; and *The Roots of Reggae* (Lyrichord LLST 7314). Jamaican quadrille and *mento* are direct forerunners of *ska* and *reggae*, and echoes of the older forms persist in contemporary Jamaican popular music, most strikingly on the Wailers's "Ska Quadrille" and more recently on Yellowman's "Skank Quadrille" (*Galong Galong Galong*! Greensleeves GREL 87) with his updated "calls."

Similar to the dances of Jamaica are those found in the Virgin Islands (such as "Seven Step" [to fife, banjo, and maracas], whose rhythm gets freer as it proceeds, and "Fourth Figure of Lanceros" [both on *Caribbean Dances*, Folkways 6840]); Trinidad and Tobago ("Reel," on *An Island Carnival*, Nonesuch Explorer Series 72090, or on *Vastindien*, Caprice CAP 2004: 1–2); Carriacou ("Gwa Belé," on *The Big Drum Dance of Carriacou*, Folkways 4011, and "First Figure" (lancer's dance) and "Second Figure Waltz" on *The Big Drum and Other Ritual and Social Music of Carriacou*, Folkways 34002); and the Bahamas, where quadrilles and other European dances are accompanied by various combinations of guitar, fife, trumpet, accordion, musical saw, maracas, and drums (although it is said that around the turn of the century singers were the only source of melody).[17] *Music of the Bahamas*, Vol. 3: *Instrumental Music from the Bahamas Islands* (Folkways 3846) provides quadrille melodies by several instrumental combinations, including one with two trumpets, mandolin, and drums that is suggestive of the early New Orleans-inspired King Oliver–Louis Armstrong jazz recordings (*King Oliver's Creole Jazz Band*, Milestone 47017).

In Panama—where many English-speaking West Indians migrated for work on the Canal in the early 1900s—the quadrille has continued to be important, with annual dance exhibitions and club competitions. *Quadrille*, by Eric Garcia y sus 5 Progresivos (SallyRuth Records SR 1004) preserves a five-part "Quadrille" and a five-part "Caledonia" (a mid-nineteenth century European quadrille innovation) by a band of tenor saxophone, clarinet, two guitars, bass, and drums. The polyphony of tenor and clarinet is reminiscent of both early New Orleans jazz and *Martiniquais biguines.*

In English Creole-speaking Belize the *bruckdown* is a quadrille-derived set dance, similar to the Jamaican *bruckins*, and semantically if not choreographically related to the U.S. "breakdown." "Bruckdown-Belize Style" by Jesus Acosta and The Professionals (*From Belize with Love*, Contemporary Electronic Systems CES 7805) has four dances (*Degagez* ["dégagé"], *Action, Ou pas Bensoiw,* and *La Lancha* ["lancers"]) threaded together by percussion interludes with rhythms suggestive of Martiniquais *cadence* drumming.

In Cuba the *contradanza* arrived by way of the French planters and slaves from Haiti who, following the 1791 slave rebellion, settled in

Oriente Province, especially in the cities of Santiago de Cuba and Guantanamo. The slaves' Tumba-Francesca societies of these cities developed drum-accompanied versions of these French dances called *cocoyé, masón, babril, catá,* and *juba*.[18] A *masón* can be heard on *Antologia de la Musica Afrocubana*, Vol. VII: *Tumba Francesca* (Areito LD-3606).

In the middle of the nineteenth century other European dance forms such as the *cuadrillos* and the *lanceros* entered urban Cuban society, and along with the evolved *contradanza*, a quick-paced double-theme form, they were the basis for creolization into the *danza*, or *habanera*, in the mid-1800s. The *danzón* was a further development of the same dance in the late 1800s, a three-musical-theme couple dance, quite similar in form and development to ragtime of the same period in New Orleans.[19] The *danzón* became especially associated with *charanga* orchestras; by the 1940s a *mambo* section was added to the end. Since the *cha-cha* developed out of the *mambo*, both these dances ultimately belong to the *contradanza* family. In other areas under the influence of Cuban music, even Dutch Curaçao, drums are important, and the Cuban *danza* seems to be a reinforcing influence ("Erani ta Malu" is an example, on *Tumba Cuarta & Ka'i*, Original Music OMC 202). By contrast, in another Spanish-speaking area, Venezuelan string band music uses no drums, but nevertheless shows its relationship to traditional *contredanse*. (Hear "Las Viejas" and "La Tremenda," examples of polka and merengue derived from the Venezuelan dance cycle, on Maria Rodriguez, *Songs from Venezuela*, World Circuit WC 001.)

In Brazil, the *quadrilha* continues as a regional dance, and is especially performed on the Festa Junina (mid-summer day), mostly in the Northeast (*Isto é Quadrilha*, Campeiro KCL 62033). And in coastal Suriname the *seti* dance is a multi-part form paralleling the *contredanse*, but using English and American melodies.

Quadrilles and other ballroom-derived set dances are by no means merely survivals of European culture in the West Indies and South America. They remain vital in their own right and also affect the development of popular music in the New World. The 1984 LP *Yélélé* (GD 0202), by Pierre-Edouard Decimus and Jacob Desvarieux (the leaders of the disco-*zouk* band from Guadeloupe, Kassav'), includes "Kavalié O Dam," which opens with the title chanted, the traditional call for gentlemen to get their partners, and then moves through a catalogue of dances (including clogging); as if this message of pan-national quadrillia weren't clear enough, a U.S.-type country fiddle enters to churn up a hoedown. All this, against a drum-machine beat and words in French Créole. Similarly, Jamaican rapper Sister Carol's "Wild Thing," from the end of the soundtrack recording of Jonathan Demme's film *Something*

Wild (1985), joins a reggae beat with U.S. country banjo and fiddle: near the end Sister Carol cries out, "schottische!"[20]

Musical creolization (the fusion of two or more historically unrelated forms) is nicely illustrated in contrast to the West Indies by the case of the Seychelles, an archipelago of islands in the Indian Ocean northeast of Madagascar, first colonized by the French in 1770–1796 and later by the English in 1796–1976. Slaves from the Malagasy and East Africa were used as laborers in the development of the spice industry. Here, in these islands whose *Créole* language, architecture, dress, and people make them seem as if they were West Indians on the wrong side of Africa, the local dance is the *kamtole*, a suite of country dances that date from contact with the European *contredanse* in the late 1700s. Their first local *contredanses* feature two violins, a mandolin, a triangle, and drum. Later, other dances were added to form suites—the polka, the schottische, and the one-step; and the accordion, banjo, and guitar were added to the orchestra. Finally, English, Scots, and Irish folk melodies were included, entering the Seychelles when the English introduced the quadrille. Today the *kamtole* suite can include the waltz, schottische, mazurka, polka, "jazz" (one-step), four *contredanses* directed by a caller who improvises calls, the *écossaire, belin* (a polka variant), and *katpas* (*pas de quatre*). These dances continue to exist alongside older African musical forms of dance and music.[21] A contrast in the opposite direction—the non-creolized—is provided by set dance music from Quebec. In rural France, like rural Quebec—areas at least culturally much closer to the urban sources for the spread of French "country" dances—the fiddle was initially the central instrument, eventually to be replaced by the accordion.

Dance Suites Among Afro-Americans in the United States

In the United States, the most common ballroom dance form in the early nineteenth century was the cotillion of five or six dances in different meters and tempos. The American sets also incorporated newer round dances such as the waltz, the polka, and the schottische. Further variations developed in the suite form to include the Lancers and Caledonia quadrilles.[22] Dance orchestras of the nineteenth century were often called social orchestras or quadrille bands, and were composed of two violins (the second often doubling as caller), a cello for the bass part and clarinets, flutes, cornets, harp, or piano. These orchestras used arrangements which allowed them to expand or contract in size (down to a trio or duet) or sometimes to switch from strings to brass. A typical ball in New Hampshire in 1859 consisted of 17 quadrilles, 2 contradances, and 4 other multiple dance forms.[23]

Freedmen and urban slaves are attested to having attended formal balls at which dance suites were the central form of activity.[24] Just how important and widespread these dances became is shown by the fact that the ex-slaves who were repatriated back to Liberia beginning in 1820 took the quadrille with them; and when they became the ruling elite of that country, they made it into something of a national dance. It continued to be popular at least well into the 1950s.[25]

Long before the emergence of ragtime there were a considerable number of Afro-American orchestra directors and composers at work on dance music. The outstanding social dance orchestra of its time was that of black Philadelphian Francis Johnson (1792–1844), violinist, horn player, dance caller, arranger, and composer of songs, concert works, and dance suites such as "La Sonnambula Quadrille Number Two" (*Come and Trip It: Instrumental Dance Music 1780s–1920s*, New World Records NW 293). The quality of his orchestra and the freshness of his music led to national and European tours. Richard Walm, a contemporary, spoke of Johnson's fame and ability to reshape songs into new quadrilles:

In fine, he is the leader of the band at all balls, public and private; sole director of all serenades . . . inventor-general of cotillions; to which add, a remarkable taste in distorting a sentimental, simple, and beautiful song, into a reel, jig, or country-dance.[26]

In addition to turning songs into dances, Johnson's orchestra wrote original songs into his quadrilles for the orchestra to sing, a bold innovation recognized in the title of his famous "Voice Quadrille" (*19th Century American Ballroom Music*, Nonesuch H-71313).[27]

Johnson was the most internationally known black musician of his time, but in the early to mid-1800s a number of others—J. W. Postlewaite, James Hemmenway, Basile Bares, and N. Clark Smith, to name a few—were leading composers of dance music in cities such as Boston, New Orleans, St. Louis, New York, and Philadelphia.[28] The published cotillions and quadrilles of these composers were multi-sectioned, multi-strained dances in various forms, including the 5-part rondo (ABACA); they were typically in 2/4 or 6/8 time; they changed key with each new section; and they were written in a variety of rhythms. (Yet everything we know about Afro-American musical performance style tells us that this music was played with greater flexibility and rhythmic subtlety than the notation of sheet music can suggest.) Even the round dances—the waltz, polka, etc.—written by these composers could be complex and suite-like. The "Rescue Polka Mazurka" (1869), for example, alternates polka and mazurka rhythms. (Compare with the Cuban "new" [c. 1898] *danzón*'s two sections of 32 measures, the first in 2/4 and the second in 6/8.) What was being developed was a form capable of absorbing folk, popular, and classical musics and molding them to new functions. A similar form with equally synthesizing power was to resurface with new rhythmic inventions at the end of the nineteenth century with the black composers of ragtime. As Floyd and Reisser put it, we can see "an unbroken line of development from the music of the early black composers of social dance . . . to the beginnings of notated ragtime."[29]

Meanwhile, folk and rural versions of set dances and dance suites were flourishing in nineteenth-century America. The ex-slaves interviewed by the WPA in the 1930s show that the dances most often remembered from slavery days were contradances, square dances, the cotillion, the waltz, and the quadrille (though the individual steps remembered for these dances seem to be strictly Afro-American—juba, buck dancing, and the like).[30] Various descendants of these dances persist today, and two states have been especially well served by recorded surveys: for Virginia, there are square dances, reels, breakdowns, and buck dances played on accordions, banjos, fiddles, harmonicas, and guitar on *Virginia Traditions: Non-Blues Secular Black Music*, Blue Ridge Institute BRI-001; and for North Carolina, reels and buck dances on guitar, banjo, and fiddle are on *Eight-Hand Sets & Holy Steps*, Crossroads C-101.

In black French areas the earliest instrumental music was mazurkas and *contredanses* played by accordion, two violins, and *bastrinque* (triangle) or just by two violins.[31] The second black creole musician to make records can be heard on *Amadé Ardoin* (Old Timey 124), but the three-minute time limit of the 78 rpm record keeps us from seeing the complex organization of these tunes as part of a dance cycle (and paradoxically reinforces our own contemporary provincial ideas about the brevity of popular music). Pops Foster, the New Orleans bass player (who began his career in small string groups), recalls playing for black and white French audiences in the country c. 1906:

They liked their music very fast and they danced to it. Some of the numbers they liked were "Lizard on the Rail," "Red, Oh Red," "Chicken Reel," and "Tiger Rag." They had a guy who called figures for them. First you'd play eight bars of a tune, then stop. Then the announcer would get up and call, "get your partners." When everybody got their partners, he'd blow a whistle and the band would start playing again. The announcer would call figures like, "Ladies Cross, Gent's Right, Promenade" and all that stuff. You'd play three fast numbers then take it down to a waltz, a slow blues, or a schottische.[32]

Though this music is usually identified with Anglo-American fiddle traditions, travelers' accounts of music in cities all across the country—Richmond, Wheeling, Baltimore, Charleston—mention black fiddlers playing and calling reels for white and black audiences.[33] And Afro-American influences on fiddling are obvious even on the earliest recordings we have of this music. Speaking of the syncretism of British and African musical

practices within the southern Piedmont and Appalachian fiddle traditions, Alan Jabbour says:

Especially notable is the way syncopations at the very heart of the music of the
American South are not simply superimposed, but actually built into the bowing
patterns. The pattern . . . which divides eight sixteenths into groups of 3-3-2 is
fundamental here and in the bowing of other fiddlers throughout the South.[34]

The fiddle was extraordinarily popular among slave musicians.[35] Even
where fiddle melodies may have been purely European-derived, fiddles were often played "African"-style: for example, a second player—a
straw-beater—was sometimes used to add rhythm to the melody, as in
this 1882 description of a cotillion dance following a corn-shucking in
Georgia:

The performer provides himself with a pair of straws about eighteen inches in
length, and stout enough to stand a good smart blow. . . . These straws are used
after the manner of drum-sticks, that portion of the fiddle-strings between the
fiddler's bow and his left hand serving as a drum. One of the first sounds which
you hear on approaching the dancing party is the *tum tee tum* of the straws, and
after the dance begins, when the shuffling of feet destroys the other sounds of
the fiddle, this noise can still be heard.[36]

When the stringed instrument was as large as the bass, however, it was
struck by sticks. (Hear drummer Ray Bauduc and bassist Bob Haggart
on the Bob Crosby band's 1939 recording, "Big Noise From Winnetka"
(Bob Crosby, *Suddenly It's 1939*, Giants of Jazz GOJ 1032.) This practice
is of Kongo origin, similar to the *ti-bwa* sticks on the side of drums in
Guadeloupe, or the *cajónero* (in Peru) on the strings of the guitar. (For examples of Kongo drumming itself in the New World, hear *juba* on *Ritual
Drums of Haiti*, Lyrichord LLST 7279, and *Tambor de Crioula*, FUNARTE,
Rio CDFB 012, from Brazil.)

The dance calls, too, were different from their European counterparts: more than mere directions, they took the shape of rhymed "raps,"
adding rhythmic subtlety and humor that helped spirit both the dancers
and band alike.[37] Willis James quotes one "caller-out" this way:

If you like the way she look
Hand the lady your pocketbook.
Swing her fancy,
    Come to the middle,
    But be careful, don't bust the fiddle.[38]

(The best parallel in another genre is cadence-counting in the military:
Afro-American drill sergeants introduced both melody and syncopated
rhythm into the pattern and permanently altered the "ONE-two-three-four"

call which had dominated Western military marching for centuries. The same could be said for the influence of black cheerleaders on audiences for American athletics.) Black square dance- and reel-calling are part of the Afro-American dance instruction song tradition which extends from "Ballin the Jack" to "The Twist" and beyond (songs which tell the dancers what to do next), and which is at least partly rooted in the older tradition in which African master drummers signal and direct dancers.[39]

It was Lafcadio Hearn who in 1876 observed the black roustabouts on the riverfront of Cincinnati dancing a quadrille to the "Devil's Dream" (accompanied by fiddle, banjo, and bass), gradually transforming it into a Virginia reel, and then changing it again, this time to a "juba dance" done to a shout-like call-and-response song.[40]

Again, there is the sense that these European dance forms were flexible and open to transformation and improvisation, at least within the performances of Afro-Americans. It seems odd, then, that many writers on ragtime and early jazz underplay their importance. Certainly the oldest jazz musicians recalled playing for quadrille and set dances around 1900: Johnny St. Cyr in New Orleans, Wilbur Sweatman in St. Louis, and Perry Bradford in Atlanta, for instance.[41] The mother of New Orleans clarinetist George Lewis recalled dance music of the 1880s this way:

At a dance, before the quadrille time—they'd give about two or three quadrilles a night—but before the quadrille came, they would play a waltz, you'd have to waltz around the floor. Lancers and varieties, that's in quadrille, and "balancé, balancé"; that's in quadrille too.[42]

Alphonse Picou's orchestra played four or five sets a night, c. 1897, each consisting of a mazurka, a waltz, a schottische, a polka, a two-step, then ending with a quadrille and a march.[43] By 1910 these sets had changed to include a two-step, slow drag, ragtime one-step, and the fox-trot. But the quadrille still remained for the midnight centerpiece.[44]

Most of the older New Orleans musicians also remember playing set dances and dance suites well after the turn of the century. (The modern jazz musician's use of the word "sets" for groups of pieces in live performance probably derives from these older dance forms.) Baby Dodds noted that "there were certain dance halls where we could only play mazurkas, quadrilles, polkas, and schottisches."[45] And those who remember Buddy Bolden, the cornetist usually given credit for being the first important jazz musician, say that he first played in a string band with cornet and/or clarinet (similar to the Cuban *charanga francesca*, c. 1898). His group "might play a schottische and follow that with a variety, 'a long thing made up of waltzes and all kinds of time'"; they played "no ragtime, 'except in the quadrilles or late at night.'"[46] (Nick La Rocca, the trumpet player for the Original Dixieland Jazz Band, the first band to record jazz, also played with string groups of the same type for the first three years of his career, 1905–1908.)[47]

These multi-strain, multi-rhythm dances were ideal forms for the development of early jazz. Under pressure to find new melodies to set against a variety of rhythms, musicians altered conventional patterns and improvised new ones. The New Orleans pianist Armand Hug said "The quadrille was a proper dance, usually limited to a certain social strata, but the Uptown bands changed it to their own style."[48] Jelly Roll Morton in his Library of Congress recordings described and illustrated just how it was changed in his account of how "Tiger Rag" came into being:

"Tiger Rag" happened to be transformed from an old quadrille that was in many different tempos, and I'll no doubt give you an idea of how it went. This was the introduction meaning that everyone was supposed to get their partners . . . it may be five minutes' lapse between the time, an' of course, they'd start it over again, and that was the first part of it . . . then the next strain would be the waltz strain . . . Also, they'd have another strain . . . mazooka time . . . that was that . . . third strain, an' that was in a differen' tempo . . . a two-four time . . . of course, they had another one, . . . now I'll show you how it was transformed . . . I also named it. It came from the way that I played it by "makin' the tiger" on my elbow.[49]

(The French jazz writer Robert Goffin recognized the "Tiger Rag" as the second dance of a quadrille he had heard as a child in Belgium.[50] And others have recognized phrases borrowed from "London Bridge is Falling Down" and the "National Emblem March," along with second chorus riffs which parody the alto part in German brass bands.[51])

New York composer and pianist James P. Johnson said that set dances and dance suites were the basis for a number of jazz compositions. In fact his own "Carolina Shout" was a ragtime arrangement of a set dance preferred by dock workers originally from the Charleston, South Carolina area:

My mother was from Virginia and somewhere in her blood was an instinct for doing country and set dances—what were called "real ['reel'?] shoutings." My "Carolina Shout" and "Carolina Balmoral" are real southern set or square dances. I think the "Carolina Balmoral" was the most spirited dance in the South. I find I have a strong feeling for these dances that goes way back—and I haven't found anyone else with it yet.

One of the men would call the figures and they'd dance their own style of square dances. The calls were . . . "Join hands" . . . "Sashay". . . "Turn around" . . . "Ladies right and gentlemen left" . . . "Grab your partner" . . . "Break away" . . . "Make a strut" . . . "Cows to the front, bulls stay back" . . .

When he called "Do your stuff" or "Ladies to the front," they did their personal dances. The catwalk, for instance, was developed from the cotillion, but it was also part of the set dances. . . .

These people were from South Carolina and Georgia where the cotillion was popular—and the "Charleston" was an offspring of that. It was a dance figure

like the "Balmoral." A lot of my music is based on set, cotillion, and other southern country dance steps and rhythms. . . .

I heard good piano from all parts of the South and West, but I never heard
real ragtime until we came to New York. Most East Coast playing was based on
cotillion dance tunes, stomps, drags, and set dances like my "Mule Walk Blues,"
"Gut Stomp," and the "Carolina Shout" and "Balmoral." They were all country
tunes.[52]

The dances they did at the Jungles Casino were wild and comical—the more
pose and the more breaks, the better. These Charleston people and the other
southerners had just come to New York. They were country people and they felt
homesick. When they got tired of two-steps and schottisches (which they danced
with a lot of spieling), they'd yell: "Let's go back home!" . . . "Let's do a set!" . . .
or "Now put us in the alley!" I did my "Mule Walk" or "Gut Stomp" for these
country dances.[53]

At a piano contest in Egg Harbor, New Jersey in 1914, Johnson first
heard other dance suites for piano which were the basis for various jazz
forms:

There was a pianist there who played quadrilles, sets, rags, etc. From him, I first
heard the walking Texas or boogiewoogie bass. The Boogiewoogie was a cotillion step for which a lot of music was composed.

Johnson's equation of the shout with the quadrille is also important.
It has usually been assumed that the shout was a strictly religious dance
derived from Africa, in which a circle of dancers shuffle counterclock-
wise around one or two dancers while others keep time and sing around
the edges of the room, the point being to bring on possession. But
Johnson was very clear on the secular function of the dance as he knew
it in late nineteenth-century New Brunswick, New Jersey:

The Northern towns had a hold-over of the old Southern customs. I'd wake up
as a child and hear an old-fashioned ring-shout going on downstairs. Somebody
would be playing a guitar or jew's-harp or maybe a mandolin, and the dancing
went to "The Spider and the Bed-Bug Had a Good Time" or "Susie." They
danced around in a shuffle and then they would shove a man or a woman out
into the center and clap hands.[54]

But it was equally clear that these shouts could serve religious functions.
Willie "The Lion" Smith said, "Shouts are stride piano—when James P.
and Fats and I would get a romp-down shout going, that was playing
rocky, just like the Baptist people sing."[55] The ring shout was a widely dif-
fused form, present in country or city, certainly wherever Sanctified or
Holiness churches were to be found. And as such, it seems to have acted
as a reservoir for a variety of African performance style features.[56] Its use
as a secular form as well as a sacred one is not well documented, but fits
patterns of multiple functions seen in the West Indies.[57]

It was Jelly Roll Morton who carried these set forms to their greatest heights in jazz. Perhaps more than any other jazz musician, Morton was concerned with balance in the structure, melody, and rhythm of his compositions. His works for his Red Hot Peppers like "Black Bottom Stomp," and "Grandpa's Spells" were wonders of contrasted texture and form, multi-thematic works in which even repetitions of a theme were varied in instrumentation, rhythm, and dynamics. As he showed with "Tiger Rag," Morton borrowed from the forms of ragtime and quadrille in order to set up sectional contrasts within his song form. This he did not do mechanically, but so creatively that Gunther Schuller suggests that he often reached a level of formal complexity which was close to or even beyond that of the rondo.

Morton's melodies were also quite often borrowed from a wide variety of sources: the blues, ragtime, creole folk songs, marches, operatic arias, Mexican pop songs, Cuban *sones*, music hall melodies, and of course French quadrille tunes. But this wholesale appropriation was not a result of a lack of originality. First, there was already a pattern of melodic borrowing within the quadrille tradition. "Quadrilles consumed melodies at a fearful rate," according to early American popular music scholar Thornton Hagert, "and it was common practice to make the music up out of bits of popular songs or snatches from opera arias."[58] As a result, the quadrille form was often the means for joining together otherwise musically incongruous materials, or for using music in unorthodox ways.[59] But Morton's intention was to "jazz" up these tunes, not merely arrange them in new settings. A certain degree of familiarity with the original melodies was required so that the variations would be understood and appreciated. Besides, as Morton put it, "Jazz is a style that can be applied to any type of tune."[60]

As has often been pointed out, Morton's greatest work appeared on record just at the point when the fashion in music was changing from the multi-strained, complex form to the 32-bar pop song. The biggest names in jazz were now improvising on these simpler forms, and, with certain exceptions, jazz was to be reduced to theme-solo-theme for many years to come. Morton resisted the trend, but it cost him an audience. He was perhaps the last in a nineteenth-century tradition of composers who worked in forms built on the contrast of themes and their variations.

Some writers on the history of ragtime have attempted to minimize the influence of dance suites and set dances, primarily on the basis of very limited notions of what these dances were like and how they were recombined. Edward A. Berlin and Eric Thacker,[61] for instance, both mention the limited possibilities for building rags on 2/4, 3/4 and 6/8 meters. But there is reason to believe that these forms were more flexible and syncretic than has been thought. Dancer Sidney Easton from Savannah, for example, said that "the colored people used a four-four, not a six-eight tempo, four couples at a time, with lots of solo work and improvised breaks by each dancer putting together steps of his own"[62] in their set dances. Certainly, Jelly Roll Morton and James P. Johnson seem to have made an effort to show how the transformations in these forms occurred. In any case, there is no particular reason to see the evolutionary sequence of dance suite-to-ragtime-to-jazz as rigidly unilinear as it has been portrayed. Until very recently at least, jazz was a music for dancing. And in New Orleans, brass bands are still playing multi-thematic musical compositions in second-line rhythm, not just as an evolutionary step towards another musical development, but as a thriving, ongoing tradition of its own.

Nor have we seen the end of the quadrille's influence on jazz. Dennis Charles—drummer with avant-gardists such as Cecil Taylor and Steve Lacy—was born and raised in St. Croix, the Virgin Islands within a family which performed West Indian quadrille music. Asked about his unique approach to playing the cymbal, he said:

What I try to do is . . . years ago in the West Indies these guys used to play and they had a guy who played triangle. The triangle is the kind of beat I try to get, ting-a-ling ting-a-ling, it's the same 3 beats you play on the cymbal, but it's that feeling I try to capture.[63]

All That Beef, and Symbolic Action Too! Notes on the Occasion of the Banning of 2 Live Crew's *As Nasty as They Wanna Be*

If I feel physically as if the top of my head were taken off, I know that it is poetry.

—Emily Dickinson

And is it art just because folklorists can analyze it?

—*"The Importance of Being Nasty,"* Newsweek

Bawdiness, lasciviousness, smut, trash, lewdness, pornography, obscenity, ribaldry, the erotic, the risqué, the salacious, the prurient, whatever you want to call it (I prefer *blue* myself), the sheer variety of terms points to a long cultural obsession. We have more words for blue texts than the Eskimos have for *snow*: surely this tells us something profound about ourselves, and about our past. Now, with the culture police moving on many fronts (and the real police right behind them), with rap music under assault and 2 Live Crew's record *As Nasty as They Wanna Be* the first recording to be banned in many years, and several of the group's members accused of violations of the Racketeer Influenced and Corrupt Organizations (RICO) Act and under arrest for performing the record live in the adults-only Futura Club in Broward County, Florida, a brief meditation on the blue seems timely, if not exactly asked for.

Blue literature is not a recent development, nor is it an exclusive product of a single culture, of the lower classes, of people of color, or of men. Although ingenuously ignored by guardians of tradition, blue comedy has been part of English literature at least since the origins of Middle English and is perpetuated today as part of the canon as taught to high school and college students.[1] Bawdy laughter is at the heart of work of such writers as Shakespeare and Chaucer, who are deified as representing the greatest ideals of the Western humanistic tradition; the same humor also resonates in the writings of such local colorists and regional writers as Robert Burns and Mark Twain. The point seems to be that if it's funny, it's not obscene.[2] "Ornery," maybe, or "cute," but not obscene. In their pornography decisions the courts have in effect been ruling on what is funny and what is not.

Whether all cultures have blue literature remains a question, since the comparative study of pornography has yet to begin. But oral literature of the world—being freer from the constraints of judges, publishers, and other arbiters of taste—suggests that the blue may well be universal. Records such as 2 Live Crew's are themselves inheritors of a variety of spoken-word traditions which include the Jody ("the Grinder") cadence-counts of the military; the routines of burlesque and standup comics; "party" records; the epic toasts of prisons and work camps; American boasting and tall-tales; the songs and verse of fraternities and sororities;[3] and Euro- and African American children's taunts, jump rope rhymes, and Mother Goose parodies. (Just how bawdy Euro-American children can be has been massively documented for English speakers by Wendy Lowenstein, Sandra McCosh, and Ian Turner; for German-speaking children by Ernest Borneman; and for the French by Claude Gaignebet.[4] Judging by these scholars' evidence, it is not kids who need protection from pornography; it's adults who need protection from children.)

Because of this tangle of cultural sources, our efforts at understanding blue material have usually been superficial or wrong. Take for example, the dozens, the game in which young black males insult each other with sexual remarks about each other's mother. In the 1960s, social scientists glibly diagnosed this contest as a consequence of slaveholders' breeding practices, matrifocal families, or a reaction to racial stereotyping; or again, as proof of sexual ambivalence, arrested development, whatever. But how differently reads this 164-year-old African account, which may be the earliest written reference to such "playing": "We must distinguish the respect, obedience and affection which they always show toward their mothers. The greatest insult one can utter is the all too familiar *sahr sa ndci* (by the genitalia of your mother). This oath has frequently been drowned in blood."[5] Needless to say, the cultural pathologists never bother to look for historical antecedents. If they did, they would have seen that blue rapping is neither recent nor especially black. To name only one case close to home, Vance Randolph's "Ribaldry at Ozark Dances" transcribes blue square dance calls from country parties in the early 1900s, where drunkenness, gang wars, gun play, and sexual assaults were also common. From Columbia, Missouri, circa 1918, here is a call for "Turkey in the Straw":

Grab her by the right leg, swing her half around,
Grab her by the left leg, throw her on the ground,
Stick it in the middle and a bobble up and down,
When you come to her ass-hole, go on around.[6]

Or from Washington County, Arkansas, circa early 1900s:

The more you fuck her, the louder she'll squeal,
The louder she hollers, the better you'll feel

Log-chain your sweetie, log-tie your honey,
Stick it up her ass, get the worth of your money[7]

It would truly be an academic exercise to attempt to determine whether these "traditional" Anglo-American texts are more or less violent and misogynous than those of contemporary Afro-American youth.

Nor is the blue domain occupied by men alone. The relative scarcity of women's bawdy texts in print is more a matter of who controls publication than it is evidence of a lack of interest. At least we know that when sound recordings became possible, gross themes flourished among many women performers: Victoria Spivey's "Handy Man" (1928), Lucille Bogan's "Shave 'Em Dry" (1935), Lizzie Miles's "My Man o' War" (1930), and Lil Johnson's "Hottest Gal in Town" (1936) are classic blues of their kind.[8] By the 1940s it was possible for a woman to build a commercial career on blue material. (Julia Lee, for example, had hits with "Snatch and Grab It," "My Man Stands Out," "Don't Come Too Soon," and "All This Beef and Big Ripe Tomatoes.") Nor is verbal sexual abuse exclusively male: Millie Jackson's recordings and performances of the 1970s seethe with caustic suggestion and censure,[9] and in more recent times Roxanne Shanté's live appearances are strewn with male-baiting and trashing.

Censorious law-makers fatuously talk about community standards, but in practice it is hard to know who is going to find what offensive. Even pornographers can be offended: Bessie Smith's "Empty Bed Blues," a favorite of Frieda von Richthofen, so enraged her lover, D. H. Lawrence, that he furiously broke the record against the wall in Harry Crosby's Paris apartment. And we are continually surprised to find out who's been working on the blue production line. Tampa Red's Hokum Jug Band 1929 recording of "How Long, How Long Blues" (a record admittedly without a single offensive word, but with such moaning, puffing, and double-entendres that its meaning is all too clear) included Georgia Tom Dorsey, the same Thomas A. Dorsey who was one of the inventors of gospel music. And Jimmie Davis—twice a fundamentalist, segregationist governor of Louisiana—had in a former life recorded such songs as "High Behind Blues" (1932) and "Tom Cat and Pussy Blues" (1932), accompanied by black guitarist Oscar Woods.

By the same token, the line usually drawn between the acceptable and the obscene is outrageously hypocritical. When the Hollywood Argyles sang, "I'm a mean motorscooter and a bad go-getter" in their 1960 hit "Alley Oop," their sly bowdlerization rested on their audience's familiarity with rough street talk.[10] In fact, all the "cute" and "ornery" double-entendres of TV, movies, and Vegas clubs depend on an underlying community of shared deeper blue meanings. And today no one raises an eyebrow over the mainstreaming (and franchising) of corporate names such as that of the Mother Truckers or the restaurant chain, Fuddruckers.[11]

Rock and *roll* are themselves words whose sexual meanings are barely concealed.[12] But these same terms also have their place in black religious discourse, as do words like the *house, daddy, baby,* being *taken higher,* and all those words of ecstasy and possession. The aesthetic of vernacular music always draws at least part of its strength from this criss-crossing of semantic domains and the teasing ambiguity that results. From its origins in burlesque, vaudeville, and the tent show, rock 'n' roll is built on a hierarchy of tease that implies that lipsyncing is singing, that the body is doing something other than dancing, that white may be black, that male may be female, and that something other than music may be about to happen—revolution, violence, spiritual revelation, sex. But when on the rare occasion that something else does actually happen, the show is over, the spell shattered. (The final phase of the decline of The Doors can be marked in 1969, when Jim Morrison exposed himself on stage in Miami.)

But what of the case in point, 2 Live Crew's *As Nasty As They Wanna Be*? Recorded by a group of young men who think of themselves as comedians and perform in the Rudy Ray Moore tradition, the record—which in another age would have been found in the "comedy" bins of stores that cater to Afro-Americans—somehow found its way under the broad category of popular music of America.[13] The record itself is a catalog of rude bumper sticker slogans, schoolyard catches, and taunts; selections of toasts; conventional male boasts and student fantasies about teachers; received sexual wisdom of the streets; perverse pillow talk; sampled disco moans and lines from *Full Metal Jacket*; advertising slogans; Latin music struts; reggae allusions; metal riffs; parodies of various ethnic dialects; and songs whose melodies are built from the speech tones and rhythms of insults and expletives. Throughout it all runs a selection of what in Anglo-American folklore is known as monstrous tools, awed maidens, lethal bitches, much mechanico-surreal sexual posturing and verbal cod pieces, and not a little bit of anxiety and distrust of women.[14] Gritty stuff, disrespectful, and only occasionally funny, but very little that couldn't also be found spread among the writings of Norman Mailer, *Finnegans Wake*, and the documented outbursts of ex-president George H. W. Bush. And nothing, for that matter, that couldn't be heard in the many X-rated records of Blowfly, an artist-producer who has been churning out blue rap unmolested in Miami for at least the last fifteen years.[15]

Offensive, yes, and especially offensive to women, but is *As Nasty As They Wanna Be* legally obscene? Does it appeal to prurient interests? Less so, I would think, than the TV soaps (where *bitch*, incidentally, is apparently an acceptable word), even among the pathologically suggestible. Does it contain patently offensive conduct? Yes, but compared to what one routinely sees in the movies? More to the point, no judge seems willing to locate both arousal and disgust within the same text or audience (and certainly not within themselves). So, as legal scholar Kathleen M. Sullivan has argued, to make *Miller v. California* work as a standard, the community must be segregated, and arousal attributed to a sexual or ethnic minority, while disgust is located within the majority.[16]

Yet the Court may still ask if there is any literary, artistic, political, or scientific value to these songs and chants. Suffice it to say that this is not very deep stuff (that Judge José Gonzalez, Jr., could get a 62-page decision out of it means nothing other than someone was paying him more per word than they are me). But at least this much about it is of value: it serves to remind us that in an age when no other forms of literature are believed to have any social force (even sedition is no longer taken seriously, and cop-killer songs seem protected by the First Amendment), obscenity is still believed to have social consequences. If that were really true we ought to be devoting ourselves to its study in order to understand its verbal magic. Yet I suspect that on the contrary, the hatred of obscenity is part of a sentimental and desperate attempt to cling to an imagined past where some form of literature mattered. But it's too late even for porn. Left to itself, it has little demonstrable effect overall, except as part of the deadening semiotic barrage that we respectfully still speak of as our culture.

I suppose the cynic will say that if 2 Live Crew or other rappers ever do time in the slammer they will at least find new ideas there for future recordings. But I would say that they could also find fresh material at less public expense in that other dwelling place of the incorrigible and the recidivistic, the library.

Addendum: 1993

After the foregoing was written, 2 Live Crew went to court and was acquitted.[17] Central to the defense argument were the testimonies of John Leland, pop music critic for *Newsday*, who argued that the defendants' material was well within the rap tradition, and that of Professor Louis Henry Gates, Jr., of Harvard, who extended Leland's point by arguing that routines such as 2 Live Crew's were part of the black folk aesthetic and were examples of literary art. In hindsight we know that the jurors claimed that the literary and cultural arguments played no part in the decision, and indeed did not even consider race in their discussions. Instead, 2 Live Crew was acquitted in part because the police could not accurately transcribe what they claimed was obscene, much less decode what they had transcribed, so that the jury and witnesses could not agree on what they were hearing. (A similar conclusion was reached by the FBI, when it gave up after two years of trying to find the obscene meaning of the Kingsmen's 1963 recording of "Louie Louie.")[18] But in spite of this, the jury had no difficulty in recognizing that the material was funny, and even asked the judge for permission to laugh. In the end the jury foreman said that they felt it wasn't obscene because it was funny.[19]

In his recent *Black Studies, Rap, and the Academy*, Houston A. Baker, Jr., struggles mightily to locate the 2 Live Crew affair outside of a strict context of race and to find a middle ground between George Will's association of rap music with the Central Park jogger rape and Gates's and Leland's literary and cultural defense of what many consider antiwomanist poetry. In fact, Baker's criticism of Gates's testimony would regard my "defense" of 2 Live Crew as being what he calls "the others do it, so why persecute we?" argument, and answers that the "widespread existence of male sexual brutality does not mean that any given appearance of it should be regarded by scholars as simply another speeding vehicle on the highway of popular culture's dark underbelly."[20] He goes on to say that 2 Live Crew was "understandably banned" and to imply that they should have been because "common sense alone suggests a correlation" between the existence of such verbal material and the incidence of violence against women in the United States, and that such violence should not be protected free speech.[21] Granting Baker the correlation (though not necessarily the significance of the correlation), one might also correlate much of Western art and literature with such violence.

I am sympathetic with Baker's plea for treating such a case in a larger framework than race. In fact, my previous comments were meant to call attention to a cultural complex that goes far beyond the American mythology of color. And I agree with his resentment of the law and the media for handing us the choice of having to defend *this* kind of verbal behavior. But we do not get much choice as to where our battles will be fought—even the trial of *Lady Chatterley's Lover* left literary critics uneasy. Leland and Gates were given a case in which still more young black men were going to jail and it was not clear what their crime was. Were they guilty of saying nasty, even violent, things about women in an unfunny way? Or of allowing a culturally specific text to be recontextualized, in terms of both audience and medium?[22] Whatever it was, they were made scapegoats of race, in long unresolved cultural matters, as part of the current demoralization of young black men. And on that point, I believe Baker would agree with me.

Chapter 21
The Real Old School

Does rap have a beginning? Where does the credit or (some might say) the blame lie? The quick answer is to say that it's an African-American form for which, on a diasporic flow chart, you could plot an unbroken line from Africa to the Caribbean and on to the United States. Or maybe bypassing the Caribbean altogether, but in any case ending with the youth of the black working class. Yet things in the United States have never been *that* simple. Or that pure. The origins of everything American twist and shout their way through history, giving and taking as they go, inventing and reinventing themselves, praising their authentic beginnings about as often as they deny them.

Americans have always been creole—and whether "creole" refers to food, speech, music, or race, it always means something made new, something emergent, not an import from Europe, Africa, Asia, whatever. Try it another way: America has been postmodern from the git-go, with everything out on the table, history unfolding, putting it all up for grabs. It is a country in which mixture is king. And as the poet said, the pure products of America would go crazy anyway.

Rap caught most of America looking, something new pitched at them when they least expected it, right at the height of the reign of disco's decorous salon society. To many it meant liberation and a return to the real stuff: 1970s dance music had buried an emotionally charged, folk-based 1960s soul music which spoke in the victorious poetic rhetoric of civil rights and black power. All those elements of black folk culture that had been denied by the elegance and pretense of the ballroom or the club came back with a vengeance on the avenues and in the parks. Performers were free again to talk that talk, to insert curses, blessings, and jokes into their raps, and to return to the funky, individually grained voices that disco had made to seem gauche. Most of all, rap put black musical performances back on a collective basis, a social mix in which the community's ethos could be affirmed, or where new and even forbidden ideas could be tested. Folks were dancing in the streets again.

But even as rap may have been a welcome innovation, something about its form also seemed vaguely familiar, even to its young advocates, who had no interest in what used to be. Rap is rhythmic talk, talk leaning toward music. Yet all speech is to some degree rhythmic, with stresses occurring at regular intervals to make sounds easier to understand (in English, for example, stresses divide sounds into equally spaced units regardless of how slow or fast the speech); and all speech is musical in that some syllables are pitched higher or lower than others. What's more, stress and pitch are related (in English, high-pitched syllables are normally stressed). Rap, then, falls somewhere between the worlds of music and talk, but sharing with both.

As a form of heightened speech, rap also finds kinship with a wide variety of other forms, some from the most innocent and primal moments of childhood, others from pop culture, still others from some of the most sublime examples of American oratory. Highly rhythmic and pitched speech has always been part of children's counting-out chants and game songs as a means of instructing and coordinating activity. One of the classics (and one which crossed over into pop song) is "Little Sally Walker":

Little Sally Walker
Sitting in a saucer
Rise, Sally, rise
Wipe your dirty eyes
Put your hand on your hip
Don't let your backbone slip

Similar routines have been used by adults for cadence-counting chants in military drills, in work songs, and in tobacco auctioneering. One of the earliest forms of popular entertainment, the square dance, was unique in the Western world for the instructions chanted out in the rhythm of the dance by the callers. And for at least one hundred years one of the most popular types of music has been the dance instruction song— like "Ballin' the Jack," "It's Pony Time," or "The Hucklebuck"—in which how-to-do-it directions are inserted between the choruses. It's no surprise that cheerleaders' chants often contain bits and pieces of all of the above.

Sometimes the instructional element of games is highlighted in the form of word puzzles, as when pig latin-like languages are used: Shirley Ellis put music to one such puzzle in "The Name Game" (1964), making it a language game you could dance to. No wonder that some of the earliest recorded raps—such as Frankie Smith's 1981 "Double Dutch Bus"— contained allusions to double Dutch jump rope as well as to a form of trick childhood speech known by the same name:

Rebecca, Lolita, Veshawn and Dawn
Everytime you do the double Dutch you really turn it on
Bilzarbra, Milzery, Milzetty, Kilsan
Tilzommy, Kilzerrance, Kilzommy, that's my man
Come on, get on my double Dutch Bus

If play is one end of the heightened speech spectrum, high oratory is the other. Martin Luther King Jr., was only the most visible of a long tradition of preachers who spoke of "singing the word," of bringing the Spirit to bear on the merely verbal, of exhorting the masses. When ministers like Jesse Jackson took to the barricades in the civil rights struggle, the meter and melody of their sermons set the standard by which the rhetoric of political figures like Malcolm X was measured.

Much has also been made of the technologically sophisticated context in which rap emerged—the use of sound processing, sampling, mixing, drum machines, and the panoply of studio apparatus typically used with today's raps—as a means of showing that rap is radically new and only secondarily beholden to folklore and tradition. But sophisticated as these productions may be, the artful logic that lies beneath them has been part of African-American aesthetics for at least a century.

You don't have to romanticize musical history to acknowledge that sound processing and effects can be found on recordings from the early part of the 1900s. Think of closely overlapped vocals in work songs as delay; growling, humming, and bent notes as fuzz effects and flanging; falsetto and false bass in vocals and early instrumental music as octave splitting and the products of harmonizers. And think of the wash and panning effects of choirs and big bands; the wah-wah of plungers and hats over horns. Scratching is heard in the early rhythmic use of sandpaper, animal jawbones, rub-boards, rattles, and gourds filled with seed, as well as in their aural equivalent in stuttered words and verbal distortions, like double Dutch speech. In fact, you'd be hard-pressed to find any new electronic effects that don't have their older African-American acoustic equivalent.

Sampling too has its roots in vocal interpolations in early African-American pop balladry and jazz instrumental "quotations," and cutting and mixing are essential to multiparted singing styles, early jazz performances, even folktales. Among the African-derived coastal people of Surinam, the interplay of folktale and songs is called *cutsingi* and "cutting" (in one language or another) is a basic term in the musical vocabulary of Haitians, Cubans, and many English-speaking West Indians, as it is among African-Americans. Even drum machines were anticipated by scat singing (and in case anyone forgot, human beat box imitations of drum machines also remind us that drums were once used to imitate voices for sending messages). No wonder hip-hop musicians treat technology with an air of casual demystification: their ancestors in-vented all of these technologies in their acoustic forms.

While rap meant a return to basics for some, for many others it was only further proof that America was already on the way to what columnist George Will called its "slide into the sewer." To them it was unprecedented, noisy black male boasting, verbalized criminality, misogyny, and raw obscenity. But was it truly without precedent? Take the boasting rap, the song of self-praise, the self-advertisement: America has always been a boasting country, its denizens seeing themselves as a breed apart, and there have always been those who were masters of the art of making their own noise. The tall-talking backwoods boasters among the early West settlers, for example: the ring-tailed roarers and those who described themselves as born of half horse-half alligator stock. You could hear them among Mark Twain's riverboat men in *Life on the Mississippi*. "Look at me!" one of them cried out. "I'm the man they call Sudden Death and General Desolation. Sired by a hurricane, dam'd by an earthquake! Look at me! I take alligators and a bar'l of whiskey for breakfast!" You could also hear them among the blues singers in the bars on the South Side of Chicago in the 1950s:

I was raised on the desert, born in a lion's den
My chief occupation is taking monkey-men's women.

I'm drinkin' TNT, I'm smokin' dynamite
I hope some screwball start a fight.

Or:

I'm sold to the devil
Trouble is all I crave
I'd rather see you dead
And layin' in your grave.

Even the gangsta raps and epics of criminal badness of performers like N.W.A, Ice Cube, the Geto Boys, and those who came after them are far from new—or even uniquely African-American. America has had a long romance with bandits, outlaws, and bad guys. Well before books and films about mass murderers and bank robbers, there were the bad man songs of the West, folk songs about John Dillinger, Pretty Boy Floyd, and Jesse James (themselves an updating of old Anglo-Saxon ballads of robbers, murderers, and warriors—in fact, Teddy Roosevelt publicly declared his patriotic delight when he realized that American serial killer Jesse James had replaced British Robin Hood as the world's most popular bandit).

Some would blame rap for the spread of obscenity and profanity into pop culture, but nasty talk has had its part to play in songs from every stratum of American society, whether it be sophisticates like Cole Porter ("Let's Do It"); fundamentalists and segregationists like country singer Jimmie Davis (twice governor of Louisiana) who in an earlier life recorded bawdy songs like "Tom Cat and Pussy Blues" and "High Behind Blues" with black musicians; or religious figures like Thomas A. Dorsey, the father of American gospel music, who as Georgia Tom Dorsey, along with Tampa Red, once recorded such lewd material as "How Long, How Long Blues." Even in the most highly sanitized days of early white rock 'n' roll, the meaning of lines like "I'm a mean motorscooter and a bad go-getter" from the Hollywood Argyles' 1960 hit "Alley Oop" depended on listeners being familiar with street talk.

Disrespectful music about women can scarcely be blamed on contemporary young black males alone. In the first decade of this century, whites at Ozark country parties (where drunkenness, violence, gunplay, gang wars, and sexual assaults were common) square-danced to calls like this one:

Log-chain your sweetie, log-tie your honey
Stick it up her ass, get the worth of your money

Women too have played a role in gender-bashing and nastiness, as can be heard from any number of records by female blues singers in the 1920s and 1930s (Lucille Bogan, Victoria Spivey, and Lizzie Miles to name a few), and by the 1940s it was possible for a singer like Julia Lee to have national hits with songs like "Snatch and Grab It" and "Don't Come Too Soon."

But having noted rap's broad affinities, its American-ness, its creole emergence, and its lack of exclusive rights to be offensive, no one would be fooled into missing the fact that it finally is also very much an African-American form. Rap departs from the regular stresses of English, redeploys them, making the sounds and words jump to a superimposed beat. It retunes English, causing pitch and stress to move independently, making speech appear even less speech-like and more musical. When the words come in a staccato beat, the syllables of English begin to take on new sounds—the familiar standard English formula of vowel-consonant-vowel gives way to the rapid-fire of consonant-vowel, consonant-vowel. (By contrast, before they figured things out, raps from Europe in the early 1980s were either simple chants or weakly rhythmic tirades.) Rappers often point to the chattering, irregular rhythms of the snare and bass drum in bebop as one source for modern rap. But well before the bop revolution of the mid-1940s, jazz musicians like Frankie Newton

("The Onyx Hop" in 1937) and Louis Prima ("House Rent Party" in 1934) were using words in the drum rhythms of their times.

But even more important, the African-American tradition that led to rap is revealed by the ease with which speech sits within music. In Europe, songs have been inserted into speech for centuries in what are called *cante fables*, where folktale-tellers break off from their stories to go into song. Among African-Americans, the pattern is just the other way around: preachers sermonize rhythmically within gospel singers' songs, doo-wop quartets testify in the middle of their ballads, and rhythm 'n' blues singers like Bo Diddley work sly insults and the dozens into conversational songs like "Say, Man." Whereas in Europe the introduction and praising of the performers occur at the beginning or endings of songs, among African-Americans they normally occur inside, while the music is still playing.

The most likely candidate for a direct forebear of modern rap is the toast, the rhymed monologue, an African-American poetic form that typically recounts the adventures of a group of heroes who often position themselves against society either as so shrewd and powerful as to be superhuman, or so bad and nasty as to be subhuman. Toasts tell stories like "Staggerlee," "The Signifying Monkey," or "The Freaks' Ball," stories that could thrive in the prisons, the army, and on the street. "The Titanic"—or "Shine," as it is sometimes known—tells the story (in first-person) of a character so strong and resourceful that he not only escapes the sinking of the great ship but also resists the pleasures of crossing racial lines for sex when it means risking death by water.

Toasts sometimes turned up completely intact in raps, as on James Brown's "King Heroin" in 1972, or in Schoolly D's first recordings. But more often they went through transformations before they returned in pop form, as in Jalal Nuriddin's influential 1973 recording of *Hustler's Convention*. Nuriddin was a member of the Last Poets, a group that joined the poetry of the prison to black militant rhetoric and processed it through beatnik and jazz sensibilities, against the crack of conga drums. Nuriddin's own solo efforts had even more direct influences on modern rap.

Radio DJs, meanwhile, had picked up something of the rhythm and the rhetoric of the toasts, and had made them part of their routines as they rhymed their way between and over records. You could hear Dr. Hep Cat from Austin, Texas, Dr. Daddy-O from New Orleans, and many others on local stations throughout the South. Later, new rhyming personalities boomed out from the high-wattage stations of the North— people like Georgie Woods in Philadelphia, Daddy-O Daylie in Chicago, or Jocko Henderson on WOV, whose routines became so popular that they were used as greetings on the street:

Be, bebop
This is your jock
Back on the scene
With a record machine
Saying "Hoo-popsie-doo
How do you do?"

Jocko's fame even reached Jamaica, when visiting producer Clement "Coxsone" Dodd heard him and returned home to show his own DJ, Count Machouki, how it was done. Soon Machouki, U-Roy, and Sir Lord Comic were talking over their massive sound systems. It was not much of a stretch, after all, as Jamaican music also had links to dance-step calling (though in their case it was quadrilles and mento dances). Soon Yellowman and Big Youth were chanting long stories in rhyme form, for which they were labeled toasters. Early influential hip-hop DJs such as Jamaican-born Kool Herc have sometimes denied direct Jamaican influence on rap, but their audiences must have at least been indirectly prepared for rap before it appeared here full-blown. just as surely the long, elaborate story-toasts of the Jamaican DJs offered models for those Americans whose first raps were simple and repetitious MC banter, for it was not too long before they expanded their routines to epic proportions.

In the late 1960s and early 1970s, poetry seemed to be everywhere in black America, and spilling over the usual barriers. There were the new academically trained poets like Amiri Baraka, Sonia Sanchez, and Stanley Crouch, recording their politically edged verse with music; urban folk poets like Gil Scott-Heron and the Last Poets with their minimalist accompaniment; or entertainers such as Melvin Van Peebles, Rudy Ray Moore, Blowfly, and even Muhammad Ali using old folk forms or vaudeville routines that nonetheless sounded fresh to the media. (Daryl McDaniels, D.M.C. of Run-D.M.C., recently said that Ali's "Float like a butterfly, sting like a bee" boast is "the most famous rap lyric ever.") Like Renaissance gentry, these figures had again made poetry relevant to society; and maybe more important in the long run, they had liberated it from the "spoken word" record bins and moved it in with music. It would fall to the next generation to take that poetry to the streets—and to take over the world.

World Views Collide—
Jazz Overseas

Chapter 22

Josef Škvorecký and the Tradition of Jazz Literature

The idea of the universality of the black experience in the West is so common that it seems too banal to mention. It comprises a subtext in the writings of Twain, Melville, Faulkner, maybe half of American literature. A smaller group of writers—Du Bois, those of the Harlem Renaissance, Norman Mailer—have told us that part of this experience is its ability to be communicated indirectly, through images of the body, through art, music, dance. The theoretical appeal of blacks also represented for late nineteenth- and twentieth-century artists an escape from industrialization and the rise of the middle class: one thinks of slumming literati such as Rimbaud in his *A Season in Hell*, his "pagan book, nigger book"; André Gide and Picasso in Africa; D. H. Lawrence in New Mexico, Australia, and those other Harlems of the European mind. (So Rimbaud may have been dealing in the slave trade in East Africa; Gide and Picasso could scarcely be called boosters of a *black* Africa; and Lawrence so hated Bessie Smith's "Empty Bed Blues" that he broke the record against Harry Crosby's wall. So what else is new?)

But there was a special attraction in the life and appearance of the black jazz musician: the double alienation of the artist and color. Whatever his occupation itself might be like, the jazz musician provided perhaps the first truly nonmechanical metaphor for the twentieth century. Not since the English Gentleman, with his modality of poise, authority, and how-one-should-be, has such an image dominated the world. Some abstraction or other of the lives of jazz performers and their followers now gives shape to the mores of street punks and media executives; it informs the muscles of professional dancers as well as the timing of stand-up comedians; and it feeds the languages and moves of fashion designers, basketball players, soldiers, and others. Now, whether one has heard of Charlie Parker or not, one inherits a notion of cool, an idea of well-etched individuality, a certain angle of descent. Such is the detachability and resale value of race and culture in our times.

Jazz has touched literature in a strange variety of ways. Sometimes the musicians and their followers have provided a rich background for period pieces such as Claude McKay's *Home to Harlem* or Langston Hughes's *Not Without Laughter,* or they have supplied allusions and intertextual shape (Ellison's *Invisible Man,* Joyce's *Finnegans Wake,* Malcolm Lowry's *Under the Volcano*),[1] maybe even a controlling figure (Ishmael Reed's *Mumbo Jumbo*). Others have found in jazz a model for improvisatory and antiphonal writing; and some have seen in the speech and writing of musicians a special kind of oral rhythm and dynamics of imagery.[2] Yet, curiously, the jazz life itself has seldom provided the basis for first-rate fiction. Perhaps the subject is at once too arcane and too restricted, too confined. What we most often see in fictional representations of jazz musicians' lives is either conventional sociological wisdom or local color dominating character.

Still, some jazz fiction is not without interest. More often than not it seems to be about relations between blacks and whites. And some very interesting fiction has been done by those who have used jazz as a keystone for constructing novels of manners that deal with race relations. Needless to say, the writers of this genre are usually white, and the white personae they create in their books are means by which the authors legitimize their creation of black characters. Here we see some justification for Mailer's remark that "it is moot if any white who had no ear for jazz can know the passion with which some whites become attached to the Negro's cause." The best documentation of the twice alienated is in the novel of the hipster. Chandler Brossard's *Who Walk in Darkness* (1952) leads into the Village and Uptown in the late 1940s, to those places where jazz and Latino musics mixed along with black and white; the book's central figure is a black man passing for white, but that fact was edited out of the first edition—a nice, reflexive fifties touch. John Clellon Holmes's *Go!* (1952) and *The Horn* (1958) also witness the period, as do Jack Kerouac's many novels, especially *Desolation Angels* (1965) and *The Subterraneans* (1958). Kerouac's books are lame in some fundamental ways, but there is a sweetness in his documentation of postwar underlife that makes him hard to resist. Jazz is everywhere in his work, and musicians such as Brew Moore, Allen Eager, and Richie Kamuca make appearances under pseudonyms, along with the legendary fan, Jerry Newman. (In a favorite passage of mine in *Visions of Cody* Jack himself secretly trails his idol, saxophonist Lee Konitz, across New York City.)

There was other hipster fiction, and a wonderful level of excess was reached in the novels of Bernard Wolfe and the short stories of Terry Southern. Wolfe is a man of remarkably diverse interests—a psychologist, a screenwriter, an associate of Trotsky in Mexico, a theorist of race relations—who first became known for the book he coauthored with white clarinetist Mezz Mezzrow, *Really the Blues* (1946). Though avowedly

Mezzrow's autobiography, the book rather crudely uses blacks as ciphers for white fantasy, and as in minstrel shows, the medium is a white man boasting of his competence in black culture by taking observers on a guided tour, complete with a glossary of native hip terms. Although Mezzrow does the talking, Wolfe's interest in Nietzsche's polarities and *The Birth of Tragedy* is always in the wings. (Nietzsche's is "the only book I know which says something about bebop," Wolfe once wrote.)

In some later essays, especially "Uncle Remus and the Malevolent Rabbit"—an essay that influenced Franz Fanon—Wolfe reversed himself (or Mezzrow, whatever) on blacks with a vengeance. Now black culture was shown to be nothing but white fantasies or the product of black reaction to those fantasies. Then, in two novels, *The Late Risers* (1954) and *The Magic of Their Singing* (1961), he introduced the hipster as the latest in a long series of literary white America's wise psychopaths. Although at times fragmented by a forced didacticism, there are some strong moments in Wolfe's books. In *The Late Risers,* for instance, there is a fine composite black character named Movement, a man who has appeared in *Carmen Jones, Cabin in the Sky, Green Pastures,* and the Katherine Dunham dance company, but who now dresses Brooks Brothers with a single gold earring and deals drugs and sundries. Hearing of the terminal illness of an aging German professor of *Afro-Amerikanische* who is seeking the help of a Haitian voodoo adept, Movement volunteers to impersonate a *houngan* with the aid of Folkways recordings and burnt cork ("I do not have to cross color lines, only observe them"). This deviation from his usually correct appearance in aid of a white man who is a professional student of the incorrect puzzles Movement's friends and leads him to justify his behavior by a weird reinterpretation of Sartre's *Anti-Semite and Jew* and Melville's *The Confidence Man.* (Concerning the professor's obsession with black culture, Movement observes, "I understand a man caught between conjure and *Das Kapital.*")

Wolfe has dozens of passages such as this, most of them amounting to a vicious satire on hipster race relations in mid-century. Even so, there is nothing in Wolfe that even approaches the viciousness of Terry Southern's treatment of the same subject in *Red Dirt Marijuana and Other Tastes* (1967). In "The Night Bird Blew for Dr. Warner" a white professor of music turns ethnographer to experience bebop in the manner of the natives. Schooled for his field trip in hip argot and eager to experience serious drugs, Dr. Warner sets out for certain neighborhoods to seek truth but ends up having his head beaten in. And in "You're Too Hip, Baby" a white fan solicits the friendship of an expatriate black musician in Paris with ultimate cool and studied restraint, only to have the tenor saxophonist offer him music lessons, his wife, and finally himself sexually in exchange. When each is rejected in turn, the musician asks what it is the white man *really* wants; when he learns that it's merely "the scene" and the "sounds," he rejects him as a "hippy and a professional nigger lover."

The metaphysics of race relations take a different turn in the jazz fiction of black writers. Where whites see jazz as a way out and treat its practitioners with a form of New Sentimentalism, blacks look to the music as a means of unifying their situation in a white-dominated society with a black collective tradition and a meaningful group history. James Baldwin, in his short story "Sonny's Blues" (1957), brings his characters in line with their culture through a moment of ritualized musical affirmation. Much the same project pervades John Williams's *Night Song* (1962) and William Melvin Kelley's *A Drop of Patience* (1965). And just such a ritual music scene is the totality of LeRoi Jones's "The Screamers" (1967). The purest version of this use of jazz as metaphor occurs in Rudolph Fisher's "Common Meter" (1930), wherein a cutting contest between two bands at the "Arcadia Ballroom" offers the winner the "jazz championship of the world" and, on a side bet, the favors of a fine dance hostess. When one band tricks the other by cutting the skins on the drum heads, denying them rhythm, the victims triumph by collective foot stomping, turning "St. Louis Blues" into a *shout.*

They had been rocked thus before, this multitude. Two hundred years ago they had swayed to that same slow fateful measure, lifting their lamentation to heaven, pounding the earth with their feet, seeking the mercy of a new God through the medium of an old rhythm, zoom-zoom. They had rocked so a thousand years ago in a city whose walls were jungle.[3]

Of course it's possible to pass over this sort of thing as yet another example of the Negro as Exotic Primitive. But in the 1930s, when Sterling Brown criticized the stereotype of the exotic as a departure from the American social norm, the act of departure had considerably different significance. At their best, these books treat the exotic as an assertion, as a transvaluation of the norm, rather than as an act born of weakness and the necessity of failure.

By the same token, when jazz fiction amounts to mere social-science melodrama, it deserves to he neglected—as has been "Blue Melody" (1948), a soggy bagel by J. D. Salinger. Here two Southern white children are befriended by a black pianist and his blues-singing niece, but their urban pastoral cannot override reality when the niece dies from a ruptured appendix as she is refused admittance to a Jim Crow hospital (yes, cf. "The Death of Bessie Smith" by Edward Albee too!). But jazz fiction that comes anywhere near its living originals has had a certain mediating force, standing between the public on one side and those peculiar moral tracts about black folks put out by sociologists and urbanologists on the other. The simple fact is that it has been difficult to reduce, say, a Charles Mingus or a Duke Ellington to crude and broken ruins of racism, or to treat a Billie Holiday or Lester Young as nothing more than—to use Ralph Ellison's phrase—the sum of their brutalization. Jazz fiction in this sense has been an ongoing refutation of the sociology of pathos.

It might seem easy to dismiss European novels on jazz as being more of the same with less detail and style. But truth be told, novels such as Ernest Borneman's *Tremolo* (1948), W. Clapham's *Come Blow Your Horn* (1958), Bennie Green's *Blame It on My Youth* (1967), A. Mitchell's *If You See Me Comin'* (1962), or John Wain's *Strike the Father Dead* (1962) are no worse and sometimes better than the American average. Yet one should treat with care jazz followers on the Continent, where the music has suffered special constraints, where some have gone to concentration camps for jazz, where some have indeed died for jazz. Many East Europeans have now suffered musical censorship under both the Nazis and nominally socialist governments with little or no difference in policy. Accounts of this repression are curiously rare in the West, so that the publication of Josef Škvorecký's "Red Music" (which is included as a preface to his two novellas published together in 1979 under the title *The Bass Saxophone*) is doubly important: it serves as both a political revelation and a necessary introduction to Škvorecký's jazz literature, a literature which is surely the most important, the best fiction we have, and in which the music has been used both as a subject for description and as a stylistic means.

When Škvorecký undertook to write about jazz beyond the American context, he was in effect freed of the burden of the racial conflict which partially motivates American jazz literature; he nonetheless inherited the esthetic oppositions and social implications of the organization of the music. The esthetics of jazz demand that a musician play with complete originality, with an assertion of his own musical individuality. (Regardless of the public's acclaim for some noted imitators, musicians give only the meanest of rewards to camp followers.) At the same time jazz requires that musicians be able to merge their unique voices in the totalizing, collective improvisations of polyphony and heterophony. The implications of this esthetic are profound and more than vaguely threatening, for no political system has yet been devised with social principles which reward maximal individualism within the framework of spontaneous egalitarian interaction. Thus when Europeans and white Americans embrace the music, they also commit a political act of far more radical dimensions than that of simply espousing a new political ideology. (True radicalism, someone once said, lies not in telling someone his politics are wrong, but in telling him his shoes are tied wrong.)

Škvorecký's fictional world is divided into those who have made this musical commitment and those who haven't, and the music becomes a metaphor for a greater revolution than one we have lived to see. *The Cowards* (1958) begins with an epigraph from Mezzrow and Wolfe's *Really the Blues* to the effect that behind the jazz played by white Chicagoans of the 1920s was a revolution in bourgeois values, a revolution carried forth by the optimism and creativity of youth. Early on in *The Cowards*, the narrator Danny says:

Some old geezer stood planted in the doorway with a half pint of beer in his hand, staring at us. I could read his mind. His eyes looked like two bugles and he had a mouth like a tuba. He certainly didn't think the stuff we were producing was music. We didn't either, really. Not *just* music. For us it was something more like the world. Like before Christ and after Christ. I couldn't even remember what it had been like before jazz. I was probably interested in soccer or something—like our fathers who used to go to the stadium every Sunday and shout themselves hoarse. I wasn't much more than a kind of miniature dad myself then. A dad shrunk down to about four foot five. And then along came Benno with his records and jazz and the first experiments in Benno's house with a trumpet, piano, an old xylophone I'd dug up in the attic and two violins that Lexa and Haryk were learning to play because their parents wanted them to. And then Jimmy Lunceford and Chick Webb. And Louis Armstrong. And Bob Crosby. And then everything else was After Jazz. So that it really wasn't just music at all. But that old geezer over there couldn't understand that. He'd been ruined a long time ago by soccer and beer and brass band music.[4]

The Cowards is an account by jazz-living youth of the events of 4–11 May 1945, the period when the Germans were withdrawing from Czechoslovakia and the Russians were moving in. Though it is in many respects a scrupulously realistic account of the times, it is also something of a manifesto of a specific cultural continuity in a period of change, a counter-continuity of anti-bourgeois values, a revolution within a revolution, a critique of the falsity of the revolution as seen from behind dark glasses and music stands. (Whatever else was happening during those days on the political front, the book opens with the playing of Jimmy Lunceford's "Annie Laurie" and ends with his "Organ Grinder's Swing.")

Škvorecký's short story "Song of the Forgotten Era" follows other jazz children forward to an incident in 1951, as reflected upon by one of them in the early 1960s. Here the act of playing a Russian military march in swing time brings the wrath of the government down upon them and permanently alters the direction of their lives. The story ends with one of the postwar youths, now an adult, singing a jazz version of "Annie Laurie," reaching back to the optimism of youth and a momentarily liberated Czechoslovakia.

I closed my eyes. It was so long ago. So terribly long ago. It was a blood sacrifice, a different, less conspicuous kind of sacrifice, for a better life of that generation

of twist-crazy chicks and youths up there. . . . Venus . . . was singing, in that forgotten voice, the song of the quickly forgotten years.[5]

In "Pink Champagne" (1969), another short story set in Prague during the same period, the period Škvorecký calls the "very intense, very
underground and generally crazy" period of his life, jazz is only a small
part of the theme; it surfaces when a group of university students pass
themselves off as English peace marchers by singing a Jimmy Rushing
blues. Later they find themselves singing the song again, now in private,
not as a trick, but as an act of unity. At first glance, "Emöke" would seem
to be something of a departure from this theme, since the blues appear
as part of a young man's scheme to seduce a Hungarian woman who has
retreated from the war and her own personal tragedies into a spirituality which she wears like a widow's mourning garb. Here the blues the
young man improvises to crack her resistance while dancing is a home-
made, very Czech version of the blues, but one which calls upon some
ancient secrets from distant mystical sources.

But now she was hearing it, a poem composed just for her by a man, a poem
flowing from a man's heart, borne by the strange magic of this crazy age of
telecommunications from the heart and throat of a half-stoned black shouter of
the Memphis periphery to the vocal chords [sic] of a Prague intellectual in this
social hall in a recreation center in the Socialist state of Czechoslovakia.[6]

Škvorecký has discovered the very unifying and affirming ritual qualities of the music which black writers had discovered in the United
States. In "Red Music" he states it again, now in opposition to a writer of
brilliant jazz criticism who could finally never get the music squarely in
line with what he calls his own "Marxist-Leninist" orientation.

And no matter what LeRoi Jones says to the contrary, the essence of this music,
this "way of making music," is not simply protest. Its essence is something far
more elemental: an *élan vital*, a forceful vitality, an explosive energy as breath-
taking as that of any true art, that may be felt even in the saddest of blues. Its
effect is cathartic.[7]

Škvorecký comes very close here to what Sidney Bechet, in his autobiography *Treat It Gentle*, said jazz was all about. Bechet explained that the
music invented by ex-slaves was something which transcended the conditions of race and servitude: "It wasn't just white people the music had
to reach to, nor even their own people, but straight out to life and to
what a man does with his life when it finally *is* his."[8]

"The Bass Saxophone," the latest of Škvorecký's works to appear in
English translation, returns again to the occupation, now to an incident
in which a young musician crosses political lines and risks everything in

order to have a chance to play a bass saxophone in a strange German band. Realism is kept to a minimum: there are no accounts of suppressed newspapers, forced labor, gas chambers, and the rest. In this war there is first and only the ban against jazz and the underground which manages to keep the music alive. Czechoslovakia thus becomes a landscape of hidden music, where apparently innocent peasant gatherings could, at the signal of a lookout, begin trucking to a Basie tune; where German *Offizierschule* bands rehearsed smuggled Chick Webb arrangements; where the Jews of Terezín had a band called the Ghetto Swingers (all but one of them to die finally in the camps); and where even in the camps other bands kept playing what the Nazis called *Judeonegroid* music. Škvorecký's obsession with this single suppressed art gives "The Bass Saxophone" a suffocating closure and an amnesiac structure. Only his sense of the absurd and the richness of his descriptions of the music keep it moving. And one does not easily forget his image of Kansas City rifts in Buchenwald.

Jazz may be something of a general motif in modern Czech fiction; Škvorecký himself has mentioned its presence in films such as *Hijacking* (1952) and *Music from Mars* (1964). I have not read Škvorecký's "The End of the Nylon Age" or "A Word I Shall Not Withdraw," but I have read Milan Kundera's *The Farewell Party* with its crude handling of jazz as exotic background and local color. What finally is unique and appealing in Škvorecký's writing is its Europeanness, the very distance between his characters' love for jazz and the sources of the music. They may live and die for jazz, but it is always someone else's music, heard through imported records and badly translated song lyrics. Readers of the fiction of jazz are not musicians, and this distance between author and subject echoes the distance between reader and living musicians. Somehow, in speaking from deep continental Europe, Škvorecký has caught the excited detachment that one once felt in looking at faded and awkwardly posed pictures of jazz heroes in old issues of *Metronome* magazine.

Chapter 23

World Views Collide: The History
of Jazz and Hot Dance

Writings on the history of music, like the histories of race they inevitably resemble, come dressed in an almost mythological language, a code that makes the evolution of traditions appear suspiciously preordained. In America, the idea of Afro-American musical tradition seems fixed at the moment, but the quiet conceals an ongoing debate that is fought in terms of social justice as well as aesthetics. We all know the story so far: dislocated, culture-shocked slaves encounter English, Christianity, and Anglo-Gaelic music and dance on the plantations, and then give these forms a cultural twist, by accident, or choice, or parodic intent. Whites, in turn, borrowed back from blacks, and new forms of music, like jazz, came into being through these oscillations. It all reads as smoothly as a social engineer's flow chart.

But the meeting of African and European music was not a benign encounter, not a case of "borrowing," "lending," and "learning"; it was more like the frisson described in Ishmael Reed's *Mumbo Jumbo*, a collision of cultures that would occur again and again on an international scale. The rise of jazz was the most stunning of modernisms, becoming a form that carried within it the theory of relativity, surrealism, primitivism, radical democracy, and a new way of *being*, all at once.

Such revisionist thoughts are provoked by *The History of Jazz and Hot Dance* (Harlequin Records) a history-shaking series of LPs of the earliest recorded jazz from Argentina, Switzerland, Russia, India, Austria, Hungary, Trinidad, Finland, Martinique, South Africa, and Australia, with forthcoming records from the Netherlands, Belgium, Denmark, Cuba, "Black Africa," Japan, Canada, and elsewhere. Produced in the UK by folklorist Bruce Bastin, the LPs (11 so far) come packaged in stark white covers, each with a different reproduction of a 78 record: there is a Czech Esta, with tax stamp still affixed; a South African Bantu Botho; an Indian Rex with a lion surrounded by the legend "British Made: Hear What You Like, When You Like."

There are revelations aplenty here, starting with the liner notes. Who now knows that there was a circuit for black song-and-dance performers and "Negro operettas" that ran from Helsinki to Moscow in the late 1800s? That Jubilee singers and cakewalkers reached India even earlier, by the mid-1800s? Or that the Swiss were producing music boxes with black songs by 1890? In other words, the exposure of the world to Afro-American culture was under way well before the Jazz Age. Jazz, as these albums attest, was a global force that simultaneously modernized and preserved traditions.

Musically, there is enough on these records to guarantee that the first few chapters of books on the history of jazz will have to be rewritten. The rediscovery of all this world music from 1910 to 1939 after so many decades is a little like the shock of, say, discovering the ruins of Troy, Babylon, and Storyville, all in the same day. Getting a handle on so much music is not easy, and one is almost forced to divide the records into those from countries where African descendants were in the majority and those where they weren't.

In *The History of Jazz and Hot Dance in Russia* (HQ 2012) we hear the music tantalizingly documented in S. Frederick Starr's scholarly *Red and Hot: The Fate of Jazz in the Soviet Union*, and it's much as Starr described it: awkward, and often played too fast. Yet there is something else here. When the Jakov Skomorovsky Orchestra rips into "Bei mir bist du schön" (1941), for example, there are home-grown innovations in evidence, such as the choir voicing of trombones, tuba, and accordion inside an otherwise ordinary dance band; or the straight-ahead, free-of-schmaltz reading they give it, suggesting that, unlike Benny Goodman in his hit version, they were comfortable with Yiddish music.

Granted, it's easy to read pathos into this proto-jazz and overpraise it when you consider the political conditions under which it was produced. When jazz fell out of the state's favor, superstars like Eddie Rosner (the Russian Harry James) found themselves in gulag camps. Luckier musicians like Alexander Tsfasman, the Leningrad stride pianist, got off lightly, merely being forced to give up music-making for a living. Politics aside, there is exhilaration in the Russian's breathless tempos, an urgency in the crisp arrangements that expresses the joy of discovery but also redefines the music and sets it apart from its more relaxed parallels in America. In the Russian context, stiff and stomping rhythm sections make a kind of sense. The Czech and Austrian records (HQ 2019 and 2014) also bristle with the interplay of the self and Other. The scene in Prague and in Vienna must have been especially rich, given the imaginative vocals and the generally high quality of musicianship on these performances. Their earliest jazz records—like those of the other European countries—sound like local folk and vernacular dance music heated up under the pressure of the rising expectations. But unlike the pattern in Russia, total mimicry of American jazz ultimately took over in these countries, and their best recordings often have obvious sources. Other countries—like India and Switzerland—imported American musicians and came to depend upon them far too much for the health of their music.

Another surprise in these records is the deep involvement of Jews with early jazz, something also noticed in the U.S. but seldom commented on. In Russia most name musicians were Jewish, and Jews were disproportionately represented on records from Austria to Argentina. Seeing these names not only helps explain Nazi and Soviet hatred of the music, it also raises the question of how much of jazz is distinctively Jewish. Why were so many Jews drawn to the music? This cannot be dismissed as merely the outcome of social exclusion, for Jews were often in the cultural mainstream in Europe. Perhaps jazz provided an outlet for the improvisations of klezmer and cantorial music.

Whatever the story, Europe was ready for jazz. Some of its musicians simply imitated American records, but others reframed the music around their own folk or avant-garde traditions. (This latter course gave us the Danish violinist Svend Asmussen, the German trombonist Albert Mangles- dorff, and the gypsy guitarist Django Reinhardt.) American nationalism encourages us to believe that because we were closer to the source—Afro- Americans—other countries' efforts must always appear underdevel- oped, perhaps even comical. *Our* jazz, after all, was a response to shifting social alignments, to urbanization, and to changing notions of freedom. And for many, it was also a break with Europe's cultural supremacy. But European jazz was also an assertion of new identity, a transformation of the continent's traditions. Paradoxically, we now find ourselves viewing de- velopments abroad with the smug ethnocentrism of nineteenth-century European imperialists.

Yet none of this prepares us for what was happening in predominantly black countries. The music of Trinidad (HQ 2016) is typical, in that it seems on first hearing to have no relevance to jazz. In fact, you could infer that there was active resistance to jazz: the earliest recordings sound like Venezuelan *passeos* and waltzes. Still, we're told that Lionel Balasco (the first recorded black instrumentalist, and, maybe not incidentally, part Sephardic Jew) performed rags by Joplin and Lucky Roberts; Jim Europe's New York–based Hell Fighters sought its clarinet players in Trinidad; and some calypsonians crossed over into jazz when they re- corded in New York City. *Something* was tying these musics together.

The clue to West Indian relations to jazz lies not in New York City, but in New Orleans, America's Caribbean city. When Jelly Roll Morton told Alan Lomax that at the heart of jazz lay the "Spanish tinge," he was talk- ing about the *habanera* rhythm (or slow drag, or tango bass). Exposure to international pop tells us that this is not so much Spanish as it is

African. This rhythm is the backbone of much Afro-American music, from W. C. Handy to Bo Diddley. Given the common cultural foundations of Trinidad and New Orleans, it is no surprise that rhythmic similarities turn up on some Morton-like piano on George Cabral's "Memories of Trinidad" (1939), or formal similarities on Sam Manning's "Recuerdos Del Pasado" (1934). But while Trinidad shared some musical rudiments with jazz, it seems to have used them for its own local purposes, developing them into calypso and soca.

What a surprise, then, that in Martinique (HQ 2018) we hear the closest kin to early jazz. Beyond the beguine rhythms, the familiar improvised polyphony and salty clarinet tone of New Orleans come through. In the 1940s and '50s, New Orleans Creole musicians like Kid Ory and Paul Barbarin made records very similar to those of Fort de France dance-hall bands, and as if to make the point, the Harlequin LP includes Sidney Bechet's "Haitian Orchestra" of 1939 playing "Sous le Palmiers." The melody may be "Haitian," but the style is Pan-Caribbean. The message from the islands is that music based on similar resources may not develop along the same course. Martinique's popular music veered off toward Congolese and Cuban pop, to form *cadance*, still the hot dance of the moment.

Finally, back to Africa, but to South Africa (HQ 2020), the wrong part as far as the origins of jazz are concerned. Traditional music here lacks the polyrhythmic engines of West and Central Africa, finding its strength instead in rich choral textures. The first recordings of "township jazz" (music played in black bars around the cities, here documented between 1946 and 1960) were jump tunes in the style of the early Nat King Cole trio, and the music later moved through the gamut of r&b to bebop and cool, only to turn around with penny-whistle swing—a folksy yet urbane street music in the 1950s. (Just how much South Africans retrenched musically can be heard on *The Indestructible Beat of Soweto*, Earth Works 5502.) As difficult as it is to generalize from this thin slice of time, it appears that South African musicians began copying black American music when it was in an advanced slate of development, only to then reject it, producing a culturally conservative pop music filled with intensely harmonized vocals and cyclical melodies and rhythms.

Listening to these non-European musics, we can marvel at the complexities of rhythmic organization and the subtleties of interplay, though still long for a guitar to rock out or a horn to cut loose, at least once in a while. But on this series we encounter people who choose *not* to emulate Americans, and have nonetheless produced musics that are coherent, continuous, and shared by entire national populations. A blunt rejection, I suppose, but also a pleasant reminder that we have not yet used up all of the world's musical resources.

Chapter 24

Way Down Yonder in Buenos Aires

Of all the chauvinisms this country has committed, that of the jazz musician is the most arrogant, the most racist, and probably the most accurate. It goes like this: only Americans can play jazz, and the best of these are black, the remainder more or less white. Oh, there are exceptions that prove the rule and some honorary mentions with heart, but who can really question what Albert Murray calls the black patrimony of jazz? It is interesting to watch the interpretative carryings-on, the twisting and turning of the paradigm, when an anomaly like Django Reinhardt turns up. In Django's case street logic had it that his great abilities stemmed from the fact that either (a) he was a Gypsy, a member of a pariah caste, and therefore homologous to a black; or (b) Gypsy culture and black-American culture shared more than either did with white Euro-American culture. (There was a third view that Django was part Negro, but who took *that* seriously?)

I bring this up to clarify the problem raised by *Oscar Alemán: Swing Guitar Legend* on Rambler. Before now I only knew of Alemán as a vague name learned from a single sentence in a jazz history and from a Tom Van Bergeyk re-creation of an unbelievable Alemán finger-picked solo on ukulele. Now I—we—have to reckon with yet another jazz musician of the first order who is not only not black, but also not even American. Alemán (1909?–1980) was born in the Choco, in Argentina, becoming first a professional *milonga* dancer, then a boxer, and finally the greatest jazz guitarist in his country, where he was known as "el negro Alemán." (Note that American chauvinism is exportable even to a country which claims to have lost or mislaid its entire black population.)

Alemán left for Europe in the late 1920s as part of a guitar duo under the management of black promoter Harry Fleming, the dancer who followed the European success of Florence Wills's *Blackbirds* with his own smaller revue, *Bluebirds*. Stranded in Paris in 1932 Alemán became the leader of Josephine Baker's orchestra, the Baker Boys, and moved to the center of Parisian musical life. From there he went on to join other bands headed by black Americans such as Freddy Taylor and

Bill Coleman, but made only a handful of recordings with them. Jazz history—such as it is—recognizes Django Reinhardt as the dominant figure on guitar in the 1930s, and it has been easy to see Alemán as an also-ran. But although Reinhardt was a great influence in Argentina (the Quinteto de Hernam Oliva continues to make fine xerox copies of the Quintet of the Hot Club of Paris), Alemán had shaped a jazz style from local resources and American jazz records even before Reinhardt was recorded.

The earliest Alemán documented on this record is from Copenhagen in 1938. The two sides with Danish musicians are perfunctory, enlightened only by Alemán's solos and the originality and bite of his backing riffs (as on "Sweet Sue"). But the two unaccompanied performances from the same session are a revelation: "Nobody's Sweetheart," for instance, condenses into three minutes all the skills of a musician who knows precisely what can be gotten from a guitar. There is simultaneous finger picking of rhythm and melody, contrapuntal lines, richly harmonized riffs, fleeting uses of double-time and overtones. "Whispering" starts with a Spanish tinge done with classical technique and gives way to flying chordal playing.

In 1939 Alemán put together an exceptional trio: John Mitchell (on rhythm guitar) had first gone to Europe with Sam Wooding's band and two years after these recordings were made was interned in Nazi camps (though he returned in 1944 and played with Jimmy Lunceford); and "Serious" Wilson Myers (on bass and vocals) had worked with Bessie Smith, King Oliver, Duke Ellington, and was later to arrange for Jimmy Dorsey. Together they were lightly but firmly in the swing tradition, Alemán suggesting some of the directions in which Charlie Christian would soon be going, and Myers scatting and bowing his bass in the manner Slam Stewart was to make famous.

History and the liner notes beg for a comparison between Django and Alemán, and their solo and trio recordings of the late 1930s give us something to contrast. Like Django, Alemán had a fondness for fast-fingering and unusual intervals, for wide, romantic vibrato, and for the back beat, and both love the suspended feeling of holding a blue note across several beats (something they probably learned from white musicians like Bix Beiderbecke). If Django was a master of the single line of the evocative improvised melody and the subtly shifting rhythms, Alemán's classical fingering gave him the edge in articulation and full use of the plectrum: he was much more the complete guitarist, and used his steel-bodied instrument like a piano.

The rest of the album follows Alemán after he returned to Argentina early in World War II. The eight recordings made in Buenos Aires between 1941 and 1945 are interesting, even charming: there is a very fine "Swinging on a Star," and a clever "Diga Diga Do" which finally turns into a vaudeville hora. But as with Django on the Quintet of the Hot Club recordings, one listens fitfully, waiting until the clouds lift for those brief moments of flash guitar. Alemán continued to be active for the next 35 years, recording as recently as 1977. But he remained in Latin America, where he never recovered the brilliance he showed on those few recordings when he played with black American musicians. Or played all alone.

Chapter 25

Improvising Under Apartheid: Afro Blue

With the first century of jazz beginning to close, a new fascination with the range and the meaning of the form is taking hold. An almost perverse scholarship is developing, which for the first time offers us a chance to see how jazz developed away from America, see what its relationship to the mother state was. There are elaborate recorded documentaries such as the British Harlequin series of the *History of Jazz and Hot Dance* around the world; portraits of hidden histories of jazz like S. Frederick Starr's *Red and Hot: The Fate of Jazz in the Soviet Union*; Chris Goddard's picture of early jazz in Europe, *Jazz Away from Home*; Jim Godbolt's *A History of Jazz in Britain*; and Michael Zwerin's account of jazz under Nazi suppression, *La tristesse de Saint Louis.*

Now it's possible to ask questions such as, What would jazz be like in a country with no black people? Or, for that matter, with no white people? And the answer appears to be that there would be none, or at least none of any originality, in such countries. Jazz seems to require a mix of both African and European musical traditions, one that, for instance, uses European and African instruments, rhythms, and melodies; provides opportunities to study them formally, but also to experiment with them; and offers the means for communicating musical traditions across class, racial, and regional lines. Typically this can only be accomplished in an urban setting. So did jazz develop in the United States, Britain, and to a lesser degree in Canada, France, Germany, Zimbabwe, South Africa, Brazil, Argentina, and Jamaica. In the United States the same pattern worked itself out regionally: most of the great innovators in jazz came from the big cities or the southern border states. Mississippi, so important to the development of rhythm and blues, has produced scarcely any jazz musicians in spite of its high proportion of blacks. The paradox of Afro-American studies is that when you trace the development of black cultural forms, they often point to a Euro-American form—"Tiger Rag" leads back to the quadrille, the *son montuno* to the Iberian *son*. It's the next step of historical searching that's missing: behind the Euro-American form, or possibly beside it, is an African one, fusing with and transforming the European, which in turn is transformed into an Afro-American one. The square dance is a lot blacker than we give it credit for being. The cultural juxtapositions of postmodernism are a lot older than they seem.

New South African recordings and reissues and David Coplan's excellent *In Township Tonight!* help us see South Africa as a test case for a comparative study of jazz origins. What keeps the study from working to perfection is that South African jazz had its origins in direct imitation of the United States—South Africa had experienced Afro-American spirituals and both white and black minstrel shows by the late 1800s, caught on to ragtime from its beginning, and followed U.S. music up through soul and 1960s expressionistic jazz. For the time being, we're making judgments from incomplete sources, recapitulating the history of commercially recorded music as captured by the British, white South Africans. Thus far, we have scattered field recordings of folk music: *ingoma ebusuku* (Zulu-Swazi choral music influenced by missionaries and Afro-American aesthetics); vocal *marabi* (multiethnic pop music developed in Johannesburg and first recorded in the 1940s); a small amount of *kwela* (penny whistle jive) of the 1950s, and Afro-rock from bands such as Jaluka. What we haven't heard is *tsaba-tsaba* (a 1940s mix of African, Latin, and swing musics); instrumental *mbaqanga* (Africanized jazz from the '50s); and much of the new jazz of the late 1960s and 1970s. As in the United States and Cuba, all these South African forms coexisted, and weren't recorded until 20 years after the fact. Unlike in America, where field recording was a venerable tradition, South Africa essentially ignored its music.

Township jazz recording began in the mid-1940s. Before this, British and South African record companies sought out only the most exotic and early mixtures, Western and African, of church and choral music. An increasing black cosmopolitanism after World War II and the exposure to British and American troops created a marketplace for home-grown jazz. You can hear it on *Jazz and Hot Dance in South Africa 1946–1959* (Harlequin), which begins in the mid-1940s with the Manhattan Brothers and the Merry Blackbirds Orchestra's "Pesheya Dwezo Ntaba" ("Playing on the Mountain Side"). The Manhattans sound like a cross between the Mills Brothers and the Golden Gate Quartet, and Peter Rezant's Blackbirds are competent late swing accompanists. The Black Broadway Boys' "Mia Mia Bounce" from 1951 is a boogie-woogie style which could also be heard in the United States in some r&b bands from the same period. Other groups from the early 1950s—the Manhattan Stars, the King Cole Boogies, the African Swingsters, the Jazz Swingcopators, and King Force Silgee's Jazz Forces—also share boogie or swing rhythms with soloists who more or less successfully imitate Ben

Webster, Ella Fitzgerald, Oscar Moore, and Nat King Cole. But the tenor saxophonist in the King Force Silgee band plays with a Wardell Gray feel, and the soloists in the Jazz Swingcopators appear to conceive their lines boppishly, even while boogie and 4/4 rhythms underpin them. It's odd that the Harlequin LP, presenting South African jazz chronologically, grows more native as time goes on. The album underscores the fact that recordings were scattershot, they didn't document the evolution of South African music chronologically. Fads—the marketplace, as usual—dictated what was recorded.

The South African equivalent of r&b—instrumental marabi—was just beginning to be recorded in the early 1950s. More of a dance music, marabi was aimed at the working class and therefore had an extremely wide audience, one mostly urban. *South African Jive*, vol. 3: *African Jazz* Ethnic Cassettes) has what sound like 1950s–1960s guitar-saxophone section small bands, with melodies that are riff-based, call-and-response efforts, and with few solos. Some bands like Mughubela and His Saxophone Jive play what sounds like kwela, the saxophone substituting for the penny whistle, with banjo rhythm behind; others, like the Country Jazz Band, seem like stripped-down Basie groups, circa 1944; the Transvaal Rocking Jazz Stars and Rex Ntuli's band mix sax trios with double guitar leads à la contemporary Zaire. But the majority—bands like Boy Masaka and His Big Ten, the Nick Mick Band, and the Zee Zee Jazz Appointment—structure their songs around backbeat brush rhythms, fulminant bass lines, and cycles of cascading riffs. They often sound like nothing less than Mbube choral songs transcribed instrumentally.

Like so many other creolized forms—salsa, the Caribbean novel—modern South African jazz reached its fullest expression not on native soil, but abroad, encouraged by foreign admirers. After apartheid laws made performance virtually impossible, a wave of avant-garde black musicians left the country for receptive continental European countries, and then eventually made their way to London in the mid-1960s. Like their counterparts in New York, they were paradoxically caught up in the same cultural heat that produced the Beatles and the second Great Awakening of rock and roll.

Pianist Abdullah Ibrahim (a/k/a Dollar Brand) was among the first to go. Coming up through Capetown vocal groups, dance bands, and the like, in 1960 he formed the Jazz Epistles, a hard bop band which included Hugh Masekela and Kippie Moeketsi, the alto saxophonist said by many South Africans to be the equal of Charlie Parker (though his solo on the Shanty Town Seven's "Unoya Kae," on the Harlequin LP, does not serve his legend well). In 1962 Ibrahim broke up the band to play in Switzerland, and with the support of Duke Ellington made recordings in the United States and played the festival circuit. A strong and idiosyncratic synthesizer of Ellington, Monk, South African folk and pop melodies, Protestant hymns, and Muslim chants, Ibrahim belongs to a select group of post-Monk pianists.

Besides the Jazz Epistles, the other early 1960s band of importance in South Africa was the Blue Notes, a seemingly Ornette Coleman–inspired group with Dudu Pukwana on alto sax, trumpeter Mongezi Feza, Johnny Dyani on bass, and pianist Chris McGregor. Since McGregor was the son of Scottish missionary parents in the Transkei Province, the band was illegally multiracial; after two years of suffering while performing semi-secretly, the Blue Notes left for Zurich in 1965 with the help of Ibrahim. From there they moved to London where they joined the circle of new British free-players like Dave Holland and John Surman, hung out with visiting Americans, including Albert Ayler, and recorded *Blue Notes for Mongezi* and *Blue Notes in Concert* (both on Dgun records).

In 1969–70, McGregor augmented the African musicians with British avant-gardists to an 18-piece orchestra, and recorded as the *Brotherhood of Breath* (RCA Neon). The results are still startling 17 years later and a fine introduction to the South African avant-garde: Dudu Pukwana's arrangement of "MRA" takes the circling riffs common to township band music and breaks them, tossing the parts from instrumental section to section, like pygmy hocketing, with the result that a short repetitious figure is played over and over while continuing to hold interest. Similarly, on "The Bride" Pukwana varies the section play so that the band seems articulated more like a finger piano or a xylophone than an orchestra. "Davashe's Dream," on the other hand, is simply a series of solos over a straightforward ballad chord progression. But the individual playing is so acute, so sharply etched, that you scarcely notice what's underneath. In its twists and slides, Pukwana's alto suggests a history of style—Ben Webster, Ornette Coleman, Johnny Hodges. Mongezi Feza—who was compared to Don Cherry—lets loose fountains of notes, in arcs of sound at incredible velocity that sometimes begin beyond the trumpet's range and emerge as rushes of air that fall into downward runs. McGregor contributed two contrasting pieces, "Night Poem," a long fantasia on African village themes and instruments, and "Union Special," which sounds like a Boer polka and continually accelerates with the thunderous drums of Louis Moholo.

Alas, none of McGregor's 10 or so recordings are in print, nor are any by Louis Moholo and Mongezi Feza. Especially missed are records with Dudu Pukwana's band Spear, such as *In the Townships* (Caroline/Virgin), perhaps the truest evocation of what these musicians were hoping to accomplish—a merger of funk, free playing, and township pop-song feeling.

With the burst of Free Jazz's creative energy in the late 1960s, there occurred an astonishing convergence of the avant-garde and the folk-loric internationally, a looping backwards of tradition which has yet to be fully accounted for. We began to again hear about simultaneous collective improvisation, for the first time since New Orleans; the memory of New Orleans funeral parades was called on to explain the seemingly out-of-tune drones of saxophonist Albert Ayler over rattling snare drum rhythms. Brazilian one-stringed berimbau player Nana Vasconcelos joined the postmodern trio Codona (even while it might never have occurred to them to record with one-string country diddly-bow players from Mississippi). Don Cherry began a personal odyssey of recording with folk musicians across the world. And some heard in the harmolodics of Ornette Coleman's Prime Time band the density and texture of brass and saxophone *rara* bands in Haiti, or that of Jamaican Count Ossie and the Mystic Revelation of Rastafari. In retrospect these were not so much the products of the experimentation of the avant-garde as they were a tacit recognition of common principles girding African-American aesthetics.

South Africa's best musicians were also compelled to reverse years of imitating Americans by finding new strength in their own folk traditions, even when it seemed artistic suicide to attempt this in a country controlled by a mythology that defined culture as race. The irony was that just as they began, they were driven out of their country in the name of European Culture by a people who understood all too well what they were attempting, only to find themselves continuing in Europe itself among people who had only vague, if sympathetic, understanding.

Just how well they succeeded aesthetically is another question. Johnny Dyani felt that émigré South African musicians were led astray by the American avant-garde, and were in danger of losing their own musical language. From Denmark, he kept his own group together (recording *Africa, Mbizo,* and *Song for Biko* for Steeplechase) and worked as one of the shapers of Pierre Dorge's New Jungle Orchestra. Chris McGregor now lives in provincial France, and he also talks about retreating from free jazz, and about excessive improvisation and structure, the sense of community and tradition necessary but missing from contemporary music. Younger instrumentalists have left South Africa since the 1970s: guitarist Lucky Ranku, drummer Churchill Jolobe (both with Dudu Pukwana's band Zila), pianist Mervyn Africa, trumpeter Claude Deppa, drummer/promoter Julian Bahula (*African Soul,* on Plane records) and Brian Abrahams (*Akuzwakale* on District Six records), and there is talk of great musicians still unable to leave South Africa. But more and more, survival demands that they work with musicians from elsewhere in Africa and

Europe. If individual exile was the precondition of modernism, a continuing tradition of exile seems to be the basis of postmodernism. But then South African musicians, like Afro-Americans, have been fusing and creolizing musics for more than three centuries, making them the true founders of postmodernism. The process isn't over. South African music is still evolving. With the explosion of available records, the fusing and creating, a good enough metaphor for freedom, will continue.

Open Works

Chapter 26

Sonny Rollins in the Age
of Mechanical Reproduction

The book on Sonny Rollins is that his recordings almost never capture his incendiary live performances, and even those are notoriously variable. Yet no one has ever accused him of leaving an audience conceptually unprovoked. His performances are exercises in generic erasure, filled with revivals of long-rejected pop songs, movie themes, operatic arias, and appropriated Third World dances. And his treatment of these melodies is unpredictable—sometimes boldly stated, with no embellishment, at other times radically resituated (by parody or odd choice of tempo) or fragmented. What keeps Rollins's eclecticism from being that of yet another borrow, shred, and cut-and-paste, emotionally homeless postmodernist is a socially based theory of assemblage. Behind his music lies an aesthetic of spontaneity and human response so intensely visceral and interactional that it is more an ethic than an aesthetic. Call it rhythm & blues sensibility, or the culture of the Blues People, whatever, it is cool without being detached, tough by way of highly developed technique, and so confident that it relishes risk, even in the form of sentimentality.

Rollins eased into the Bottom Line last weekend and leaped into aggressive versions of "Where or When," "I'm Glad There Is You," and "Long Ago and Far Away," setting the pattern for the evening's improvisations: two or four bars of the original melody, followed by double- and triple-time outside bursts so fast and so reckless that he sometimes skipped and stumbled over the rhythm, only to recover and plunge forward again. Between the ballads and show tunes, Rollins played an unusual number of calypsos, which seem to have taken on a renewed significance for him. In spite of their simple melodies they provide him with vehicles capable of staying with his audacious detailing. Especially on "The Duke of Iron" (dedicated to Cecil Anderson, a calypsonian whose career was based mostly in New York) his playing was richly reticulated and dramatic. Though other jazz musicians have tried calypsos— Shake Keane, Joe Harriott, John Surman, even Charlie Parker—most of them have stuck close to the curb. But on an evening as loaded as Friday was with carnival songs, it became apparent that West Indian music has shaped his improvising. (Particularly noticeable is a staggered triplet in the choral responses of older calypsos, which can often be heard in his up-tempo ballads.)

The physicality of Rollins's performance mimes his music: lunging, crouching, sweating, playing out and up, he conveys the belief that with work anything is possible, that with an extra surge of energy the most banal piece of material can be taken to the edge. When it doesn't happen, at least the audience knows it might have, and they were witness to the struggle. And when a new record, like *Here's to the People* (Milestone), doesn't capture all this promise, it nonetheless keeps the covenant alive, especially on jaunty revivals like "Lucky Day" and "Why Was I Born."

Rollins has been playing like this, night after night, for forty-four years, where he has come to be expected to improvise with that legendary level of intensity that brings an audience to its feet, shouting, and sends them dizzy out into the night. Yet this artist in an age of mechanical reproduction has been copied like few others in their own lifetimes: with his music transcribed and studied, his entire career scrupulously recorded, Rollins's playing has been caught on the wing and made permanent and repeatable by others. Every performance now becomes a test of his ability to resist self-plagiarism, a challenge to add something of significance without relying on his past progress. In managing this, he has already surpassed masters like Louis Armstrong, Thelonious Monk, and Coleman Hawkins. And to see him wrestle with his own achievements puts to shame those players who toil in the ice caves of what they so grimly call the Tradition.

Chapter 27

Sun Ra, 1914–1993

The news that Sun Ra had left the planet at age seventy-nine on Sunday, May 30, sent waves of dismay and trepidation through many. Some, I'm sure, rushed to consult astrological tables and numerological treatises; others, less spiritually adept, browsed balefully through their record collections. So when the Bottom Line announced an Arkestra concert for this last Saturday it was taken to be a good sign. And indeed it was, for with Amiri Baraka pronouncing the in/evocation and guests such as Stanley Jordan swelling the band to 25, it was clear that the music was still here and that Sun Ra's legacy lives.

But what is the legacy of a musician who thrived on paradox and mystery, and made contradiction an art form? How do you come to terms with a man who made a lifelong effort (like Father Divine and Elijah Muhammad) to obscure many of the facts of his earlier life, all of which if known would have shown him to be a prodigy, an outstanding scholar, and a musician who had more than paid his way into the tradition? A musician so devoted to the written score that he often rewrote an arrangement again and again, but who also reintroduced collective improvisation into free jazz in the 1960s? A man whose work includes poetry (*The Immeasurable Equation*, Volumes I and II), painting, and film, and whose influence was ubiquitous during the 1960s and 1970s (light shows, the writing of Henry Dumas, *Close Encounters of the Third Kind*—some have said Spielberg drew inspiration from Sun Ra's underground film *Space Is the Place*). A man who worked with artists ranging front Katherine Dunham, Lil Green, and Olatunji to LeRoi Jones, John Coltrane, and John Cage? How do you grasp the range of an artist who was the first to bring electronics into jazz, but also kept alive the repertory of Fletcher Henderson and Duke Ellington? Whose recorded output was so great that not only has no one assayed it, no one can even claim to have heard it all? An artist said to be so marginal and obscure that he has never been honored at American jazz festivals or at Lincoln Center, but who taught at the University of California at Berkeley and was inducted into the Alabama Music Hall of Fame by Governor George Wallace?

In later years it was easy to be puzzled by Sun Ra's Afro-Platonic neo-hermeticism or for some to laugh at his excesses (*he* certainly did). But in the 1970s his six-hour multimedia barrages could be genuinely frightening experiences. The music moved from stasis to chaos and back again, with shrieks and howls pouring out of an Arkestra dressed like the Archers of Arboria; dancers swirled through the audience ("butterflies of the night," a French critic called them); fire-eaters, gilded muscle-men, and midgets paraded in front of masks, shadow puppets, and films of the pyramids. Performance rules were being broken one-a-minute. Nothing like it had been seen since Wagner's throwdowns at Bayreuth. Somehow Sun Ra's spectacles seemed to capture all the promise and the threat of the 1960s—especially since no one in the audience had a clue as to what was going on.

In tireless interviews and endless jeremiads to his audiences, Sunny tried to communicate that it was time to rethink the assumptions on which our daily existence rests, and that, unlike philosophies and religions, his message affirmed life and did not "deal with death." And in that spirit, reflecting on Sun Ra's passing I realize that some may remember him as one of the great avant-gardists of the second half of the twentieth century; others may think of him as a Black cultural nationalist, one who extended Afrocentricity from Egypt to the heavens. And they will all be right, though his sense of tradition was too strong to tolerate innovation for its own sake, and his spirit too lavishly universalistic ("omniversalistic," he would have corrected me) to stop at the vulgar limits of race and history.

I prefer to see him as the last of the great Romantic composers, driven by a hunger for a totality that only music could express. Like the Romantics—who were inspired by the Pythagoreans—he saw that harmony and mathematics were fundamental to both music and the universe; and like Nietzsche and Schopenhauer, he understood that music symbolized the unity in diversity that is the cosmos, the big band its space vehicle, Afro-American aesthetics its culture-synthesizing principle. His compositions are programmatic in the grandest Romantic sense: pictures and guide-paths to emotional and spiritual states. Over 20 years ago Sun Ra was saying that jazz was virtually extinct, and that most musicians were now merely actors. He saw that great music—its social and economic functions stripped away—is always rooted in emotion. When it isn't, it becomes merely referential, mannered, and earth-bound dull. And given the sublime role he saw for music in life, it is also a sinful waste. Such a legacy was God's truth in the 1960s (and the 1860s, for that matter), but, as even Sun Ra admitted, a tough sell in the postmodern 1990s. Still, all things considered, I'd keep my eyes on the skies.

Chapter 28

!Ornette Coleman: ?Civilization

Kurt Masur stepped into Avery Fischer Hall on the first of two nights devoted to Ornette Coleman's 1972 symphonic work, *Skies of America.* Before he even raised his baton to conduct Aaron Copland's shopworn *Fanfare for the Common Man,* my attention fell on what the spotlight revealed at the edge of the podium: a white plastic saxophone. It was the emblem which once signified to some the arrival of the glories of free jazz, an Excalibur stuck in the rock of conventional art. To others it was a cheap, childlike horn which signaled fraud, or worse, anti-jazz; the badge of a whacked-out, shabbily dressed, fuzzy-headed, strange-talking group of musicians from what was just beginning to be called the Lower East Side. But to Coleman it was just a horn with a dry sound, one "in which you could almost see the shape of the breath of a note." Now, with the horn illuminated and the New York Philharmonic beginning to tune up, the harmolodics had started before Coleman even appeared on stage.

Under the cryptic cipher of "?Civilization," Ornette Coleman occupied a week of the Lincoln Center Festival (a venue where he has not been welcome by the jazz division), the latest of his mysterious comings and goings on the New York scene. In his first public manifestation, almost forty years ago, Coleman appeared with Charlie Haden, Don Cherry, and Billy Higgins, a quartet which now wears a mantle in jazz history equal only to that of Louie Armstrong's Hot Five or Jelly Roll Morton's Red Hot Chili Peppers. Just at the point when some musicians were growing tired of conventional pop song structure and slowing down harmonic movement through modal playing, Coleman arrived to take things a step further, liberating musicians from having to improvise on chordal patterns altogether. Like poets of the day, he let the limits of his breath determine structure. "I analyzed where I was taking the changes, the harmonies and other elements, and using them as ideas. Not using them to get to ideas." Added to this was his wandering, free-ranging tonality, which eventually changed everyone's ears so that post-Coleman, tonality became a conscious choice, not just a matter of wrong or right, and the door was opened for free-tempered singers to come, like John Lydon circa PIL's "Swan Lake."

No sooner than the shock from the initial group was wearing off, Coleman announced himself as a classical composer by first writing some chamber works with conventional instrumentation and then writing and scoring the set of compositions he called *Skies of America*. He said that there was no difference in his writing for a symphony orchestra and for his small group: with the quartet, "what I was doing was to try and write a melodic line that sounded like it was structured orchestratedly. I was trying to play orchestrated music in a small context." And the spirit of that original quartet could be heard in the orchestra at Lincoln Center.

Coleman (whose clothes have always been as ahead of style as his music) this night joined the Philharmonic on stage with the octet Prime Time wearing a black-and-white-checked suit and a dark summer hat, and the work began with massed strings whose spread harmony is apparently meant to express the sky. At times the strings were given Ornette's nursery-bop themes, at others they sighed with bent notes of the oldest sort. But the octet and the Orchestra also bounced themes around, one triggering reactions in the other (sometimes they seemed to be taking twos—exchanging licks), or joining together in what appeared to be moments of mutual swing (though Prime Time's amplification often overwhelmed the orchestra). There were also held chords by the orchestra which allowed the octet some solo space, and when Coleman's turn came he managed to play notes that sounded as if they had never been played before.

The work has its lighter moments, but it is not easy listening: there are no obvious thematic linkages, no big climaxes; in fact, like much of African American popular music it was filled with many small climaxes. Coleman has said that *Skies of America* is about clefs, that is, about the differences between the tunings of the instruments of the symphony orchestra, and therefore about *difference*, but also a certain way of rebalancing. He's argued that all notes should be equal; and while Arnold Schoenberg also said something to the same effect, Coleman meant it. His aim is nothing less than a complete revision of American musical thinking, a transformation of language, and in *Skies of America*, a subversion of symphonic methodology.

Thursday night hundreds were turned away at the box office because the faithful and the curious knew the original quartet was to be united, minus the late Don Cherry. The evening began with a trio of Coleman, Charlie Haden on bass, and Billy Higgins on drums. Haden now could be clearly heard at last, all low-end rumblings and sliding chromatic lines that hinted at dozens of other songs. Higgins emerged again as a great drummer, championing rhythms of the street, African and African American, yet full of light and shadow, and often delicate to the point of near inaudibility. And Coleman (in peacock blue silk suit) proved himself still capable of the cocked phrase that leaves you spinning. In the second half trumpeter Wallace Roney and pianist Kenny Baron joined the group, Baron playing sparsely or not at all behind Coleman, but sometimes soloing a cappella with sublime clarity. When singers Lauren Kinhan and former Prime Time bassist Chris Walker joined them to sing their own and Coleman's songs, the audience witnessed the most avant-garde group in jazz history in the role of a nightclub backup band. But it was also a rare chance to hear Coleman play accompanying obbligatos, many of which were in straight r&b form, though a bit more wistful than one might have expected.

On the final night Coleman returned (in painter's-palette suit) with Prime Time, the group that he has held together in one manifestation or other since 1972, and one which has resisted full public acceptance for just as long. The fact is that, as with his early quartet, we do not yet hear Prime Time as the band Coleman hears. Patiently he explains that it is an attempt to remove the distinction between melody, harmony, and rhythm, that players are free to roam without the "caste system of sound" maintained by keys, cadences, returns: "harmolodics allow a person to use a multiplicity of elements to express more than one dimension at one time"; "harmolodics means the loss of a style in music." To many listeners Prime Time is just a rock band, albeit a very peculiar one, with its strong beats canceled by weak ones and with no obvious focus. But Coleman has always seen the guitars and amplification as the smallest format he could use and still get a full orchestral sound. The listener's problem may be that (as Coleman complains) his saxophone has not been mixed down enough, that he is not a soloist. Or that the way we hear music is still too concert-oriented, too linear and one-dimensional—having heard Prime Time in the round, I can affirm that they sound like six or seven different bands depending on the listener's location. What he seems to want is a music of such density of information, yet also open, that all of its sources become equal, with their chance to shine, even if ambiguously—asking listeners to experience or maybe even perform the work in their heads.

Was this Coleman's intention on the last night, filling the show with rappers, dancers, contortionists, jugglers, sword swallowers, glass walkers, a near three-hour video which became a kind of museum of ethnology, and lastly Lou Reed and Laurie Anderson, all of them connected by an obscure syntax that was not easily read? One easy answer is that he sought to return us to the functional music of another era, and like Sun Ra immerse us in the logic of black cabaret with its shake dancers, freak acts, and exotics; another would be that Coleman seeks a tactile expression of a new age of race-, gender-, and shape-changing which is the visual equivalent of note-changing, bringing the music back to its corporeal base in dancing, procession, and ecstatic release.

Whatever his aim, in the still center of it all stood Ornette Coleman, like a point of perspective which seemed at times to be vanishing—fragile, alone with a vision he longs to share, his white saxophone that big inverted and reversed question mark still hanging over us.

Chapter 29

The Local and the Express:
Anthony Braxton's Title-Drawings

From a distance the history of the art produced by African-Americans might be seen as a series of swings from the ethnic to the universal and back again. What is perceived or claimed at one moment as distinctively African becomes at another moment African-American, or American, or even European. This ambiguity may be a specific instance of a more general rule: that all American art is indeterminate in source, bound as it is to the instability created by the shifting myths surrounding race in the West. In any case, one of the most striking features of the contributions of musicians who are ascribed as African-Americans is that they cannot be easily understood either as simply the result of the direct continuity of African tradition or a variation on European tradition, but only as a unique product of the cultural process of creolization. And music, along with language, is the example par excellence of the process of creolization in operation.

"Creole" is a word common to all parts of the New World and even to some of the Old, but one about which there is little agreement. Sometimes applied to a style of cuisine, a mode of behavior, or a person of a certain "color" or social status, it seems always to refer to a certain means of creating culture, and to a way, a style, of doing things. Creole languages are sometimes referred to as "broken," or bastardized versions of standard, national languages. If regarded as words on a list, as discrete objects, written in a European writing system, they do look strangely—possibly even comically—European. But linguists tell us that when put into speech, the grammars of creoles show principles of organization that owe little to European language history. Rather than being seen as dialects of European languages, creoles might be better understood as converged and reassembled languages, products of the joining together of two or more historically distinct languages under very pressurized circumstances.

What makes this kind of language situation even more complicated is that creoles virtually always coexist with standard languages. For instance in the Caribbean, Martinique standard French is considered by the government and the schools to be the standard language, even while most of the population speaks *Créole*. (*Créole*, in addition to being the language of the underclass, is the language of pop songs, joking, and the emotions.)

Generalizing from the creation of creole languages to other domains, we come face-to-face with this paradox: while it may be possible to identify the sources of individual components, when put into use, new combinations and totalities come into being which have no apparent specific relationship to their historical sources. In the case of language this means that while particular sounds and words can be traced to particular languages, the total speech that results is a new and emergent product. The same is true of music. Even if one can trace the sources of particular instruments, ensembles, and rhythms, when we hear them combined in performance, their sources are moot at best.

The process of creolization is often understood as being the result of raw necessity, as a make-do phenomenon among the poor and oppressed, or as a function of secrecy. But expediency and privacy seem secondary to the process of interpretation between different systems of values and meanings. When one system of interpretation is dominant, the minority system is sometimes forcibly translated into dominant terms, particularly where the parallels between the two are few.

All of this is complicated by the fact that in the twentieth century much of the art by African-Americans has entered the broader public realm by having been adopted by commercially cultivated audiences of white youth. When musics originally created by African-American musicians for their own people were spread to a more general audience, the primary meanings were often lost or distorted. Describing the way that late 1960s black soul music entered the world of the white teenager, Ian Hoare argues that what had for African-Americans been a broad-based, shared aesthetic, became for whites an alien art used in order to reject and contradict their own tradition:

This often means that black music is appropriated by way of a series of crude (and false) antitheses. Toughness is espoused because it is preferable to sentimentality; repression is opposed by license rather than liberation, bodilessness by brainlessness, a highly developed musical technique by an almost calculated technical incompetence.[1]

It was by means of just such reductive misunderstandings that the spirituals came to be seen as sorrowful, dixieland as good-time music, the blues as self-pitying, etc. Such narrow aesthetic readings have had the effect of constraining African-American performers and artists, of holding them to social roles that are at best stereotypically benign. The music made by African-Americans is usually seen by whites as exclusively "social," because it is a music which is often developed in interaction, through performance, rather than through solitary composition. Yet it is this very process of aesthetic-through-process that makes the music not just a style but an ethic. Many musicians have struggled against these narrowed perspectives, sometimes by demanding the same respect given to European classical music; sometimes by broadening the terms to include dimensions such as spirituality, soul, and metaphysics, and by reaching for deeper historical and cross-cultural ties (in Egypt and other parts of Africa, for example); sometimes by simply denying the existence of the imposed categories (so, in the early 1970s, jazz began to become a marked term, sometimes enclosed by quotes, sometimes prefixed with the same verbal flag of alert used by the Nation of Islam: "so-called").

Anthony Braxton began a rigorous campaign in the 1970s to relocate the music created by himself and other African-Americans. First, he introduced a metalanguage to redefine the music and short-circuit facile interpretations (using terms such as "affinity dynamics," "pulse track structures," and "vibrational alignment," all of which, incidentally, no longer seem so strange); and second by extending the sources of the music beyond the usual limits of Africa, slavery, the ghetto, and the like, to world history, anthropology, and (with other composers of the 1960s and 1970s such as Sun Ra, Leo Smith, and John Coltrane) even to the solar system and the cosmos. Braxton ceased to give verbal titles to his compositions and performances as per the usual European practice, and instead used formulas, cabbalistic constructions, and miniature drawings, which from "Composition 105A" forward also began to incorporate human figures. And with "Composition 113" his titles also became multi-dimensional and visually dramatic. Now, if critics wished to write about a Braxton performance or recording, they were obliged to reproduce the pictorial titles, or undertake a difficult description of these titles/pictures.[2]

As jarring as Braxton's titling first seems, it is possible to find precedents for it among African-American musicians. Many of the earliest jazz recordings were given arcane or extremely local names.[3] By the bop era, titles were often based on sounds alone (Charlie Parker's "Klactoveesedstene"), rhythms (Thelonious Monk's "Let's Call This"), or speech-inflected instrumental figures (Miles Davis' "So What").[4]

As yet, Braxton has not asked musicians to "read" these later titles/drawings musically, nor has he offered complete interpretations of them. Still, it is possible to recognize elements which seem to transcend his private musical world. One marked feature of these drawings is the presence of elements which also appear in a configuration of works that Africanist/art historian Robert Farris Thompson has identified as Kongo-inspired African-American folk art.[5] These patterns especially appear in rural yard art, that is African-American yards which are "swept" free of grass, and are decorated and "dressed" with found objects, painted stones, bottles, "non-lawn furniture," and arcane symbols. All of these elements seen in yard art are also found in Braxton's titles: *containment* (markers, boundaries, and wires); *figuration* (toy-like objects, simplified animals); *medicine* (plants); and most persistently, *motion* (ladders, wheels, tires, boats, bicycles, cars and trucks, highways and railroads). To these one might add—following Thompson's lead and recent research by Grey Gundaker[6]—*flash* (searchlights and spotlights) and *enthronement* (chairs, seats). Yet this break from the European tradition of yard and garden is often read by whites as being no art at all, merely the untidy accumulation of junk.

If we focus on only one of these elements—motion—we note the presence of railroad tracks and trains, and indeed Braxton often increasingly refers to the interplay in his compositions in terms of trains, tracks, and the operations of switching and movement. The blues and jazz have always contained programmatic musics based on trains (Ellington's "Daybreak Express"), and, later, cars (Eddie Vinson's "Cadillac Blues"), buses (Walter Coleman's "Greyhound Blues"), airplanes (Lionel Hampton's "Flying Home"), and spaceships (Sun Ra's "Rocket Number Nine"). But trains have far and away dominated the imagination of those who titled music in terms of travel. Seemingly, every known American railroad line has had a praise song.

Lionel Hampton, for example, describes the departure of the Special from Birmingham, Alabama at six o'clock every evening in the early 1900s, as a celebration so important that crowds gathered and cheered, and where the spirit of the moment extended to the train crew who gave away food and even coal.[7] That Braxton's father worked for the railroad in Chicago (like Hampton's grandfather or Sun Ra's father and mother in Birmingham) reinforces the trains' importance as icons. They continue to be obsessions of contemporary African-American artists like David Hammons, whose 1989 installation at Exit Art Gallery in New York City had a model train running through piles of coal and upturned piano lids, while recordings of John Coltrane's "Blue Trane," James Brown's "Night Train," and Thelonious Monk's "Little Rootie Tootie" played (Braxton is also a model train enthusiast). Yet even here railroads bring Euro-American and Anglo-Christian symbolism (think of country music's hellbound trains or Nathaniel Hawthorne's "Celestial Railway") into conjunction with African-American images of optimism and earthly escape. (Black railroads, however, run underground, as well as on the surface and elevated to the skies.)

The comparison of the rise of the new black music of the 1960s and 1970s to folk art of the yard is not as capricious as it may seem, because during that period a basic reexamination of musical resources was under way: the accepted principles of tonality were questioned; a rebalancing of the relations of harmony, melody, and rhythm was undertaken; and the functions and even the proper venues of the music were heatedly discussed. For those who did not follow this new consciousness, much of the music seemed unprincipled and without focus. Since it was no longer "entertainment" music for drinking and dancing, it was not clear to many how one should listen to it, or what it was for. Like yard art, it was seen as artless, the product of the incompetent and the charlatan.

It might be suggested that Anthony Braxton's title-drawings are "about" the same thing as many African-American folk arts; that they derive from common sources and have benefited from the same experiences so as to converge on similar grounds from circuitous routes; that they are, in other words, exclusively part of the African-American aesthetic. But it could also be said that what they share, and what we can learn from them together, is that they both employ creole ways of doing things and making meaning, ways which result in a kind of art that Umberto Eco calls the "open work": a creation susceptible "to countless different interpretations which do not impinge upon its unadulterable specificity," a work which offers an unusually high degree of possibilities in the amount of information provided and in the form of ambiguity entailed, and one which makes every reception of it "both an *interpretation* of it and a *performance* of it, because in every reception the work takes on a fresh perspective for itself."[8] It is this openness, this ambiguity, this emergent quality, which makes the art of African-Americans seem both perpetually modern, and a model for the postmodern.

Chapter 30

Magnificent Declension: *Solibo Magnificent*

All novels, Mikhail Bakhtin says, are about language. Narratives may engage, characters may inspire empathy or stir up antagonism, but it's the layering and interweaving of languages, the confrontation of speech styles and dialects that best define the novel as a form. And it is the novel that best represents the multilingual babel that is the nature of every human society, even the smallest village or tribe. Yet it is typically those societies on the fringes of the centripetally nationalistic West—those of the Caribbean, pre-Soviet Russia, Africa, Latin America—which offer up the truly centrifugal, multilingual novel.

Case in point: Patrick Chamoiseau, author of the critically acclaimed *Texaco*, writes from Martinique, the Caribbean country most closely allied with France, the New World territory where French is the most cultivated, and the island that produced perhaps the twentieth century's finest French poet, Aimé Césaire. On Martinique, the primary languages are French and Créole, the latter existing uneasily (like all creoles) alongside the standard language with which it shares kinship; like a bastard child, Créole is inevitably considered inferior, a mark of the underclass, and—worse for the middle class—an audible reminder of the island's status as an outpost of Empire. For an educated person to speak Créole is either absurd or revolutionary; and though the form of the novel gives a kind of license to its representation, to put Créole in print for the world is to give it greater status that it has in Martinique, where it is usually restricted to humor magazines.

Solibo Magnificent, though an earlier work than *Texaco*, is more daring in its bold use of speech and dense characterization.[1] Though Chamoiseau draws equally on both languages of Martinique, working them together to create new forms, he unashamedly writes under the sign of Créole, and so represents people who are not usually heard from. By doing so, he also has available an emotional and intellectual register not part of standard French. (Créole, according to Derek Walcott, another Caribbean writer with a creole in his background, is richer in nuance, "audibly aware of its melody, its pauses and flourishes, its direction toward laughter even in tragedy.") Chamoiseau's people speak in a phantasmagoria of words composed in the meter of dreamtime which he throws down before the received pronunciation of French:

it's Soliboscape Solibo from the depths-without-depth Solibo of the forgotten Solibo of the traces without path without Tiger without Rabbit Solibo without sugar without salt natal total hospital congenital bottle municipal jackal clubpodal local grammatical.

Though composed of police reports, authorial descriptions, ethnographic notes, the testimonies of fourteen witnesses (one of whom is the "author"), even drum rhythms, the plot of *Solibo Magnificent* is surprisingly straightforward and coherent: Solibo, a storyteller and "wordsman" of the folk, is performing an oral epic in a park before a ragtag group of listeners during Carnival in Fort-de-France, when suddenly (in medias res so to speak), he chokes to death on his own words, setting off a police investigation that turns his entire audience into suspects and eventually escalates into threats, humiliations, beatings, and two deaths. As a story it's not much—maybe even less, once we realize that Solibo's death is intended as a symbol of the dying of an oral culture. But as an account of the lives and adventures of languages, a depiction of the social laminations and interpretations of discourses in an ex-colonial society, the novel is remarkable.

But what language is this American edition written in? The original French-Créole compound, subdivided by various dialects and argots, was complex enough. Once translated (by the team who also translated *Texaco*), several other strata of language appear. There is a glossary to aid the reader when the untranslatable peeks through the English (or perhaps Englishes, for the translators manage to find words between the cracks of English and American slang, misfiring only when their choice of equivalents seems either dated or too hip). The complexities grow and intertwine, a rich and heady mix, but one not unique in the history of literature—multiple languages and even glossaries could be found in the earliest English novels before writers like Jane Austen flattened and homogenized the voices of class, race, gender, and age. Like Samuel Richardson, Chamoiseau evokes a divided community of talkers, in which some are incomprehensible to others, or one group pretends not to understand another (or pretends *to* understand another). For instance, when the French-trained Inspector and the Chief Sergeant interrogate one of the witnesses, they both speak French to him, but translate in terms of class: "your age, profession, and permanent address?" "Huh?" "The Inspector asks you what hurricane you were born after, what you do for the béké, and what side of town you sleep at night?" And over it all, unheard, falls the shadow of the *békés* (the white descendants of the old planter class), who never make an appearance, but nonetheless penetrate every domain.

Martinique has a long history of literary factions (such as Negritude and *antillanité*). Chamoiseau is a leading figure in Créolité, a movement that seeks to locate a unique voice and identity in their past and work it into a literary form called "oraliture." From this base, Créolité promises to reach beyond the local and the folkloristic to the rest of the world. Their aim is neither to create their own classics, nor to replace the world's classics in an act of totalitarian universality, but to reach toward "diversalité," the creation of a "world diffracted but recomposed, the conscious harmonization of preserved diversities," as Chamoiseau and his colleagues put it in their 1989 manifesto, *Éloge de la créolité*.

The languages are new, the locale tropical, but the project is reminiscent of another "diversalité," modernism, and the striving of James Joyce and even T. S. Eliot to build a universal art on the vernaculars of the world (a modernism in which we pretend as if we understood one another). Chamoiseau also reminds us that the black world has played a central role in the creation of modernism, and that its influence has not yet run its course.

Chapter 31

Metaphors of Incommensurability

> *"Notes is good enough for you people, but us likes a mixtery."*
> —*Jeannette Robinson Murphy, "The Survival of African
> Music in America"*

The old black woman who gave Jeannette Robinson Murphy an account of how spirituals were created reminds us that it is "mixture" that lurks behind the vast array of words that have been used over the last four hundred years to describe the processes and products of cultural contact in the Americas and elsewhere in the world: words like *nomadism, deterritorialization, transnationalism, modernism,* and *postmodernism,* all of which attempt to characterize some of the conditions under which people come into contact and produce new cultural forms; or *marronage, border culture, heterogeneity, cosmopolitanism, multiculturalism,* and *pluralism,* terms used to name the social results of such encounters, results that social scientists have also called *transculturalization, oppositional culture,* or *contra-acculturation.*

These are only a small part of a field of terminology that is rich to the point of obsession, an obsession that perhaps thinly disguises the fear that race and culture are inextricably—perhaps even causally—linked, a fetishization that sees things, like people, in the process of dissolving and reforming before the eyes. Despite the refutation of just such a linkage by anthropologists since the time of Boas, terms for racial intermixing are still used to describe the pollution and degradation that results when cultural forms are changed through contact between social groups (especially those in which one group is dominant), terms such as *mongrelization, bastardization, corruption, métisage,* or *mestizaje,* and the recent more polite or ironic terms, *symbiosis* and *hybrid.* But this is the terminology of those who speak from positions of dominance; the view from the bottom often yields quite different terms, such as the food and cooking metaphors *gumbo, callaloo, massala,* and *sancocho,* or those of violence and disruption, like *broke-up,* or of mock or transvalued opprobrium, like *bad*. Similarly, the defenders of the arts of the dominant describe the products of the contact between what they perceive as high and low arts as *pastiche, macaronic, aping,* or at best, as *mimicry, ventriloquism, parody,* or *mockery*. (But compare how the same individuals speak of the arts that result from contact of peoples of relatively equal social status—especially across national lines; the words are *borrowing, influence, loan,* and so on.) It is only among the more radical and political elements of the art worlds of the West that we find terms such as *bricolage, détournement, montage, fusion,* and *collage,* words that originally surfaced in art movements like dada, surrealism, and lettrism, and that attempt to complicate the nature and sources of creativity. (That those very art movements may also have been inspired by products of such cultural contact should at least be noted in passing.)

In the Americas the oldest known term for these processes is *creole,*[1] itself apparently created in creole fashion from the Portuguese *criar* ("to bring up") and *crioulo* ("native") and who-knows-what-else and merged into a term with both adjectival and noun forms. The discourse of creolization has continued now for four centuries, an ongoing dialogue which remains remarkably open and inviting of participation. The concept of creole has been used across a great deal of geographical and intellectual territory in the New World (and to a lesser degree even in parts of the Old). From Cotton Mather's description of Harvard graduates ("shining criolians") to the offspring of Russians and Aleuts in the Bering Strait, from the children of French planters in Louisiana to the children of newly arrived slaves, the concept has always meant a new product, something emergent, something else. It has been fought over and claimed by various peoples, and as such retains a certain residual ambiguity and variability. It has referred to foods, spices, clothing, language, architecture, literature, and styles, as well as to individuals and entire races; it has been said to be an impure state of being, but also the purest state possible. (Is something new purer than the old, or is it the essence of corruption?) But in whatever way it has been used, it has raised questions about the appropriateness of such concepts as "descent," "origins," and the very status of *being*.

In spite of a long and widespread history of the folk use of the idea of creole, academic thinking on creolization has until very recently been focused primarily on Afro-Caribbean and African American populations, and more often than not on the languages of these peoples. Some of the highlights of this academic work deserves at least a brief overview, since it has given us our clearest and most sustained view of the concept of creolization, one that ultimately raises fundamental questions about the nature of language and even society itself.

A Brief History

Melville J. Herskovits conceptualized the relations between African and European cultures with a set of processual terms, the key one of which was *reinterpretation*, a concept refined out of an earlier African Americanist concept, *syncretism.*[2] Where syncretism was used to describe the situation within which African cultural forms fused with European forms of similar configuration, reinterpretation encompassed situations in which a cultural form from one society can be given another society's function or value, or in which a newer alien form can be assimilated to older functions and values. (The classic case of reinterpretation is the joining of African deities to Catholic saints in Haiti, Brazil, Trinidad, and elsewhere.) Herskovits saw this process as describing the reinterpretation of African forms into European terms. It could work both ways, however, as Alfred Métraux in *Voodoo in Haiti* (1959) seemed to imply that imposed European forms and values were reinterpreted into African forms and functions.[3]

To this notion of reinterpretation the linguist Douglas Taylor—himself a native of Dominica in the West Indies—added the concept of *remodeling*, a notion apparently borrowed from classical philology. The essence of this idea was that forms are not only reinterpreted, but also gradually changed and transformed to resemble their cultural environment—African words come to seem Portuguese, Portuguese to seem English, English to seem Dutch, and so on. In an example, Taylor traced the transformation of the early Surinam maroon language Saramaccan word *sinda* ("sit") into *sindo*, the modern Saramaccan word with the same meaning, to *sidon*, the Sranan (the Surinam creole) term with equivalent meaning.[4] Positing a missing form, **sindon*, the evolutionary sequence then becomes

sinda > sindo > *sindon > sidon

Assuming that the original *sinda*, like Haitian Créole *sita* and the Dutch West Indies Papiamentu *sinta*, has its roots in Ibero-Romance (Ptg. *assentar*, Sp. *assentar*, Sp. *sentado*), *sidon* ends up resembling the English "sit down." The problem that this presents for historical linguistics is, at what point did the word change its genetic relationship? That is, at what point did it change from Portuguese to English?

Karl Reisman later articulated the dynamics of remodeling and reinterpretation as a constant creative process in relations between creoles and lexically similar European languages, permitting a given element, motif, or syllable to take on one cultural garb and context of meaning or another, but also to oscillate (not simply switch) unclearly between forms; he introduced the term *transvaluation* for the point where these movements occur.[5] Reisman put this process within a context of the duality of cultural identities, a theme elaborated by black writers in the Caribbean and the United States (the theme of *masking* and *doubleness* in W. E. B. Du Bois, Ralph Ellison, and George Lamming) as well as by folklorists (e.g., Roger D. Abrahams on tea meeting in the Anglophonic West Indies, and John Szwed and Morton Marks on set dances).[6]

The Brazilianist Roger Bastide refined and extended these ideas by distinguishing between material reinterpretations—those that remain and continue on the same cultural level and thus do not profoundly influence modes of thought (to return to an earlier example, African deities and Catholic saints could be considered as existing in a substitutive, masked relationship)—and formal reinterpretations, in which forms are comprehended in light of newly acquired values and conceptions (e.g., mystical trance reinterpreted as a form of spiritualism and then used as a means of upward mobility within a national, organized church setting; such a case is Umbanda in Brazil). Bastide noted that the first and more typical form of reinterpretation occurs in segregated social settings, the latter in more "racially democratic" societies.[7]

It is important to remind ourselves that all of these African American cultural developments took place either under slavery or in societies at their fringe, the various maroon communities, and were shaped by Africans and their descendants. It was the special historical and social complexities of these societies that next needed to be elaborated in order to show the wider social contexts impinging upon them—that is, to develop a historical model of creolization and relate it to cultural process—and Edward Kamau Brathwaite has been at work on this for the last thirty years, most notably in *Contradictory Omens*.[8] He notes that much of the analysis of the West Indies has been caught in the trap of dualism, such as white/black, or colonizer/colonized, while the creative force of the creole experience (the interchange and transformation of cultural and social elements) has been slighted. Indeed, these dualities may have blinded many to the emergent and creative qualities of West Indian life. One thinks of V. S. Naipaul's assertion that "nothing has ever been created in the West Indies, and nothing will ever be created,"[9] and Derek Walcott's response that "nothing will always be created in the West Indies . . . because what will come out of there is like nothing one has ever seen," a response that manages simultaneously to transvalue "nothing" into a positive, a presence rather than an absence, as well as perhaps to present a basis on which to challenge received notions of art and mimesis.[10] Yet while Brathwaite emphasizes the emergent quality of creole life, he also insists (possibly to the distress of some anti-essentialists) that there remains in all parties to the creole experience an engagement with ancestral relationships, with what he calls *nam*, the apparently irreducible core or essence that coexists with the cosmopolitan and processual qualities of creolization. And it is the interplay of these factors, he suggests, which determines the outcome.

Creole Languages

Though the general features of creole languages have been understood for some time, the descriptions of them typically have been simplistic. In part this is the result of premature attempts to universalize them through a typology, as part of a unilinear evolutionary process wherein pidgin languages always turn into creole languages; and in part it is a consequence of attempting to oversystemize languages, to reduce their inherent variation in the name of science. The most widely recognized creole languages are found in the Caribbean, in parts of South America, the United States, Sierra Leone, in what are mistakenly called the pidgins of West Africa, the islands of the Indian Ocean, and early Afrikaans in South Africa. These languages all coexist in a complex relationship with English, Dutch, French, or Portuguese in the same areas. All these creoles share common features in verb system, aspect, syllable remodeling, serial verbs, stress and tone independence, semantic shift in common words, and a heritage of African words and syntax. Though they may be crudely characterized as the languages of the enslaved or the conquered because of their origins in the plantation system, they also have the ability to conquer, and have become the intimate and folkloric languages of whites in some areas, the vehicular language of East Indians and Middle Easterners in others, and have been spread through migration and popular culture to the rest of the world.

These creoles are more than the result of the meeting and interaction of European and African languages. They are also the consequences of the encounter of the different styles, forms of expression, and beliefs associated with these languages. And once in place they exist in opposition to—but also overlapping with—the imposed European languages. The creolized forms thus also came to exist in a peculiar relationship between African systems of stylization and means of interpretation of forms and meaning on the one hand, and their European equivalents on the other. While never fully resolved in this social state, they are realized in an oscillation of forms, a movement back and forth across the Euro-African scale.

What all this adds up to is that linguistic creolization involves the merging and dissolving of language images, the ambiguous play of language forms and meanings, of forms and styles, all decentered, with no clear sense of which language is primary or foregrounded, all maintained under an apparent merging of languages with no apparent fixed boundaries of distinct linguistic systems, or of nonshared syntaxes.

Of course, all languages may be said to exist between the poles of systematic structural features on the one hand, and contextual adaptation and creation and the varying valences and ranges of individual items of form and meaning on the other. Yet if grammar or syntax is conceived of as a relation of form and interpretation, creolized languages seem to create unusual amounts of division between formal systems and meanings. In some cases they seem to be able to move in relative independence from each other, leading to the remodeling of new forms on the one hand and the reinterpretation of "Afro-" and "Euro-" forms on the other.

One of the other results of the creole process is that there is a greater ambiguity in the relation of form and meanings, and the production of a multiplicity of meanings beyond that found in most languages. Further, the nature of the search for multiplicity seems to carry certain specifically "African"- and some specifically "Creole"-style features and ways of handling and interpreting meaning (thus paralleling Brathwaite's insistence on the continuity of core ancestral values within the creole experience).

Considered as a whole, creole languages provide one instance of human creativity closely resembling what Umberto Eco calls the "open work" of art, a work that offers an unusually high degree of possibilities in the amount of information provided and in the form of ambiguity entailed. It is a creation susceptible "to countless different interpretations which do not impinge upon its unadulterable specificity," and one that makes every reception of it "both an interpretation of it and a performance of it, because in every reception the work takes on a fresh perspective for itself."[11] It is this openness, this ambiguity, this emergent quality, which has made art of the Americas in general (and African American art in particular) seem both perpetually modern, and a model of the postmodern.[12]

Yet open though they may be, creole forms are not completely indeterminate, and in fact often seem to carry with them cues to interpretation, and, by modeling the process in front of us, even provide the means for understanding the processes that gave rise to them. All art may have such interpretive cues built into it, but creole forms cue the observer/listener/participant into a position that also dislocates a single frame, monologic point of view, thus virtually assuring the production of new meanings. If we return again to the woman quoted by Jeannette Robinson Murphy (where "mixtery" creolizes "mixture" and "mystery" at the same time as it asserts a contrast between written and nonwritten forms—i.e., "notes" opposed to a "mix"), we see the creolization process demonstrated for us. Think also of W. E. B. Du Bois's opening chapter in *The Souls of Black Folk,* where in delineating double-consciousness among African Americans, he converges at least three distinct threads of meaning: the well-established nineteenth-century meaning of double consciousness as an abnormal condition, a form of multiple personality; the revision of that meaning by transcendentalist and European Romantics into the notion of the artist as exemplar of true understanding warring with "the social forces inhibiting genuine self-realization" (as Emerson put it); and the African American folk conception of those born with "double vision," those able to see into both the spiritual and material realms.[13] Yet Du Bois, like Murphy's anonymous informant, does not belabor the multiplicities or spell out the possibilities, but leaves them floating, open, free to be interpreted by those who could and would do so.

Creolization, whether called by that name or not, has often been a highly conscious process and has served as the locus of new and radical artistic and political developments in a variety of New World areas. There were, for example, the aesthetic proclamations of the Martin Fierro group in Argentina, or the *Anthropophagous Manifesto* of the Brazilian "cannibals" in the 1920s.[14] In more recent times developments in the West Indies and Mexico have led to the examination of their own folklore and a reckoning with creolization that has incited political and artistic potential. Over the last thirty years in Martinique, for example, there has been increasing reaction to implications of the literary politics of negritude as articulated in the work of Aimé Césaire. "Antillanité," a position with which Edouard Glissant is often associated, stresses creativity rather than preservation as a basis for political and artistic activity.[15] And even if those of Glissant's persuasion view their folkloric background ambivalently, they nonetheless draw strength from the transformative and complex possibilities of their culture. Now we see in Martinique a new movement called "créolité" (as represented by Jean Bernabé, Patrick Chamoiseau, Raphael Confiant, and others), which expresses renewed interest in folklore (especially in the work of their own folklorists) not so much as a means of reconstructing a real or imaginary past, but as a basis for a new creative openness. It offers them a sense that what they have discovered in their own cultural history provides a model for the world, not in timeless values or the Western notion of universality, but in *diversalité,* "the great opportunity of a world diffracted but recomposed, the conscious harmonization of preserved diversities."[16] Such movements provide us with more than opportunities for the study of exotic folklore. They have much to teach us about our own cultural processes.

Creolization, Mixture, or Something Else?

Perhaps creolization is a concept broad enough to serve parallel phenomena in areas beyond the Americas; perhaps its lessons will reach
across historical and linguistic lines. Perhaps other terms might serve
just as well. But to my mind, none has yet emerged. True, in recent years
the concept of hybridity has attracted an unusually large following. Yet I
think its usage has been by and large uncritical, and, though super-
ficially open and indefinite, ultimately too limited. The modern use of
the term *hybrid* derives from postcolonial studies, especially those concerned with India, and was developed around a particular use of "text,"
and one that is textual in a rather narrow sense (at least from the perspective of linguistics). "Hybridity" is a biological and sexual metaphor,
usually applied oppositionally (though not necessarily as oppositionally
as when some West Indian intellectuals many years ago spoke of the
power of "mongrelization" in New World art). And, in spite of some writers' interest in ambiguity in hybrid states, there is nonetheless often a
crude duality behind the term that distorts the complexity of the process
described; worse, there is also the assumption of an essentially pure past
for all parties before encounter. In spite of the progressive intentions of
its users, hybridity is too often the controlling metaphor of a rather shallow and ahistorical analysis.

    This is not to say that *creolization* is always used with precision. Indeed
it, too, often functions as a shallow (and even mystical) metaphor for the
merging of previously "untainted" elements into a single new form. For
example, it is often said that jazz was created out of the meeting of the
harmony of Europe and the rhythm of Africa (or, similarly, that creolized languages are constructed from a European vocabulary imposed
on an African syntax). But surely this is oversimplification to the point
of ignorance. Who among such commentators knows "African harmony"
well enough to be able to show that it had no influence? Would they, for
example, rule out the complex and multiparted Ekonda choral music of
the Kongo as being nonharmonic? For that matter, who among them
knows the array of relevant "European rhythms" well enough to dismiss
their influence? And who knows enough of both creole and African languages to make such judgments about the influence of the latter's vocabularies? Even if these characterizations could be shown to be correct,
surely such a crude lamination would not resemble jazz or any known
creole language. Such simplifications are at best uninformed shorthand
descriptions; at worst they are racist projections, Europe always on top.

    In fact, if we can generalize from what we know of the creation of cre-
ole languages to cultural creations in other domains, we come face to
face with this paradox: while it may be possible to identify the history

and sources of individual components, when put into use, new combinations and totalities come into being which have no apparent specific relationship to their historical sources. In the case of language this means that while particular sounds and words can be traced to particular languages, the total speech that results is a new and emergent product. The same is true of music. Even if one can trace the sources of particular instruments, rhythms, and forms of ensembles, when we hear them combined in performance, their sources are moot at best.

If the virtue of creolization lies in its organic history as a native concept in the Americas, its fault stems from the specificity of its New World history and the timidity of its users in applying it elsewhere. Since it is normally only applied to situations of black and white contacts in the Americas with their attendant inequities, creolization is often understood as being merely one of the weapons of the weak, the result of raw necessity, a make-do phenomenon, or a function of secrecy. But surely expediency and privacy are secondary to the process of interpretation, not only a result of adjusting to divergent cultural forms, but also an act of mediation between different systems of values and meanings. Such processes are not limited to the oppressed and the abject. As Ralph Ellison once said of African American culture, it surely must amount to more than the sum of its brutalization.

There are, in fact, situations worldwide which seem remarkably parallel to New World creole events. A few brief examples: the culture contact situations of Europe have for too long been the preserves of historians and literary scholars, groups with vested interests in maintaining certain territorial boundaries and alignments. Gilles Deleuze and Félix Guattari, on the other hand, have demonstrated how European literature can be rethought from the margins by using Kafka's notion of minor languages and literature, in which minority languages such as "Czech German" are seen as functioning to undermine the stability of a major language like German.[17] By simultaneously intensifying and impoverishing the dominant language, deterritorializing it, setting it into motion, turning it into just another dialect, the minor language tends to reduce the major to minor status. In his dialogics, Mikhail Bakhtin, too, came close to approximating a creolist position, while using only the languages of Europe from the perspective of what was then a minor language, Russian.[18]

Whatever the terms chosen to encompass the phenomena discussed here, the mixture of cultural materials is ultimately what is of concern, and we need to ask to what degree and at what levels is mixture possible? Is anything conceivable, everything up for grabs? Or is there some limiting order here, a set of parameters, or at least a range in which mixture takes place? These are big questions, but we might at least make a start by thinking of some of the varieties and possibilities of mixture within one domain, language, since it is the cultural exemplar par excellence and thus a model for culture itself (as well as one of the sites at which it is easiest to see mixture at work). The following might serve as a preliminary list:

1. Mixture within the structure of a language—such as in the cases which we call creoles and pidgins (and though such cases may seem obvious, it is worth remembering how long linguists stubbornly resisted even the idea of the possibility of mixed grammar).
2. Mixture within the repertoires of individual speakers—either (a) by means of mixing various codes together in what is typically called "switching," or (b) by the creation of individualized private codes. Christopher Columbus is said to have used both of these strategies, speaking Mercantile Latin, as well as Spanish with Portuguese interference.
3. Mixture in the speech of segments of the population, as in street slang, the vocabulary of literary scholars, and so on.
4. Mixture within the use of different styles of speaking—essentially style-switching (though "switching" is again too simple a designation for what occurs in most instances).

   The possibilities here include an enormous range of processes, including parody and mimicry, artificial language construction (as in macaronics), oscillation of languages, and the carnivalization of speech. One literary example: the manner in which Ezra Pound, James Joyce, and T. S. Eliot style-switch within levels of literature and speech in their particular brands of literary modernism (crudely put, Pound creolizes "up" from a Eurocentric perspective, Joyce creolizes "down," and Eliot—at least in "The Waste Land"—moves in both directions).
5. Large mixed repertoires developed within individuals and groups for use in linguistic navigation—such as in trading, criminal activities, and journalism.

Mixture also implies commingling and crossing of social levels and strata in a variety of circumstances: the local vs. the metropolitan, the local vs. the global, the colonized vs. the colonizer, the emergent vernacular vs. the standard language, the as-yet-unrecognized vs. the hegemonic, and so on, for the regional, the religious, and the ethnic. Mixture suggests the presence of a multiplicity of codes, voices, styles, meanings, and identities (all of which, incidentally, surface as part of the development of written literature).

Whatever the ultimate terminology, we will at least always be in debt to creole linguistics for placing into doubt the idea of genetic linguistic models, and having forced our attention toward all languages (not only the "distressed" languages) as being involved in social processes and characterized by high variability. And as a result we benefit from a creolist view of society that rejects monolithic visions (even those that are pluralistic) of society as a sacred, political entity whose principal product is nationality, in favor of a notion of peoples in potentially equal, differing cultures, developing distinct ways of being and doing from ancestral sources, but also exchanging and sharing with each other and developing new forms, meanings, and interpretations. *This* is something new.

Notes

Chapter 2. Musical Style and Racial Conflict

Note: An earlier form of this paper, "'Soul' Music: Style and Racial Conflict in Jazz," was read at the Central States Anthropological Society meetings in Columbus, Ohio, May 1961. I am obviously indebted to the reports on the "Jazz Life" provided by Nat Hentoff.

1. J. S. Slotkin, "Jazz and Its Forerunners as an Example of Acculturation," *American Sociological Review* 7 (August 1946): 570–75; Howard S. Becker, "The Professional Dance Musician and His Audience," *American Journal of Sociology* 57 (September 1951): 135–44; Norman M. Margolis, "A Theory on the Psychology of Jazz," *American Image* 2 (Fall 1954): 263–91 and Francis Newton, *The Jazz Scene* (Baltimore, 1961), 252–69.

2. Slotkin, "Jazz and Its Forerunners," 570.

3. John S. Wilson, "Expanding Market for Better Jazz," *New York Times*, March 12, 1961, X15.

4. Nat Hentoff, "Race Prejudice in Jazz," *Harper's* 28 (June 1959): 75.

5. Ibid., 74.

6. Nat Hentoff, "The Murderous Modes of Jazz," *Esquire* (September 15, 1960): 91.

7. Hentoff, "Race Prejudice," 72.

8. John Tynan, "Les McCann and the Truth," *Down Beat* 27 (September 15, 1950): 21.

9. Leonard Feather, "The Racial Undercurrent," in *Down Beat's Music 1961* (Chicago, 1960), 46.

10. John Tynan, "Funk, Soul, Groove," *Down Beat* (November 24, 1960): 19.

11. Leonard Feather, *The Book of Jazz: A Guide to the Entire Field* (New York: Horizon, 1957), 39–53.

12. Nat Hentoff, "Jazz and Jim Crow," *Commonweal* 73 (March 24, 1961): 658.

13. Feather, *Book of Jazz*, 51.

14. Morroe Berger, "Jazz: Resistance to the Diffusion of a Culture Pattern," *Journal of Negro History* 32 (October 1947): 461.

15. For an "environmentalist" conception of Negro musical superiority in jazz, see "Racial Prejudice in Jazz," *Down Beat* 29 (March 15, 1962): 20–26; and "Inside the Cannonball Adderley Quintet," *Down Beat* 28 (June 8, 1961): 19–22.

16. James Baldwin, "A Negro Assays the Negro Mood," *New York Times Magazine*, March 12, 1961, 104.

17. C. Eric Lincoln, *The Black Muslims in America* (Boston: Beacon Press, 1961), 22.

18. Nat Hentoff, "The New Faces of Jazz," *Reporter* 25 (August 17, 1961): 50.

19. LeRoi Jones, *Blues People: Negro Music in White America* (New York: William Morrow, 1963), 219.

Chapter 3. *Musical Adaptation Among Afro-Americans*

A somewhat different version of this paper was read at the sixty-sixth Annual Meeting of the American Anthropological Association in Washington, D.C., December 1, 1967. This paper is dedicated to Alan Lomax, to whom it owes so much

1. Melville J. Herskovits, *The Myth of the Negro Past* (1941; reprint Boston: Beacon Press, 1958), 261–69.

2. Alan Lomax, "Song Structure and Social Structure," *Ethnology* 1 (1962): 425–51; Alan Lomax, "Special Features of the Sung Communication," in *Essays on the Verbal and Visual Arts: Proceedings of the 1966 Annual Spring Meeting of the American Ethnological Society,* ed. June Helm (Seattle: AES, 1967), 109–27; and Alan Lomax, *Folk Song Style and Culture* (Washington, D.C.: AAAS, 1968).

3. Norman E. Whitten, Jr., "Personal Networks and Musical Contexts in the Pacific Lowlands of Colombia and Ecuador," *Man* 3 (1968): 50–63.

4. Jeannette Murphy, "The Survival of African Music in America," *Popular Science Monthly* 55 (1899): 660–72.

5. See John A. Lomax and Alan Lomax, *Folk Song U.S.A.* (New York: Duell, Sloane, and Pearce, 1966), 106–9; Alan Lomax, *The Folk Songs of North America in the English Language* (Garden City, N.Y.: Doubleday, 1960), 226.

6. Alan Lomax, *Folk Songs of North America,* xxix. Lomax is probably quoting Zora Neale Hurston.

7. The following are representative: Paul Oliver, *Conversation with the Blues* (New York: Horizon Press, 1965), 17–18; Dorothy Scarborough, *On the Trail of Negro Folksongs* (Hatboro, Pa.: Folklore Associates, 1963), 97–98: Lydia Parrish, *Slave Songs of the Georgia Sea Islands* (Hatboro, Pa.: Folklore Associates, 1965), 93; Samuel Charters, *The Poetry of the Blues* (New York: Oak, 1965), 35; Bernard Klatzko, album notes to *In the Spirit, No. 1 and* 2, Origin Jazz Library Records OJL-12, OJL-13; Chris Strachwitz, "An Interview with the Staples Family," *American Folk Music Occasional No. 1,* ed. Chris Strachwitz (New York: Oak, 1964), 16–17.

8. Pete Welding, "Tapescripts: Interview with Rev. Robert Wilkins. T7–155," *John Edwards Memorial Foundation Newsletter* 3 (1967): 55.

9. Zora Neale Hurston, *Jonah's Gourd Vine* (Philadelphia: J.B. Lippincott, 1934), 271.

10. Harriet J. Ottenheimer, "Blues: Pattern and Variation," paper presented to the Society for Ethnomusicology, Albuquerque, N.M., November 13, 1965, p. 2.

11. Alan Lomax, private communication.

12. Roger D. Abrahams, *Deep Down in the Jungle … Negro Narrative Folklore from the Streets of Philadelphia* (Hatboro, Pa.: Folklore Associates, 1964; reprint Chicago: Aldine, 1970), 62–63.

13. Charles Keil, *Urban Blues* (Chicago: University of Chicago Press, 1966), 148.

14. William Francis Allen, Charles Pickard Ware, and Lucy Kim Garrison, *Slave Songs of the United States* (New York, reprint Medford, Mass: Applewood, 1995, 1867), v.

15. Lomax, "Song Structure," 425–51.

16. Lomax "Special Features," 120–21; Lomax, *Folk Song Style and Culture*, chaps. 6 and 7.

17. Anthony F. C. Wallace, *Religion: An Anthropological View* (New York: Random House, 1966), 106.

18. Leonard Feather, "A Talk with Mahalia Jackson," *American Folk Music Occasional No. 1*, ed. Chris Strachwitz (New York: Oak, 1964), 46.

19. Paul Oliver, *Conversation with the Blues* (New York: Horizon Press, 1965), 164–65.

20. For similar points concerning Negro song in general, see Janheinz Jahn, *Muntu: The New African Culture* (New York: Grove Press, 1961), 224–25, and Alfons M. Dauer, *Der jazz, seine Ursprunge und seine Entwicklung* (Kassel: Röth-Verlag, 1958), 74.

21. Oliver, *Conversation with the Blues*, 165.

22. Alan Lomax, *The Rainbow Sign: A Southern Documentary* (New York: Duell, Sloane, and Pearce, 1959), 7–8.

23. Mimi Clar Melnick, "'I Can Peep Through Muddy Water and Spy Dry Land': Boasts in the Blues," in *Folklore International*, ed. D. K. Wilgus (Hatboro, Pa.: Folklore Associates, 1967), 139–49.

24. Keil, *Urban Blues*, 152.

25. Arna Bontemps, "Rock, Church, Rock," in *Anthology of American Negro Literature*, ed. Sylvestre C. Watkins (New York: Modern Library, 1944), 431.

26. E. Franklin Frazier, *The Negro Church in America* (New York: Schocken, 1964), 75.

27. Kenneth Lee Karpe, album notes to *Ray Charles at Newport*, Atlantic Records 1289.

28. Jacob D. Elder, "Evolution of the Traditional Calypso of Trinidad and Tobago: A Socio-Historical Analysis of Song-Change" (Ph.D. dissertation, University of Pennsylvania, 1966).

29. For a discussion of the aggressive roots of calypso, see Andrew Pearse, "Mitto Sampson on Calypso Legends of the Nineteenth Century," *Caribbean Quarterly* 4 (1956): 250–62; Daniel J. Crowley, "Toward a Definition of Calypso," *Ethnomusicology* 3 (1959): 55–66, 117–24; J. D. Elder, "Kalinda-Song of the Battling Troubadours of Trinidad," *Journal of the Folklore Institute* 3 (1966): 192–203.

30. Daniel J. Crowley, "The View from Tobago: National Character in Folklore," in *Folklore International*, ed. D. K. Wilgus (Hatboro, Pa.: Folklore Associates, 1967).

31. Whitten, "Personal Networks"; Norman E. Whitten, Jr., and Aurelio Fuentes, "¡Baile Marimba! Negro Folk Music in Northwest Ecuador," *Journal of the Folklore Institute* 3 (1966): 169–91.

32. Whitten, "Personal Networks," 61.

33. Lerone Bennett, Jr., *The Negro Mood and Other Essays* (New York: Ballantine, 1964), 85–86.

Chapter 4. An American Anthropological Dilemma: The Politics of Afro-American Culture

The preparation of this essay was accomplished with the support of the National Institute of Mental Health, U.S. Public Health Service, Grant No. MH-I7216. It has also benefited from discussions with my colleagues Erving Goffman, Dell Hymes, and Dan Rose.

1. See, for example, Ira Katznelson, "White Social Science and the Black Man's World: The Case of Urban Ethnography," *Race Today* (February 1970): 47–48.

2. Eric R. Wolf and Joseph G. Jorgensen, "Anthropology on the Warpath in Thailand," *New York Review of Books* (November 19, 1970): 26–35; William S. Willis, "Skeletons in the Anthropological Closet," in *Reinventing Anthropology*, ed. Dell Hymes (New York: Random House, 1969).

3. Sidney W. Mintz, foreword to *Afro-American Anthropology: Contemporary Perspectives*, ed. Norman E. Whitten, Jr., and John F. Szwed (New York: Free Press, 1970), 1–15; William S. Willis, "Anthropology and Negroes on the Southern Colonial Frontier," in *The Black Experience in America*, ed. James C. Curtis and Lewis L. Gould (Austin: University of Texas Press, 1970); Ann Fischer, "The Effect upon Anthropological Studies of U.S. Negroes of the Professional Personality and Subculture of Anthropologists" presented at the annual meeting of the Southern Anthropological Association, New Orleans, March 13–15, 1969.

4. Willis, "Anthropology and Negroes," 36.

5. Fischer, "Effect upon Anthropological Studies."

6. Franz Boas, *The Mind of Primitive Man* (1938; reprint New York: Macmillan, 1963), 240.

7. Quoted in Melville J. Herskovits, *Franz Boas* (New York: Scribner, 1953), 111. It is incidentally worth noting that the details of Boas's involvement with black leaders and causes are generally missing from his numerous biographers' writings.

8. Cf. the following statement from Boas, *Mind of Primitive Man*, 238:

We have found that no proof of an inferiority of the Negro type could be given, except that it seemed barely possible that perhaps the race would not produce quite so many men of highest genius as other races, while there was nothing at all that could be interpreted as suggesting any material difference in the mental capacity of the bulk of the Negro population as compared with the bulk of the white population. There will undoubtedly be endless numbers of men and women who will be able to outrun their white competitors, and who will do better than the defectives whom we permit to drag down and retard the healthy children of our public schools.

It is possible that Herskovits also confused anthropometric and cultural data in the same way early in his career. William Stewart has suggested that it was this earlier seductive encounter with "science" that later led Herskovits to be so wary of the use of physical science as a model for anthropology. See Melville J. Herskovits, "The Ahistorical Approach to Afroamerican Studies," *American Anthropologist* 62 (1960): 559–68.

9. Ruth Benedict, *Race: Science and Politics* (1940; reprint New York: Viking Compass, 1959), 86–87.

10. Ruth Benedict, *Patterns of Culture* (1934; reprint New York: New American Library, Mentor Books, 1959), 26.

11. See, for example, M. F. Ashley-Montagu, *Man's Most Dangerous Myth: The Fallacy of Race* (New York: Harper and Brothers, 1942).

12. Charles Valentine, *Culture and Poverty: Critique and Counter Proposals* (Chicago: University of Chicago Press, 1968), 20–24.

13. E. Franklin Frazier, "Traditions and Patterns of Negro Family Life in the United States," in *Race and Culture Contacts*, ed. E. B. Reuter (New York: McGraw-Hill, 1934), 194.

14. Gunnar Myrdal, *An American Dilemma: The Negro Problem and Modern Democracy* (New York: Harper and Row, 1944), 928.

15. Ibid., 928–29.

16. For a critique of the concept of deficit culture, see Stephen S. Baratz, "Social Science's Conceptualization of the Afro-American," in *Black America*, ed. John F. Szwed (New York: Basic Books, 1970), 55–66.

17. Quoted in Lerone Bennett, Jr., "The World of the Slave," *Ebony* 26 (February 1971): 56.

18. Kenneth B. Clark, *Dark Ghetto* (New York: Harper and Row, 1965); Christopher Lasch, *The Agony of the American Left* (New York: Vintage, 1969), 125–26; Michael Harrington, *Toward a Democratic Left* (New York: Vintage, 1968), 80; Lee Rainwater, "The American Working Class and Lower Class: An American Success and Failure," in *Anthropological Backgrounds of Adult Education*, ed. Sol Tax et al., Notes and Essays on Education for Adults 57 (Boston: Center for the Study of Liberal Education for Adults, 1968), 41–42; William H. Grier and Price M. Cobbs, *Black Rage* (New York: Basic Books, 1968), 114–29; Abram Kardiner and Lionel Ovesey, *The Mark of Oppression: Explorations in the Personality of the American Negro* (New York: Meridian, 1962), 333–34.

19. Nathan Glazer and Daniel P. Moynihan, *Beyond the Melting Pot* (Cambridge, Mass.: MIT Press, 1963), 53. A revised edition of this work renounces this statement, however.

20. Stanley M. Elkins, *Slavery: A Problem in American Institutional and Intellectual Life* (Chicago: University of Chicago Press, 1959), 93, 107.

21. Milton Gordon, *Assimilation in American Life* (New York: Oxford University Press, 1964), 179.

22. Ibid., 79.

23. Given all the pronouncements over the years, it is shocking to realize that in 1969 an anthropologist could truthfully claim to be publishing the first ethnographic, community-based study of black lower-class child-training practices in the United States. See Virginia H. Young, "Family and Childhood in a Southern Negro Community," *American Anthropologist* 72 (1970): 269–88.

24. Ralph Ellison, *Shadow and Act* (New York: New American Library, Signet Books, 1966), 129–30.

25. Thomas S. Szasz, "Blackness and Madness: Images of Evil and Tactics of Exclusion," in Szwed, ed., *Black America*, 67–77.

26. See, for example, Zora Neale Hurston, *Mules and Men* (Philadelphia: J.B. Lippincott, 1935). See also Lorenzo D. Turner, *Africanisms in the Gullah Dialect* (Chicago: University of Chicago, 1949).

27. Paul Radin, "Status, Fantasy, and the Christian Dogma," in *God Struck Me Dead*, ed. Clifton H. Johnson (1945; reprint Philadelphia: Pilgrim Press, 1969), vii–xiii (originally issued in 1945 by the Fisk University Social Science Institute, Nashville, Tennessee, from a typescript written before 1930); Hortense Powdermaker, *After Freedom: A Cultural Study in the Deep South* (New York: Viking Press, 1939).

28. Melville J. Herskovits, *The Myth of the Negro Past* (1941; reprint Boston: Beacon Press, 1958).

29. For a discussion of the criticism of Herskovits, see the introduction to Whitten and Szwed, eds., *Afro-American Anthropology*, 28–30.

30. Herskovits published and lectured extensively on racist policies and practices; his articles appeared in the liberal political journals of the 1920s and 1930s and in the NAACP and Urban League magazines. And, like his mentor Boas, he was involved with W. E. B. Du Bois in such ventures as the Fourth Pan-African Congress in 1927.

31. Melville J. Herskovits, "The Negro's Americanism," in *The New Negro*, ed. A. Locke (New York: Charles and Albert Boni, 1925), 359–60.

32. Melville J. Herskovits, "The Negro in the New World: The Statement of a Problem," in *The New World Negro*, ed. Frances S. Herskovits (1930; reprint Bloomington: Indiana University Press, 1966), 6.

33. Melville J. Herskovits, "What Has Africa Given America?" *New Republic* 84, 1083 (1935): 92–96.

34. Herskovits, *Myth of the Negro Past*, 32.

35. Lasch, *Agony of the American Left*, 121–22.

36. For plastic arts, crafts, and architecture, see Robert Farris Thompson, "African Influence on the Art of the United States," in *Black Studies in the University: A Symposium*, ed. Armstead L. Robinson, Craig C. Foster, and Donald H. Ogilvie (New Haven, Conn.: Yale University Press, 1969), 122–70; and Roger D. Abrahams, "Social Uses of Space in an Afro-American Community," presented at the Conference on Traditional African Architecture, Yale University, New Haven, Connecticut, May 7–9, 1970. For verbal arts see Roger D. Abrahams, *Positively Black* (Englewood Cliffs, N.J.: Prentice-Hall, 1970); Roger D. Abrahams, *Deep Down in the Jungle . . . Negro Narrative Folklore from the Streets of Philadelphia* (1964; reprint Chicago: Aldine, 1970); and Bruce A. Rosenberg, *The Art of the American Folk Preacher* (New York: Oxford University Press, 1970). For music, see LeRoi Jones, *Blues People* (New York: William Morrow, 1963); Gunther Schuller, *Early Jazz: Its Roots and Musical Development* (New York: Oxford University Press, 1968); Charles Keil, *Urban Blues* (Chicago: University of Chicago Press, 1966); Paul Oliver, *Savannah Syncopators* (New York: Stein and Day, 1970); Alan Lomax, "The Homogeneity of African-Afro-American Musical Style," in Whitten and Szwed, eds., *Afro-American Anthropology*, 181–201; and John F. Szwed, "Afro-American Musical Adaptation," in Whitten and Szwed, *Afro-American Anthropology*, 219–27). For dance, see Marshall and Jean Stearns, *Jazz Dance: The Story of American Vernacular Dance* (New York: Macmillan, 1968).

For speech, see J. L. Dillard, *Black English* (New York: Random House, 1972); David Dalby, *Black Through White: Patterns of Communication*, African Studies Program, Indiana University (Bloomington: Indiana University Press, 1970); Karl Reisman, "Cultural and Linguistic Ambiguity in a West Indian Village," in Whitten and Szwed, eds., *Afro-American Anthropology*, 129–44; Abrahams, *Positively Black*; Thomas Kochman, "Toward an Ethnography of Black American Speech Behavior," in Whitten and Szwed, eds., *Afro-American Anthropology*, 145–62; William Stewart, "Towards a History of American Negro Dialect," in *Language and Poverty: Perspectives on a Theme*, ed. Frederick Williams (Chicago: Markham Publishing, 1970), chap. 7; and William Labov et al., *A Study of the Non-Standard English of Negro and Puerto Rican Speakers in New York City*, vol. 2, Final Report, Cooperative Research Project No. 3288 (Washington, D.C.: Office of Education, 1968).

For oral history, see Sterling Stuckey, "Through the Prism of Folklore: The Black Ethos in Slavery," *Massachusetts Review* 9 (1968): 417–37; Sterling Stuckey, "Twilight of Our Past: Reflections on the Origins of Black History," in *Amistad 2*, ed. John A. Williams and Charles F. Harris (New York: Vintage, 1971), 261–95; William L. Montell, *The Saga of Coe Ridge* (Knoxville: University of Tennessee Press, 1970); Lawrence W. Levine, "Slave Songs and Slave Consciousness: An Exploration in Neglected Sources," presented at meetings of the American Historical Association, December 28, 1969; and Robert Blauner, "Black Culture: Myth or Reality?" in Whitten and Szwed, eds., *Afro-American Anthropology*, 347–66.

On religion, see Morton Marks, "Trance Music and Paradoxical Communication," presented at the American Anthropological Association meetings, New Orleans, November 1969.

On style and interpersonal behavior, see Alan Lomax, *Folk Song Style and*

Culture (Washington, D.C.: American Association for the Advancement of Science, 1968); Ellison, *Shadow and Act*; Karl Reisman, "Contrapuntal Communications in an Antiguan Village," Working Paper 3, Penn-Texas Working Papers in Sociolinguistics, 1970.

37. On the slave trade, see Philip D. Curtin, *The Atlantic Slave Trade: A Census* (Madison: University of Wisconsin Press, 1969); Vincent Harding, "Religion and Resistance Among Antebellum Negroes, 1800–1860," in *The Making of Black America: Essays in Negro Life and History*, ed. August Meier and Elliott Rudwick (New York: Atheneum, 1969), 179–97; and Roy S. Bryce-Laporte, "The Conceptualization of the American Slave Plantation as a Total Institution" (Ph.D. dissertation, University of California, Los Angeles, 1968).

38. On Afro-American kinship, see Ulf Hannerz, *Soulside: Inquiries into Ghetto Culture and Community* (New York: Columbia University Press, 1969).

39. On the Caribbean and South America, see Roger Bastide, *Les amériques noires* (Paris: Payot, 1967); Morton Marks, "El santo en Nueva York," presented at the meetings of the American Anthropological Association, San Diego, November 22, 1970; and Alfonso A. Narvaez, "Where Religion and Superstition Mix in the City," *New York Times*, September 15, 1970, 41.

40. On insights for the understanding of Africa, see Joseph H. Greenberg, "An Application of New World Evidence to an African Linguistic Problem," in *Les afro-américains*, Mémoire 27 (Dakar: Institut français d'Afrique noire, 1957), 129–31; Robert Farris Thompson, "The Sign of the Divine King," *African Arts* (Spring 1970): 8–17; and Robert Farris Thompson, "From Africa," *Yale Alumni Magazine* (November 1970): 16–21.

41. M. G. Smith, "The African Heritage in the Caribbean," in *Caribbean Studies: A Symposium*, ed. Vera Rubin (Seattle: University of Washington Press, 1960): 45.

42. The fact that "cultural deprivation" of the black poor should have become an issue just at the point where many white middle- and upper-class youths were finding their own culture meaningless is a sad commentary on social scientists' sense of paradox.

43. See, for example, Melvin M. Tumin, "Some Social Consequences of Research on Racial Relations," in *Recent Sociology*, vol.1; *On the Basis of Politics*, ed. Hans Peter Dreitzel (New York: Macmillan, 1969), 256–59.

44. Two examples are (1) the successful efforts of Andrew Pearse and Melville J. Herskovits in support of the Spiritual Baptists of Trinidad against repressive government legislation; and (2) Jean Price-Mars's and others' use of voodoo and folk culture as a basis for nationalism during the United States occupation of Haiti.

45. Gary T. Marx, "Two Cheers for the National Riot Commission," in Szwed, ed., *Black America*, 82–84. Cf. the analysis of a priori and "schematizing" responses to the 1956 Soviet intervention in Hungary in Jean-Paul Sartre, *Search for a Method*, trans. Hazel E. Barnes (New York: Vintage, 1963), 29–30, n. 8.

it matters little a priori that the Communist commentators believed that they had to justify the Soviet intervention. What is really heartbreaking is the fact that their "analyses" totally suppressed the originality of the Hungarian fact. Yet there is no doubt that an insurrection at Budapest a dozen years after the war, less than five years after the death of Stalin, must present very particular characteristics. What do our "schematizers" do? They lay stress on the faults of the Party, but without defining them. These indeterminate faults assume an abstract and eternal character which wrenches them from the historical context so as to make of them a universal entity; it is "human error." The writers indicate the presence of reactionary elements, but without showing their Hungarian reality. Suddenly these reactionaries pass over into eternal Reaction. Finally, those commentators present world imperialism as an inexhaustible, formless force, whose essence does not vary regardless of its point of application. They construct an interpretation which serves as a skeleton key to everything. . . . In short, nothing new has happened. That is what had to be demonstrated.

46. Bronislaw Malinowski, introduction to Fernando Ortiz, *Cuban Counterpoint* (New York: Knopf, 1947), viii–ix.

47. For a discussion of the influence of Afro-American political style on other parts of the world, see Gilberto Freyre, *The Racial Factor in Contemporary Politics*, Occasional Papers of the Research Unit for the Study of Multi-Racial Societies, University of Sussex (London: MacGibbon and Kee, 1966), 18–21. A specific example of this influence is Pierre Vallières, *White Niggers of America* (New York: Monthly Review Press, 1971), on the Front de Libération du Québec.

Chapter 5. Reconsideration: The Myth of the Negro Past

1. Melville J. Herskovits, *The Myth of the Negro Past* (1941; reprint Boston: Beacon Press, 1958).

Chapter 6. Reconsideration: Lafcadio Hearn in Cincinnati

Lafcadio Hearn, *Selected Writings*, ed. Henry Goodman (New York: Citadel Press, 1949). Other editions that include Hearn's Cincinnati writings are *Barbarous Barbers*, ed. Ichiro Nishizaki (Tokyo: Hokuseido Press, 1939); *Children of the Levee*, ed. O. W. Frost (Lexington: University of Kentucky Press, 1957); *An American Miscellany*, 2 vols., ed. Albert Mordell (New York: Dodd, Mead, 1924); and *Occidental Gleanings*, 2 vols., ed. Albert Mordell (New York: Dodd, Mead, 1925).

Chapter 7. The Forest as Moral Document: The Achievement of Lydia Cabrera

1. Kenneth Bilby, "The Carribean as a Musical Region," in *Carribean Contours*, ed. Sidney W. Mintz and Sally Price (Baltimore: Johns Hopkins University Press, 1994), 181–218.

2. For a general discussion of these matters in the Miami area, see Mercedes C. Sandoval, "Santeria as a Mental Health Care System: An Historical Overview," *Social Science and Medicine* 13B (1979): 137–51.

3. Alexander H. Leighton, Thomas A. Lambo, C. C. Hughes, J. M. Murphy, and D. Macklin, *Psychiatric Disorder Among the Yoruba* (Ithaca, N.Y.: Cornell University Press, 1963), 105.

4. Ann Petry, *The Street* (Boston: Houghton Mifflin, 1946), 136.

5. Susan Sontag, *On Photography* (New York: Delta, 1977), 23.

6. For a guide to Carpentier's book, see Roberto González Echevarría, "Socrates Among the Weeds," *Massachusetts Review* 24 (1984): 545–61.

7. Lydia Cabrera, *El Monte* (Havana: Ediciones C.R., 1954), 13.

Chapter 8. Race and the Embodiment of Culture

Acknowledgment is gratefully expressed for support from the U. S. Public Health Service, National Institute for Mental Health Grant No. MH 17,216, which aided preparation of this essay.

1. For a short overview of scientific anti-racism, see Thomas F. Gossett, *Race: The History of an Idea in America* (New York: Schocken Books, 1965), 409–30.

2. Fynes Moryson, *An Itinerary*, 4 vols. (London, 1617), quoted in David Beers Quinn, *The Elizabethans and the Irish* (Ithaca, N.Y.: Cornell University Press, 1966), 71–72, 63.

3. Edmund Spenser, *Faerie Queene* (Macmillan, 1970); William Camden, *Britain, or a Chorographicall Description of . . . England, Scotland, and Ireland*, trans. Philemon Holland (London, 1610).

4. Christine Bolt, *Victorian Attitudes to Race* (London: Routledge and Kegan Paul, 1971), 136–51; Quinn, *Elizabethans and the Irish*, 25–26.

5. James Redfield, *Comparative Physiognomy or Resemblances Between Men and Animals* (New York: Redfield, 1852), 253–58, quoted in L. Perry Curtis, Jr., *Apes and Angels: The Irishman in Victorian Caricature* (Washington, D.C.: Smithsonian Institution Press, 1971), 12.

6. Curtis, *Apes and Angels*, passim.

7. John Beddoe, *The Races of Britain* (London: Arrowsmith, 1885), quoted in Curtis, *Apes and Angels*, 119–21.

8. Much of the following is indebted to Roger D. Abrahams, "Stereotyping and Beyond," in *Language and Cultural Diversity in American Education*, ed. Roger D. Abrahams and Rudolph C. Troike (Englewood Cliffs, N.J.: Prentice-Hall, 1972), 19–29.

9. Abrahams, "Stereotyping and Beyond," 25.

10. See the quotes and references throughout Felix N. Okoye, *The American Image of Africa: Myth and Reality* (Buffalo, N.Y.: Black Academy Press, 1971).

11. Sidney W. Mintz, foreword to *Afro-American Anthropology: Contemporary Perspectives*, ed. Norman E. Whitten, Jr., and John F. Szwed (New York: Free Press, 1970), 4–5.

12. Ray L. Birdwhistell, *Kinesics and Context: Essays on Body Motion Communication* (Philadelphia: University of Pennsylvania Press, 1971).

13. Alan Lomax, *Folk Song Style and Culture* (Washington, D.C.: American Association for the Advancement of Science, 1968).

14. Ibid., 170–203.

15. Marvin Harris, *Patterns of Race in the Americas* (New York: Walker, 1964), 56.

16. William Camden, *Britain*, 2nd ed., vol. 2 (London, 1722), 1423.

17. Statutes of Kilkenny (1366), quoted in David H. Greene, *An Anthology of Irish Literature* (New York: Modern Library, 1954), 298.

18. Allen Walker Read, "British Recognition of American Speech in the Eighteenth Century," *Dialect Notes* 6 (1933): 329, quoting from the *London Magazine*, 1746.

19. B. [Beverly] Carradine, *Mississippi Stories* (Chicago: Christian Witness Co., 1904), 98–99. I am grateful to William Stewart for calling this reference and the one in the preceding note to my attention.

20. Matthew Gregory Lewis, *Journal of a West India Proprietor* (London, 1834).

21. For a novel that develops the background for *Jane Eyre*, see Jean Rhys, *Wide Sargasso Sea* (New York: Norton, 1966).

22. Carl Wittke, *Tambo and Bones: A History of the American Minstrel Stage* (Durham, N.C.: Duke University Press, 1930), passim.

23. Steve Voce, "It Don't Mean a Thing," *Jazz Journal* 24 (1971): 16.

24. Willie Morris, *North Toward Home* (Boston: Houghton Mifflin, 1967), 81.

25. Ibid., 79.

26. Leslie Fiedler, *Waiting for the End* (New York: Stein and Day, 1964), 134.

27. Colin M. Turnbull, "The Mbuti Pygmies of the Congo," in *Peoples of Africa*, ed. James L. Gibbs, Jr. (New York: Holt, Rinehart and Winston, 1965), passim.

28. Frank M. Snowden, Jr., *Blacks in Antiquity: Ethiopians in the Greco-Roman Experience* (Cambridge, Mass.: Harvard University Press, 1970), passim.

29. For further development of this argument, see John F. Szwed, "An American Anthropological Dilemma: The Politics of Afro-American Culture," in *Reinventing Anthropology*, ed. Dell Hymes (New York: Pantheon, 1973).

30. Paul Riesman, review of Carlos Castenada, *Journey to Ixtlan*, *New York Times Book Review*, October 22, 1972, 7.

31. G. K. Chesterton, "Celts and Celtophiles," in *Heretics* (London: Bodley Head, 1905), 176–77.

32. Friedrich Engels, *The Condition of the Working Class in England in 1844*, quoted in Patrick O'Farrell, *Ireland's English Question: Anglo-Irish Relations, 1534–1970* (New York: Schocken, 1971), 144; Sidney and Beatrice Webb, 1892, quoted in Janet Beveridge, *An Epic of Clare Market* (London: G. Bell, 1960), 9.

33. Roger Bastide, *African Civilizations in the New World* (London: C. Hurst, 1971), 224.

34. Claude Lévi-Strauss, "The Scope of Anthropology," *Current Anthropology* 7 (1966): 122.

Chapter 9. After the Myth: Studying Afro-American Cultural Patterns in the Plantation Literature

1. Roger Bastide, *African Civilizations in the New World* (London: C. Hurst, 1971).

2. See Raymond Williams, *The Country and the City* (New York: Oxford University Press, 1973).

3. Melville J. Herskovits, *The Myth of the Negro Past* (1941; reprint Boston: Beacon Press, 1958).

4. Melville J. Herskovits, *The Interdisciplinary Aspects of Negro Studies*, Bulletin 32 (Washington, D.C.: American Council of Learned Societies, 1941).

5. Robert Farris Thompson, "African Influence on the Art of the United States," in *Black Studies in the University: A Symposium*, ed. Armstead L. Robinson, Craig C. Foster, and Donald H. Ogilvie (New Haven, Conn.: Yale University Press, 1969), 139–40; and Robert E. Perdue, Jr., "African Baskets in South Carolina," *Economic Botany* 22 (1968): 289–92.

6. William R. Bascom, *Shango in the New World* (Austin: University of Texas African and Afro-American Research Institute, 1972).

7. Richard Price, "Saramaka Woodcarving: The Development of an Afro-American Art," *Man* (1970): 375.

8. George E. Simpson and Peter B. Hammond, "Discussion," in *Caribbean Studies: A Symposium*, ed. Vera Rubin (Seattle: University of Washington Press, 1960), 48.

9. Ibid., 50.

10. Sidney W. Mintz, foreword to *Afro-American Anthropology: Contemporary Perspectives*, ed. Norman E. Whitten, Jr., and John F. Szwed (New York: Free Press, 1970), 7–8.

11. Daniel J. Crowley, "American Credit Institutions of Yoruba Type," *Man* 53 (1953): 80; William R. Bascom, "Acculturation Among the Gullah Negroes," *American Anthropologist* 43 (1941): 43–50; Ira De A. Reid, "Mrs. Bailey Pays the Rent," in *Ebony and Topaz: A Collectanea*, ed. Charles S. Johnson (New York: National Urban League, 1927), 144–48.

12. Ruth Landes, review of *Afro-American Anthropology*, ed. Norman E. Whitten,

Jr., and John F. Szwed, *American Anthropologist* 73 (1971):1306–10; Melville J. Herskovits, "The Social Organization of the Candomble," *Anais do XXXI Congresso Internacional de Americanistas* (São Paulo, 1954), 505–32; Lydia Cabrera, *El Monte*, 2nd ed. (Havana: Ediciones C.R., 1954); and William R. Bascom, "The Focus of Cuban Santeria," *Southwestern Journal of Anthropology* 6 (1952): 64–68.

13. M. G. Smith, *Kinship and Community on Carriacou* (New Haven, Conn.: Yale University Press, 1962); Benjamin Henry Latrobe, *Impressions Respecting New Orleans, Diary and Sketches, 1818–1829* (New York: Columbia University Press, 1951); John P. Watson, *Annals of Philadelphia and Pennsylvania, in the Olden Times* (Philadelphia: Edwin S. Stuart, 1857), 2: 261.

14. Herskovits, *Myth of the Negro Past*, 167–86.

15. John Luffman, *A Brief Account of the Island of Antigua, Together with the Customs and Manners of Its Inhabitants, White as Well as Black* (London: T. Cadell, 1788), 94–95.

16. Peter H. Wood, "'It Was a Negro Taught Them,' A New Look at African Labor in Early South Carolina," in *Discovering Afro-America*, ed. Roger D. Abrahams and John F. Szwed (Leiden: E.J. Brill, 1975).

17. William Beckford, *A Descriptive Account of the Island of Jamaica* (London: T. and J. Egerton, 1790), 225.

18. J. B. Moreton, *Manners and Customs in the West Indian Islands* (London: W. Richardson, 1793).

19. Trelawney Wentworth, *A West Indian Sketch Book* (London: Whittaker, 1834), 1: 66.

20. Eugene D. Genovese, *Roll Jordan Roll: The World the Slaves Made* (New York: Pantheon, 1974).

21. Alan Lomax, *Folk Song Style and Culture* (Washington, D.C.: American Association for the Advancement of Science, 1968).

22. Henri Baudet, *Paradise on Earth: Some Thoughts on European Images of Non-European Man* (New Haven, Conn.: Yale University Press, 1965), 47.

23. Eldred D. Jones, *The Elizabethan Image of Africa* (Charlottesville: University of Virginia Press, 1971).

24. Robert Pierpoint, "Negro, or Coloured, Bandsmen in the Army," *Notes and Queries* 2 (1916): 303–4; Leigh Hunt, *The Wishing Cap Papers* (Boston: Lee and Shepard, 1873).

25. Martin Cooper, *Beethoven: The Last Decade, 1817–1827* (New York: Oxford University Press, 1970), 33; Pierpoint, "Negro, or Coloured, Bandsmen," 303.

26. Morton Marks and John F. Szwed, "Afro-American Cultures on Parade," presented at the American Anthropological Association annual meeting, New York, 1971.

27. Peter Wilson, "Reputation and Respectability: A Suggestion for Caribbean Ethnology," *Man* 4, 1 (1969): 37–53.

28. Roger D. Abrahams and Richard Bauman, "Sense and Nonsense on St. Vincent: Speech Behavior and Decorum in a Caribbean Community," *American Anthropologist* 73, 3 (1971): 262–72; Roger D. Abrahams, "Talking My Talk: Black English and Social Segmentation in Black Communities," *Florida F/L Reporter* 10 (1972): 29–38; and Roger D. Abrahams, *Talking Black* (Rowley, Mass.: Newbury House, 1976).

29. Jerome C. Handler and Charlotte J. Frisbie, "Aspects of Slave Life in Barbados: Music and Its Cultural Context," *Caribbean Quarterly* (1972): 14.

30. Peter Marsden, *An Account of the Island of Jamaica, with Reflections on the Treatment, Occupation, and Provision of the Slaves* (Newcastle: S. Hodgson, 1788), 33, our emphasis.

31. Beckford, *Descriptive Account*, 1: 392, our emphasis.

32. H. T. De La Beche, *Letter from the West Indies* (London, 1846), 40.

33. James Stewart, *A View of the Past and Present State of the Island of Jamaica* (London: Oliver and Boyd, 1823), 269–70.

34. Matthew Gregory Lewis, *Journal of a West India Proprietor* (London, 1836), 45, 97; Michael Scott, *Tom Cringle's Log* (Edinburgh: Blackwood, 1833), 204.

35. Karl Reisman, "Cultural and Linguistic Ambiguity in a West Indian Village," in *Afro-American Anthropology*, ed. Whitten and Szwed.

36. Morton Marks, "Performance Rules and Ritual Structure in Afro-American Music" (Ph.D. dissertation, University of California at Berkeley, 1972), 5.

37. Roger D. Abrahams, *Positively Black* (Englewood Cliffs, N.J.: Prentice-Hall, 1970).

38. Keith Whinnom, "The Origin of European-Based Creoles and Pidgins," *Orbis* 14 (1965): 511–26; William A. Stewart, "Sociolinguistic Factors in the History of American Negro Dialects," *Florida F/L Reporter* 5, 2 (1967): 11–29; William A. Stewart, "Continuity and Change in American Negro Dialects," *Florida F/L Reporter* 6, 1 (1968): 3–14; J. L. Dillard, *Black English: Its History and Usage in the United States* (New York: Random House, 1972).

39. Roger D. Abrahams, "Traditions of Eloquence in the West Indies, *"Journal of Inter-American Studies and World Affairs* 12 (1970): 505–27; Abrahams, "Talking My Talk"; Abrahams, *Talking Black*.

40. Paul Radin, foreword to *God Struck Me Dead: Religious Conversion Experiences and Autobiographies of Ex-Slaves*, ed. Clifton H. Johnson (Philadelphia: Pilgrim Press, 1969), ix.

Chapter 10. Speaking People, in Their Own Terms

1. James Agee and Walker Evans, *Let Us Now Praise Famous Men* (Boston: Houghton Mifflin, 1941).

Chapter 18. From "Messin' Around" to "Funky Western Civilization": The Rise and Fall of Dance Instruction Songs

1. Ann Hutchinson Guest, *Dance Notation: The Process of Recording Movement on Paper* (New York: Dance Horizons, 1984).

2. Alec Wilder, *American Popular Song* (New York: Oxford University Press, 1972), uses the term "'dance instruction' song." We use his term. but without the quotation marks. Marshall W. Stearns and Jean Stearns, *Jazz Dance: The Story of American Vernacular Dance* (New York: Macmillan, 1968), call these "dance-songs with instructions."

3. "The Jerk," for example, originally recorded by the Larks in 1964, gave rise to a long line of successors: for instance, Clyde and the Blue Jays' "The Big Jerk," Bob and Earl's "Everybody Jerk," and even the Larks' follow-up, "Mickey's East Coast Jerk." See Steve Propes, "The Larks and the Jerk," *Goldmine*, August 26, 1988.

4. For further comments on dance crazes, see Katrina Hazzard-Gordon, *Jookin': The Rise of Social Dance Formations in African American Culture* (Philadelphia: Temple University Press, 1990); and Stuart Cosgrove, "The Erotic Pleasures of the Dance-Craze Disc," *Collusion* (February–April 1983): 4–6. Also, see Jim Dawson, *The Twist: The Story of the Song and Dance That Changed the World* (Boston:

Faber and Faber, 1995); Ron Mann, dir., *The Twist* (1992; reissued Chicago: Home Vision Entertainment, 2003, DVD).

5. William B. Smith, "The Persimmon Tree and the Beer Dance" (1838), reprinted in *The Negro and His Folklore in Nineteenth-Century Periodicals*, ed. Bruce Jackson (Austin: University of Texas Press, 1967), 3–9.

6. Thomas W. Talley, *Negro Folk Rhymes* (New York: Macmillan, 1922), 258–62.

7. Dance instruction songs have also been noted in the carnivals of Haiti and Trinidad, and in Argentinian tango, areas with either a majority of peoples of African descent, or with a history of significant African cultural influence.

8. On African American musicians and callers, see Paul Oliver, *Songsters and Saints: Vocal Traditions on Race Records* (Cambridge: Cambridge University Press, 1984), 22.

9. Bessie Jones and Bess Lomax Hawes, *Step It Down: Games, Play, Song, and Stories from the Afro-American Heritage* (New York: Harper and Row, 1972), discuss the African American version of this "ring play" song.

10. Roger D. Abrahams, "There Is a Brown Girl in the Ring," in *Two Penny Ballads and Four Dollar Whiskey*, ed. Kenneth S. Goldstein and Robert H. Byington (Hatboro, Pa.: Folklore Associates, 1966), 121–35.

11. See Stearns and Stearns, *Jazz Dance*, 100–102; Oliver, *Songsters and Saints*, 33–34.

12. Stearns and Stearns, *Jazz Dance*, 100–101, 117; the Stearnses spell the name of the first dance invoked the Bumbishay, while Oliver spells it Bombashay.

13. "One Step Instruction" was part of a newspaper promotion give-away. See *Early Syncopated Dance Music*, Folkways Records RBF 37.

14. Stearns and Stearns, *Jazz Dance*, 98–99.

15. Ibid., 107.

16. Ibid., 110–11.

17. Clyde E. B. Bernhardt, as told to Sheldon Harris, *I Remember: Eighty Years of Black Entertainment, Big Bands, and the Blues*, foreword by John F. Szwed (Philadelphia: University of Pennsylvania Press, 1986), 26.

18. See Stearns and Stearns, *Jazz Dance*, 140–59, on black musicals in the 1920s. Also, see Allen Woll, *Black Musical Theatre: From Coontown to Dreamgirls* (Baton Rouge.: Louisiana State University Press, 1989).

19. Stearns and Stearns, *Jazz Dance*, 100–101.

20. Ibid., 113–14.

21. Rod Gruver, "The Origins of the Blues," *Down Beat Music 71* (Chicago: Maher, 1971), 16–19.

22. But see also African American songs which describe animals dancing in Africa, such as the Ideals' "Mo Gorilla."

23. "Public spaces," however, were, and to some degree still are, segregated: *American Bandstand*, the television show which did the most to spread new dances in the United States, was initially restricted to whites.

24. Vernon [and Irene] Castle, *Modern Dancing* (World Syndicate Co., by arrangement with New York: Harper and Brothers, 1914). Reid Badger, *A Life in Ragtime: A Biography of James Reese Europe* (New York: Oxford University Press, 1995) describes the relationship between the Euro-American Castles and James Europe, their African American bandleader, and names black dancers such as Johnny Peters and his partner Ethel Williams, who taught the Castles African American dances.

25. "Gee" and "haw" (or "hoy") are commands used for horses or mules in the South. Their use in the 1950s and 1960s suggests that the influence of rural-based "animal" dances was still vital.

26. As we will discuss below, "The Shout," contrary to what its title might suggest by way of vocalization, is actually an African American religious dance. See Lynn Fauley Emery, *Black Dance in the United States from 1519 to 1970* (New York: Dance Horizons, 1980).

27. Stearns and Stearns, *Jazz Dance*, 104.

28. There is an obvious sexual meaning here, to be discussed below.

29. Quoted in Roger St. Pierre, liner notes, Rufus Thomas, *Jump Back*, Edsel Records ED 134, 1984.

30. Again, there is an obvious sexual reference here.

31. Morton Marks, "'You Can't Sing Unless You're Saved': Reliving the Call in Gospel Music," in *African Religious Groups and Beliefs*, ed. Simon Ottenberg (Meerut, India: Archana Publications, 1982), 305–31.

32. See Barry Michael Cooper, "Kiss Me Before You Go-Go," *Spin*, June 1985, 65–67.

33. Michael Freedberg, "Dust Their Blues," *Boston Phoenix*, October 16, 1992; Michael Freedberg, "Rising Expectations: Rick James Gets Down," *Village Voice*, October 11, 1983.

34. Ramon Guirao, *Orbita de la poesia afrocubana, 1928–37* (Havana: Ucar, García y Cía,, 1938).

35. Stearns and Stearns, *Jazz Dance*, 27.

36. See Emery, *Black Dance*, 120–26. Also see Jones and Hawes, *Step It Down*, 45–46, for the distinction between religious and secular shout steps.

37. Jones and Hawes, *Step It Down*, 144–45. After each line sung by the leader, the group respond, "Daniel," and performs a mimetic action.

38. See Stearns and Stearns, *Jazz Dance*, 105, on the various titles of the dances.

39. William Moore, "Ragtime Crazy," quoted in Oliver, *Songsters and Saints*, 33.

40. In fact, the earliest recorded dance calls for European set dances and dance suites were performed by African Americans. See John F. Szwed and Morton Marks, "The Afro-American Transformation of European Set Dances and Dance Suites," *Dance Research Journal* 20, 1 (1988).

41. This has complex cross-cultural repercussions, especially since, as several theorists have argued, black music and dance (on both sides of the Atlantic) are key agents in the articulation of cultural memory. See, for instance, Paul Gilroy, *The Black Atlantic: Modernity and Double Consciousness* (London: Verso, 1993).

42. Conveniently collected together are the following sets of dance songs without dances: *It's Finking Time': 608 Punk vs. Dancing Junk* (Beware Records LP Fink 1); *Bug Out Volume One: Sixteen Itchy Twitchy Classics* (Candy Records LP4); *Bug Out Volume Two: Sixteen Itchy Twitchy Classics* (Candy Records LP3); *Land of 1,000 Dunces: Bug Out Volume 3* (Candy Records LP 7). A selection from the three Candy discs is available as *Best of the Bug-Outs* (Candy CD7).

43. Lena Williams, "Three Steps Right, Three Steps Left: Sliding into the Hot New Dance," *New York Times*, April 22, 1990.

44. On Madonna's appropriation of Voguing, see Cindy Patton, "Embodying Subaltern Memory: Kinesthesia & the Problematics of Gender and Race," in *The Madonna Connection: Representational Politics, Subcultural Identies, and Cultural Theory*, ed. Cathy Schwichtenberg (Boulder, Colo.: Westview Press, 1993), 81–105.

45. See Theodor S. Adorno, *The Culture Industry: Selected Essays on Mass Culture*, ed. Jeremy M. Bernstein (London: Routledge, 1991).

46. In "Why Do Songs Have Words?" in *Music for Pleasure: Essays in the Sociology of Pop* (New York: Routledge, 1988), Simon Frith cites two such theorists: David Riesman, "Listening to Popular Music," *American Quarterly* 2 (1930), and

Norman Denzin, "Problems in Analyzing Elements of Mass Culture: Notes on the Popular Song and Other Artistic Productions," *American Journal of Sociology* 75 (1969). Frith notes that this was the typical view of sociologists of rock and pop music in the 1970s.

47. Frith, "Why Do Songs Have Words?" traces this view back to 1930s Leavisite mass-culture criticism.

48. The authors would like to thank Roger Abrahams, Robert F. Thompson, Noel Carroll, Laurence Senelick, Michael McDowell, David Krasner, Gerri Gurman and her Memorial High School dance class, Amy Seham, Toni Hull, Juliette Willis, and Margaret Keyes, as well as Brooks McNamara, Richard Schechner, and the faculty and students in the Department of Performance Studies, New York University, for their help with this article.

Chapter 19. The Afro-American Transformation of European Set Dances and Dance Suites

We wish to acknowledge the help given us by John Forrest and by the anonymous referees for *Dance Research Journal.*

1. For the European background of set dances and dance suites, see Jean Michel Guilcher, *La Contredanse et les renouvellements de la danse française* (Paris: École Practique des Hautes-Études et Mouton, 1969); and Philip J. S. Richardson, *The Social Dances of the Nineteenth Century in England* (London: Herbert Jenkins, 1960).

2. Jay D. Dobbin, *The Jombee Dance of Montserrat: A Study of Trance Ritual in the West Indies* (Columbus: Ohio State University Press, 1986).

3. Compare to *bambuala* and *babalao*, as well as to the Gaelic drum, the *bodhrán.* John C. Messenger, "Montserrat: The Most Distinctively Irish Settlement in the New World," *Ethnicity* 2 (1975): 298–99.

4. Dobbin, *Jombee Dance*, 136–37. Dobbin also provides an exceptionally vivid and complete presentation of a dance he witnessed (60–96).

5. Melville J. Herskovits, *Trinidad Village* (New York: Knopf, 1947), 88, 160–62; Andrew Pearse, "Aspects of Change in Caribbean Folk Music," *Journal of the International Folk Music Council* 8 (1955): 31–32; Donald R. Hill, notes to *The Big Drum and Other Ritual and Social Music of Carriacou*, Folkways 34002; Molly Ahye, *Golden Heritage: The Dance in Trinidad and Tobago* (Trinidad: Heritage Cultures, 1978), 99.

6. *The Original Quadrille Saint Croix Cultural Dance* (U.S. Virgin Islands: no publisher, no date, c. 1982), 4.

7. Jocelyne Guilbault, "A St. Lucian *Kwadril* Evening," *Latin American Music Review* 6 (1985): 31–57. This discussion is indebted to Guilbault's extensive research.

8. Very little St. Lucian folk music is available on record, but a sample of *masouc* (mazurka) played on violin, *cuatro*, and *shak-shak* appears on *An Island Carnival*, Nonesuch Explorer Series 72090, and also on the Swedish LP *Vastindien*, Caprice CAP 2004:1–2.

9. Some of the most exciting work on Afro-American dance outside of the United States is being done by the West Indian anthropologist Marie-Céline Lafontaine. Cf. her "Musique et société aux Antilles," *Présence Africaine* 121–22 (1982): 72–108; "Le Carnaval de l''autre,'" *Témps Modernes* 441–42 (April–May 1983): 2126–73; and *Alors ma chère, moi . . .* (Paris: Editions Caribéennes, 1987).

10. Two other examples of complete quadrilles from Marie-Galante—an island which is part of Guadeloupe—are on *La musique à Marie-Galante*, Société d'histoire de la Guadeloupe ATP 82–1. And an example of a mazurka from

Martinique can be found on *Caribbean Dances* (Folkways 6840), where the notes to the record suggest that the much accelerated mazurka of the French West Indies is a prototype of the *biguine*.

11. Hear, for instance, Fremont Fontenot's "Contredanse" with accordion and triangle on *Zodoco: Louisiana Creole Music*, Rounder 6009, or "Contredanse & Shoefly Swing" on *Louisiana Creole Music*, Folkways 2622.

12. Lafontaine, "Musique et société," 101–5.

13. Cf. Jacqueline Rosemain, *La musique dans la société antillaise 1635–1902* (Paris: L'Harmattan, 1986; Maurice Jallier and Yollen Lossen, *Musique aux Antilles: Mizik boo kay* (Paris: Éditions Caribéennes, 1985).

14. For a description of a set dance in the Maroon area of Jamaica, see Katherine Dunham, *Journey to Accompong* (New York: Henry Holt, 1946), 22–27.

15. Cheryl Ryman, "The Jamaican Heritage in Dance: Developing a Traditional Typology," *Jamaican Journal* 44: 11, 13. Ryman is a principal dancer with the National Dance Theatre Company of Jamaica, and she has developed a core vocabulary of dance moves for the company that includes quadrille patterns. Cf. Rex Nettleford, *Dance Jamaica: Cultural Definition and Artistic Discovery* (New York: Grove Press, 1985), 181.

16. Walter Jekyll, ed., *Jamaican Song and Story* (1906; reprint New York: Dover, 1966), 216–17. Jekyll includes words and music to 79 quadrille songs.

17. Norris Stubbs, "Major Musical Forms in the Bahamas," in *Third World Group: Bahamas Independence Issue* (Bahamas: Bahamas Printing and Litho, 1973), 101–2, as quoted by Basil C. Hedrick and Jeanette E. Stephens, *In the Days of Yesterday and in the Days of Today: An Overview of Bahamian Folkmusic*, Research Records No. 8 (Carbondale: University Museum, Southern Illinois University at Carbondale, 1976), 32.

18. Lisa Lekis, *Folk Dances of Latin America* (New York: Scarecrow Press, 1958), 226.

19. John Santos, liner notes to *The Cuban Danzón*, Folkways 4066.

20. This cry occurs *only* on the recording, not on the film soundtrack.

21. Liner notes to *Seychelles: danses et romances d'ancienne France*, Ocora 558534.

22. Thornton Hagert, liner notes to *Come and Trip It: Instrumental Dance Music 1780s–1920s*, New World Records NW 293; Charles Hamm, *Music in the New World* (New York: Norton, 1983), 297–306.

23. Notes to *Homespun America: Marches, Waltzes, Polkas and Serenades of the Manchester [New Hampshire] Cornet Band . . . and Manchester Quadrille Orchestra*, Vox Records, SVBX 5309.

24. See, for example, Eyre Crowe, *With Thackeray in America* (New York: Scribner's Sons, 1893), 147–48; and the New Orleans sources referred to in John W. Blassingame, *Black New Orleans, 1860–1880* (Chicago: University of Chicago Press, 1973), 145–46.

25. John Collins, *E. T. Mensah: King of Highlife.* (London: Off the Record Press, 1986), 34.

26. Richard Walm (Peter Atall, Esq.), *The Hermit in America on a Visit to America* (Philadelphia: M. Thomas, 1819), as quoted by Eileen Southern, *The Music of Black Americans* (New York: Norton, 1971), 113.

27. This was long before a parallel musical development in 1920s Cuba: the *danzonete*—borrowing from the Afro-Cuban *son*—added voices to the *cheranga* orchestra (cf. John Santos, album notes to *The Cuban Danzon*, Folkways 4066).

28. Samuel A. Floyd, Jr., and Marsha J. Reisser, "Social Dance Music of Black Composers in the Nineteenth Century and the Emergence of Classic Ragtime,"

Black Perspective in Music 8, 2 (Fall 1980): 161–94; Samuel A. Floyd, Jr., "A Black Composer in Nineteenth-Century St. Louis," *Nineteenth Century Music* 4 (November 1980): 151–67; Southern, *Music of Black Americans,* 114; Charles D. Jerde, "Black Music in New Orleans: A Historical Overview," *Black Music Research Newsletter* 9, 1 (Spring 1987): 6.

29. Floyd and Reisser, "Social Dance Music," 175.

30. Robert B. Winans, "Black Instrumental Music Traditions in the Ex-Slave Narratives," *Black Music Research Newsletter* 5, 2 (Spring 1982): 4.

31. Ann Allen Savoy, *Cajun Music: A Reflection of a People,* vol. 1 (Eunice, La.: Bluebird Press, 1984), 304–5. The second violin was also called a *bastrinque,* calling attention to its rhythmic function in this music.

32. Pops Foster, *The Autobiography of Pops Foster, New Orleans Jazzman, as Told to Tom Stoddard* (Berkeley: University of California Press, 1971), 7–8.

33. See Southern, *Music of Black Americans;* and Winans, "Black Instrumental Music." See also Dena Epstein, *Sinful Tunes and Spirituals: Black Folk Music to the Civil War* (Urbana: University of Illinois Press, 1977); and Lynne Fauley Emery, *Black Dance* (Palo Alto, Calif.: National Press Books, 1972).

34. Alan Jabbour, liner notes to *The Hammons Family,* 25. See also Robert Cantwell, *Bluegrass Breakdown: The Making of the Old Southern Sound* (Urbana: University of Illinois Press, 1984).

35. Sterling Stuckey, *Slave Culture: Nationalist Theory and the Foundations of Black America* (New York: Oxford University Press, 1987), 20–22; Winans, "Black Instrumental Music," 3.

36. David C. Barrow, Jr., "A Georgia Corn-Shucking," *Century Magazine* 24 (1882): 878.

37. Ibid.

38. Willis James, "The Romance of the Negro Folk Cry in America," *Phylon* 16 (1950): 18.

39. Hear Otis Redding's recording of "The Hucklebuck," where his vocal part, set in the midst of the melody as played by the Memphis Horns, cuts across the beat like an African talking drum.

40. Lafcadio Hearn, "Levee Life," in *An American Miscellany,* ed. Albert Mordell, vol. 1 (New York: Dodd, Mead, 1924). Dunham describes a Jamaican Maroon set dance that follows a similar pattern of Europe-to-Africa style change through the progression of the dances.

41. St. Cyr is quoted in "As I Remember: Johnny St. Cyr," *Jazz Journal* 19, 9 (September 1966): 7; Sweatman and Bradford in Marshall and Jean Stearns, *Jazz Dance* (New York: Macmillan, 1968), 23.

42. Tom Bethell, *George Lewis: A Jazzman from New Orleans* (Berkeley: University of California Press, 1977), 21.

43. European-derived dances such as the mazurka and the schottische had become thoroughly nativized and regionalized by the late 1800s. In light of this, it is interesting that John Storm Roberts seems to consider them "Latin influences" in his *The Latin Tinge: The Impact of Latin American Music on the United States* (New York: Oxford University Press, 1979), 31–37.

44. Samuel B. Charters, *Jazz: New Orleans 1885–1963,* rev. ed. (New York: Oak Publications, 1963), 18.

45. Baby Dodds, *The Baby Dodds Story as Told to Larry Gara* (Los Angeles: Contemporary Press, 1959), 10.

46. Louis Jones, quoted in Donald M. Marquis, *In Search of Buddy Bolden: First Man of Jazz* (Baton Rouge: Louisiana State University Press, 1978), 107; see also

Beatrice Alcorn, quoted in Marquis, *In Search of Buddy Bolden*, 94; and Charlie Love's and Harrison Barnes's interviews ("'Buddy Bolden was a Tall Man . . .'") in *The Music of New Orleans*, vol. 4: *The Birth of Jazz* (Folkways 2464).

47. H. O. Brunn, *The Story of the Original Dixieland Jazz Band* (Baton Rouge: Louisiana State University Press, 1960), 9.

48. Marquis, *In Search of Buddy Bolden*, 101.

49. Transcribed in Rex Harris, *Jazz*, 2d ed. (London: Penguin, 1953), 66–67.

50. Robert Goffin, *Jazz from Congo to Swing* (London: Musicians Press, 1946), 19.

51. Wilfrid H. Mellers, *Music in a New Found Land: Themes and Developments in the History of American Music* (New York: Knopf, 1965), 289.

52. Tom Davin, "Conversations with James P. Johnson," *Jazz Review* 2, 5 (June 1959): 15–17. See also Walter "One-Leg Shadow" Gould's comment that "Old Man Sam Moose was ragging the quadrilles and schottisches before I was born. . . . He was born way before the [Civil] war." Rudi Blesh and Harriet Janis, *They All Played Ragtime*, 4th ed. (New York: Oak Publications, 1971), 190. One contemporary observer also drew attention to the square dance qualities of the Big Apple, a popular dance of the 1930s, which was said to have originated in Columbia, South Carolina. See Kyle Crichton, "Peel That Apple—The Story of the 'Big Apple'," *Life*, August 9, 1937, p. 22, and Robert S. Gold, *Jazz Talk* (Indianapolis: Bobbs-Merrill, 1975), 18.

53. Davin, "Conversations with James P. Johnson (II)," *Jazz Review* 2, 6 (July 1959): 12–13.

54. Blesh and Janis, *They All Played Ragtime*, 190.

55. Ibid., 188. In August Wilson's play "Joe Turner's Come and Gone," an after-dinner secular ring shout at a Pittsburgh rooming house turns into a possession ritual.

56. See Marshall Stearns, *The Story of Jazz* (New York: Oxford University Press, 1953), 13, on the importance of the form for preserving style. Sterling Stuckey provides the best overview of the evidence for the presence of the ring shout in the United States and in West Africa. *Slave Culture*, 3–97.

57. There may also be reason to see an East Coast tradition at work here, one with roots in the coastal areas of Northern Florida and South and North Carolina, and extending (by migration) to Washington, D.C., Wilmington, Delaware, Philadelphia, New Jersey, and New York. Sharing the characteristics of 3–3–2 additive rhythm, shifting meters, etc., this tradition produced the Broadway influences of James P. Johnson and Eubie Blake (Baltimore), the pop music of Jerry Lieber (Baltimore), the gospel music of Philadelphia, North Jersey, and New York City, the bebop of Dizzy Gillespie (South Carolina) and Thelonious Monk (North Carolina), and the avant-garde playing of John Coltrane (North Carolina.)

58. Hagert, liner notes, 1.

59. "Quadrille," *The New Grove Dictionary of Music and Musicians*, vol. 15 (Washington, D.C.: Grove's Dictionaries of Music, 1980), 491. Examples include the *Bologna Quadrilles* (based on Rossini's *Stabat Mater*), Chabrier's *Souvenirs de Munich* (based on themes from *Tristan und Isolde*), and Fauré and Messager's *Souvenirs de Bayreuth* (based on themes from *The Ring*).

60. As quoted in Gunther Schuller, *Early Jazz: Its Roots and Musical Development* (New York: Oxford, 1968), 139. Schuller's work was an invaluable source for these comments on Morton.

61. Edward A. Berlin, *Ragtime: A Musical and Cultural History* (Berkeley, Calif.: University of California Press, 1980), 118–19; Eric Thacker, "Ragtime Roots," *Jazz & Blues* 3, no. 8 (November 1973): 6.

62. Stearns and Stearns, *Jazz Dance*, 23.

63. "Dennis Charles," interviewed by Ludwig Van Trikt, *Cadence* 13, 10 (October 1987): 6.

Chapter 20. All That Beef, and Symbolic Action Too! Notes on the Occasion of the Banning of 2 Live Crew's As Nasty as They Wanna Be

1. Some of the most important blue folkloric texts are kept in print by university presses (Vance Randolph's 1976 *Pissing in the Snow and Other Ozark Folktales*, for example, is published by the University of Illinois Press), and the most erotic of Jelly Roll Morton's songs are preserved in the Library of Congress.

2. For an early discussion of this distinction, see Ralph Bass's account of his dispute over Hank Ballard and the Midnighters' 1954 hit, "Work with Me Annie," on the Jack Parr TV show, in Michael Lydon and Ellen Mandel, *Boogie Lightning: How Music Became Electric* (New York: Dial Press, 1974), 84.

3. Nasty's "Fraternity Record," a song of intragreek insults, suggests that 2 Live Crew is the latest in a long series of Southern college gross-out house party bands such as the semi-legendary Doug Clark and the Hot Nuts.

4. Wendy Lowenstein, *Shocking, Shocking, Shocking: The Improper Play-Rhymes of Australian Children* (Melbourne: Fish and Chips Press, 1974); Sandra McCosh, *Children's Humour: A Joke for Every Occasion* (London: Panther/Granada, 1979); Ian Turner, *Cinderella Dressed in Yella* (Melbourne: Heinemann, 1969); Ernest Borneman, *Studien zur Befreiung des Kindes*, 4 vols. (Often, Switzerland: Walter-Verlag, 1973–76); Claude Gaignebet, *Le folklore obscène des enfants* (Paris: Maisonneuve and Larose, 1977).

5. Jacques-François Roger, *Fables sénégalaises recueilles de l'Ouolof* (Paris: Nepveu, 1828).

6. Vance Randolph, "Ribaldry at Ozark Dances," *Mid-America Folklore* 17 (1989): 17.

7. Ibid., 14–15.

8. Paul Oliver, *Screening the Blues: Aspects of the Blues Tradition* (London: Cassell, 1968).

9. See, for example, Millie Jackson, *Feelin' Bitchy*, Spring Records, 1977.

10. Kenneth Goldstein's ground-breaking "Bowdlerization and Expurgation: Academic and Folk," *Journal of American Folklore* 80 (1967): 374–86, was an inspiration for this paper.

11. See, for example, older blues song/dozens euphemisms like *fudderrucker* and *feathermucker.*

12. In an interview published in the *Village Voice* during the 1988 presidential campaign, candidate and warning-label advocate Al Gore laughed when it was pointed out to him that his generation had their own form of objectionable pop songs such as Little Richard's "Good Golly Miss Molly" ("she sure likes to ball"); he allowed that the difference was that you weren't supposed to know such things then.

13. For 2 Live Crew's claim to being comedians, see Martha Frankel, "2 Live Doo-Doo," *Spin* (October 1990): 62, quoting their interview from *Hitmakers*. For a survey of Rudy Ray Moore's career, see Charles Kilgore, "Rudy Ray Moore: The Life and the Laughter," *Uncut Funk* (Winter 1990): 24–25. Not only was *Nasty* self-labeled as potentially offensive, but it also was issued in a sanitized version, *As Clean as You Wanna Be.*

14. To many, it seems, "bitch" is the most offensive word in the rap vocabulary, yet response to it appears to be distributed along cultural lines not yet fully understood. In the Afro-American domain, at least, its use sometimes appears to be more literal, as in "Men are dogs; women are bitches." For some women rappers' views of the word, see Kim France, "5 Slammin' Women Rappers Bitch, Cuss, Sound Off, Get Down, Let Loose, and Get Nasty as They Wanna Be and You've Never Heard Dis like This," *Egg* (March 1991): 64–69.

15. For an interview with Blowfly that surveys his career, see "The Weird World of Blowfly," *Ungawa!* (c. 1992).

16. Kathleen M. Sullivan, "2 Live Crew and the Cultural Contradictions of *Miller*," *Reconstruction* 1 (1990): 19–20.

17. For accounts of the record banning, arrests, and trial, see Lisa Jones, "2 Live For You," *Village Voice*, October 12, 1990; Lisa Jones, "The Signifying Monkees," *Village Voice*, November 6, 1990; Todd Loren, "2 Live Crew: 1 Bad Mother," *Rock 'n' Roll Comics* (April 1991); Luther Campbell and John R. Miller, *As Nasty as They Wanna Be: The Uncensored Story of Luther Campbell of the 2 Live Crew* (Fort Lee, N.J.: Barricade Books, 1992); and *2 Live Crew Comics* 1 (June 1991).

18. See Dave Marsh, *Louie Louie: The History and Mythology of the World's Most Famous Rock 'n' Roll Song* (New York: Hyperion Press, 1993). Other commentators claimed to have no problems in understanding the 2 Live Crew text and transcribing it. See George Will, "America's Slide into the Sewer," *Newsweek*, July 30, 1990.

19. *New York Times*, October 21, 1990, 30.

20. Houston A. Baker, Jr. *Black Studies, Rap, and the Academy* (Chicago: University of Chicago Press, 1993), 72.

21. Ibid., 73–74.

22. To my knowledge, *As Nasty As They Wanna Be* was never played on the radio or television. Nor was it turned into print until George Will followed the lead of religious and political journals (and in doing so, I believe, reprinted erroneous transcriptions).

Chapter 22. Josef Škvorecký and the Tradition of Jazz Literature

1. Perle Epstein, "Swinging the Maelstrom: Malcolm Lowry and Jazz," *Canadian Literature* 44 (Spring 1970): 51–66.

2. Edward Kamau Brathwaite, "Jazz and the West Indian Novel," *Bim* 11, 44 (1967): 275–84; *Bim* 12, 45 (1967): 39–51; *Bim* 12, 46 (1968): 115–26; Jason Berry, "Jazz Literature: Through a Rhythm Joyously," *Village Voice*, May 8, 1978, 61–82; Jason Berry, "Jazz Literature," *Southern Exposure* 6, 3 (Fall 1978): 40–49.

3. Rudolf Fisher, "Common Meter," in *Black Voices: An Anthology of Afro-American Literature*, ed. Abraham Chapman (New York: New American Library, 1968), 74–86.

4. Josef Škvorecký, *The Cowards*, trans. Jeanne Němcová (New York: Grove, 1970), 30–31.

5. Josef Škvorecký, "Song of the Forgotten Years," in *New Writing in Czechoslovakia*, ed. and trans. George Theiner (Baltimore: Penguin, 1969), 80.

6. Josef Škvorecký, "Emöke," in *The Bass Saxophone: Two Novellas*, trans. Káča Poláčková-Henley (New York: Knopf, 1979), 83.

7. Josef Škvorecký, "Red Music," in *The Bass Saxophone*, 3–4.

8. Sidney Bechet, *Treat It Gentle* (London: Cassell, 1960); quoted in Martin Williams, *Jazz Masters of New Orleans* (New York: Macmillan, 1967), xix.

Chapter 29. The Local and the Express: Anthony Braxton's Title-Drawings

1. Ian Hoare, "Mighty, Mighty Spade and Whitey: Black Lyrics and Soul's Interaction with White Culture," in *The Soul Book*, ed. Ian Heart, Tony Cummings, Clive Anderson, and Simon Frith (New York: Dell, 1975), 193. Cf. Anthony Braxton's discussion of the role of the white jazz critic in *Tri-Axium Writings*, vol. 3 (San Francisco: Synthesis Music, 1985), 235–308.

2. Winston Smith, "Let's Call This: Race, Writing, and Difference in Jazz," *Public* 4/5 (1990): 71.

3. Eric Townley, *Tell Your Story: A Dictionary of Jazz and Blues Recordings, 1917–1950*, Nos. 1, 2 (Essex: Storyville, 1976, 1987).

4. Smith, "Let's Call This Race," 72. The European and Euro-American tradition of experimental music titling also converges with the African-American, but I lack the competence to discuss it here. It should be noted, however, that there is a direct connection between these composers' titles and the titles used by twentieth-century painters.

5. Robert Farris Thompson, "The Song That Names the Land: The Visionary Presence of African-American Art," in *Black Art: Ancestral Legacy: The African Impulse in African-American Art*, ed. Alvia J. Wardlaw and Robert V. Rozelle (Dallas, Tex.: Dallas Museum of Art; New York: Abrams, 1989), 123–24.

6. Grey Gundaker, "Tradition and Innovation in African-American Yards," *African Arts* 26, 2 (April 1993): 58–71, 94–96.

7. Lionel Hampton with James Haskins, *Hamp: An Autobiography* (New York: Warner, 1989), 3.

8. Umberto Eco, *The Open Work* (1962; reprint Cambridge, Mass.: Harvard University Press, 1989), 4.

Chapter 30. Magnificent Declension: Solibo Magnificent

1. Patrick Chamoiseau, *Solibo Magnificent*, trans. Rose-Myriam Réjouis and Val Vinokurov (1988; New York: Pantheon, 1997); *Texaco*, trans. Rose-Myriam Réjouis and Val Vinokurov (1992; New York: Pantheon, 1997).

Chapter 31. Metaphors of Incommensurability

1. I am indebted to Karl Reisman for first introducing me to many of the ideas in this essay.

2. Melville J. Herskovits, *The Myth of the Negro Past* (1941; reprint Boston: Beacon Press, 1958).

3. Alfred Métraux, *Voodoo in Haiti* (New York: Oxford University Press, 1959).

4. Douglas Macrae Taylor, review of Antoon Donicie and Jan Voorhoeve, *Sarama Kaanse Woordenschat*, *International Journal of American Linguistics* 30 (1964): 436.

5. Karl Reisman, "Cultural and Linguistic Ambiguity in a West Indian Village," in *Afro-American Anthropology*, ed. Norman E. Whitten, Jr., and John F. Szwed (New York: Free Press, 1970), 129–44.

6. On tea meeting, see Roger D. Abrahams, "The Training of the Man-of-Words in Talking Sweet," in *The Man-of-Words in the West Indies* (Baltimore: Johns Hopkins University Press, 1983), 109–21; on set dances, see John Szwed and

Morton Marks, "Afro-American Transformations of European Set Dances and Dance Suites," *Dance Research Journal* 20 (1988): 29–36.

7. Roger Bastide, *The African Religions of Brazil* (1960; reprint Baltimore: Johns Hopkins University Press, 1978).

8. Edward Kamau Brathwaite, *Contradictory Omens: Cultural Diversity and Integration in the Caribbean* (Mona, Jamaica: Savacou Publications, 1974).

9. V. S. Naipaul, *The Overcrowded Barracoon, and Other Articles* (London: Andre Deutsch, 1972), 8.

10. Derek Walcott, "The Caribbean: Culture or Mimicry?" *Journal of Interamerican Studies and World Affairs* 6 (1974): 9. Walcotts's retort to Naipaul is yet another example of the creolization process.

11. Umberto Eco, *The Open Work* (1962; reprint Cambridge, Mass.: Harvard University Press, 1989), 4.

12. John Szwed, "Vibrational Affinities," in *The Migrations of Meaning: A Sourcebook,* ed. Judith McWillie and Inverna Lockpez (New York: INTAR Gallery, 1992), 59–67.

13. W. E. B. DuBois, *The Souls of Black Folk* (Chicago: McClurg, 1938);and Grey Gundaker, *Signs of Diaspora/Diaspora of Signs: Literacies, Creolization, and Vernacular Practice in African America* (New York: Oxford University Press, 1998), 22–26.

14. Jean Bernabé, Patrick Chamoiseau, and Raphael Confiant, "In Praise of Creoleness," *Callaloo* 13 (1990): 866–909.

15. Edouard Glissant, *Caribbean Discourse: Selected Essays* (Charlottesville, Va.: University of Virginia Press, 1989).

16. Bernabé, Chamoiseau, and Confiant, "In Praise of Creoleness," 903.

17. Gilles Deleuze and Félix Guattari, *Kafka: Toward a Minor Literature* (Minneapolis: University of Minnesota Press, 1986), 16–27.

18. Mikhail Bakhtin, *The Dialogic Imagination* (Austin: University of Texas Press, 1981)

Bibliography

Abrahams, Roger D. *Deep Down in the Jungle . . . Negro Narrative Folklore from the Streets of Philadelphia*. Hatboro, Pa.: Folklore Associates, 1964. Reprint Chicago: Aldine Press, 1970.

———. *The Man-of-Words in the West Indies*. Baltimore: Johns Hopkins University Press, 1983.

———. *Positively Black*. Englewood Cliffs, N.J.: Prentice-Hall, 1970.

———. "Social Uses of Space in an Afro-American Community." Paper presented at the Conference on Traditional African Architecture, Yale University, New Haven, Connecticut, May 7–9, 1970.

———. "Stereotyping and Beyond." In *Language and Cultural Diversity in American Education*, edited by Roger D. Abrahams and Rudolph C. Troike, 19–29. Englewood Cliffs, N.J.: Prentice-Hall, 1972.

———. "Talking My Talk: Black English and Social Segmentation in Black Communities." *Florida F/L Reporter* 10 (1972): 29–38.

———. "There Is a Brown Girl in the Ring." In *Two Penny Ballads and Four Dollar Whiskey*, edited by Kenneth S. Goldstein and Robert H. Byington, 121–35. Hatboro, Pa.: Folklore Associates, 1966.

———. "Traditions of Eloquence in the West Indies." *Journal of Inter-American Studies and World Affairs* 12 (1970): 505–27.

———. "The Training of the Man-of-Words in Talking Sweet." In *The Man-of-Words in the West Indies*. Baltimore: Johns Hopkins University Press, 1983.

———. *Talking Black*. Rowley, Mass.: Newbury House, 1976.

Abrahams, Roger D. and Richard Bauman. "Sense and Nonsense on St. Vincent: Speech Behavior and Decorum in a Caribbean Community." *American Anthropologist* 73, no. 3 (1971): 262–72.

Abrahams, Roger D. and John F. Szwed, eds. *Discovering Afro-America*. Leiden: E.J. Brill, 1975.

Abrahams, Roger D. and Rudolph C. Troike, eds. *Language and Cultural Diversity in American Education*. Englewood Cliffs, N.J.: Prentice-Hall, 1972.

Adorno, Theodor S. *The Culture Industry: Selected Essays on Mass Culture*. Edited with an introduction by Jeremy M. Bernstein. London: Routledge, 1991.

Agee, James and Walker Evans. *Let Us Now Praise Famous Men*. Boston: Houghton Mifflin, 1941.

Ahye, Molly. *Golden Heritage: The Dance in Trinidad and Tobago*. Petit Valley, Trinidad: Heritage Cultures, 1978.

Allen, William Francis, Charles Pickard Ware, and Lucy McKim Garrison. *Slave*

Songs of the United States. New York, 1867. Reprint Medford, Mass.: Applewood Books, 1995.

Badger, Reid. *A Life in Ragtime: A Biography of James Reese Europe.* New York: Oxford University Press, 1995.

Baker, Houston A., Jr. *Black Studies, Rap, and the Academy.* Chicago: University of Chicago Press, 1993.

Bakhtin, Mikhail. *The Dialogic Imagination.* Austin: University of Texas Press, 1981.

Baldwin, James. "A Negro Assays the Negro Mood." *New York Times Magazine,* March 12, 1961.

Baratz, Stephen S. "Social Science's Conceptualization of the Afro-American." In *Black America,* edited by John F. Szwed, 55–66. New York: Basic Books, 1970.

Barrow, David C., Jr. "A Georgia Corn-Shucking." *Century Magazine* 24 (1882): 878.

Bascom, William R. "Acculturation Among the Gullah Negroes." *American Anthropologist* 43 (1941): 43–50.

———. "The Focus of Cuban Santeria." *Southwestern Journal of Anthropology* 6 (1952): 64–68.

———. *Shango in the New World.* Austin: University of Texas African and Afro-American Research Institute, 1972.

Bastide, Roger. *African Civilizations in the New World.* London: C. Hurst, 1971.

———. *The African Religions of Brazil.* 1960. Reprint Baltimore: Johns Hopkins University Press, 1978.

———. *Les Amériques noires.* Paris: Payot, 1967.

Baudet, Henri. *Paradise on Earth: Some Thoughts on European Images of Non-European Man.* New Haven, Conn.: Yale University Press, 1965.

Bechet, Sidney. *Treat It Gentle.* London: Cassell, 1960.

Becker, Howard S. "The Professional Dance Musician and His Audience." *American Journal of Sociology* 57 (September 1951): 135–44.

Beckford, William. *A Descriptive Account of the Island of Jamaica.* London: T. and J. Egerton, 1790.

Beddoe, John. *The Races of Britain: A Contribution to the Anthropology of Western Europe.* London: Arrowsmith, 1885.

Benedict, Ruth. *Patterns of Culture.* 1934. Reprint New York: New American Library, Mentor Books, 1959.

———. *Race: Science and Politics.* 1940. Reprint New York: Viking Press, Compass Books, 1959.

Bennett, Lerone, Jr. *The Negro Mood, and Other Essays.* New York: Ballantine, 1964.

———. "The World of the Slave." *Ebony* 26 (February 1971): 56.

Berger, Morroe. "Jazz: Resistance to the Diffusion of a Culture Pattern." *Journal of Negro History* 32 (October 1947): 461.

Berlin, Edward A. *Ragtime: A Musical and Cultural History.* Berkeley, Calif.: University of California Press, 1980.

Bernabé, Jean, Patrick Chamoiseau, and Raphael Confiant. *Éloge de la créolité.* Paris: Gallimard/Presses Universitaires créoles, 1989.

———. "In Praise of Creoleness." *Callaloo* 13 (1990): 866–909.

Bernhardt, Clyde E. B., as told to Sheldon Harris. *I Remember: Eighty Years of Black Entertainment, Big Bands, and the Blues.* Foreword by John F. Szwed. Philadelphia: University of Pennsylvania Press, 1986.

Berry, Jason. "Jazz Literature." *Southern Exposure* 6, no. 3 (fall 1978): 40–49.

———. "Jazz Literature: Through a Rhythm Joyously." *Village Voice,* May 8, 1978, 61–82.

Bethell, Tom. *George Lewis: A Jazzman from New Orleans*. Berkeley, Calif.: University of California Press, 1977.

Beveridge, Janet. *An Epic of Clare Market*. London: G. Bell, 1960.

Bilby, Kenneth. "The Carribean as a Musical Region." In *Carribean Contours*, edited by Sidney W. Mintz and Sally Price, 181–218. Baltimore: Johns Hopkins University Press, 1994.

Birdwhistell, Ray L. *Kinesics and Context: Essays on Body Motion Communication*. Philadelphia: University of Pennsylvania Press, 1971.

Blassingame, John W. *Black New Orleans, 1860–1880*. Chicago: University of Chicago Press, 1973.

Blauner, Robert. "Black Culture: Myth or Reality?" In *Afro-American Anthropology: Contemporary Perspectives*, edited by Norman E. Whitten, Jr., and John F. Szwed, 347–66. New York: Free Press, 1970.

Blesh, Rudi and Harriet Janis. *They All Played Ragtime*. 4th ed. New York: Oak Publications, 1971.

Boas, Franz. *The Mind of Primitive Man*. 1938. Reprint New York: Macmillan, 1963.

Bolt, Christine. *Victorian Attitudes to Race*. London: Routledge and Kegan Paul, 1971.

Bontemps, Arna. "Rock, Church, Rock." In *Anthology of American Negro Literature*, edited by Sylvestre C. Watkins, 431. New York: Modern Library, 1944.

Borneman, Ernest. *Studien zur Befreiung des Kindes*. 4 vols. Olten, Switzerland: Walter-Verlag, 1973–76.

Brathwaite, Edward Kamau. *Contradictory Omens: Cultural Diversity and Integration in the Caribbean*. Mona, Jamaica: Savacou Publications, 1974.

———. "Jazz and the West Indian Novel." *Bim* 11, 44 (1967): 275–84; 12, 45 (1967): 39–51; 12, 46 (1968): 115–26.

Braxton, Anthony. *Tri-Axium Writings*. Vol. 3. San Francisco: Synthesis Music, 1985.

Brunn, Harry O. *The Story of the Original Dixieland Jazz Band*. Baton Rouge: Louisiana State University Press, 1960.

Bryce-Laporte, Roy S. "The Conceptualization of the American Slave Plantation as a Total Institution." Ph.D. dissertation, University of California, Los Angeles, 1968.

Cabrera, Lydia. *El Monte*. Havana: Ediciones C.R., 1954.

Camden, William. *Britannia, or A Chorographical Description of Great Britain and Ireland*. London, 1722.

———. *Britain, or a Chorographicall Description of the Most Flourishing Kingdomes of England, Scotland, and Ireland*. Translated by Philemon Holland. London, 1610.

Campbell, Luther, and John R. Miller. *As Nasty as They Wanna Be: The Uncensored Story of Luther Campbell of the 2 Live Crew*. Fort Lee, N.J.: Barricade Books, 1992.

Cantwell, Robert. *Bluegrass Breakdown: The Making of the Old Southern Sound*. Urbana: University of Illinois Press, 1984.

Carradine, B. [Beverly]. *Mississippi Stories*. Chicago: Christian Witness Co., 1904.

Castle, Vernon [and Irene Castle]. *Modern Dancing*. World Syndicate Co., by arrangement with New York: Harper and Brothers, 1914.

Chamoiseau, Patrick. *Solibo Magnificent*. Trans. Rose-Myriam Réjouis and Val Vinokurov. 1988; New York: Pantheon, 1997.

Chamoiseau, Patrick. *Texaco*. Trans. Rose-Myriam Réjouis and Val Vinokurov. 1992; New York: Pantheon, 1997.

Charters, Samuel B. *Jazz: New Orleans 1885–1963*. Rev. ed. New York: Oak Publications, 1963.

Charles, Dennis. "Dennis Charles: Interview with Ludwig Van Trikt." *Cadence* 13, no. 10 (October 1987): 6.

———. *The Poetry of the Blues.* New York: Oak Publications, 1965.

Chesterton, G. K. "Celts and Celtophiles." In *Heretics.* London: Bodley Head, 1905.

Clark, Kenneth B. *Dark Ghetto.* New York: Harper and Row, 1965.

Collins, John. *E. T. Mensah: King of Highlife.* London: Off the Record Press, 1986.

Cooper, Barry Michael. "Kiss Me Before You Go-go," *Spin,* June 1985, 65–67.

Cooper, Martin. *Beethoven: The Last Decade, 1817–1827.* New York: Oxford University Press, 1970.

Cosgrove, Stuart. "The Erotic Pleasures of the Dance-Craze Disc." *Collusion,* February–April 1983, 4–6.

Crowe, Eyre. *With Thackeray in America.* New York: Scribner's Sons, 1893.

Crowley, Daniel J. "American Credit Institutions of Yoruba Type." *Man* 53 (1953): 80.

———. "Toward a Definition of Calypso." *Ethnomusicology* 3 (1959): 55–66, 117–24.

———. "The View from Tobago: National Character in Folklore." In *Folklore International,* edited by D. K. Wilgus. Hatboro, Pa.: Folklore Associates, 1967.

Curtin, Philip D. *The Atlantic Slave Trade: A Census.* Madison: University of Wisconsin Press, 1969.

Curtis, James C., and Lewis L. Gould, eds. *The Black Experience in America.* Austin: University of Texas Press, 1970.

Curtis, L. Perry, Jr. *Apes and Angels: The Irishman in Victorian Caricature.* Washington, D.C.: Smithsonian Institution Press, 1971.

Dalby, David. *Black Through White: Patterns of Communication.* African Studies Program, Indiana University. Bloomington: Indiana University Press, 1970.

Dauer, Alfons M. *Der Jazz, seine Ursprunge und seine Entwicklung.* Kassel: E. Röth-Verlag, 1958.

Davin, Tom. "Conversations with James P. Johnson." *Jazz Review* 2, no. 5 (June 1959): 15–16.

———. "Conversations with James P. Johnson." *Jazz Review* 2, no. 6 (July 1959), 12.

Dawson, Jim. *The Twist: The Story of the Song and Dance That Changed the World.* Boston: Faber and Faber, 1995.

De La Beche, H. T. *Letter from the West Indies.* London, 1846.

Deleuze, Gilles, and Félix Guattari. *Kafka: Toward a Minor Literature.* Minneapolis: University of Minnesota Press, 1986.

Denzin, Norman. "Problems in Analyzing Elements of Mass Culture: Notes on the Popular Song and Other Artistic Productions." *American Journal of Sociology* 75 (1969).

Dillard, J. L. *Black English: Its History and Usage in the United States.* New York: Random House, 1972.

Dobbin, Jay D. *The Jombee Dance of Montserrat: A Study of Trance Ritual in the West Indies.* Columbus: Ohio State University Press, 1986.

Dodds, Baby. *The Baby Dodds Story as Told to Larry Gara.* Los Angeles: Contemporary Press, 1959.

Dreitzel, Hans Peter, ed. *Recent Sociology.* Vol. 1, *On the Basis of Politics.* New York: Macmillan, 1969.

Du Bois, W. E. B. *The Souls of Black Folk.* Chicago: McClurg, 1938.

Dunham, Katherine. *Journey to Accompong.* New York: Henry Holt, 1946.

Eco, Umberto. *The Open Work.* 1962. Reprint Cambridge, Mass.: Harvard University Press, 1989.

Elder, Jacob D. "Evolution of the Traditional Calypso of Trinidad and Tobago: A Socio-Historical Analysis of Song-Change." Ph.D. dissertation, University of Pennsylvania, 1966.

———. "Kalinda—Song of the Battling Troubadours of Trinidad." *Journal of the Folklore Institute* 3 (1966): 192–203.

Elkins, Stanley M. *Slavery: A Problem in American Institutional and Intellectual Life.* Chicago: University of Chicago Press, 1959.

Ellison, Ralph. *Shadow and Act.* New York: New American Library, Signet Books, 1966.

Emery, Lynne Fauley. *Black Dance in the United States from 1519 to 1970.* Palo Alto, Calif.: National Press Books, 1972. Reprint New York: Dance Horizons, 1980.

Epstein, Dena. *Sinful Tunes and Spirituals: Black Folk Music to the Civil War.* Urbana: University of Illinois Press, 1977.

Epstein, Perle. "Swinging the Maelstrom: Malcolm Lowry and Jazz." *Canadian Literature* 44 (Spring 1970): 51–66.

Feather, Leonard G.. *The Book of Jazz, a Guide to the Entire Field.* New York: Horizon Press, 1957.

———. "The Racial Undercurrent." In *Down Beat's Music 1961.* Chicago, 1960, 44–46.

———. "A Talk with Mahalia Jackson." In *American Folk Music Occasional No. 1,* edited by Chris Strachwitz, 46. Berkeley, Calif., 1964.

Fiedler, Leslie. *Waiting for the End.* New York: Stein and Day, 1964.

Fischer, Ann. "The Effect upon Anthropological Studies of U.S. Negroes of the Professional Personality and Subculture of Anthropologists." Paper presented at the annual meeting of the Southern Anthropological Association, New Orleans, March 13–15, 1969.

Fisher, Rudolf. "Common Meter." In *Black Voices: An Anthology of Afro-American Literature,* edited by Abraham Chapman, 74–86. New York: New American Library, 1968.

Floyd, Samuel A., Jr. "A Black Composer in Nineteenth-Century St. Louis." *Nineteenth Century Music* 4 (November 1980): 151–67.

Floyd, Samuel A., Jr., and Marsha J. Reisser. "Social Dance Music of Black Composers in the Nineteenth Century and the Emergence of Classic Ragtime." *Black Perspective in Music* 8, 2 (Fall 1980): 161–94.

Foster, Pops. *The Autobiography of Pops Foster, New Orleans Jazzman, as Told to Tom Stoddard.* Berkeley: University of California Press, 1971.

France, Kim. "5 Slammin' Women Rappers Bitch, Cuss, Sound Off, Get Down, Let Loose, and Get Nasty as They Wanna Be and You've Never Heard Dis Like This." *Egg* (March 1991): 64–69.

Frankel, Martha. "2 Live Doo-Doo." *Spin* (October 1990): 62.

Frazier, E. Franklin. *The Negro Church in America.* New York: Schocken Books, 1964.

———. "Traditions and Patterns of Negro Family Life in the United States." In *Race and Culture Contacts,* edited by E. B. Reuter, 191–207. New York: McGraw-Hill, 1934.

Freedberg, Michael. "Dust Their Blues," *Boston Phoenix,* October 16, 1992.

———. "Rising Expectations: Rick James Gets Down." *Village Voice,* October 11, 1983.

Freyre, Gilberto. *The Racial Factor in Contemporary Politics.* Occasional Papers of the Research Unit for the Study of Multi-Racial Societies, University of Sussex. London: MacGibbon and Kee, 1966.

Frith, Simon. "Why Do Songs Have Words?" In *Music for Pleasure: Essays in the Sociology of Pop*. New York: Routledge, 1988.

Gaignebet, Claude. *Le folklore obscène des enfants*. Paris: Maisonneuve and Larose, 1977.

Genovese, Eugene D. *Roll Jordan Roll: The World the Slaves Made*. New York: Pantheon, 1974.

Gibbs, James L., Jr., ed. *Peoples of Africa*. New York: Holt, Rinehart and Winston, 1965.

Gilroy, Paul. *The Black Atlantic: Modernity and Double Consciousness*. London: Verso, 1993.

Glazer, Nathan and Daniel P. Moynihan. *Beyond the Melting Pot*. Cambridge, Mass.: MIT Press, 1963.

Glissant, Edouard. *Caribbean Discourse: Selected Essays*. Charlottesville, Va.: University of Virginia Press, 1989.

Godbolt, Jim. *A History of Jazz in Britain, 1919–1950*. London: Quartet Books, 1984.

Goddard, Chris. *Jazz Away from Home*. New York: Paddington Press, 1979.

Goffin, Robert. *Jazz from Congo to Swing*. London: Musicians Press, 1946.

Gold, Robert S. *Jazz Talk*. Indianapolis: Bobbs-Merrill, 1975.

Goldstein, Kenneth S. "Bowdlerization and Expurgation: Academic and Folk." *Journal of American Folklore* 80 (1967): 374–86.

Goldstein, Kenneth S. and Robert H. Byington, eds. *Two Penny Ballads and Four Dollar Whiskey*. Hatboro, Pa.: Folklore Associates, 1966. González Echevarría, Roberto. "Socrates Among the Weeds." *Massachusetts Review* 24 (1984): 545–61.

Gordon, Milton. *Assimilation in American Life*. New York: Oxford University Press, 1964.

Gossett, Thomas F. *Race: The History of an Idea in America*. New York: Schocken Books, 1965.

Greenberg, Joseph H. "An Application of New World Evidence to an African Linguistic Problem." In *Les afro-américains*, 129–31. Mémoire 27. Dakar: Institut français d'Afrique noire, 1957.

Greene, David H., ed. *An Anthology of Irish Literature*. New York: Modern Library, 1954.

Grier, William H., and Price M. Cobbs. *Black Rage*. New York: Basic Books, 1968.

Gruver, Rod. "The Origins of the Blues." In *Down Beat Music 71*. Chicago: Maher, 1971.

Guest, Ann Hutchinson. *Dance Notation: The Process of Recording Movement on Paper*. New York: Dance Horizons, 1984.

Guilbault, Jocelyne. "A St. Lucian *Kwadril* Evening." *Latin American Music Review* 6 (1985): 31–57.

Guilcher, Jean Michel. *Le contredanse et les rénouvellements de la danse française*. Paris: École Practique des Hautes-Études et Mouton, 1969.

Guirao, Ramón. *Orbita de la poesía afrocubana, 1928–37*. Havana: Ucar, García y Cía, 1938.

Gundaker, Grey. *Signs of Diaspora/Diaspora of Signs: Literacies, Creolization, and Vernacular Practice in African America*. New York: Oxford University Press, 1998.

———. "Tradition and Innovation in African-American Yards." *African Arts* 26, no. 2 (April 1993): 58–71, 94–96.

Hamm, Charles. *Music in the New World.* New York: Norton, 1983.

Hampton, Lionel, with James Haskins. *Hamp: An Autobiography.* New York: Warner, 1989.

Handler, Jerome C., and Charlotte J. Frisbie. "Aspects of Slave Life in Barbados: Music and Its Cultural Context." *Caribbean Quarterly* (1972): 5–46.

Hannerz, Ulf. *Soulside: Inquiries into Ghetto Culture and Community.* New York: Columbia University Press, 1969.

Harding, Vincent. "Religion and Resistance Among Antebellum Negroes, 1800–1860." In *The Making of Black America: Essays in Negro Life and History,* edited by August Meier and Elliott Rudwick, 179–97. New York: Atheneum, 1969.

Harrington, Michael. *Toward a Democratic Left.* New York: Vintage Books, 1968.

Harris, Marvin. *Patterns of Race in the Americas.* New York: Walker, 1964.

Harris, Rex. *Jazz.* 2nd ed. London: Penguin, 1953.

Hazzard-Gordon, Katrina. *Jookin': The Rise of Social Dance Formations in African American Culture.* Philadelphia: Temple University Press, 1990.

Hearn, Lafcadio. *An American Miscellany.* 2 vols. Edited by Albert Mordell. New York: Dodd, Mead, 1924.

———. *Barbarous Barbers.* Edited by Ichiro Nishizaki. Tokyo: Hokuseido Press, 1939.

———. *Children of the Levee.* Edited by O. W. Frost. Lexington: University of Kentucky Press, 1957.

———. *La Cuisine Créole: A Collection of Culinary Recipes, From Leading Chefs and Noted Creole Housewives, Who Have Made New Orleans Famous for Its Cuisine.* New Orleans: Hansell, 1885.

———. "Levee Life." In *An American Miscellany,* edited by Albert Mordell, vol. 1. New York: Dodd, Mead, 1924.

———. *Occidental Gleanings.* 2 vols. Edited by Albert Mordell. New York: Dodd, Mead, 1925.

———. *Selected Writings.* Edited by Henry Goodman. New York: Citadel Press, 1949.

Heart, Ian, Tony Cummings, Clive Anderson, and Simon Frith, eds. *The Soul Book.* New York: Dell, 1975.

Hedrick, Basil C., and Jeanette E. Stephens. *In the Days of Yesterday and in the Days of Today: An Overview of Bahamian Folkmusic.* Research Records 8. Carbondale: University Museum, Southern Illinois University at Carbondale, 1976.

Helm, June, ed.. *Essays on the Verbal and Visual Arts: Proceedings of the 1966 Annual Spring Meeting of the American Ethnological Society.* Seattle, American Ethnological Society, University of Washington Press, 1967.

Hentoff, Nat. "Jazz and Jim Crow." *Commonweal* 73 (March 24, 1961): 658.

———. "The Murderous Modes of Jazz." *Esquire* (September 15, 1960): 91.

———. "The New Faces of Jazz." *Reporter* 25 (August 17, 1961): 50.

———. "Race Prejudice in Jazz." *Harper's* 28 (June 1959): 75.

Herskovits, Frances S., ed. *The New World Negro.* 1930. Reprint Bloomington: Indiana University Press, 1966.

Herskovits, Melville J. "The Ahistorical Approach to Afroamerican Studies." *American Anthropologist* 62 (1960): 559–68.

———. *Franz Boas.* New York: Scribner's, 1953.

———. *The Interdisciplinary Aspects of Negro Studies.* Bulletin 32. Washington, D.C.: American Council of Learned Societies, 1941.

———. *The Myth of the Negro Past.* 1941. Reprint Boston: Beacon Press, 1958.

———. "The Negro in the New World: The Statement of a Problem." In *The New*

World Negro, edited by Frances S. Herskovits. 1930. Reprint Bloomington: Indiana University Press, 1966.

———. "The Negro's Americanism." In *The New Negro: An Interpretation,* edited by Alain Locke, 353–60. New York: A. and C. Boni, 1925.

———. "The Social Organization of the Candomble." *Anais do XXXI Congresso Internacional de Americanistas,* 505–32. São Paulo, 1954.

———. *Trinidad Village.* New York: Knopf, 1947.

———. "What Has Africa Given America?" *New Republic* 84, no. 1083 (1935): 92–96.

Hoare, Ian. "Mighty, Mighty Spade and Whitey: Black Lyrics and Soul's Interaction with White Culture." In *The Soul Book,* edited by Ian Heart, Tony Cummings, Clive Anderson, and Simon Frith. New York: Dell, 1975.

Hunt, Leigh. *The Wishing Cap Papers.* Boston: Lee and Shepard, 1873.

Hurston, Zora Neale. *Jonah's Gourd Vine.* Philadelphia: J. B. Lippincott, 1934.

———. *Mules and Men.* Philadelphia: J. B. Lippincott, 1935.

Hymes, Dell, ed. *Reinventing Anthropology.* New York: Random House, 1969.

"Inside the Cannonball Adderley Quintet." *Down Beat* 28 (June 8, 1961): 19–22.

Jackson, Bruce, ed. *The Negro and His Folklore in Nineteenth-Century Periodicals.* Austin: University of Texas Press, 1967.

Jahn, Janheinz. *Muntu: An Outline of the New African Culture.* New York: Grove Press, 1961.

Jallier, Maurice and Yollen Lossen. *Musique aux Antilles: Mizik boo kay.* Paris: Edition Caribéennes, 1985.

James, Willis. "The Romance of the Negro Folk Cry in America." *Phylon* 16 (1950): 18.

Jekyll, Walter, ed. *Jamaican Song and Story.* 1906. Reprint New York: Dover, 1966.

Jerde, Charles D. "Black Music in New Orleans: A Historical Overview." *Black Music Research Newsletter* 9, no. 1 (spring 1987).

Johnson, Clifton H., ed. *God Struck Me Dead: Religious Conversion Experiences and Autobiographies of Ex-Slaves.* Philadelphia: Pilgrim Press, 1969.

Jones, Bessie and Bess Lomax Hawes. *Step It Down: Games, Play, Song, and Stories from the Afro-American Heritage.* New York: Harper and Row, 1972.

Jones, Eldred D. *The Elizabethan Image of Africa.* Charlottesville: University of Virginia Press, 1971.

Jones, LeRoi. *Blues People.* New York: William Morrow, 1963.

Jones, Lisa. "2 Live for You." *Village Voice,* October 12, 1990.

———. "The Signifying Monkees." *Village Voice,* November 6, 1990.

Kardiner, Abram, and Lionel Ovesey. *The Mark of Oppression: Explorations in the Personality of the American Negro.* New York: Meridian, 1962.

Katznelson, Ira. "White Social Science and the Black Man's World: The Case of Urban Ethnography." *Race Today* (February 1970): 47–48.

Keil, Charles. *Urban Blues.* Chicago: University of Chicago Press, 1966.

Kilgore, Charles. "Rudy Ray Moore: The Life and the Laughter." *Uncut Funk* (Winter 1990): 24–25.

Kochman, Thomas. "Toward an Ethnography of Black American Speech Behavior." In *Afro-American Anthropology: Contemporary Perspectives,* edited by Norman E. Whitten, Jr., and John F. Szwed, 145–62. New York: Free Press, 1970.

Labov, William, et al. *A Study of the Non-Standard English of Negro and Puerto Rican Speakers in New York City.* Vol. 2, *Final Report.* Cooperative Research Project 3288, Office of Education. New York: Columbia University, 1968.

Lafontaine, Marie-Céline. *Alors ma chère, moi . . .* Paris: Éditions Caribbéennes, 1987.

———. "Le carnaval de l' 'autre.'" *Témps Modernes* 441–42 (April–May 1983): 2126–73.

———. "Musique et société aux Antilles." *Présence Africaine* 121–22 (1982): 72–108.

Landes, Ruth. Review of *Afro-American Anthropology,* edited by Norman E. Whitten, Jr., and John F. Szwed. *American Anthropologist* 73 (1971): 1306–10.

Lasch, Christopher. *The Agony of the American Left.* New York: Vintage, 1969.

Latrobe, Benjamin Henry. *Impressions Respecting New Orleans, Diary and Sketches, 1818–1829.* New York: Columbia University Press, 1951.

Leighton, Alexander H., Thomas A. Lambo, C. C. Hughes, J. M. Murphy, and D. Macklin. *Psychiatric Disorder Among the Yoruba.* Ithaca, N.Y.: Cornell University Press, 1963.

Lekis, Lisa, *Folk Dances of Latin America.* New York: Scarecrow Press, 1958.

Levine, Lawrence W. "Slave Songs and Slave Consciousness: An Exploration in Neglected Sources." Paper presented at meetings of the American Historical Association, December 28, 1969.

Lévi-Strauss, Claude. "The Scope of Anthropology." *Current Anthropology* 7 (1966): 122.

Lewis, Matthew Gregory. *Journal of a West India Proprietor.* London, 1834.

Lincoln, C. Eric. *The Black Muslims in America.* Boston: Beacon Press, 1961.

Lomax, Alan. *The Folk Songs of North America in the English Language.* Garden City, N.Y.: Doubleday, 1960.

———. *Folk Song Style and Culture.* Washington, D.C.: American Association for the Advancement of Science, 1968.

———. "The Homogeneity of African-Afro-American Musical Style." In *Afro-American Anthropology: Contemporary Perspectives,* edited by Norman E. Whitten, Jr., and John F. Szwed. New York: Free Press, 1970.

———. *The Rainbow Sign: A Southern Documentary.* New York: Duell, Sloane, and Pearce, 1959.

———. "Song Structure and Social Structure." *Ethnology* 1 (1962): 425–51.

———. "Special Features of the Sung Communication." In *Essays on the Verbal and Visual Arts: Proceedings of the 1966 Annual Spring Meeting of the American Ethnological Society,* edited by June Helm, 109–27. Seattle, American Ethnological Society, University of Washington Press, 1967.

Lomax, John A, and Alan Lomax. *Folk Song U.S.A.* New York: Duell, Sloane and Pearce, 1966.

Loren, Todd. "2 Live Crew: 1 Bad Mother." *Rock 'n' Roll Comics,* April 1991.

Lowenstein, Wendy. *Shocking, Shocking, Shocking: The Improper Play-Rhymes of Australian Children.* Melbourne: Fish and Chips Press, 1974.

Luffman, John. *A Brief Account of the Island of Antigua, Together with the Customs and Manners of Its Inhabitants, White as Well as Black.* London: T. Cadell, 1788.

Lydon, Michael, and Ellen Mandel. *Boogie Lightning: How Music Became Electric.* New York: Dial Press, 1974.

Malinowski, Bronislaw. Introduction to Fernando Ortiz, *Cuban Counterpoint.* New York: Knopf, 1947.

Mann, Ron, dir. *The Twist.* 1992. Reissued Chicago: Home Vision Entertainment, 2003, DVD.

Margolis, Norman M. "A Theory on the Psychology of Jazz." *American Image* 2 (Fall 1954): 263–91.

Marks, Morton. "Performance Rules and Ritual Structure in Afro-American Music." Ph.D. dissertation, University of California at Berkeley, 1972.

———. "El santo en Nueva York." Paper presented at the meetings of the American Anthropological Association, San Diego, November 22, 1970.

———. "Trance Music and Paradoxical Communication." Paper presented at the American Anthropological Association meetings, New Orleans, November 1969.

———. "'You Can't Sing Unless You're Saved': Reliving the Call in Gospel Music." In *African Religious Groups and Beliefs*, edited by Simon Ottenberg, 305–31. Meerut, India: Archana Publications, 1982.

Marks, Morton and John F. Szwed. "Afro-American Cultures on Parade." Paper presented at the American Anthropological Association annual meeting, New York, 1971.

Marquis, Donald M. *In Search of Buddy Bolden: First Man of Jazz.* Baton Rouge: Louisiana State University Press, 1978.

Marsden, Peter. *An Account of the Island of Jamaica, with Reflections on the Treatment, Occupation, and Provision of the Slaves.* Newcastle: S. Hodgson, 1788.

Marsh, Dave. *Louie Louie: The History and Mythology of the World's Most Famous Rock 'n' Roll Song.* New York: Hyperion Press, 1993.

Marx, Gary T. "Two Cheers for the National Riot Commission." In *Black America*, edited by John F. Szwed, 78–96. New York: Basic Books, 1970.

McCosh, Sandra. *Children's Humour: A Joke for Every Occasion.* London: Panther/ Granada, 1979.

Meier, August and Elliott Rudwick, eds. *The Making of Black America: Essays in Negro Life and History.* New York: Atheneum, 1969.

Mellers, Wilfrid H.. *Music in a New Found Land: Themes and Developments in the History of American Music.* New York: Knopf, 1965.

Melnick, Mimi Clar. "'I Can Peep Through Muddy Water and Spy Dry Land': Boasts in the Blues." In *Folklore International: Essays in Traditional Literature, Belief, and Custom in Honor of Wayland Debs Hand*, edited by D. K. Wilgus, 139–49. Hatboro, Pa.: Folklore Associates, 1967.

Messenger, John C. "Montserrat: The Most Distinctively Irish Settlement in the New World." *Ethnicity* 2 (1975): 298–99.

Métraux, Alfred. *Voodoo in Haiti.* New York: Oxford University Press, 1959.

Mintz, Sidney W. Foreword to *Afro-American Anthropology: Contemporary Perspectives*, edited by Norman E. Whitten, Jr. and John F. Szwed, 1–15. New York: Free Press, 1970.

Mintz, Sidney W., and Sally Price, eds. *Carribean Contours.* Baltimore: Johns Hopkins University Press, 1994.

Montagu, M. F. Ashley. *Man's Most Dangerous Myth: The Fallacy of Race.* New York: Harper and Brothers, 1942.

Montell, William L. *The Saga of Coe Ridge.* Knoxville: University of Tennessee Press, 1970.

Moreton, J. B. *Manners and Customs in the West Indian Islands.* London: W. Richardson, 1793.

Morris, Willie. *North Toward Home.* Boston: Houghton Mifflin, 1967.

Moryson, Fynes. *An Itinerary*, 4 vols. London, 1617.

Murphy, Jeannette. "The Survival of African Music in America." *Popular Science Monthly* 55 (1899): 660–72.

Myrdal, Gunnar. *An American Dilemma: The Negro Problem and Modern Democracy.* New York: Harper and Row, 1944.

Naipaul, V. S. *The Overcrowded Barracoon, and Other Articles.* London: Andre Deutsch, 1972.

Narvaez, Alfonso A. "Where Religion and Superstition Mix in the City." *New York Times,* September 15, 1970, 41.

Nettleford, Rex. *Dance Jamaica: Cultural Definition and Artistic Discovery.* New York: Grove Press, 1985.

The New Grove Dictionary of Music and Musicians. Washington, D.C.: Grove's Dictionaries of Music, 1980.

Newton, Francis. *The Jazz Scene.* Baltimore, 1961.

O'Farrell, Patrick. *Ireland's English Question: Anglo-Irish Relations, 1534–1970.* New York: Schocken Books, 1971.

Okoye, Felix N. *The American Image of Africa: Myth and Reality.* Buffalo, N.Y.: Black Academy Press, 1971.

Oliver, Paul. *Conversation with the Blues.* New York: Horizon Press, 1965.

———. *Savannah Syncopators.* New York: Stein and Day, 1970.

———. *Screening the Blues: Aspects of the Blues Tradition.* London: Cassell, 1968.

———. *Songsters and Saints: Vocal Traditions on Race Records.* Cambridge: Cambridge University Press, 1984.

Ortiz, Fernando. *Cuban Counterpoint.* New York: Knopf, 1947.

Ottenberg, Simon, ed. *African Religious Groups and Beliefs.* Meerut, India: Archana Publications, 1982.

Ottenheimer, Harriet J. "Blues: Pattern and Variation." Paper presented at the meetings of the Society for Ethnomusicology, Albuquerque, November 13, 1965.

Parrish, Lydia. *Slave Songs of the Georgia Sea Islands.* Hatboro, Pa.: Folklore Associates, 1965.

Patton, Cindy. "Embodying Subaltern Memory: Kinesthesia and the Problematics of Gender and Race." In *The Madonna Connection: Representational Politics, Subcultural Identies, and Cultural Theory,* edited by Cathy Schwichtenberg, 81–105. Boulder, Colo.: Westview Press, 1993.

Pearse, Andrew. "Aspects of Change in Caribbean Folk Music." *Journal of the International Folk Music Council* 8 (1955): 31–32.

———. "Mitto Sampson on Calypso Legends of the Nineteenth Century." *Caribbean Quarterly* 4 (1956): 250–62.

Perdue, Robert E., Jr. "African Baskets in South Carolina." *Economic Botany* 22 (1968): 289–92.

Petry, Ann Lane. *The Street.* Boston: Houghton Mifflin, 1946.

Pierpoint, Robert. "Negro, or Coloured, Bandsmen in the Army." *Notes and Queries* 2 (1916): 303–4.

Powdermaker, Hortense. *After Freedom: A Cultural Study in the Deep South.* New York: Viking Press, 1939.

Price, Richard. "Saramaka Woodcarving: The Development of an Afro-American Art." *Man* (1970): 375.

Propes, Steve. "The Larks and the Jerk." *Goldmine,* August 26, 1988.

Quinn, David Beers. *The Elizabethans and the Irish.* Ithaca, N.Y.: Cornell University Press, 1966.

"Racial Prejudice in Jazz." *Down Beat* 29 (March 15, 1962): 20–26.

Radin, Paul. Foreword to *God Struck Me Dead: Religious Conversion Experiences and Autobiographies of Ex-Slaves,* edited by Clifton H. Johnson. Philadelphia: Pilgrim Press, 1969.

———. "Status, Fantasy, and the Christian Dogma." In *God Struck Me Dead:*

Religious Conversion Experiences and Autobiographies of Ex-Slaves, edited by Clifton H. Johnson, vii-xiii. Philadelphia: Pilgrim Press, 1969. (Originally issued in 1945 by the Fisk University Social Science Institute, Nashville, Tenn., from a typescript written before 1930.)

Rainwater, Lee. "The American Working Class and Lower Class: An American Success and Failure." In *Anthropological Backgrounds of Adult Education*, edited by Sol Tax et al., 29–46. Notes and Essays on Education for Adults 57. Boston: Center for the Study of Liberal Education for Adults, Boston University, 1968.

Randolph, Vance. *Pissing in the Snow and Other Ozark Folktales*. Urbana: University of Illinois Press, 1976.

———. "Ribaldry at Ozark Dances." *Mid-America Folklore* 17 (1989): 17.

Read, Allen Walker. "British Recognition of American Speech in the Eighteenth Century." *Dialect Notes* 6 (1933): 329.

Redfield, James. *Comparative Physiognomy, or Resemblances Between Men and Animals*. New York: Redfield, 1852.

Reid, Ira De A. "Mrs. Bailey Pays the Rent." In *Ebony and Topaz, a Collectanea*, edited by Charles S. Johnson, 144–48. New York: National Urban League, 1927.

Reisman, Karl. "Contrapuntal Communications in an Antiguan Village." Working Paper 3, Penn-Texas Working Papers in Sociolinguistics, 1970.

———. "Cultural and Linguistic Ambiguity in a West Indian Village." In *Afro-American Anthropology: Contemporary Perspectives*, edited by Norman E. Whitten, Jr., and John F. Szwed, 129–144. New York: Free Press, 1970.

Reuter, E. B., ed. *Race and Culture Contacts*. New York: McGraw-Hill, 1934.

Rhys, Jean. *Wide Sargasso Sea*. New York: Norton, 1966.

Richardson, Philip J. S. *The Social Dances of the Nineteenth Century in England*. London: Herbert Jenkins, 1960.

Riesman, David. "Listening to Popular Music." *American Quarterly* 2 (1930).

Riesman, Paul. Review of *Journey to Ixtlan*, by Carlos Castaneda. *New York Times Book Review*, October 22, 1972, 7.

Roberts, John Storm. *The Latin Tinge: The Impact of Latin American Music on the United States*. New York: Oxford University Press, 1979.

Robinson, Armstead L., Craig C. Foster, and Donald H. Ogilvie, eds. *Black Studies in the University: A Symposium*. New Haven, Conn.: Yale University Press, 1969.

Roger, Jacques-François. *Fables sénégalaises recueillies de l'Ouolof*. Paris: Nepveu, 1828.

Rosemain, Jacqueline. *La musique dans la société antillaise, 1635–1902*. Paris: L'Harmattan, 1986.

Rosenberg, Bruce A. *The Art of the American Folk Preacher*. New York: Oxford University Press, 1970.

Rubin, Vera, ed. *Caribbean Studies: A Symposium*. Seattle: University of Washington Press, 1960.

Ryman, Cheryl. "The Jamaican Heritage in Dance: Developing a Traditional Typology." *Jamaican Journal* 44: 11, 13.

Sandoval, Mercedes C. "Santeria as a Mental Health Care System: An Historical Overview." *Social Science and Medicine* 13B (1979): 137–51.

Sartre, Jean-Paul. *Search for a Method*. Translated by Hazel E. Barnes. New York: Vintage Books, 1963.

Savoy, Ann Allen. *Cajun Music: A Reflection of a People*. Vol. 1. Eunice, La.: Bluebird Press, 1984.

Scarborough, Dorothy. *On the Trail of Negro Folksongs*. Hatboro, Pa.: Folklore Associates, 1963.

Schuller, Gunther. *Early Jazz: Its Roots and Musical Development*. New York: Oxford, University Press, 1968.

Schwichtenberg, Cathy, ed. *The Madonna Connection: Representational Politics, Subcultural Identies, and Cultural Theory*. Boulder, Colo.: Westview Press, 1993.

Scott, Michael. *Tom Cringle's Log*. Edinburgh: Blackwood, 1833.

Simpson, George E., and Peter B. Hammond. "Discussion." In *Caribbean Studies: A Symposium*, edited by Vera Rubin, 46–53. Seattle: University of Washington Press, 1960.

Škvorecký, Josef. *The Cowards*. Translated by Jeanne Nemcová. New York: Grove, 1970.

———. "Emöke." In *The Bass Saxophone: Two Novellas*. Translated by Káča Poláčková-Henley. New York: Knopf, 1979.

———. "Red Music," in *The Bass Saxophone: Two Novellas*. Translated by Káča Poláčková-Henley. New York: Knopf, 1979.

———. "Song of the Forgotten Years." In *New Writing in Czechoslovakia*, edited and translated by George Theiner. Baltimore: Penguin, 1969.

Slotkin, J. S. "Jazz and Its Forerunners as an Example of Acculturation." *American Sociological Review* 7 (August 1946): 570–75.

Smith, M. G. "The African Heritage in the Caribbean." In *Caribbean Studies: A Symposium*, edited by Vera Rubin, 34–46. Seattle: University of Washington Press, 1960.

———. *Kinship and Community on Carriacou*. New Haven, Conn.: Yale University Press, 1962.

Smith, William B. "The Persimmon Tree and the Beer Dance." 1838. Reprinted in *The Negro and His Folklore in Nineteenth-Century Periodicals*, edited by Bruce Jackson, 3–9. Austin: University of Texas Press, 1967.

Smith, Winston. "Let's Call This: Race, Writing, and Difference in Jazz." *Public* 4/5 (1990): 71.

Snowden, Frank M.. *Blacks in Antiquity: Ethiopians in the Greco-Roman Experience*. Cambridge, Mass.: Harvard University Press, 1970.

Sontag, Susan. *On Photography*. New York: Delta, 1977.

Southern, Eileen. *The Music of Black Americans*. New York: Norton, 1971.

Spenser, Edmund. *The Faerie Queene*. Macmillan, 1970.

St. Cyr, Johnny. "As I Remember: Johnny St. Cyr." *Jazz Journal* 19, no. 9 (September 1966): 7.

Starr, S. Frederick. *Red and Hot: The Fate of Jazz in the Soviet Union, 1917–1980*. New York: Limelight, 1994.

Stearns, Marshall W.. *The Story of Jazz*. New York: Oxford University Press, 1953.

Stearns, Marshall W., and Jean Stearns. *Jazz Dance: The Story of American Vernacular Dance*. New York: Macmillan, 1968.

Stewart, James. *A View of the Past and Present State of the Island of Jamaica*. London: Oliver and Boyd, 1823.

Stewart, William A. "Continuity and Change in American Negro Dialects." *Florida F/L Reporter* 6, no. 1 (1968): 3–14.

———. "Sociolinguistic Factors in the History of American Negro Dialects." *Florida F/L Reporter* 5, no. 2 (1967): 11–29.

———. "Towards a History of American Negro Dialect." In *Language and Poverty: Perspective on a Theme*, edited by F. Williams, chap. 7. Chicago: Markham, 1970.

Strachwitz, Chris, ed. *American Folk Music Occasional No. 1*. Berkeley, Calif., 1964.
———. "An Interview with the Staples Family." In *American Folk Music Occasional No. 1*, edited by Chris Strachwitz, 16–17. Berkeley, Calif., 1964.
Stubbs, Norris. "Major Musical Forms in the Bahamas." In *Third World Group: Bahamas Independence Issue*. Nassau: Bahamas Printing and Litho, 1973.
Stuckey, Sterling. *Slave Culture: Nationalist Theory and the Foundations of Black America*. New York: Oxford University Press, 1987.
———. "Through the Prism of Folklore: The Black Ethos in Slavery." *Massachusetts Review* 9 (1968): 417–37.
———. "Twilight of Our Past: Reflections on the Origins of Black History." In *Amistad 2*, edited by John A. Williams and Charles F. Harris, 261–95. New York: Vintage Books, 1971.
Sullivan, Kathleen M. "2 Live Crew and the Cultural Contradictions of *Miller*." *Reconstruction* 1 (1990): 19–20.
Szasz, Thomas S. "Blackness and Madness: Images of Evil and Tactics of Exclusion." In *Black America*, edited by John F. Szwed, 67–77. New York: Basic Books, 1970.
Szwed, John F. "Afro-American Musical Adaptation." In *Afro-American Anthropology: Contemporary Perspectives*, edited by Norman E. Whitten, Jr., and John F. Szwed, 219–27. New York: Free Press, 1970.
———. "An American Anthropological Dilemma: The Politics of Afro-American Culture." In *Reinventing Anthropology*, edited by Dell Hymes. New York: Pantheon, 1973.
———, ed. *Black America*. New York: Basic Books, 1970.
———. "Vibrational Affinities." In *The Migrations of Meaning: A Sourcebook*, edited by Judith McWillie and Inverna Lockpez, 59–67. New York: INTAR Gallery, 1992.
Szwed, John F., and Morton Marks. "The Afro-American Transformation of European Set Dances and Dance Suites." *Dance Research Journal* 20, no. 1 (1988): 29–36.
Talley, Thomas W. *Negro Folk Rhymes*. New York: Macmillan, 1922.
Tax, Sol et al., eds. *Anthropological Backgrounds of Adult Education*. Notes and Essays on Education for Adults 57. Boston: Center for the Study of Liberal Education for Adults, Boston University, 1968.
Taylor, Douglas Macrae. Review of *Sarama Kaanse Woordenschat*, by Antoon Donicie and Jan Voorhoeve. *International Journal of American Linguistics* 30 (1964): 436.
Thacker, Eric. "Ragtime Roots." *Jazz & Blues* 3, no. 8 (November 1973): 6.
Thompson, Robert Farris. "African Influence on the Art of the United States." In *Black Studies in the University: A Symposium*, edited by Armstead L. Robinson, Craig C. Foster, and Donald H. Ogilvie, 122–70. New Haven, Conn.: Yale University Press, 1969.
———. "From Africa." *Yale Alumni Magazine* (November 1970): 16–21.
———. "The Sign of the Divine King." *African Arts* (Spring 1970): 8–17.
———. "The Song That Names the Land: The Visionary Presence of African-American Art." In *Black Art: Ancestral Legacy: The African Impulse in African-American Art*, edited by Alvia J. Wardlaw and Robert V. Rozelle. Dallas, Tex.: Dallas Museum of Art; New York: Abrams, 1989.
Townley, Eric. *Tell Your Story: A Dictionary of Jazz and Blues Recordings, 1917–1950*. No. 1. Essex: Storyville, 1976.
———. *Tell My Story*, No. 2. Essex: Storyville, 1987.

Tumin, Melvin M. "Some Social Consequences of Research on Racial Relations." In *Recent Sociology*, vol.1, *On the Basis of Politics*, edited by Hans Peter Dreitzel, 242–62. New York: Macmillan, 1969.

Turnbull, Colin M. "The Mbuti Pygmies of the Congo." In *Peoples of Africa*, edited by James L. Gibbs, Jr. New York: Holt, Rinehart and Winston, 1965.

Turner, Ian. *Cinderella Dressed in Yella*. Melbourne: Heinemann, 1969.

Turner, Lorenzo D. *Africanisms in the Gullah Dialect*. Chicago: University of Chicago, 1949.

Tynan, John. "Funk, Soul, Groove." *Down Beat* (November 24, 1960): 19.

———. "Les McCann and the Truth." *Down Beat* 27 (September 15, 1950): 21.

Valentine, Charles. *Culture and Poverty: Critique and Counter Proposals*. Chicago: University of Chicago Press, 1968.

Vallières, Pierre. *White Niggers of America: The Precocious Autobiography of a Quebec "Terrorist"*. New York: Monthly Review Press, 1971.

Voce, Steve. "It Don't Mean a Thing." *Jazz Journal* 24 (1971): 16.

Walcott, Derek. "The Caribbean: Culture or Mimicry?" *Journal of Interamerican Studies and World Affairs* 6 (1974): 9.

Wallace, Anthony F. C. *Religion: An Anthropological View*. New York: Random House, 1966.

Walm, Richard [Peter Atall, Esq.]. *The Hermit in America on a Visit to America*. Philadelphia: M. Thomas, 1819.

Wardlaw, Alvia J., and Robert V. Rozelle. *Black Art: Ancestral Legacy: The African Impulse in African-American Art*. Dallas: Dallas Museum of Art; New York: Abrams, 1989.

Watkins, Sylvestre C. *Anthology of American Negro Literature*. New York: Modern Library, 1944.

Watson, John P. *Annals of Philadelphia and Pennsylvania, in the Olden Times*. Philadelphia: Edwin S. Stuart, 1857.

"The Weird World of Blowfly." *Ungawa!* circa 1992.

Welding, Pete. "Tapescripts: Interview with Rev. Robert Wilkins. T7–155." *John Edwards Memorial Foundation Newsletter* 3 (1967): 55.

Wentworth, Trelawney. *The West India Sketch Book*. London: Whittaker, 1834.

Whinnom, Keith. "The Origin of European-based Creoles and Pidgins." *Orbis* 14 (1965): 511–26.

Whitten, Norman E., Jr. "Personal Networks and Musical Contexts in the Pacific Lowlands of Colombia and Ecuador." *Man* 3 (1968): 50–63.

Whitten, Norman E., Jr., and Aurelio Fuentes. "¡Baile Marimba! Negro Folk Music in Northwest Ecuador." *Journal of the Folklore Institute* 3 (1966): 169–91.

Whitten, Norman E., Jr., and John F. Szwed, eds. *Afro-American Anthropology: Contemporary Perspectives*. New York: Free Press, 1970.

Wilder, Alec. *American Popular Song*. New York: Oxford University Press, 1972.

Wilgus, D. K., ed. *Folklore International: Essays in Traditional Literature, Belief, and Custom in Honor of Wayland Debs Hand*. Hatboro, Pa.: Folklore Associates, 1967.

Will, George. "America's Slide into the Sewer." *Newsweek*, July 30, 1990.

Williams, Frederick, ed. *Language and Poverty: Perspectives on a Theme*. Chicago: Markham Publishing, 1970.

Williams, Lena. "Three Steps Right, Three Steps Left: Sliding into the Hot New Dance." *New York Times*, April 22, 1990.

Williams, Martin. *Jazz Masters of New Orleans*. New York: Macmillan, 1967.

Williams, Raymond. *The Country and the City*. New York: Oxford University Press, 1973.

Willis, William S. "Anthropology and Negroes on the Southern Colonial Frontier." In *The Black Experience in America*, edited by James C. Curtis and Lewis L. Gould. Austin: University of Texas Press, 1970.

———. "Skeletons in the Anthropological Closet." In *Reinventing Anthropology*, edited by Dell Hymes. New York: Random House, 1969.

Wilson, John S. "Expanding Market for Better Jazz." *New York Times*, March 12, 1961, Section X, 15.

Wilson, Peter. "Reputation and Respectability: A Suggestion for Caribbean Ethnology," *Man* 4, 1 (1969): 37–53.

Winans, Robert B. "Black Instrumental Music Traditions in the Ex-Slave Narratives." *Black Music Research Newsletter* 5, no. 2 (Spring 1982): 4.

Wittke, Carl. *Tambo and Bones: A History of the American Minstrel Stage*. Durham, N.C.: Duke University Press, 1930.

Wolf, Eric R., and Joseph G. Jorgensen. "Anthropology on the Warpath in Thailand." *New York Review of Books* (November 19, 1970): 26–35.

Woll, Allen. *Black Musical Theatre: From Coontown to Dreamgirls*. Baton Rouge: Louisiana State University Press, 1989.

Wood, Peter H. "'It Was a Negro Taught Them,' A New Look at African Labor in Early South Carolina." In *Discovering Afro-America*, edited by Roger D. Abrahams and John F. Szwed. Leiden: E.J. Brill, 1975.

Young, Virginia H. "Family and Childhood in a Southern Negro Community." *American Anthropologist* 72 (1970): 269–88.

Zwerin, Michael. *La tristesse de Saint Louis: Jazz Under the Nazis*. New York: Beech Tree, 1987.

Index

Acknowledgments

This book owes its existence to the skill, kindness, and erudition of three great editors: Peter Agree, Terry McKiernan, and Robert Christgau.

My debt to Roger Abrahams continues to grow through the years. I also owe much to Carol Parssinen, Morton Marks, and Robert Farris Thompson, each a singular scholar, and a coauthor of several of these pieces.

Many thanks to Matthew Sakakeeny for his careful help and good advice in preparing the manuscript for this book, and to Joe Levy, Eric Weisbard, and Gary Giddins, each of whom is responsible for guiding some of these pieces into print for the *Village Voice*.

Earlier versions of these chapters were previously published as follows. All are used by permission.

Chapter 2. "Musical Style and Racial Conflict." *Phylon* 27, 4 (1966): 358–66.

Chapter 3. "Musical Adaptation Among Afro-Americans." *Journal of American Folklore* 82 (1969): 112–21.

Chapter 4. "An American Anthropological Dilemma: The Politics of Afro-American Culture." In *Reinventing Anthropology*, ed. Dell Hymes. New York: Pantheon, 1973, 153–81.

Chapter 5. "Reconsideration: The Myth of the Negro Past." *New Republic*, June 24, 1972, 30–32.

Chapter 6. "Reconsideration: Lafcadio Hearn in Cincinnati." *New Republic*, October 7, 1972, 32–33

(Chapter 7 has not been previously published.)

Chapter 8. "Race and the Embodiment of Culture." *Ethnicity* (1975): 19–33.

Chapter 9. "After the Myth: Studying Afro-American Cultural Patterns in the Plantation Literature." *Research in African Literatures* 7, 2 (1976): 211–32.

Chapter 10. "Speaking People, in Their Own Words." In *Walker Evans: Photographs from the* Let Us Now Praise Famous Men *Project.* Michener Galleries, University of Texas at Austin. 1974, 3–6.

Chapter 11. "The Lizards Fake the Fake." *Village Voice,* July 15, 1981, 80.

Chapter 12. "As It Is Prophesied, So It Used to Be." *Village Voice,* February 10, 1982, 79–80.

Chapter 13. "Greenwich's Good Gnosis." *Village Voice,* February 7, 1984, 70–71.

Chapter 14. "Free Samples: Roy Nathanson and Anthony Coleman." *Village Voice,* August 23, 1992, 82–83.

Chapter 15. "Milling at the Mall." *Village Voice,* June 16–22, 1999, 71–72.

Chapter 16. "Childhood's Ends." *Village Voice,* April 23, 1985, 98.

Chapter 17. "Sweet Feet." *Village Voice,* August 6, 1985, 77.

Chapter 18. "From 'Messin' Around' to 'Funky Western Civilization': The Rise and Fall of Dance Instruction Songs." *New Formations* 27 (1995): 59–79.

Chapter 19. "The Afro-American Transformation of European Set Dances and Dance Suites." *Dance Research Journal* 20, 1 (Summer 1988): 29–36.

Chapter 20. "All That Beef and Symbolic Action Too! Notes on the Occasion of the Banning of 2 Live Crew's *As Nasty as They Wanna Be.*" In *Don't Stop 'til You Get Enough: Essays in Honor of Robert Christgau,* ed. Tom Carson, Kit Rachlis, and Jeff Salamon. Privately published. Austin: Nortex Press, 2002, 205–10.

Chapter 21. "The Real Old School." In *The* Vibe *History of Hip Hop,* ed. Alan Light. New York: Three Rivers, 1999, 3–11.

Chapter 22. Josef Škorvecký and the Tradition of Jazz Literature." *World Literature Today* 54, 4 (Autumn 1980): 586–90.

Chapter 23. "World Views Collide: The History of Jazz and Hot Dance." *Village Voice,* February 26, 1986, 73–74.

Chapter 24. "Way Down Yonder in Buenos Aires." *Village Voice,* January 18, 1983, 83.

Chapter 25. "Improvising Under Apartheid: Afro-Blue." *Village Voice,* August 25, 1987, 11–12.

Chapter 26. "Sonny Rollins in the Age of Mechanical Reproduction." *Village Voice,* December 3, 1991, 70.

Chapter 27. "Obituary: Sun Ra." *Village Voice,* July 22, 1997, 3, 70.

Chapter 28. "!Ornette Coleman: ?Civilization." *Village Voice,* July 22, 1997, 55, 57.

Chapter 29. "The Local and the Express: Anthony Braxton's Title Drawings." In *Mixtery: A Festschrift for Anthony Braxton,* ed. Graham Lock. Exeter: Stride, 1995, 207–12.

Chapter 30. "Magnificent Declension: *Solibo Magnificent.*" *Bookforum,* Spring 1998, 29.

Chapter 31. "Metaphors of Incommensurability." Special issue on creolization, Journal of American Folklore 116, 2 (Winter 2003): 9–18.